The Laws of *ah!*

The Laws of *ah!*

and our *Boundless Mindscapes*

Written and illustrated by

Michael I Christie

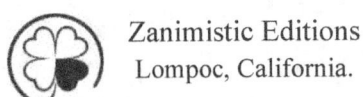

Zanimistic Editions
Lompoc, California.

Note to the reader
The material presented in this book is for information only, and should not be construed as advocating the use of psychedelics or any other practice outside what is legally sanctioned in the reader's place of residence and, even if legally permitted, should always occur under the recommended professional supervision.

Cover design: Studio E Books, Santa Barbara, CA
Cover photo: Michael I. Christie

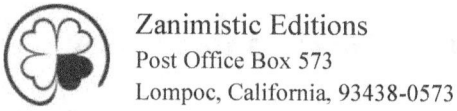
Zanimistic Editions
Post Office Box 573
Lompoc, California, 93438-0573

Suggested cataloging information:

Christie, Michael I, author
      The Laws of ah! and our Boundless Mindscapes.
      Includes bibliographical references.
      ISBN 979-8-9934641-1-4 (pbk)
      ISBN 979-8-9934641-2-1 (ebook)

      1.Title
      1. Philosophy, Practical and Integrative
      2. Psychology, Transpersonal – Spirituality

Her Dad asked the young Barry Stevens:

Why do you want to leave school?

Because half the things they teach are wrong!

So why don't you just take the other half?

Because I can't tell which is which!

to our 'kids,' their kids, and the *Barry Stevens* of the world!

*With the hope that it will help them grow
and live more fully minded.*

Table of Contents

List of Chapters, Figures, and Tables

Preface ---- XV

Book I – Beginnings

Why *ah!* - ---- 3

I.1 – Posing the problem ---- 5

I.2 – The Book of Ken – on the nature of Reality ---- 8

– Reality, act one ---- 9

– Reality, act two ---- 9

I.3 – Muddled terminology ---- 15

I.4 – Issues of semantics and application, round two ---- 20

– Additional problems ---- 22

I.5 – The Book of Isaac ---- 25

I.6 – The Book of Dmitri Ivanovic – *the Laws of ah!* – Part II -- 28

I.7 – *The Laws of ah!* – part III ---- 33

I.8 – Reality, Act Three ---- 34

I.9 – The Book of Sigmund – the structuring of our subjectivity -- 36

– We all believe what we were taught as kids ---- 41

I.10 – The Book of Alexander – from catalogs to systems ---- 44

I.11 – The Book of Pichon ---- 46

I.12 – Summary of the first round ---- 55

– The domains are complimentary, existence is simultaneous - 58

I.13 – Teaser – the subject and the Queen ---- 60

– Subject - Object and the use of subjective – objective ---- 62

– The object - subject dilemma, used as nouns ---- 62

I.14 – Life and Reproductive Strategies ---- 66

I.15 – The Book of Pierre – evolution by groping ---- 68

I.16 – Relatedness – califragilistic… ---- 70

I.17 – There never was an Adam, never an Eve, and there never will be - 72

I.18 – Sex in Nature and the nature of Sex ---- 76

I.19 – Morals and ethics in Nature ---- 79
I.20 – Putting these ideas in a historical framework ---- 81
    – The two paths to power ---- 82
I.21 – The Book of Ken revised: deconstructing the 'classic' view ---- 86
I.22 – What does 'collective' mean in different spheres? ---- 94
I.23 – The mystery of altruism & the structure of social domains ---- 98
I.24 – How did they parcel out the cake? The birth of modernity ---- 108
I.25 – Four Spiritualities – Four Gods – Four Yogas ---- 113
I.26 – The shadow and our 'split' personalities ---- 119
I.27 – The inter-subjectal and postmodernity ---- 123
I.28 – The Book of Richards ---- 126
I.29 – We widened the horizon of everyday reality, but *how far*? ---- 130
I.30 – Intention, action, interaction ---- 134
I.31 – Book I, in a nutshell… ---- 136
I.32 – Changes of state, decoupling of scales, theoretical ladders,
          and free will ---- 143
I.33 – Epilogue and Prologue – So then, what is a religion? ---- 148

Book II – Arabesques ---- 155
    – Growing numbers and complexity in material systems ---- 156
Book II – Types of complexity
II.34 – Complex minded … between the simple and the chaotic ---- 156
    – The myth of 'multitasking' ---- 162
    – Playing as a team ---- 163
Book II – Mings – Scales – Complexity – Reproduction ---- 164
II.35 – From our surroundings to our cosmic neighborhood ---- 164
    – Incredibly small ---- 166
II.36 – Can you think like a Roman? ---- 168
II.37 – Human population yesterday, today, tomorrow – ---- 169
II.38 – Grasping the scale of mings (material things) ---- 174
II.39 – Quantity, and more quantity, to hell with quality! – ---- 175

– The Charge of the Blight Brigade   - - - - 177

II.40 –The tyranny of 'normality'   - - - - 179

II.41 – Masters of Creation   - - - - 180

II.42 – Worldviews   - - - - 184

– A change of paradigm?   - - - - 185

Book II – Ideas – Experience – Education – Preaching   - - - - 187

II.43 – A 'scientific' ploy   - - - - 188

II.44 – Another turn of the spiral – the tricks of perception   - - - - 189

II.45 – Teaching versus Preaching   - - - - 192

– How can you tell education from preaching?   - - - - 195

II.46 – Attachment and detachment   - - - - 196

II.47 – Not what they found, rather *how* they found it   - - - - 198

II.48 – When being subjective plays against you   - - - - 200

II.49 – The chicken or the egg? – Exploring ideas   - - - - 204

Book II – Bonds® – Systems – Politics – Legislation   - - - - 206

II.50 – The Path of Possessions   - - - - 206

– The dance of the goods and their bads   - - - - 209

II.51 – *God by Decree!* – Legitimizing Political Power   - - - - 210

II.52 – The perfect Ponzi Scheme   - - - - 213

II.53 – Revolutionize?   - - - - 214

II.54 – Spread the Word (and keep the Numbers)   - - - - 216

II.55 – Kings and kingdoms have been notoriously ephemeral   - - - 217

II.56 – The organizational pyramid and representation   - - - - 220

– Bottom up or top down? The transformation of delegates - - 222

– An organization is NOT an organism   - - - - 226

– So then, what's the deal, loyalty or rebelliousness?   - - - - 227

– Common elements that lead to abuse and corruption   - - - - 229

– How is this so?   - - - - 232

– A question of numbers…   - - - - 234

II.57 – Politics and subjectivity   - - - - 235

x

II.58 – Averroes' koan ---- 239
  – Money, money, money… ---- 242
II.59 – Politics and complexity ---- 244
  – And then again... (tedious, but it's important) ---- 247
  – Why does Politics polarize? The mediator's predicament ---- 250
  – The down side of arrogance ---- 253

Book II – Links© **– Tradition – Science – Religion** ---- 254
  – Back to the intersubjectal. ---- 254
II.60 – The eternal cultural dilemma: tradition or innovation? ---- 255
II.61 – About the relationship between science and religion ---- 257
  – The irony: Science converges - Religions diverge ---- 261
II.62 – A universe without gods? God and his creation?
Unfolding within God? ---- 261
II.63 – Conversion ---- 262
  – What are the advantages and limitations of religion? ---- 263
II.64 – The owners of Truth – What do we mean by 'prophet'? ---- 264
II.65 – People of *The Book* ---- 268
II.66 – How *respectful* is religious preaching? ---- 270
II.67 – Guilt ---- 272
II.68 – A recovering *catholic* ---- 275
II.69 – Testimonials, a lure for suckers? ---- 277
II.70 – Provincialism ---- 278
II.71 – *ah!* loves evolution! ---- 281
II.72 – Sexocracies, sins, and scandals ---- 283
  – Again, is this 'subjective' or is it 'objective'? ---- 285
II.73 – The perfect *lekking* system... a 'just so' story ---- 286
II.74 – Back to the drawing board ---- 293
  – The great cycles ---- 295
II.75 – The laws of men ---- 300
II.76 – Beyond materialism ---- 304
  – Genesis revisited ---- 305

Book III – *Boundless mindscapes* - - - - 311
III.77 – What are we? - - - - 312
III.78 – Honoring our spiritual heritage - - - - 316
III.79 – The Book of Stan - - - - 322
III.80 – Huston, we have a problem… - - - - 330
    – The prophet's dilemma - - - - 338
III.81 – Stan II - transpersonal psychology: new maps of the psyche - - - 343
III.82 – The Nature of Spirit - - - - 348
III.83 – Why did an all-powerful god create this universe? - - - - 353
III.84 – A deeper look at the cosmos: information and holography - - - 356
    – Footprints in the sands of time - - - - 359
III.85 – Just how intelligent is *'Intelligent Design'*? - - - - 361
III.86 – Clare Graves and Spiral Dynamics® - - - - 369
III.87 – Old and new paths to spiritual growth (the return journey) - - - - 373
III.88 – Wisdom in the nature of Water - - - - 378
III.89 – Creating the Creator - - - - 381
III.90 – Beyond *The Books* - - - - 389
    – Beyond re-litics and po-ligion - - - - 391
    – Faith, a good servant, a terrible overlord - - - - 393
III.91 – What's next…? - - - - 397
III.92 – Boundless mindscapes - - - - 402

– Appendix: Summary of the Michael Christie Integrative Model - - - - 405
– Definitions and glossary - - - - 407
– Acknowledgements - - - - 417
– Sources: citations and notes - - - - 419
– Suggested reading and viewing - - - - 428
– About the author - - - - 429

– An Index for this edition is available at www.zanimistic.com

List of Figures:

Figure 1. Terms used by Ken Wilber ---- 11
Figure 2. A hypothetical example of correspondence ---- 13
Figure 3. Relationships in a holarchy ---- 14
Figure 4. My version of the terminology ---- 19
Figure 5. Fractals ---- 27
Figure 6. The elements of personality ---- 40
Figure 7. A stressed personality ---- 42
Figure 8. A balanced personality ---- 43
Figure 9. The simplest group is two ---- 48
Figure 10. The basic intersubjectal ---- 50
Figure 11. Group health ---- 53
Figure 12. An alternative set of tensing opposites ---- 54
Figure 13. The domains and us ---- 56
Figure 14. The generation of collectives, as per Michael Christie --- 58
Figure 15. Sketch of the Expanding Universe ---- 60
Figure 16. Reticular heredity in a nutshell ---- 74
Figure 17. Ken Wilber's original model ---- 88
Figure 18. Aspects of Power ---- 93
Figure 19. The new formulation of the domains as per Michael Christie - 113
Figure 20. The styles of spiritual paths ---- 116
Figure 21. *The true Laws of ah!* ---- 139
Figure 22. The Complexity Ladder ---- 140
Figure 23. The structuring of complexity ---- 159
Figure 24. Accumulated human knowledge ---- 166
Figure 25. Our universe scaled by mass ---- 167
Figure 26. Preaching versus Teaching ---- 196
Figure 27. Structural hierarchy in a private firm ---- 223
Figure 28. Structural hierarchy in a labor union ---- 224
Figure 29. Structural hierarchy in a corporation ---- 233
Figure 30. Frequency distributions ---- 248
Figure 31. The Four Bulls of Discord ---- 251
Figure 32. A vane of Political Polarities ---- 253
Figure 33. Increasing stratification of global hierarchies ---- 299

Figure 34. The *Mysticum* and the Practicum - - - - 334

Figure 35. The new maps of the psyche - - - - 345

Figure 36. A cycling cosmos - - - - 350

Figure 37. The outbound journey of existence - - - - 351

Figure 38. The Mass scale and the Electromagnetic Spectrum - - - - 358

Figure 39. Evolution unfolds in steps and stages - - - - 367

Figure 40. A change of Paradigm - - - - 368

Figure 41. The Wheel of Karma - - - - 377

Figure 42. The Return Journey - - - - 378

Figure 43. At the base of manifestation are three essentials - - - - 382

Figure 44. Creating the creator - - - - 386

Figure 45. Surfing from the Practicum to the *Mysticum* - - - - 388

Figure 46. Through the books - - - - 395

Figure 47. The Escherboros - - - - 404

List of Tables:

Table 1. Original terminology as used by Ken Wilber - - - - 12

Table 2. The basic terminology with the new terms proposed in this essay - 18

Table 3. Areas of knowledge versus modality of approach - - - - 24

Table 4. A very sketchy example of a holarchy - - - - 136

Table 5. The Commandments on the imperative Scale of *ah!* - - - - 142

Table 6. Frequency distribution of the sum of two dice thrown at random - - 247

Table 7. The order of natural Evolution and the sequence in Genesis - - - - 307

Preface

The Laws of ah! is a personal attempt to understand the world we live in. In the '90s I studied the works of Ken Wilber, which was a good starting point. But there seemed to be some problems and contradictions in his model, so I wrote some drafts and tried to grasp what they were. Two were clearly important, but understanding exactly the whys of the flaws, and, above all, finding a solution proved tricky. Challenging Ken's ideas was a daunting prospect, so I let the issues sit, mulling over the problems from time to time, writing and rewriting drafts. An ongoing discussion, perhaps. I needed to be certain I understood the issues well enough to defend my thesis, but I also needed to feel that I mastered the issues. I put together all the notes and came up with a small book, but I was still stuck on some key issues. All of this went on in English, I might add, even though I was living and working in Spanish at the time.

Curiously, many of the blocks unraveled when the opportunity arose to work on a Spanish version. I translated the whole essay to Spanish and then edited it with the help of a friend and colleague with whom I had worked in consensus-building in the past, Patricia Liljesthrom. We had discussed these issues before, so she was a most fruitful counterpoint. Each language has its own hang-ups and ambiguities, so when you do the switch, the glitches crop up in different places and forms. Very illuminating!

The end-result is an informal tour through what we perceive as *reality* in all or most of its variety, with one eye on matter (atoms to armies and the complexities of our brains), and the other on meaning (from baby-babbles to the elaborate cultural edifices that govern our lives), including a good look at the ongoing mystical revival and our understanding of the spiritual realms.

The tour is abstract at times, but rooted in practical examples where possible. It attempts to understand the dramatic shift from a world dominated by concrete material realities to one increasingly rooted in virtual, and ever more subjective constructs and values. The age of objective business and science is passing. Value has shifted. The gold is in the mind, not the matter! Hence, minding the business of your own mind is paramount to your well-being and progress.

In order to see the impact they have on our lives, I have done my best to understand and redefine the roles of science, politics, religion, and spirituality from a novel perspective, all in the context of the increasingly complex world we live in. Yet, as Hollywood likes to say, *"any similarity with real people or institutions is purely coincidental."* Inevitably, anything that pleases one person or group is sure to annoy someone else (and vice versa). It is impossible to analyze widespread problems without touching on someone's sore points, so please hold your horses, this is primarily an exploration of possibilities, food for thought and discussion.

The analysis is approached in three steps: **Book I** discusses the nature of reality, reformulates some of the premises that still dominate western thinking, proposes a novel frame of reference, and some new terms to get beyond current muddles in terminology. **Book II** addresses problems of global scales and complexity, and some of the limitations of old religious and political notions in this new context. **Book III** looks at advances in transpersonal psychology and cosmology, proposing novel perspectives on religion and spirituality.

To round this off, keep in mind that though I took considerable care to be well informed, and several people proofread and assisted with sections of the English version (see Acknowledgements), the book covers such a broad spectrum of issues that it is impossible to be up to date on every detail. In particular, statistics, dates, and numbers in general change constantly as our knowledge advances, so most are provided only for general orientation, to help situate you either in time or in the orders of magnitude of the different dimensions we are dealing with.

I hope you enjoy the read ... Cheers.

=================== 0 ===================

Book I

BEGINNINGS

ah!

Divinity. Countless names! Shame most of the familiar ones are so loaded.

Seriously, it is impossible to choose one in particular without biasing the conversation. Religions often argue about what the proper name of their deity is, might be, should be.

Some even say it should never be spoken out loud. And yet, we are compelled to do so.

I have no idea what gods would call themselves, but if we were suddenly in the presence of true Divinity, I am pretty sure I know what would happen!

We'd be **speechless**!

When we recover a bit, I am also pretty sure our first utterance would be an awed

aaahhh!

or something to that effect.

Perhaps that's why the syllable crops up in so many of the names:

All-a*h!*

Amon r-*ah!*

Budd-*ah!*

Jehov-*ah!*

Krishn-*ah!*

Shiv-*ah!*

So why not simply - *aaahhh!* - or - *ah!* - for short

It's not only natural, it's neutral. Hence

The Laws of *ah!*

==================== I ====================

Book I

BEGINNINGS

Chapter **I.1** –

Posing the problem

No doubt you have been in those situations where a discussion turns completely sterile, dogmatic, a struggle between opposing stances without any inkling of reason or prospect of resolution. A dilemma. He is convinced that preaching their philosophy is life's mission. You have your own opinion and consider that their philosophy is archaic, flawed or whatever.

Or the pitch is to convince you to sign up with their political party, adopt a religion, or donate money to some supposedly *noble cause*. The most suspicious ones are those that rant about it all being *"for your own good."* But in any event, they insist, almost forcing you into a decision (the *"call now"* ploy). How do you know if what they are preaching is true? - if the arguments are valid? - if they are honest or if they are just trying to manipulate you? Indeed, they might be perfectly honest, yet be totally confused! That's why I am always in my right... to question, to demand proof, or to verify who is behind the whole scheme.

Then they appeal to a supposed *authority*. It varies according to the issue at hand but the most common are either scientific, ideological (political) or moral (religious). But that is often just a smoke screen without any real basis. Or they claim a scientific basis to uphold a religious claim, and so on... So then, how do you know if the argument is valid, or if the authority they claim is legitimate for the issue you are considering? Are they objective or are they being subjective? Do you know the difference? This is fundamental, because **if you don't quite understand what's at issue, there is a good chance you'll get conned**.

Let's start by pointing out that in denying God the *scientific revolution* started off on the wrong foot, which is not to say that gods necessarily exist. It's just that 'science' has been as incapable of proving that gods

don't exist as religion has been in proving that their gods **do** exist. That is, nobody has demonstrated that gods **don't** exist to a believer's satisfaction and, conversely, nobody has demonstrated that gods **do** exist to a disbeliever's satisfaction. Since nobody has found an irrefutable answer to this issue, let's leave the gods out of the discussion for the moment. Whereas we can postpone the issue of the divine, we cannot avoid including organized religion in the discussion.

Most people think they have a good command of their native language, but that is part of the problem. Quite likely we do not agree on the definition of many common words, what words like politics and religion really mean! They are just words, and each word has meanings that depend on the culture and time period you consider. If the word has one meaning for you but means something else to me, then we will have a hard time understanding each other or, as my friend John put it: "*an easy time misunderstanding each other and a hard time recognizing it.*"

We are so convinced we *know* our language that when these flaws underlie the conversation the difficulties can appear to be insurmountable. (New or ambiguous words are defined in the glossary).

Even everyday words like art refer to two completely different notions, those beautiful objects created by us, or the ability to create things or perform them artfully, as in *arts and crafts*, or *martial arts*.

When we speak of research, science, or scientific, what do we mean? During the 20th century, **science** gained much prestige, so saying something is *scientific* or *scientifically proven* makes a statement more credible to some. When it is used commercially by competing sides to boost contradictory claims, the ploy becomes suspect. Besides, much of the knowledge we use in everyday life is not scientific, nor will it ever be. *Grass is green ..., rainbows are beautiful ..., I am tired or hungry ..., honey is sweet ...,* all these statements are true, but you don't need science to tell you that. Now, if you ask "W*hy is honey sweet?*" or "*What produces a rainbow?*", then you move into the sphere of science. Understanding how things work gives rise to **technology**.

Next, we have **politics**. If science and technology establish the best way to make a cake, then politics is a means to decide who is allowed to bake it, **who pays for it and who has the right to eat it**. These rules are defined by laws, sometimes based on moral or ethical concepts, but ultimately dictated by those who are in power.

Mixed in with all this jumble are the '...*isms*' (anarchism, capitalism, communism, elitism, poorism, populism, ...), plus the '...*ocracys*' (aristocracy, autocracy, bureaucracy, democracy, theocracy, ...) and all the other forms of government. Theocracy, for instance, means '*the governance by a religious elite*,' such as the ayatollahs in Iran.

Here enters religion, also a complex term covering a range of notions and actions. Throughout history religions have often occupied the role now assigned to politics. Even in modern democracies where power is often not directly religious, different religious groups are constantly lobbying for or against different motions or propositions. Religion has also been used as a core component of ethnic and/or geopolitical identity.

But I think it is fair to say the primary role of **religion** is assumed to be about our relationship with the beyond and the divine. This includes all those religious mandates which are claimed to be *The Will of God*. The problem here is that there are hundreds of versions of these gods and what they supposedly want. It's not a question of denying the divine. Rather, we need to better understand what is the acceptable role of religion in a modern society, and thus if the mandates and dogmas they are trying to impose are acceptable or not.

Here is where the problems worsen, because it is not clear if the definitions we currently use are solid, or to what extent is it legitimate for one area to meddle in the terrain of the others. Religious conceptions not only overlap with politics, but with science as well. Politicians have few qualms about telling us how things should be done. Until fairly recently these overlaps were complete because it was believed that everything of importance there was to know about the world was contained in the *sacred books*. Historically, religious leaders have self-proclaimed the right to tell us how to make the cake, who should pay for it, and who is entitled to eat it, and have created a whole string of excuses, stories, and mythologies to justify why this is *true*, unchallengeable mandates from none other than 'god.' A lot of this seems to be crass politics, but there is such confusion of terms and roles that at times you get the impression that even they don't know where they stand! Besides, at times these notions seem out of tune with the increasing complexity of the modern world.

So, is there a better way to define and understand these areas of human endeavors? For instance, when people insist that you cannot question *(their)* religious beliefs, is this valid? Which would be the 'protected' area of religious claims and dogmas? Religions insist there is a *sacred* untouchable core, but to an external observer this is not at all obvious!

These dilemmas can't be solved on the same level at which they are perceived. Much of the problem is that **some of the underlying terms and premises are flawed**. When the foundations contain flaws, it is best to start from scratch. I start in *Book I* by condensing a frame of reference that covers the basic spectrum of 'reality' of this complex world we live in, based on a revised version of Ken Wilber's work. Then I go on to more complex problems to see if these new perspectives help us get out of some of the muddles and see more clearly. Since starting from scratch is essential, I ask for a little patience.

Before we can improve our world, we need better tools to understand it.

=================== I ===================

Chapter I.2 –

The Book of Ken – on the nature of Reality

Everybody knows the nature of reality, right? Well, maybe, maybe not! In any event, even though both you and I have direct personal experience with reality, when we want to discuss it, arguments can be confusing because we may have very different ideas about it. Also, we may be using and understanding our language in different ways. Defining and understanding 'reality' is actually a difficult and often controversial issue.

My analysis kicks off with the model proposed by Ken Wilber starting in 1977 with *The Spectrum of Consciousness*, across some twenty other books with well over 6,000 pages, to his summary volume *The Integral Vision* in 2007. Since few people have the inclination or can afford the time to read 6,000 pages of revelations, I will go over the useful aspects of that model that are most important to the discussions that follow, just to be sure we're on the same page.

Ken's summary of the world's philosophies, religions, sciences, cosmologies, and spiritual practices is awesome. Yet, though the model he proposes is a step forward, it needs some fundamental changes in structure and a few tweaks in the terminology to correct several critical issues that are central to this quest. Okay, let's go. Please take mental note of the scene the following passage evokes for you.

Reality, act one

Daniel goes out to get some fresh air. Fido wags his tail, fetches a stick, drops it at Daniel's feet and waits. Daniel picks up the stick and throws it, and Fido runs after it, picks it out of the bush and brings it back, dropping it again at Daniel's feet. The cycle repeats itself till Daniel overthrows and the stick flies over the fence and disappears. Fido starts after the stick, follows it with his gaze, stops for an instant and takes off running in the opposite direction, towards the gate. After a while he comes back through the gate with the stick, panting.

This simple scene contains many familiar elements of everyday life. The person, the dog, the stick and the bush, the fence, the gate, and the different actions are all 'in sight.' We know that those elements form ensembles with other things that are not mentioned, but that must be there, that we can imagine (Daniel's clothes, the house, perhaps a family, the surroundings, a street or road, the neighborhood, etc.). These relationships are so constant that, in fact, when we look at a scene or read a description, we automatically fill in these missing things to build a more complete imaginary scene.

On the one hand we have objects, things, actions, the I, the ***individual***. In addition, there is the ensemble, the behavioral sequences, the us, the ***collective***, composed of sets of things.

Reality, act two.

The man looks at the sun, enters the house and reemerges with a pot. Daniel Boone puts the pot on the ground: "Here, have some grub, Fido." He then picks up his raccoon-skin cap and heads for the barn to saddle his horse.

What happened to your imagined scene? The time and place, the house, the neighborhood? The first paragraph could be anywhere, anytime, but the addition of a few details likely changed much of the scene you were imagining. The name, the detail of the cap and the horse in the barn imply a different time, a specific style of dress, rural surroundings, and so on. The ensemble refers us to a more specific geography, time, and culture. But nothing material has changed (we are still looking at a page with strings of letters, sentences and so on), only the *mental images* evoked by the *symbolic language* and the **cultural *constructs in our minds*** have changed.

In addition to the material reality there is another sphere that we do not see but that we can *infer*. When Fido brings the stick, he has a *wish*, an *expectation*, and by his actions he ***communicates*** it to Daniel, who *understands* the *intention* and complies by throwing the stick. Daniel *understands* what the dog's gestures *mean*, and we *suppose* he can also communicate by speech, but till he speaks we don't *know* what language he *knows*. If the language is foreign to us, we hear the words, but we don't *understand* their *significance*. When he enters the house, he has a *purpose*. None of the terms in *italics* in this paragraph refer to objects in the material sense. Unfortunately, the terms we are currently using to name these aspects are ambiguous. To avoid this problem, we need to develop a neutral terminology.

The first aspect we perceive relates to the material, the '**exterior**' of things, but the material aspect is not all. There is also a non-material aspect. The ideas, the abstract, constitute the '***interior***' of things. This distinction is less obvious, but it is essential, so it merits more elaboration. As used by Ken, the **exterior** refers to all the levels of the tangible, what is perceived by the senses, be it directly or with the help of instruments, even if placed physically inside the individual, like the stomach for instance. The ***interior*** refers to the *sensations*, *emotions*, *dreams*, *concepts*, *ideas* that can only be perceived with the *mind*, such as a *pain* in the stomach. The gesture of pain, a behavior, is exterior and can be seen by another person, but *the pain itself* is only perceived by the individual. It cannot be photographed, and our only means of access is by way of *inference* or *communication*. The *significance* of the words Daniel speaks also belong to this sphere, what he is *thinking* and the cultural *climate* he lives in. How about the dog? Even if we do not know exactly what he *feels*, we can *infer* that when he brings the stick he *awaits* (*wishes, expects...*) something on the part of Daniel. When the stick falls behind the fence, instead of chasing after it, Fido makes a detour through the gate. To *solve* this problem the dog must have a *memory*, a *mental image* of the garden and surroundings, and *know* that to get to the other side of the fence he must go through the gate. There is no *reason* to *suppose* that these abilities of the animal are qualitatively different from their human equivalents.

Of course, many people might say that all the *interior* states mentioned are just energy states or patterns of the material substrate. Notions like *sensations (pain), feelings and emotions (joy, love)* certainly seem very close to that. But how about *ideas* and so on? Consider these: **two and two is four**; 2 + 2 = 4. We could read this out loud and someone listening would get it: two plus two is equal to four; *dos por dos es igual a cuatro...* hmm..., maybe they wouldn't get it! **Twice two is four**; two times two is four; two squared is four; $2^2 = 4$; etc. So, we have a number of material patterns or renderings of the same 'thing.'

If so, what is the nature of that '**thing**'? And how do we perceive it?

Thus, we have two axes, the individual-collective* and the material-abstract. Combined, these two axes conform or define 'domains' of reality that Ken calls *"the four corners of the cosmos."* In the simplest form, they make up a 2 x 2 table with the four domains mentioned before (Figure 1). As we will see, this division of reality is useful to organize knowledge and activities pertaining to both the natural sphere and the cultural one.

The Terminology as used by Ken Wilber

		E X T E R I O R		
Exterior-individual			Exterior-collective	
Objective			**Inter-objective**	
—INDIVIDUAL—		+	— COLLECTIVE—	
		I N T E R I O R		
Interior-individual			Interior-collective	
Subjective			**Inter-subjective**	

Figure 1. **Terms used by Ken Wilber**. The names of the domains of 'reality' used by Ken. His original terminology is represented here for ease and consistency, but note that I flipped the axes. Also, some of these terms are confusing and need to be revised (see below).

Figure 1 represents the domains as they appear in Ken's books. I will introduce the proposed changes in subsequent figures. It is important to note that Ken also uses the idea of the *'four quadrants,'* alluding to the four areas of the figure. I prefer to abandon this use because giving the domains a spatial location creates obstacles down the line. Using the left half for the mental aspects and the right half for the material aspects works well at the human level, but can be problematic at other levels, so I will change the format as needed.

The terms *interior, exterior, individual, and collective** are fine, but saying 'exterior-individual-domain' each time gets tedious. The figure format is OK, but has some restrictions. In time hopefully these concepts will become independent of the figure.

The *asterisks* in Table 1 (below) signal a problem.

Note that everybody, including Ken, use each of these terms ('collect**ive**' - 'subject**ive**' - 'object**ive**' - 'inter-subject**ive**' and 'inter-object**ive**') with at least two different meanings. This is the first fundamental muddle that needs to be resolved to avoid confusion[1].

I propose using new words to separate these meanings. The simplest solution to make this difference explicit is to change the ending when the words are used as '*pertaining to ...*':

– collectiv**al** – subject**al** – object**al** – intersubject**al** – interobject**al** –

Since this change is important, a more extensive justification is provided in Chapter I.3.

We can also arrange these terms as a simple 2 x 2 table:

AXIS	interior	exterior
individual	*subjective*	*objective*
collective	*inter-subjective*	*inter-objective*

Table 1. Original terminology as used by Ken Wilber - (asterisks are explained above).

Naturally, in a specific situation there are correspondences between the four domains. A hypothetical example will help reveal the relationships (Figure 2): economic crisis makes us anxious; this affects our bodies, which show stress syndrome, and we experience increased discord in our dealings with others. These four aspects are all present simultaneously.

---

[1] The same can be said for 'individual' which we use both as a noun and an adjective. If a distinction is needed, an alternative **noun** would be individ**uum** (*e.g.*, Figure 9). We can then restrict 'individual' to being the adjective.

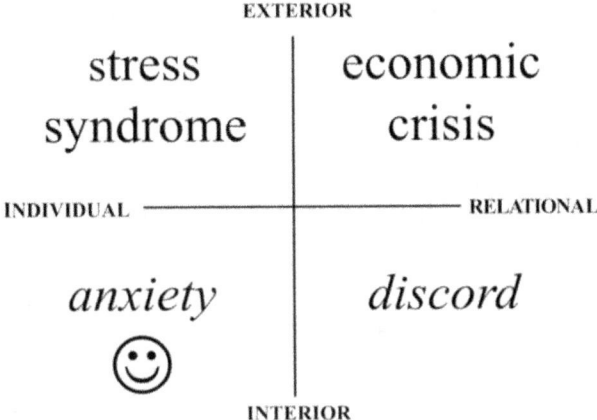

*Figure 2. **A hypothetical example of correspondence.** - In any normal situation there is a correspondence in the states between domains. - In this hypothetical case, the icon seems out of place. If we replace 'anxiety' by 'joy' - ☺ - this creates a lack of correspondence of the individual-interior state with respect to the states in the other domains. - Note: When the distinction is useful, I use italics for the **subjectal** and block for the **objectal** aspects.*

Based on these concepts, Ken organizes all aspects of the elements of our reality into four equivalent and interlinked hierarchies using an additional feature that has been recognized for some time: **increasing complexity**.

For instance, going from simple to complex, the individual-exterior domain might produce the following sequence: atoms, molecules, prokaryotes, eukaryotes, neuronal organisms, neural cord, reptilian brain stem, limbic system, neocortex and complex neocortex (Ken Wilber, 1996). The first two correspond to the physical world and could be subdivided down further to separate subatomic particles, or up by dividing inorganic from organic molecules for instance, but the details are less important than the notion of **complexity** as an organizing principle. The upper tiers correspond to the successive stages of biological evolution, as reflected by their most novel and complex feature, the nervous system.

Wilber uses the criterion of the *'holon'* proposed by Arthur Koestler in 1976, who recognized that everything is something that has parts and **at the same time** is a part of something more complex, or a **'whole/part.'** A person is a holon composed of organs, constructed of cells formed by molecules, etc. And at the same time every person is a member of a family, part of a community that integrates a tribe, a nation, etc. Each unit that belongs to a higher level is more complex and includes more parts, but is less numerous. Thus, as complexity increases, each level has fewer members, forming a natural hierarchy. All our universe is composed of holons inside holons constructing '**holarchies**.' An ensemble of individuals and/or things constitutes a **collective**.

We can use the structure of language itself as an example. The basic test of the sequence in a holarchy is to see what element can stand without the other. For instance, in our written language I can have letters without words, but I cannot have words without letters. Thus, language and writing follow the patterns described above. We have: letters, words, phrases, sentences, paragraphs, sections, chapters, a book. For instance, when I prepared Figure 3, the preceding *"Wilber uses..."* paragraph had 595 letters, 123 words, 7 sentences and 1 paragraph. Again, individual units at each successive 'level' include more parts but, as complexity increases, each level has fewer units belonging to it, down to only 1 paragraph, the most complex item in this example (Figure 3).

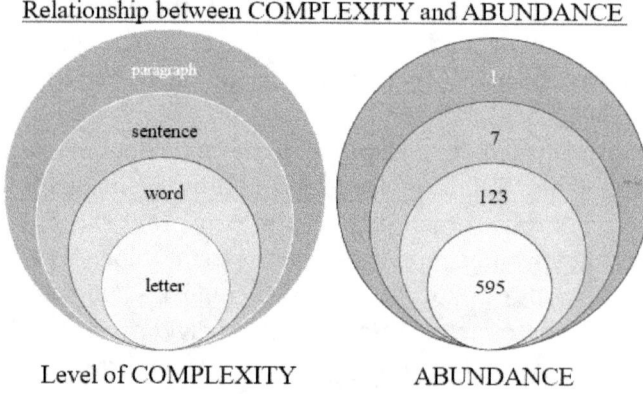

Relationship between COMPLEXITY and ABUNDANCE

Level of COMPLEXITY   ABUNDANCE

*Figure 3. **Relationships in a holarchy**. Left: levels of complexity in a paragraph. - Right: the number of units in each level in the "Wilber uses ..." paragraph in the text above. Complex levels subsume all the simpler levels.*

Higher complexity always correlates with lower abundance of units in that level.

Our first hunch is that there must be a limit, but you can continue up or down the scale virtually indefinitely. Up is easy: edition, series, collected works..., library... How about down? We tend to think of letters rather as was the case with atoms, the smallest indivisible part. But a letter is made up of different strokes of the pen or of a multitude of vibrations in the voice, and so on.

Also notice the horizontal variations: start with UPPER and lower case, normal and *italics*. Then you have the font styles. Take the 'a': - a, A, ₐ, ℚ, *a, A,* **a, A**, ···· and so on, and even within these, different people would show enough variation for each handwriting to be identifiable. Then, the 'a' represents several different sounds, as in '*a cat laughs aloud,*' not to mention the fact that you can recognize dialects and regional variations, and even individual voices by minute differences in inflection. All these variations complicate matters, but they do not make them more complex. For a more extensive treatment of the complexity issue please see Chapter II.34 (Complex minded.).

Each domain has its own holarchy. In fact, initially Ken tried to put everything into a single sequence, but found this was not possible, which was what led him to the idea of the four domains. Though each domain has its own holarchy, there is correspondence between the holarchies of the different domains, but we need not go into the details.

Just keep in mind the general notion that the huge diversity of material things we find in our universe can be organized by levels of complexity, the atomic being the most basic, then comes inorganic compounds, organic compounds, unicellular and multicellular organism, which in turn range from simple cells to very complex ones like birds and mammals, including us.

======================= I =======================

Chapter I.3 –

Muddled terminology

Currently both '*objective*' and '*subjective*' are used with two distinct meanings each: to designate domains, as in 'the objective and the subjective aspects of reality,' and to qualify a statement or attitude.

For instance, B. Alan Wallace in '*The Taboo of Subjectivity*' states that: "A central aim of this book is to unveil the ideological constraints that have long been impeding scientific research in the study of **consciousness and other subjective mental states**." (2004, p. 4, my emphasis). Note that in this statement it is not clear if he means: –mental states belonging to a 'subject,' a person–, or –mental states that are not factual, 'objective'–.

This is confusing. In the previous section I proposed **objectal** and **subjectal,** and their derivatives, as alternative words when used as *'pertaining to ... '*.

However, before we can go further, we need to make another distinction. In this context, the word 'subject' is also used with two distinct meanings: to designate an issue or to allude to a person. This is also confusing. I propose capitalizing 'Subject' when referring to a person rather than an issue, as in: *the Queen rants about subjects that bore her Subjects*. I use this distinction throughout the book. Chapter I.13 provides a more detailed justification.

More specifically, we need to stop using '**subjective**' to designate the non-material category that includes all 'mental states.' All knowledge and theories originate and exist only in minds of *Subjects* (people). Hence, under current use, all of science is '*subjective.*' Scientists are often oblivious to this glitch.

Consider the statement: "How can we reconcile **the physical and the subjective** with one another?" Note that the **-al** ending in '*physical*' has one implication, whereas the **-ive** ending in '*subjective*' has a different implication (see below). If taken literally, it is like trying to reconcile apples with attitudes or atoms with actions!

These are primarily *linguistic* traps. Knowledge and theories about any issue should be defined as '**subjectal,**' as in '*parental*' rather than '*parentive,*' things that only exist **in the domain of a Subject**, and which may or may not be '*subjective,*' a qualifier denoting **a specific methodological or attitudinal condition**. Even when knowledge is about an object, the knowledge itself belongs to the subjectal domain.

If I say "all knowledge is subjective" it is impossible to avoid the implication that it is also illusory or false. Since SCIENCE is about being 'objective,' and anything '*subjective*' is considered a no-no, the only possible non-contradictory solution to deal with these things under the current wording of the paradigm is to consider 'consciousness' as an epiphenomenon of matter, something new that emerges as the result of some forms of organization of matter.

Instead, 'the study of *consciousness and other subjectal states*' does *not* carry the implication that they are *necessarily* an epiphenomenon of the brain. This allows for the possibility that subject and object are two basic aspects of a single reality, just as 'particle' and 'wave' are two aspects of a photon. If consciousness is a property of some systems, it could well be a property of all systems, though not always perceptible by conventional means, just as electrical potential is universal, but only detectable with special instruments when it is out of balance. It might help to point out that focusing on 'consciousness' in this context can be a bit misleading because consciousness, as we understand it in humans, is a very complex and sophisticated attribute. But if you take into account that 'sensing' or awareness is one of the essential components of consciousness, then it is much easier to see that some degree of awareness can be present at least all the way down to unicellular microorganisms.

To discuss these issues 'objectively' a change in the terminology is necessary: the recommended qualifier referring to objects is '**objectal**,' and the one referring to subjects is '**subjectal**.' The terms '**objective**' and '**subjective**' must be restricted to qualify notions like methodologies, beliefs, and attitudes. This avoids second guessing what the speaker meant or was alluding to, and allows us to state our own thoughts in an unambiguous way. The reformulation of current discussions on the nature of reality using these distinctions should help reveal if the *subjectal* should continue to be treated as an epiphenomenon or should be granted equal standing as the objectal.

Part of the problem is that materialistic science has made astounding advances in areas that were previously considered the domains of 'spirit.' The correlation between thoughts and brain activity is undeniable and the discovery of a battery of drugs that alter our emotional states support the idea that our sense of 'I' and all that it implies is a product of the brain.

The notion that the subjectal is a basic property of existence underlies most people's view of the social 'universe' and it is easy to extend the idea to the world in general. To some monistic scientists this might at first seem like a legitimization of Cartesian 'spirit.' I think the distinction merely pushes back the Cartesian duality argument. Many find the reductionist materialistic view untenable because our *subjective* perception is so real, as real as matter itself. In fact, our *subjective* perception is the only way we know we are alive! It's no wonder then that many cultures consider the *dream world* to be the real one, and our waking existence only an *illusion*. Perhaps the majority of the world's citizens take this for granted, so it is the hard-core materialists who need to become more flexible.

What materialists would do well to concede is the possibility that all forms of perceptions, feelings, emotions, insight, cognitive skills, and consciousness itself are the complex expression of some basic property of existence as we understand it. This linked object-*subject* reality then permeates all of existence, at least in the space-time continuum that we have direct experiential access to.

There is another problem with these terms. They tend to be interpreted as a form of opposing or excluding dualism. Something is either objective or it is subjective. No gray areas. But the concepts are fluid and form a continuum (see Chapter I.4).

Still, there is an aspect of perception that seems to us to be independent of or external to circumstances, what many perceive as beyond this reality, something we call 'spirit.' What the defenders of this spiritual reality ascertain, but still need to prove, is that this last link of our being, the *seer* or *observer*, is other than material, – *in this world, but not of it* –, and that it is capable of existing without the support of a *sub-objectal* substrate.

Given the current developments in quantum physics, the notion of a self-sustaining spirit seems as hard to disprove as it is to prove. But moving the boundary to the outer edge of '*subjectal*' gives die-hard materialistic science a lot more elbow room without the need to resolve this ultimate problem. It opens a whole universe of exploration and should help bridge the gap between science and spirituality.

In a nutshell, here is my new terminology in the form of a table and of a figure (Figure 4).

AXES	interior	exterior
individual	**subjectal**	**objectal**
collectival	**intersubjectal**	**interobjectal**

Table 2. The basic terminology with the new terms proposed in this essay.

To see if this helps, we need to consider some concrete examples. For instance, '*I am tired*.' Is this statement objective or is it subjective? I analyze this in the next chapter.

-------------------- o --------------------

As for the issue of spirit and spirituality, consider David Bohm talking about the concept of 'ether':

The positivists said that entities which are unobservable should never be considered in physics. From this it followed that we should drop the ether. This was a correct step, but the principle behind it was wrong. Let me explain. Thousands of years ago Democritus proposed the notion of atoms. Nobody was able to observe them for 1500 years or more, but gradually people found out how to observe atoms. Now if you were to say that you would not even think about atoms until you were able to see them and you could not see them with your naked eye or with simple instruments, then you would never find them at all. I **must consider the idea of something unobservable if I am ever going to find it. First, I must think about it. I must think how I am going to find it if it is there. Then I look and see if I can find it. If I say that it is of no significance until it comes before my eyes, I am stuck.**[2]

For instance, we can't yet detect dark matter, but we know it exists because we see its effects.

-------------------- O --------------------

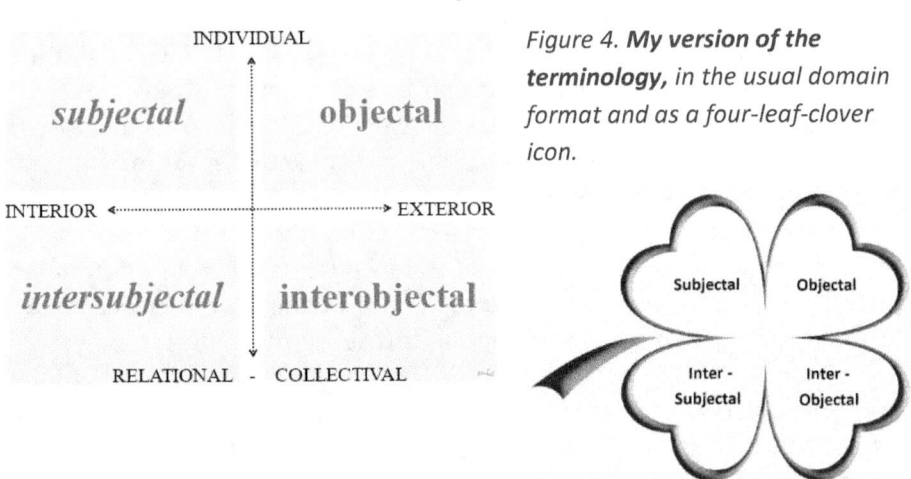

Figure 4. **My version of the terminology,** in the usual domain format and as a four-leaf-clover icon.

I use this terminology throughout the book when appropriate.

===================== I =====================

[2] David Bohm, 1978. *The Implicate Order: A New Order for Physics.* Process Studies, Vol. 8, # 2, Summer, pp. 73-102.

Chapter I.4 –
Issues of semantics and application, round two

Mixed up semantics leads to mixed up concepts. If we reduce the semantic ambiguity the conceptual side should become clearer. Though it is necessary to clarify the semantics first, it is difficult to do one without discussing the other.

The modern use of the term 'object' is unfortunate. Apparently, Rene Descartes considered it to apply only to the ideas held by the mind reflecting the perception that ideas, concepts, theories, etc. are 'objects' of the mind that can be 'manipulated' and on which it is possible to 'operate,' as in 'mathematical operations,' etc. In his terminology, material objects were 'things.' Today 'object' is applied as much to material things ('mings,' see Chapter I.12), as to conceptual ones, but the derived term 'objective' has come to mean '*with reference to material objects* (or material reality),' a curious mutation from the original sense given to the word by Descartes (see the M Bunge quote in Chapter I.41, Worldviews). This catch is hard to escape since 'matter' and 'material' can be used in a similar way (*e.g.,* 'we discussed the *matter*' or 'the *material* in your essay is ...'). If we accept the Cartesian distinction between mind and body, this gives rise to two fairly independent ways of knowing. Even if we don't accept the mind-body distinction, it's hard to deny that there are object-related and subject-related aspects to existence. For a long time, science shunned *subjectivity*, but the irony is that science could not exist without it.

Concepts and theories are intuited or constructed from information taken from the environment, but they do not belong to the environment. They belong to the mind of a Subject. In this sense no science is 'objective' and objectivity is as applicable to the study of material objects as it is to the study of subjects. Phrases such as "*objective subjectivity*" (Reason and Rowan, 1981) attempt to deal with this, but we still feel it sounds contradictory or phony. As mentioned, the time has come to coin some words to reduce the ambiguity or plurality of meaning that has crept into the object-subject discussion.

The ending *–ive*, as in objec*tive*, means 'that executes, that has a tendency to ...' We have proposed using the ending *–al* meaning '*relative to...; pertaining to...,*' as in globe – global, concept – concept*al*.

Thus, we proposed to refer to the concrete, material aspects of reality and the sciences that study those objects as 'objectal aspects' and 'objectal sciences' and to refer to the abstract, immaterial domains and those sciences that study them as '*subjectal* aspects' of reality and '*subjectal* sciences' in order to distinguish the reference to the <u>focus of study</u> from the reference to the <u>modality of appreciation</u> (the qualifiers 'objective' and 'subjective'). However, this distinction is difficult or impossible to sustain. The use of 'object' for the mental domain is almost inevitable due to the structure of grammar. Since all verbs must have a subject and an object, for any verb referring to mental states or operations both the subject and the object are in the mind (*e.g.*, as in '*I remember an <u>idea</u>,*' where 'idea' is the grammatical object of the sentence). But also, in a more literal sense, something in the mind can change state: "therapy . . . helps the individual become more conscious of the sub-personalities, thus converting them from 'hidden *subjects*' to 'conscious objects,' . . ." (Ken Wilber, 2000, p. 102).

Collective is an adjective, as in 'collective nouns.' We also use it as a noun, as in 'the collective,' therefore the domain should be 'collectiv**al**' – that is, 'belonging or pertaining to the collective sphere' (analogous to 'individual'). **Collectival** works in some contexts, **Relational** is better in others (see glossary and Chapter I.22). I will use both as analogous. It is also unfortunate that English has adopted 'individual' to stand for both meanings. In Spanish the noun differs from the adjective: *individu**o** – individu**al***. As mentioned earlier, 'individuum / individual' works well.

Don't despair, I don't intend to go over every case in print. Hopefully I conveyed the idea. Usage will do the rest.

Now, let's go back to the issue of whether '*I am tired*' is objective or subjective. In the grammatical sense it is both, in the scientific sense it is only objective. Let me explain. In the grammatical sense "I" is both the object and the subject of the sentence, so the verb and descriptor refer simultaneously to both. But the sentence could be rewritten as 'my body is tired, and I feel tired.' Now, in this version the first part is clearly *objective* in the scientific sense since it is an 'objective' observation on an object, my body. The second part is trickier. If by 'subjective' you mean something pertaining to the subject (the observer), then you might interpret that the comment is 'subjective,' which would imply it is scientifically questionable or false. This, of course, must be nonsense, making no sense. If my body is physically tired, the feeling of tiredness must clearly be appropriate, true, and therefore 'objective.' Hence, '*objective subjectivity*' is not as contradictory as it sounds!

So, what do we really mean when we say something is '*subjective*' in the epistemological scientific sense? Well, we mean that the observer, the Subject, is 'projecting' his or her beliefs or feelings on an outside thing (the object) and attributing these qualities to that thing. Or perhaps, **that his emotions and prejudices are clouding his judgment**. An example may help. Seals have big watery eyes. When unacquainted people see seals, in a zoo for instance, they frequently say "*Oh, poor thing, it looks so **sad**.*" Now, there are two problems with this observation. Seal eyes 'water' to protect them from dryness out of water and this is not related to their emotional state, which is quite different from the emotional interpretation of *watery eyes* in humans. The second aspect is that 'sad' is a feeling we can only identify in humans as humans, ourselves. As simple observers we had no way of knowing if seals had any form of feeling that could be considered equivalent to human sadness. The past tense, 'had,' is because the study of brain activity and chemistry are giving us tools that may allow us to make that sort of leap with increasing confidence.

But in the case of '*I am tired*' there can be no 'projection' because 'the thing out there' is still me! This clarifies if we restate the qualification. *It is an objective comment about a Subject*, me. Or an objective comment about an aspect of me that is *interior*, emotional. Note that I cannot use 'subjective' to describe 'interior' without falling in the trap again. What if we try the *–al* ending? If we say: "*The comment is an objective assessment of my subjectal state,*" then there is no contradiction, no ambiguity of meaning.

Contrast that to the 'sad seal' example. The comment is subjectively *subjectal*, which is to say, the person is giving an interpretation of the seal's *interior (subjectal)* status which is distorted or biased by his interpretation of what *watery eyes* mean among humans.

Additional problems

The subjective-objective is often, if implicitly, portrayed as a white-or-black dichotomy. However, most situations, descriptions and so on seem to be part subjective, part objective. In fact, rather than a dichotomy, it is a continuum. Consider the following:

People believe in some notion that we can call 'R.' A curious mind imagines a better, empirical, explanation. In scientific terms he has developed a new hypothesis. But where does it lie? So long as it is not tested it is certainly not 'objective.' Even if it is based on good empirical information, it is just an idea inside the mind of a Subject (*i.e.*, say 95% subjective). After it withstands a first round of testing, the null hypothesis is discarded with a significant probability (p<0.001). Does this make it objective? Well, not quite. A string of additional tests later, the researcher is convinced that the hypothesis is correct and, maybe, elevates it to the status of a *theory* and publishes the results. Now the idea has been materialized (it has material existence), but it still needs peer review. At this stage, what percent objective/subjective is it? After years of additional testing, experimenting, peer discussions and reviews no one can find reason to discredit it and it is now taken for a law, the 'S' law.

A century or a millennium later better experimental and analytic tools show that, in fact, it was not quite correct. Closer than 'R' perhaps, but still false or partial. Hypothesis 'V' is proposed. And so on...

Of course, if you researched the evolution of thought about this subject you would find that explanation 'R' was put forth to correct the earlier explanations 'M' and 'M₂,' and there is some evidence of an even earlier archaic explanation 'A.' This is typical of the evolution of most ideas and theories. We can express them as successive percentages (the actual values are unimportant; they are only meant to give an idea of progression).

So, then we can say that:	
the belief in 'A' is animistic, or about	~ 99 % subjective
explanation 'M' is magical	~ 90 % subjective?
and explanation 'M₂' is mythic,	~ 80 % subjective?
then explanation 'R' is religious	~ 70 % subjective? . . .
Towards the other extreme we have:	
explanation 'S', which is scientific, or	~ 60 % objective?
explanation 'U' is unitive	~ 80 % objective?
and explanation 'V' is 'vision-logic'	~ 99 % objective?

In this sequence the 100% objective will presumably be the absolute explanation. Now, here we are coming to yet another problem. We are either running out of room on the continuum or we truly have to enthrone this latest understanding as dogma. Presuming that the current version is the 'absolute' one has been the fallacy of all times. Better we stretch the continuum[3]. The irony is that the absolute explanation, if it exists at all, will almost certainly be at least in part *subjective* for the simple reason that no explanation can be absolute if it does not include us, the Subjects, consciousness, and the whole issue of subjectivity *per se*. Thus, the Z explanation will not be merely scientific. Zen, perhaps?

Of course, there may be problems with the formulation. Here again we seem to have a mix of issues and semantic problems.

We can separate the understanding of subjects and of objects as different approaches to knowledge, (*i.e.*, as subjectal and objectal knowledge), each of which can be postulated or obtained by subjective or by objective methods. Then we have:

UNDERSTANDING OF	MODALITY	
	objective approach	subjective approach
objectal reality	medicine	*animism*
subjectal reality	psychology	*politics – religion*

Table 3. Areas of knowledge versus modality of approach. Separating these concepts allows us to redefine the areas of knowledge and the possible modes of intervention. Here I include just a few terms as examples. The placement of 'politics and religion' is debatable, but remember, in an 'absolute' explanation they will have to fit in somewhere.

After years of writing and rewriting this section, I can find no way of profitably sustaining the use of object/ objectal/ objective and subject/ subjectal/ subjective in any other than the strictly grammatical context and its implied senses. As for the two domains of reality, even if we do not use the above, we still have a long list of terms, a sure sign that none does the job well enough to stand alone: concrete/ abstract - body/ mind - matter/ mind - material/ immaterial - exoteric/ esoteric - physical/ mental - exterior/ interior (as used by Wilber) - etc. Doctors speak of

---

[3] An analogous situation could be a vendor who claims his antiseptic is *99% effective* against germs. This could be valid for a specific cocktail of germs. But if we start adding resistant strains the effectiveness would decrease quite a bit. Adding strains is like stretching the continuum.

'psychosomatic' ailments, so why not psyche and soma? Extreme materialists would argue that all abstract internal states are energy states. How about matter versus energy states? Mystics might say OK, energy states are a property of matter, but that's not what we mean by 'mind,' *the seer*. The basic question remains: What is consciousness?

To make the matter (!) worse, along comes relativity and quantum physics and tells us the distinction between matter and energy is not quite true: an atom is a bundle of bound energy. It can undergo processes such as radioactive decay, transforming into something materially distinct, and releasing part of the energy. This free energy can be infused to a system (as when heated) without it changing the basic nature of the atoms. A wave, as a function, has entity[4] regardless of its energy content (above zero?). A particle becomes a wave and back again according to how you look at it. Perhaps the dichotomy is misconceived at its very roots. What is 'energy'? In physics it is understood as *the potential to cause change or do work*. This tells us what it does, but not what it is.

========================= I =========================

Paraphrasing George Orwell,
All laws are equal, but some are more equal than others!

Chapter I.5 –
The Book of Isaac

So, what are ... *the Laws of ah!* ... ?

Many people think of the Ten Commandments and similar statements as the 'laws' of gods. But those are just suggestions, rules, or commands that you can choose to obey or not. There might be earthly punishments if you don't, but still, they are laws only at the political level. Besides, they only hold here and there, in some cultures strongly, in other cultures not at all. In fact, they are pretty temperamental. And of course, none of them hold outside the sphere of human endeavors, let alone in other parts of the universe!

Divine laws on the other hand you'd expect to be unbreakable. There are a number that qualify nicely, though none of them can be found in the *scriptures (The Books)*.

---

[4] 'Entity' meaning "with distinct and independent existence."

Take the Law of Gravity. You are allowed to circumvent it under certain conditions, but break it? Not recommended; it will break you. Instant retribution! And it applies everywhere.

Then you have the Laws of Thermodynamics. They also apply everywhere, even in other planets, stars, galaxies. In fact, as far as we can tell, in all the known universe.

You could add many more Laws that are universal. Many of these were Revealed to one of our greatest modern prophets, Isaac, so if you want to get acquainted read the works of Isaac (they usually include 'Physics' in their titles). They are important because they are the ones that define the rules of the arena that *ah!* set out for this universe! Ignore them at your own risk and peril!

But don't worry. You don't need to know them scientifically, though that can be very useful at times. Take birds for instance, they know nothing of our theoretical ramblings about the Laws of Aerodynamics, yet they are accomplished masters of the skies. They do need a bit of practice when they start, but very soon they are intuitive experts! With a little practice and dedication, we can learn to be just as proficient in our worlds. Still, a greater understanding of these Laws helps and there are levels of excellence that are very hard to attain if you don't know what you are doing and why.

But even these Laws may be of a second order. The ones that truly define '*the rules of the cosmic game*' are even more abstract and most were not Revealed till very recently, less than a hundred years ago in most cases, though a few were Revealed to the classic Greeks or earlier.

David Bohm has called it the '**implicate**' or 'enfolded' order. The point is simple enough: things like numbers, mathematical rules, geometric figures and a host of other concepts are 'givens,' somehow intrinsic features or properties of reality that seem to exist as abstract models in some state before the *Big Bang* or *Creation*. They are like germs of possibility, the building blocks and constraints of creativity. If we see - *** - we say there are 'three' asterisks, but then we can hold the idea of '3' without there being any set of three things in sight. Once you understand them, such patterns begin to appear all over the place. If a single egg divides (the usual cell division), you get two cells, right? And if each of these divides in sync you get four, then eight, sixteen, and so on (but you never get 'seven' by this process). Now take a pizza and cut it in half, then again and again and you get 2, 4, 8, and 16. Bingo! Same progression. That's the thing, the progression seems to be independent of the material substrate. For lack of a better word, I will refer to all these seemingly intrinsic elements, relationships, and constraints underlying the structure of reality, the ground of existence, as '***ahxioms***.'

Perhaps the most amazing of these is the Revelation of **fractals**. Fractals are bundles of relatively simple commands that produce astonishingly complex, and often beautiful, images: ... 'walk one step, make a right-angle to your left, take another step and turn again; now walk 1+1 steps, turn left, walk 2 more and face left; walk 2+1 steps, turn, walk 3 steps, face left; take 3+1 steps, turn, another 3+1, face left; repeat as desired.' The resulting trace looks like a growing labyrinth (Figure 5).

A simple FRACTAL

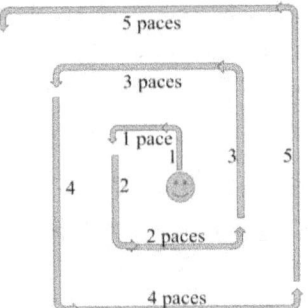
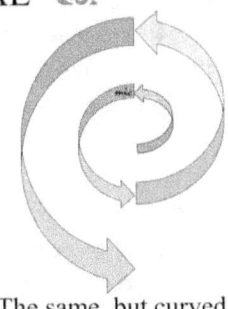

The same, but curved, produces a SPIRAL

*Figure 5. **Fractals**.*

A design generated by a formula (see explanation in the text). Variations in the formula produce different shapes and types of spirals.

These basic patterns seem to in-form nature and produce many of the forms we are familiar with, such as the huge variety of spiraled snails and seashells.

If you take small steps and barely turn, the shape becomes rounder till you end up with a perfect spiral. It's a bit like the mirrors in a kaleidoscope that take the images of the colored shards at the bottom and repeat them indefinitely, making very attractive arabesques. If you reshuffle the fragments, you get a new design.

The exact shape of the spiral can be changed by changing the values in the formula (changing the angle of the turns or the length of the steps), but the whole design is contained in the formula, and different formulas produce different designs. Even this simple pattern appears in nature at every scale, in snails, hurricanes and galaxies. Fractal designs have been shown to underlie a wide range of natural features and patterns, such as fern leaves and snow crystals. This is what allows us to create virtual realities, including things like science fiction films. We can safely assume that a pizza in *Pandora* will divide into 8 pieces, just as it does here. What makes *Avatar*'s Pandora truly sci-fi is that *unobtanium* defies gravity! Wow!

There is a huge amount of information out there on this line of Revelations, so I will not dwell on this (besides, I am no expert). But you would do well to inform yourself of the basics.

What about those other 'laws' preachers talk about all the time? Well, for the most part they are hardly different from socio-political rules and regulations. Oh, yes, preachers will assure you that their particular set was legitimized by 'God' (their god, of course). But you see, if you look around a little you will soon find that there are hundreds of versions of these rules scattered all over the world. It's more like they are little sets of rules to play different Games of Life. Am I saying they are unimportant? No, not at all. They can be very, very important if you want to play in any given place and time, but don't be fooled. At times they are imposed, but often you consent to follow them. If you don't like these rules, you could consider moving to another context of landscape with rules that better fit your needs for growth or fit whatever you think is most important for you. There are plenty to choose from.

Think of holy books as early attempts to create a virtual reality. For hundreds of years naïve tribesmen all over the world have been completely caught up by these stories and led to believe they were 'true,' but they are just as 'virtual' as any modern sci-fi video game. It can be great fun to play, just don't get fooled into thinking you must live your life by those rules. Besides, one of the virtues of the better video games is that you can choose what roles you want to play, whereas in most religious proposition someone else plays 'Preacher' and the only role left for you is to play 'Believer.'

==================== I ====================

Chapter I.6 –

The Book of Dmitri Ivanovic – *the Laws of ah!* – Part II

We talked about the Nature of Reality and *ahxioms* and the structure of the universe. Then some about Physics. This is like a building. You start with the foundations and then build up from there, all the way to the roof and the decorations. The material universe is built up one step at a time by increasing complexity. Physics deals with the basic nature of matter and how it is constructed: quarks and other subatomic particles that make up protons, neutrons, and electrons, which in turn are the building blocks that make up atoms. What comes next? Well, out of those three particles, Nature[5] has made 94 elements that occur spontaneously in nature, plus another 24 we have made in labs. The key player in this was our friend Dmitri Ivanovich, who gave us the periodic table. His grasp of the patterns structuring this complexity allowed him to predict the existence of several elements unknow to us in his time, a true act of prophecy. The last one to be identified in 2002, initially referred to as '*un.un.octium*,' the one-one-eighth element, is now officially called Oganesson. That would be an almost 40-times increase in complexity.

But the real fun begins when you get to the level of Chemistry and start combining those 94 elements. Complexity explodes. The number of possible chemical compounds is hard to grasp. A decade ago, we had identified about 60 million, but the theoretical number is much higher, in the billions. Though basic inorganic chemistry is orders of magnitude more complex than physics, it is still quite deterministic. Scientists can often predict the properties of a particular combination of elements or work out the possible structure that might have certain properties.

Complexity increases dramatically when you get into organic compounds, the basic components of life. As complexity increases, predictability decreases. This seems to be one of those very basic *Laws of our universe* that works at every level of organization, and it is one we need to keep in mind for later discussions.

There is no point in going into the details of chemistry, but it is worth spending some minutes on complexity. We tend to underestimate complexity. Elements are a little bit like letters. Some are especially good at binding, like the vowels. Others are more exclusive and only combine with special friends, so to speak. The fact is that if you have just five or six vowels and twenty or so consonants you can make up all the tens of thousands of words in the English language, plus again as many for each of their equivalents in the hundreds of other known languages. So now try to

---

[5] Or God: at these basic levels of organization the distinction is of little relevance. To a believer, the nature of God is expressed in Nature, so for the moment I will refer only to Nature.

imagine how many codes you might make up with an alphabet of 94 letters! Just to give you some idea, a string of three would have 94 x 94 x 94 possible sequences, over 830,000. Used as letters, strings of three plus strings of four plus strings of five of these elements would add to about 7.5 billion different combinations, or almost enough to code for every person on the planet. These rather simple sets make up most of what is known as inorganic chemistry. There is diversity, but it does not organize.

The really interesting stuff kicks off when you get into organic chains. The element Carbon has the capacity to link with itself to form long chains and rings. Each carbon atom has four 'arms,' so to speak, that can bind with and hold onto some other atom. Most often, two or three are used to bind to the adjacent Carbon atoms in the chain, but that leaves the other(s) to bind with something else. The Carbon chain acts a bit like the imaginary line under this sentence that holds the letters in a special fixed sequence. If you took all the letters in the sentence and put them in a blender the meaning they now convey would evaporate. It's not the letters but their different combinations and sequences that allow us to code meaning. Pretty much the same goes for organic compounds. As the chains get longer and longer, Nature can build more and more sophisticated structures and coding systems. The pinnacle goes to nucleic acid chains that form the basis of genetic coding, RNA and DNA, which no doubt you've heard of before. Each of our cells has a total of about 2.9 billion base pairs, two copies of each. It takes three base pairs to code each 'letter,' called a codon. Our genetic 'book' has about one billion codons, packed into a microscopic space! We only need 21 of these trios to code for protein sequences (many are synonyms), but even with this limited set the number of possible sequencies would approach 21 x 21 x 21 ... ... multiplied a billion times! That's a lot of possibilities, and a lot of information!

By now you must be thinking 'What on earth is this guy trying to get to?' Simple. The world of biochemistry and biology is **astronomically** complex. Millions of species each of which can have billions of slightly different versions on a theme. Currently, we humans are close to eight billion in number, and every one of us is unique in some respect. But note that over 99% of our DNA is *fixed*, which means that every person on earth that has been tested has identical copies for that 99%. All the variation you see the world over is the result of minute differences in that 1% of our genetic material (plus some variation produced by the environment that we develop in and our personal history). This sobering fact is what makes much of our tortuous histories of *ethnic cleansing* so utterly absurd. An additional reason is explained below.

Fast forward a bit. The simplest free-living organisms are one-celled animals and plants, starting with tiny bacteria and going up to some macroscopic cells. Viruses are smaller, but they are not free living. The largest cells are several centimeters across, so you can see them with the naked eye. Thousands of unicellular species are known, but as usual the real diversity appears with increasing complexity, in the multicellular level.

We are multicellular. Each cell in us has two copies of DNA, one from our mom and the other from our dad. Why would we need that? Well, it turns out our DNA is like the director of our chemical factory. It regularly sends out chemical messengers that keep the factory rolling. But that creates a problem. These chemical messengers cannot travel far, so large conglomerates of cells need to have many copies of DNA scattered all over the place in order to keep the machinery going. This puts a very real limit to cell size, and that's why we have so many cells (see below).

OK, so we have the beginnings of multicellular critters. Initially they develop fine, but then they seem to hit a ceiling. As I mentioned above, the problem is that they are totally dependent on contact chemistry. Simple aggregates of cells cannot get beyond a certain size because molecules can only react with others they bump into, so the chemical reactions that keep life going only work over a very limited area. Our senses of smell and taste are chemical, and both need to be in direct contact. That is why you bring flowers to your nose or taste a morsel in your mouth. On the other hand, sound and sight work fine at a distance.

Larger aggregates must use different strategies, including the circulation of liquids that can carry chemical signals to distant organs, more sophisticated chemical messenger-receptor systems, special cells that can transmit electrical impulses at a distance, and a few other tricks like the division of labor and the specialization of cell groups to form tissues and organs.

These innovations gave rise to yet another explosion in complexity and diversity. Estimates vary, but consider 3 to 10 million species of plants and animals as a plausible range, but the total could be much higher. Multicellular means a conglomerate of many cells, but just the name does not capture the living realities at all. The average person is made up of about 10,000,000,000,000 cells (10^{13}) or ten trillion. And then each of us is populated by about 500 different species of microorganisms in the skin, the gut and so on. Each of these bugs is much smaller than our cells, but they are about ten times as many in number. Multiply each of these bundles by eight billion humans …, and we begin to get into the sphere of what our limited minds simplify as "*infinite*":

80,000,000,000,000,000,000,000 -! … and that's just 'us' …

You could say we are walking biological libraries. Each DNA copy would be equivalent to around 2000 small books. If you add all the microorganisms, then it would be over 2500 books per set. The notable thing is that in the process of somatic cell differentiation, each human DNA set often acquires so many unique epigenetic traits that it becomes a personal signature or identifier of each and every person on earth.

Please keep in mind that this essay is not intended as a catalogue of verified facts. Many facts and figures change frequently as our knowledge of the world and the cosmos progresses, and will likely continue to change in the future. Dates, statistics, and quantities in general are provided as guidelines or reference points to situate the reader in the appropriate time or scale of things, and should not be taken too rigorously.

In case the issue of possible combinations is not obvious to some readers, here goes an explanation of sorts. Let's say you want to make up codes for the license-plates of cars in your State with the usual alphabet of 26 letters. For the first letter you have 26 choices (A or B or C or … … Z). Got one? OK, now you can choose the second letter. Since you can repeat all the letters as many times as you wish, you still have 26 to choose from, and another 26 options for the third. This gives 26 x 26 x 26 which equals 17,576 unique three-letter combinations. If you happened to be in California, you'd run out of codes very quickly, so now add three numbers: same thing, you have ten possible digits (1, 2, … 8, 9, 0) which produce 10 x 10 x 10 or 1,000 combinations. Since you can combine each letter combination with each of the number combinations, now you can make unique codes for 17,576,000 cars, which might just be enough in some states, but not in California. They had to add another digit. With sets of three letters and sets of four digits you can get over 175 million codes (if you mix the letters and numbers, it's over ten billion). Easy. Now get your calculator and try 20 'letters' multiplied a billion times. Actually, don't, your calculator might burn out … *Mind boggling!*

====================== I ======================

Chapter I.7 –

The Laws of ah! - part III

Hopefully in the previous sections I managed to convey how matter and life evolved through stages or levels involving successively more complex levels of organization. We got as far as the general idea of multicellular organisms and just how complex they really are. If you want the details, feel free to go to a biology book or the web. You'll find more than you'll ever need to know.

But there are some features about this level of organization that might be relevant and worth pulling out from the sea of information on the subject. The great advantage of multicellular over unicellular life is that if you cooperate, each part can differentiate and then specialize to do specific jobs more efficiently. Assuming you are not in some barren desert, just look around and you'll see the diversity of life that surrounds you! Clearly this innovation has proved very successful. Again, we are talking about increasing levels of complexity.

Unicellular beings do well in water or on the surface of solids (slimes), but they can't stand up like a tree can. To do that you need to have different types of tissues: hard ones for support, leathery ones to protect and keep in moisture, green ones to catch the sun's energy. And once you learn to do that, new possibilities and complexities again explode! Don't even try to do the numbers, except to note one important property. Complex organisms are more flexible and can learn in more complex ways.

Simple organisms tend to be preprogrammed. '*If too hot, sink*' might be a good reflex for some critter living in a lake (deeper water is usually cooler). But it would be counterproductive if the 'lake' was now on the kitchen stove! We call these automated responses *instincts*, which can range from simple stimulus-response ones like the one mentioned above to fairly complex sequences in some species, like building nests or singing. Instincts don't suffer from learning flaws and work fine if the environment is predictable, but they are rather rigid. Most organisms can also learn. Learning allows instinct to be tailored to changing conditions, different locations and so on.

At least in animals, as they get more and more complex, instinct plays a smaller role and learning becomes much more important. Which brings us to a critical generalization: **there is an inverse relationship between**

complexity and determinism. Simpler systems are always more rigid and deterministic than complex ones - a direct consequence of the number of possible configurations and arrangements available to each level. Flexibility (freedom) increases with complexity. It's as if the Laws of *ah!* were releasing their grip. Oh, don't be fooled, many restrictions still apply, but also more plasticity, more choice if you wish.

Perhaps it's worth mentioning some of those restrictions. There are many advantages to being more complex, but also some flaws. Complex systems are more vulnerable and inevitably break down with time. Nature (or *ah!* or Life, whatever you prefer) has solved this problem by complete systems-replacement. It seems to be easier to just trash the old one and build a new one. In other words, all complex beings are born, live for a time, and then die. If their way of living is to continue in this world, they must make new copies of themselves before they die. Reproduction has thus become a very major concern of life in general, and we humans are no exception. And then you can leave the game early, perhaps, but there is no way to reenter halfway through (you can't be born as a teenager). And there is no way to rewind either (if you make a mistake, for instance). What's done is done.

We are still in the sphere of the Laws of *ah!*

=================== I ===================

Chapter I.8 –

Reality, Act Three

Enough of nature and biology for the moment. Much of what we reviewed so far belongs to the objectal-individual aspect, with a few things taken from the objectal-collectival to hold it all together. If we want to move to the more human aspects, we need to include the *subjectal* side of reality.

In the objectal domain it was quite easy to start from the most basic components of matter and follow the sequence as matter organizes into progressively more complex systems, but this would be harder to do with *subjectal* reality. Part of the problem is that the only way we have access to this aspect of reality is through introspection. But most of us would have difficulty remembering how we felt and thought as two-year-old toddlers, or how that changed when we turned four. Yet, we can certainly concede that there was a progression, and that our mental constructs get more and more complex as we grow up.

We can also talk about it with fellow seekers, but we have no way of chatting about it with our pet; or asking the cows in the pasture out there how they are feeling today. Yet, as I posited earlier (Chapter I.2), we must assume all critters show some degree of *subjectal* perception. If you have been able to read this far you must be very conditioned to think and communicate with language, but that is certainly not the only way we can 'think.' In her book *Thinking in Pictures,* Temple Grandin has given us a description of how animals might see the world. In the last few decades this has been borne out by many animal trainers that stopped trying to break horses or tame other animals and started reading the body-language used by their charges and communicating with them through that body language. The results have been really spectacular! If you use the proper language, animals can and will learn in a few gentle hours what used to take months of brutal training. Animals are not dumb; it's more like we were being dumb. It was like trying to communicate with someone who is color-blind with color-coded messages. He just can't perceive them, which doesn't mean he's stupid (color-blindness occurs predominantly in males, by the way).

It is thus difficult to get a first-hand grasp on the way the *subjectal* domain is built up. Earlier I used language as an example of a holarchy (letter, word, phrase, sentence, paragraph ...). Since these are obviously symbolic representations of ideas and mental constructs, I think we can safely assume that language reflects aspects of the way our *subjectal* world is put together. This is reflected in the structure and sequence of preschool and school education. For the moment, at least, that's close enough. A better understanding of these processes has made teaching and learning languages much easier, for instance.

Here is where the other dimension begins to appear. Even though maturation and learning are an internal physical and subjectal process (ones that occurs in the interior of each individual), the context in which they occur and several of the elements we mentioned have more to do with the **interactions** between individuals than with the individual's inner world. It is essential to learn language and other forms of **communication**, and the 'rules' of **social interactions**. On the one hand the teacher is teaching us what is what, but at the same time he is showing us which word we could use to refer to that thing if we need to ask for it or to talk about it. And all this occurs in a very specific context where different individuals play different **roles**: teacher, student, classmate, director, etc. Of course, nobody stops to point out that this or that is 'subjectal' or anything of the sort. These events have always happened spontaneously. We just pick it up almost without thinking. It has only been a few decades since we (humanity) have started to study how these processes develop and play out.

==================== I ====================

Chapter I.9 –

The Book of Sigmund – the structuring of our subjectivity

Clearly, we Humans have been dealing with complex levels of symbolic subjectivity for millennia. The origins of speech are lost in the mists of prehistory, but we know that the oldest rock painting is over 50,000 years old. These paintings are often linked to evidence of shamanic rituals. The first scripts go back to at least 5,000 years before the present. (To avoid constant adjusting, let's fix this '**present**' as '*years before 2000,*' or **yb²** for short). These dates keep being pushed back in time, so the first attempts could be much older.

Strangely, nobody seems to have studied how all these abilities actually work till the end of the 19th century and the beginning of the 20th. They seem so natural that we take them for granted, they simply are, and work for us without us needing to think about them. There have always been some individuals who had the intuitive gift of managing their own subjectivity and of manipulating it in others, but if anyone ever studied how, he made sure to bury the secrets with him. And the little that was known was heavily laden with superstitions. To begin with, it was thought that the conscious human had total control over himself. If he behaved badly, it was due to his own malice or because he had been 'possessed' by some demon. Something of the kind was attributed to madness, and addiction was the product of the lack of moral integrity.

However obvious it might seem today, it must be stressed that what allows us to perceive the world that surrounds us (the senses), be conscious, and have a memory of how our lives have played out, is the nervous system. It was not always so. Different cultures imagined and placed our being, the soul, in a variety of ways, mostly in the heart. Even

René Descartes (1596 - 1650), the instigator of the scientific method, considered the *soul* as distinct from the body, a duality, mind **and** body. But as we advanced in the study of anatomy and physiology it became clear that the seat of our perception and biological consciousness is the nervous system.

One of the fundamental steps was given by accident by Luigi Galvani around 1780, when he established a relationship between muscle activity and electricity. That is, an electric discharge produces a reaction in the muscle, which is where the expression '*galvanized into action*' comes from. That rapidly changed the focus and started the process to understand how the nervous system works to provide us with both our senses and our behavior. Together with other discoveries, it was the kickoff for the emergence of modern medicine, including sophisticated tools like the electrocardiogram and electroencephalogram. For a time, we held the illusion that medicine centered on the material body would find the solution to all health problems, including aliments of the soul.

But it only took about a century for it to become evident that some dysfunctions and pathologies of the soul did not seem to have a physical (material) base. While he was working on hysteria cases in the Pitié Salpêtrière Hospital in Paris, the neurologist Jean M. Charcot discovered that hypnosis modified the behavior of patients, suggesting that it was possible to treat these ailments without physical interventions. One of his disciples, Sigmund Freud, picked up on these ideas and developed what we now know as *psychology*. *'Psyche'* was the word for soul in ancient Greek, thus 'the study of the soul.'

Around the end of the 1800's and the beginning of the 1900's, with Sigmund Freud's work, the issue began to gain notoriety and became the object of systematic studies, *"scientifically"* (the quotes because it was assumed that science did not meddle with subjective issues). Even so, materialistic science slowly gained ground in areas that had previously been considered the domain of spirituality. The link between thoughts and mental activity is undeniable, and the discovery of a whole battery of drugs that alter our emotional states support the notion that our self, and all that it implies, is tied to our nervous system. We can see where there is neuronal activity with a variety of material scanners, even where and what type of activity (visual, motor, etc.), but to understand the details of what is actually happening we have to access the 'Subject.'

The new-born comes into the world with a functional nervous system that allows it to survive, that is, to take care of all the basic physiological needs. As it grows, it learns to handle its body and acquires a host of abilities, including spoken language in humans, which is what allows us to operate in our family and social environment. The process is interesting but extensive. We only need to pick out a few ideas.

Perhaps the most important idea Sigmund developed is the discovery of our unconscious. This basically destroyed the myth that a conscious man had total control over himself and his actions. But better start with simpler things. A puppy or a baby has to fully concentrate in order to stand and take its first steps. Any distraction, and he stumbles. Walking requires a fairly long learning process, which may take days or months. But, as we grow and progress, walking becomes more and more automatic until we master it so efficiently, we hardly need to pay attention. The same happens with running, swimming, driving a vehicle, and so many other activities. The fundamental issue here is to realize that a large part of our daily functioning goes on in a sort of auto-pilot mode, without the intervention of our conscious self. If you think about it, this is essential, even in animals. To catch its prey a predator needs to focus fully on what the prey is doing. If it stops to think about where and how to walk, chances are it will lose the prey. Much of this gets processed automatically below the level of consciousness.

In an everyday context, think of a chat with a friend in a bar. Our ears are receiving sound from multiple noises and conversations, but the mind has the faculty of filtering out most and providing consciousness only those that are of interest to us. Our more basic vital processes (breathing, the beat of our heart, digestion, etc.) function most of the time without our conscious intervention, even when we are asleep. Fantastic, but also a limitation.

For this to work, the brain has developed mechanisms by which most of the information is filtered before it gets to consciousness. If we had to think it over, that would be a distraction. It seems our attention can only cope with one issue at a time. If something else distracts us, we lose the thread of what we were doing. That is the cause of many accidents of every kind and color. If you are driving at 60 or 70 miles per hour, a one second distraction can be fatal – literally. Tricksters, scammers and pickpockets have known this from times immemorial, but it seems science has been rather slow to catch on.

Here is where Sigmund comes in, when he realizes that this filter can also be used to block uncomfortable or stressful sensations and feelings. He called this mechanism *repression*. By 1915 he was developing his first topic, where the mind was divided into three levels or compartments: the **conscious**, the **preconscious** and the **unconscious** (the repressed part). The **preconscious** is not conscious much of the time, but it is easily accessible to consciousness. Instead, the **unconscious** is not accessible at will.

Later Sigmund developed his second topic, in which he subdivided the mind from a different perspective: he identified the **ego**, the **superego** and the **id**. The Id is the underlying biological part that usually plays out below the level of consciousness. The Ego is what we understand as our conscious personality, the part that interacts and links with the environment and with others. The Superego is the part that includes the parental, social and religious mandates, which are acquired without much conscious analysis during childhood and youth, and which we often feel as our own even though they were planted there by outside interests (Figure 6).

All these structures play a role in the operational and mental dynamics of the individual. Surely in a simpler world of prehistoric humans they were well adapted to the levels of social requirements of the times. In hunter-gatherer societies tied directly to their environment there was little room for artificial elaborations.

The problems have developed as the societies have become more complex, where these basic natural tendencies have exposed us to increasing levels of error and manipulation. In a modern society that operates largely on the basis of symbolic constructs the situation changes radically. Today we speak of *introjecting* (projecting inwards), which means something like 'taking for oneself' something from the outer world, believing it is a part of us. The process is unconscious. The individual identifies and adopts the ideas and conducts of others, what they are told or what they see in the external world. This can be a valid form of learning, of acquiring values. But here is where the risk zone lies. The young mind has few resources to evaluate which values are acceptable and which are manipulations that will play against his own interests. Later, as an adult, the poor soul ends up being a prisoner of these ideas, even though they are hampering or damaging him. When they feel uncomfortable and we deny them, or if we try to dissociate from them as a form of defense of our emotional self, these ideas slip into the **unconscious**. They retain part of their emotional charge, which is why they still affect us, but we lose the capacity to manage them consciously. In fact, they manage us!

In a nutshell, becoming aware of these hidden dimensions in our mental structure is an essential first step towards becoming more autonomous. A practical way of seeing these interactions is imagining various groups of elements that intersect, with the self or EGO in the center (see Figures 6, 7 and 8). In the following sketches the arrows depict the relationships and the dominant direction of the influences.

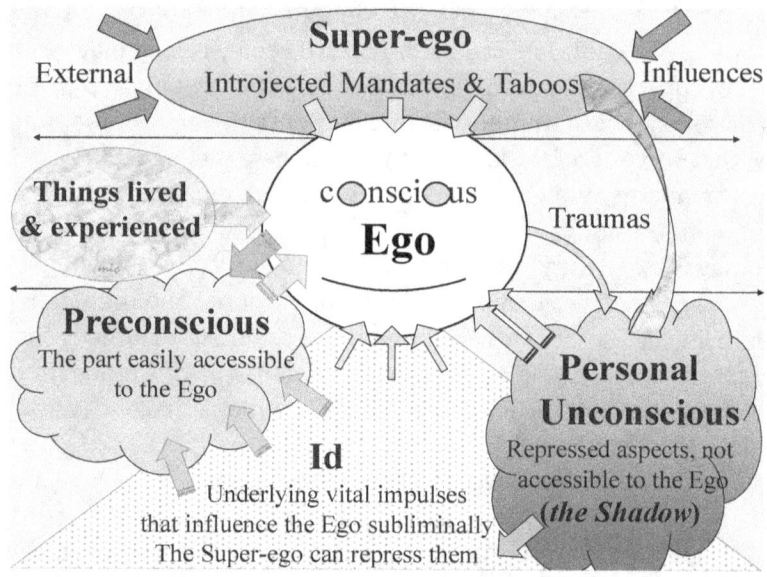

*Figure 6. **The elements of personality**. - A sketch of the basic structures of our personalities, adapted from Sigmund Freud's topics. The arrows indicate the main interactions and the dominant direction of the influences.*

For instance, the functioning of the digestive system is largely autonomous, part of the **id**, but as time passes from our last meal it starts sending messages to the preconscious that begins to awaken the sensation of wanting to eat, till the issue gains strength and the message passes directly to our consciousness, something like *"We're hungry!"* We can suppress the sensation for a time, but it will become stronger, and stronger, till it becomes impossible to avoid thinking of food. Something similar occurs with our other basic needs like urinating or defecating. No matter how much self-control, education and sophistication a person might have, in the end their biology takes command!

This is a good point in which to stress **a basic premise**: increasing complexity gives us increasing liberty, but it is ALWAYS rooted to, and limited by, all the underlying levels. Perhaps we can 'fly' with our minds, but our body continues to be bound to earth by gravity; to function we need the chemical energy provided by the food we eat; our biology demands that we comply with a number of basic self-care routines (sleep regularly, for instance), and so on. Free will is something we can enjoy AFTER we have taken care of all these requirements.

But keeping all these constraints in mind, no doubt we are very complex beings with the capacity to learn, to think, to communicate, to analyze complex problems, make decisions and provisions for the future, and even to imagine completely novel ideas and create new things. To a large extent all these abilities depend on our sophisticated nervous system and on an extended infancy and youth that allows us to accumulate a large body of information and behavioral abilities.

But, as with all complex systems, it is also vulnerable to derailments, errors and manipulations. The learning process is long and complex, and it requires the intervention of many people during many years of the youngster's life. There is always the risk that some of these people will be too authoritarian, violent, or that they use the access provided by their roles to abuse the youth under their care, be it physically or via manipulative conditionings. Besides, by its very nature, our development and life itself can expose us to traumatic experiences that leave emotional scars on our psyche. These negative experiences are not forgotten, rather they are buried in the depth of our minds, where they can produce all kinds of symptoms, such as anxieties and phobias, and thus negatively affect our lives through what Sigmund called the **unconscious** (Figure 7).

We all believe what we were taught as kids

There is a ton of historical and anthropological evidence that shows us that we believe what we were told to believe when we were kids, what our native culture believes. This includes a bundle of 'operating instructions' that under normal circumstances help us navigate the world we live in, both the natural and the social spheres. But, in addition, you almost always get a number of infiltrated concepts that are not operating instructions. I mean the social mandates, political ideologies and religious beliefs, all of which change from one society to another. If you were born and raised in a Taoist culture you will believe in the Tao; if you grew up in the Altiplano of Bolivia you will almost certainly believe in Pachamama. Had you been born in the Viking world you would have believed in Odin; and so on.

Priests and preachers know this very well. *"Give me a child and I will give you a Christian"* (or a Taliban, an anarchist, a communist, whatever strikes your fancy). That's why it is so important to pay attention and monitor what is being taught in educational institutions.

The result is that the youngster introjects a complete package of ideas that he perceives as something that belongs to him, but which in reality is a bundle of external mandates that were imposed on him. This is what Sigmund called the **superego**. Without a doubt it is a useful structure in its correct measure, but it can very easily become oppressive if the social context around the child was very authoritarian or manipulative. In the next two figures I first sketch a pathological condition and then a more balanced personality developed in a healthy environment (Figures 7 and 8).

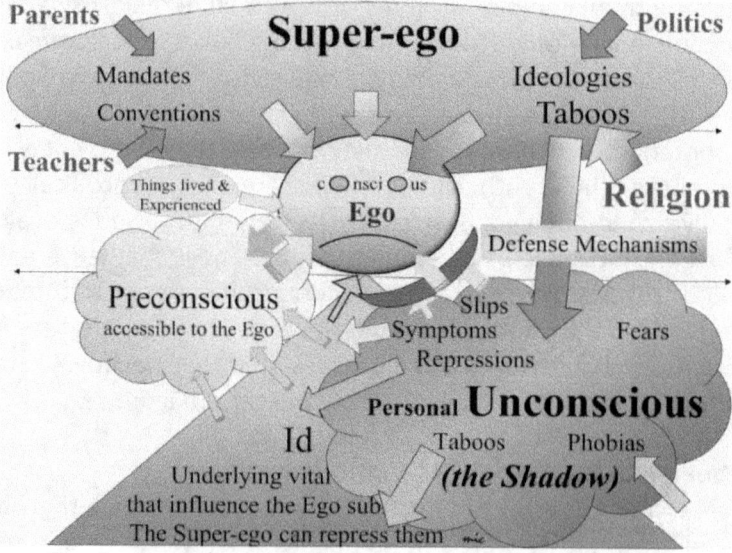

Figure 7. ***A stressed personality.*** *- A personality very dominated by external influences (mandates, prejudices, repressions) with an invasive* ***superego*** *and a strong* ***shadow*** *that dampens almost everything. The conscious* ***ego*** *is poorly developed and weak.*

It's important to emphasize that we protect our conscious Ego from many stressful or threatening situations or issues by a variety of **defense mechanisms**: introjection, projection, dissociation, denial, etc. These mechanisms protect us, but at the same time they act as screens or filters that alter the way we perceive the world around us. Our perceptions and interpretations are frequently distorted by these phobias and prejudices that operate hidden from our conscious awareness.

Perhaps because they had the good fortune to grow up with few traumas and with parents and teachers who taught them to discriminate, or because they have gone through a thorough cleanup process, many people manage to develop balanced and fluid personalities (Figure 8).

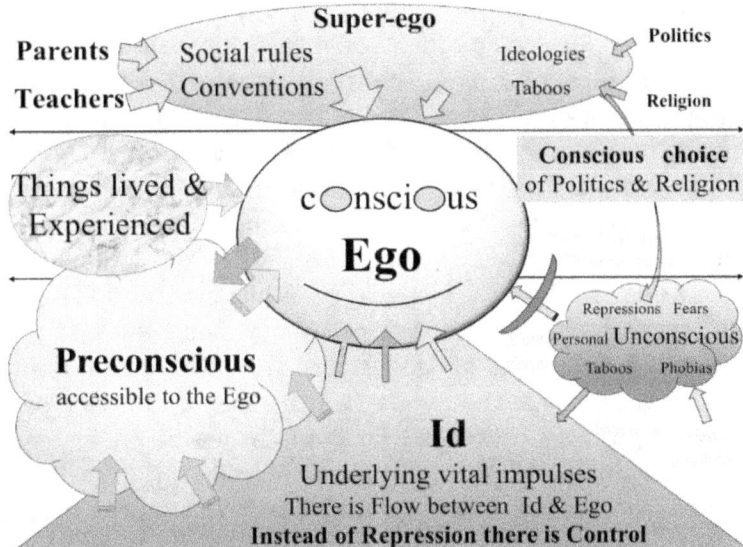

*Figure 8. **A balanced personality**.*
The conscious **ego** is strong and expansive, in fluid contact with the preconscious and with the **id**. Limited external influences: political and religious affiliations adopted as an adult with free will. A **superego** oriented towards an appropriate social insertion and a limited, weak **shadow**.

This is a brutally sketchy synthesis. We are very complex beings. But these sketches should be enough for the level of analysis we are considering at this point.

===================== I =====================

Chapter I.10 –
The Book of Alexander – from catalogs to systems

Even if implicitly, when we spoke of levels of complexity we always spoke of individuals: the atom, the molecule, the organism. Broadly, we looked at the sequence of growing complexity: subatomic particles, atoms, inorganic molecules, organic molecules, simple organisms, etc. Now, I am not saying this is the end of the story, rather just the beginning. When we move from the individual to the collectival, each level can become progressively more complicated. That is, the resulting ensembles are more complicated, but not more complex. A jigsaw puzzle is complicated, but it is not complex.

Nowadays these notions seem fairly obvious, but at the end of the 18th century in much of Europe and the Middle East, the idea was that God had created the world just as it was, and that was that. The only task left for 'natural theology' to do was to describe and catalog the things created by God. One of the prophets that opened the way to move from natural theology to natural history, and from there to the notion and comprehension of natural systems, was Alexander von Humboldt (1769 – 1859). But better we start with simpler things.

In our world things are repeated by the billions and trillions, forming aggregates that have unique properties. For instance, think of those tiny particles that we call grains of sand. On their own they don't amount to much, but if you collect thousands, you can make an hourglass; with several million you have a sandbox for the kids; several trillion make up a lovely beach; and who-knows-how-many trillions of trillions, the magnificent Sahara Desert dunes. *But they are still just grains of sand!*

Or again, with something as simple as the molecule of water, H_2O, you can create a snow crystal, the vapor of a kettle, a dewdrop, a puddle, a rivulet, clouds, a pond, rain, a river, a lake, glaciers, a waterfall, the Amazon, a sea, the polar ice caps, the ocean, waves, and a thousand things more. Experts say there are no two identical snow crystals. One single substance, an infinity of forms.

In these aggregates you find fluid forms, but no stable structures.

This aspect of reality is what Ken calls a *'collective,'* in the preceding examples from the objectal-collectival domain, the material side of the collectival. Each individual element and each level give rise to some form of collective. Broadly, atoms give rise to planets, stars, and galaxies. There are direct relationships between the behavior at the atomic level and astronomic (cosmic) dynamics. The chemical level gives us a huge diversity of substances like water and silex, the main component of sand mentioned above, which form the basis of almost everything we are familiar with in our immediate surroundings: geology, the atmosphere, the scenery, the climate, and the material base for life. The atmosphere and climate are devilishly complicated, but their basic composition is relatively simple.

Some of these aspects can be so complicated in themselves that they have given rise to branches of science and specific specializations of their own: astronomy, geology, climatology, oceanography, etc. But the basis is always the same, a variable mixture of a bunch of things. It is one of the important differences between the individual and the collectival. As a rule, the individual objects of any category or class have fairly regular forms and compositions. Instead, collectives can differ enormously in composition, form or size, as we can see in the infinite variety of clouds. In general, we perceive great categories or classes, but the borders tend to be diffuse, often with gradual transitions from one form to the next one. This is one reason why the sciences dealing with collectives came of age much later than those dealing with the individual aspects. Also, in the case of aggregates you first need to identify the parts before you can begin to understand their relationships. In most cases we started by making different kinds of catalogs, just listings without any particular structure. This marked the first efforts to study and comprehend the world of living beings: describe and catalog the existing diversity. It wasn't till mid-18th century that Carl Linnaeus attempted a more systematic ordering within each of the great groups, giving rise to modern **taxonomy**.

But, as I anticipated, Alexander von Humboldt was the first to realize that in nature everything was related to everything else (see Andrea Wulf, 2015). He broke out of the static, immutable creationist mold when he perceived that as you moved from one geography to another all the flora and the wildlife changed in predictable ways. In particular, life forms seemed to repeat from one geography to the next, but with different conglomerates of species. In other words, he realized there was unity underlying the diversity, and that this unity could be explained by physical and climatic factors. It was the beginning of the science of modern **ecology**.

Not so much, 'What are these things?'

Rather, **'How are they related?'** and **'How do they interact?'**
All this has to do with material aggregates and collectives in their different levels of organization, and the resulting mixtures. At the biological level we speak of social animals and sociobiology, at the human level specifically of societies and sociology, and at the social level of economy and institutions, just to give a few examples. These conceptions gave rise to more dynamic visions of organizations and the passage from simple linear thinking of 'actions' to the relational concept of **'interactions'** as the driving force, the idea that underlies the notion of dialectic relationships. There is no point in going into too much detail of the material aspects because they are relatively well documented and accessible (systems theories and the likes), but there is one aspect in the old classifications that needs to be replaced.

The growing complexity of holons forms a well-defined *complexity ladder* (Figure 22, Chapter I.31). On the other hand, no such order can be found in the range of 'collectives,' which can be a mixture of holons from almost any level of complexity (*e.g.*, an ecosystem). But the underlying forces that generate these collectives at each level of organization are unique and constant. This fundamental distinction motivates and justifies the change from a descriptive treatment of 'collectives' to one driven by the underlying forces (links and bonds) that generate and govern the dynamics of those collectives, the *forces* that underlie 'aggregatedness.' This issue and conceptual change is further discussed and incorporated in Chapter I.12.

What is relatively obvious in the material domain is quite elusive in the subjectal domain.

===================== I =====================

Chapter I.11 –

The Book of Pichon

Each of us is an individual, but we also all belong to a family, and in the days of yore each family belonged to a clan. In a simple society a hunting party might be made up of several men with no particular leader. In fact, leadership might rotate according to what's going on. The fastest might lead the chase, the strongest might take over to bring the animal down, the most skilled at butchering will process the carcass, and so on.

But as groups get bigger some form of leadership emerges. And as they come together to form more complex groups, so do the roles get more complex and specialized. Some form of rank appears and is usually indicated by visible signs such as a feather in their cap. Clan bosses that unite several hunting groups might have three feathers, and the head of a group of clans that make up a Tribe deserves a full headdress! Finer still will be the ritual dress of the Great Chief that leads all the tribes that make up the Nation, perhaps a full headdress that has long 'tails' to the ground. There comes a point when adding more to the headdress becomes impractical, so the boss of bosses that rules a Kingdom replaces the headdress with a crown. The details vary a lot from culture to culture, but the general principles are surprisingly universal.

Now, you might think this explains the collective, but it doesn't. What I have just described is simply the visible external result. You need to ask yourself, what keeps these units together? What is the **glue** that underlies a 'nation'? There are some external material props, no doubt: a shared territory, a Proper name, and a flag being amongst the most obvious. But as important are the family ties, shared language, history, myths, customs (such as dress, food, etc.), and a sense of common origin and destiny. Also, the knowledge that there are *others* out there that are different and often dangerous, enemies that we must beware of and ward off.

Note that much of this entails different types of links between people. Leadership, roles, ranks, bossing, leading, obeying, ruling, family ties, language, shared history, myths, friendships, arguments... All these notions only make sense in the context of groups and collectives, so they are in some sense *inter*. At the same time, most involve mental states, abstract interactions, communication, ideas that go back and forth across the community. Hardly any of this could fit into the inter-objectal domain. So, where does it fit? Many of these things belong to the inter-subjectal.

This seemingly elusive muddle began to unravel around the middle of the 20th century, after Humboldt had provided the ideas of systems and interactions, and Freud had given us his psychology. Several schools in Europe and the Americas started working out different aspects, but the man who put together the coherent theory and practice that I am familiar with was a psychiatrist who worked in Argentina, whom everybody called *Pichon*. Enrique Pichon-Rivière (1907-1977), was born in Switzerland, but grew up and studied medicine in Argentina, specializing in Psychiatry. He later went on to study psychoanalysis, but eventually broke away when he realized there was another sphere that was not covered by standard psychology (Pichon is yet another Freudian "renegade"). In time he developed his own school to study and operate in this sphere which he called *Social Psychology*. Pichon's *Social Psychology* closely matches what I understand as the inter-subjectal, which is why he will be our guide.

Many of the processes that underlie the dynamics of groups and societies belong to the sphere of '*social psychology*,' which studies and operates on the inter-subjectal within groups and collectives. But what, exactly, is inter-subjectal? One way to look at it is this: *subjectal* is all that goes on **inside** of a Subject[6] (a person, inside your head), like feelings, emotions, ideas, images, dreams, intentions, ….

Inter-subjectal is what happens **between** Subjects, what jumps from one Subject to another, and much of that has to do with communication (Figure 9).

Figure 9. **The simplest group is two.**
 A chat with a friend or dining with a date. If a friend proposes a 'blind date,' you will surely ask if he is handsome or is she pretty, charming, young or not quite, and so on. Let's say all this sounded OK, even intriguing, so you accepted, only to discover that your date just arrived from abroad and only speaks Manipuri.
Not a word of English! Rats, and now?

We can transmit a lot of information with our bodies, besides its size and shape. Virtually all animals use their bodies to transmit information by means of posture, colors, smells, sounds, and displays. They even have specially modified appendages to stress some gestures and make them more visible at a distance. Even the direction of the gaze is important in social animals, including humans of course. In fact, scientists consider that an important part of the message we transmit in a normal conversation is through our **body language**. It is worth mentioning that once an animal adopts a color, form, or gesture to transmit a specific message, that feature

---

[6] The use of a capitalized '**S**ubject' applied to people is explained in Chapter I.13.

tends to become exaggerated and, if it is advantageous to the sender, ways to either fake the message or its magnitude will crop up and evolve. Even though the vehicle for the message is material, the interpretation of its **significance** requires a receptor Subject, an 'other.'

After millions of years of living up in trees, our monkey, ape, and protohuman ancestors gradually lost much of their capacity to smell. But for terrestrial mammals, producing and perceiving odors is an extremely rich form of communication that can serve either to attract or to repel other members of their species, and to pass on information about identity, age, sex, physiological status, reproductive condition, and so on.

Sound is another important means of communication. Songs, growls, purrs, tweets, and a whole cacophony of calls populate any natural environment. Human speech is the most complex form of communication we are aware of, but certainly not the only one. A music score is probably just as complex, but it has completely different symbols and structure. It allows a composer to tell a group of musicians how he wants them to play the music he imagined.

But the supreme form of communication is through **symbolic language**. An important advantage of symbolic language is that it can transmit information at a distance about things that are not physically present, and even about totally intangible and abstract ideas (Figure 10). This gives us the basis. Once we have a **shared language**, we can also share a multitude of issues: our current situation, feelings, thoughts and needs, our past and future, stories, ideas, methods and belief systems. In short, a shared language also means a shared culture and history.

All this sounds great, but communication is not without its perils. Once you replace the real object with any form of symbol, it becomes increasingly possible to cheat, so Nature takes precautions. A stag that wants to communicate its health and fitness grows huge antlers. Antlers are reliable signals because they require a huge amount of energy both to grow and to move around with. There's no way a sickly individual could fake it. That's also what makes a lot of very expensive items reliable signs of wealth and status. Almost anybody can fake a fancy suit. A very fancy car is not so easy. It takes flying around in your private jet to push most of the competition out of the game. Faking, however, is not only limited to physical signals. Language itself is highly prone to distortions of many kinds, plain lying being the most obvious.

Figure 10. **The basic intersubjectal**. – The relationship of the subjectal (clouds) to the intersubjectal (boxes), in a gender toned interaction. – Symbolic language is an essential aspect of human communication. – What we say is seldom a true rendering of what we think. - Another aspect of the intersubjectal are the roles we play in an interaction (see text).

Yet, communication is only a part of the **intersubjectal**. Roles are another important element of this domain. I'm not referring to what actors do, though that is where the concept originated. When two people interact, they tend to take on different roles, such as dominant or subordinate, helpful or obstructing, and so on. These postures are not necessarily conscious. In fact, usually they are unconscious. For instance, someone in a group might boycott systematically without being aware of it. Also note that terms such as 'leader' or 'collaborator' can only occur within a group. You might be accustomed to the idea that a 'leader' is someone who was nominated and holds some sort of special rank. But that's only partly so. Leaders may be concrete people, but 'leadership' is abstract, a state of mind that must be awarded and accepted, and may be completely transitory, floating from individual to individual, as we saw above. These roles can become frozen in an institutional structure, but still, that's just a variation on the theme.

When Wilber and others speak of this domain, they tend to go directly to the upper levels of complexity within the domain, using words such as culture or religion. These are hypercomplex concepts that span many facets, including aspects from all the domains. Pichon-Rivière's conception is more appropriate for this stage or level because it is based on the dynamics of small groups, the basic components of this huge structure that we call intersubjectivity. In the English-speaking milieu, people such as Paul Watzlawick on communication theory, and Eric Berne on group dynamics come to mind.

We have all grown up in family groups and social contexts of diverse natures and complexities, to such a degree that we often take all this social stuff as a given. Most of us can navigate in social contexts intuitively, but to operate in the social sphere professionally you need to know how social dynamics works in general, how to read social situations, and master the appropriate tools for interventions.

The only way to gain this expertise is to be a part of and work in groups centered on a task. Studying is a task; *group conformation* is also a task (see below). These groups will slowly show all the social dynamics, which allows the student to see and feel the interactions *in the flesh*, always with the guidance of a facilitator adept at noting and interpreting these situations. Just as the psychologist must practice his share of introspection in order to learn to recognize the elements of his inner world, so the social psychologist must participate in group interactions for a number of years to be able to perceive those fleeting instances of subtle interactions that constitute the basis of group and social dynamics.

A note on group *'conformation.'* The usual meaning of the word in English is to comply with some format or standard, except in chemistry where it also refers to the different spatial arrangements or 'conformations' a molecule can adopt. This is the sense given by Pichon to his *"conformación grupal,"* which goes beyond the mere formation of a group. If I invite a few friends to dinner, I *formed* a group, but this alone does not define how the group will organize and interact, how it will *conform*. In this sense, **group conformation** is a process that takes time and can spin off in many directions.

In the previous chapters on the material aspects of reality it was possible to make comparisons of the different levels of complexity and their complications. Here we find a slightly different situation. Since we have no direct way of accessing and understanding intersubjectivity in lower animals, our starting point must be at the level of complex organisms with an evolved neocortex and relatively advanced social systems, with basic symbolic language as a minimum. When we shift from the subjectal to the intersubjectal, we are dealing with situations that are at the same time complicated and complex. Getting this across without using math is a challenge.

Let's play. Using the 'a' as grains of sand we can produce various aggregates of 'a's:

---

chains: aaaaaaaaaaa ---- calligraphies: A ₐ @ a A **a A**

ladders: AAAAAA --- waves: aaaaaaaaaaaaaaaaaaa

Amusing, but not very useful.

With syllables we could hold long conversations:

Pi pi pi. ¡Muuuu! Tweet, tweet. Baaa. Woof, Woof. Oink…

This is the level of complexity attained by most animals. There is communication, but the range of information they can transmit is limited, and in general refers to current tangible things and situations. We also use monosyllables for many basic concepts, so don't underestimate monosyllables.

It just takes chains of syllables for the number of combinations to explode. Add strings of words, phrases, sentences, and the possibilities are unlimited, infinite, even with lowly monosyllables: *We will ask Pat why she went to her own art show in the big red car full of wet mud*. This is what allows us to encode and communicate names and terms for millions of people, things, ideas and situations, including abstract concepts and complex plots. **It is the basis of our culture**.

Something similar happens when we go from the individual to groups and communities. We are adding the complication of a multiplicity of interactions and cultural variations to the already complex biology of the individual. This is what enables the fantastic richness of interactions between humans. The possibilities, for better or for worse, are unlimited, virtually infinite.

We spoke of communication and of roles. Another aspect of the *intersubjectal* is related to the notion of links and ties between individuals. The primary ties are those formed in the heart of family, those that last a lifetime. Then we go through a multitude of variably durable relationships and other more fleeting acquaintances: friendships, dates, significant others, colleagues, competitors, enemies, partners, allies, opposers. Note that I have included a number of relationships that would normally be considered 'negative,' but these are also forms of linkage. It is important to stress that if we have, say, ten types of links, and ten or fifteen individuals with shifting dynamics such as complicities, love triangles, bullying, supporting, scapegoating and so on, the number of possible situations and combinations escalates astronomically. This is what makes 'reading' complex social interactions a challenging art.

As Leo Buscaglia proposed, the opposite of love is indifference, not hate. This is another important aspect in the dynamics of groups, small and big. What is the tension that marks the current dynamics of this group now? And what might be its resolution? This is important when the intention is to help the group solve its problems and improve its functioning, transforming these polarities into a synthesis. A conflictive love-hate situation might be resolved if we can get the parts to gain some degree of acceptance, even indifference towards the situation (Figures 11 and 12).

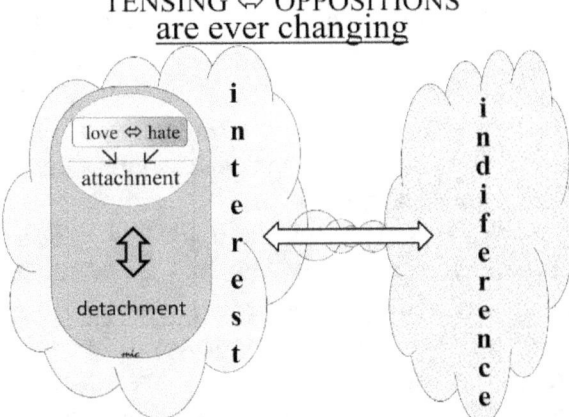

TENSING ⇔ OPPOSITIONS
are ever changing

*Figure 11. **Group health**.*
In a healthy interpersonal and group dynamics the oppositions or polarities are, precisely, **dynamic and ever changing!** The sequence can move in both directions (start with indifference and move towards a love-hate relationship or the opposite).

As the groups go through the different stages of formation and development, the polarities tend to change spontaneously, even without intervention. Which brings us to another aspect of intersubjectal evolution, the stages of group conformation: tele, communication, relevance, affiliation, cooperation, belonging and learning.

Though the process of group conformation has a directionality, it cannot be reduced to a linear process. Pichon saw it as a spiral. The group goes through these stages and then reenacts the same sequence of stages, each time deepening the ties and transforming the relationships, a process which he referred to as a **dialectic spiral**.

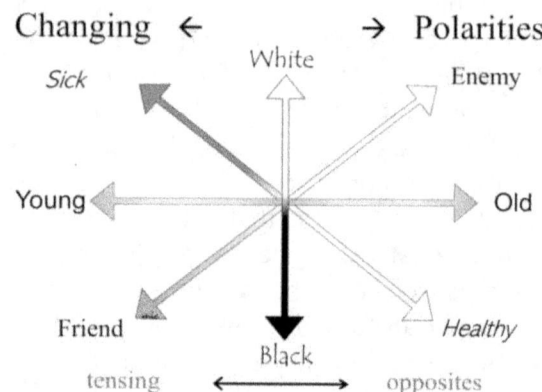

Changing ← → Polarities

Figure 12.
An alternative set of tensing opposites.

In group relationships the axis that dominates depends on each group, the stages of group conformation, the task at hand and the external influences of the moment.

With this very sketchy outline of group dynamics in mind, let's return to the issue of communication, which by definition always takes place in a group, be it real or virtual. It was Paul Watzlawick who defined the five axioms of communication. For instance, the first axiom posits that it is impossible to not communicate in a social situation (that is, even silence provides information). It is also useful to keep in mind the eight stages of communication, starting with the emitter who must have some idea he wished to transmit, he codifies it (puts it into words), he transmits it via some channel (gestures, oral or written), at which point the process switches to the receptor who must perceive the message, decodify it, accept it (take it in), use it, and in an ideal situation provide feedback (*i.e.*, return an appropriate response to the sender). It's important to keep this chain in mind because the process can fail or err in any of these stages, **or it can be deliberately distorted, interfered with, or misinterpreted** in some of them.

This is not the place to develop a whole treatise on social psychology, but I hope this sketch is enough to make it clear that **the intersubjectal is a domain with its own identity**, just as complicated and complex as the interobjectal domain. These basic elements make up the pieces that form the web that structures all the sociocultural world, including politics and religion. But, in my opinion, even though culture and its derivatives, politics and religion, use and are heavily influenced by these basic dynamics, the derived constructs cannot be reduced to them. In addition to the increase in the intrinsic complexity, the construction of any area of culture requires the participation of many other aspects from all the domains. In other words, 'culture' is a **level of organization**, not a domain.

In keeping with the idea of a dialectic spiral, it's time to make a synthesis and then see if we can develop a second round of complexification.

================== I ==================

Chapter I.12 –
Summary of the first round

When we try to visualize the idea of the domains in our world, all this about – subjectal | objectal | individual | collectival – and their variants 'interobjectal' and 'intersubjectal' are viable, but we are still using qualifiers to refer to nouns. Which, then, might those nouns be? At the most basic level, the simplest adequate solution would look something like this: - Ideas | Things | Links | Bonds -.

Note, though, that I used 'things' for lack of a better word. We are again stuck without a good word for 'material things,' in contrast to the more general sense the word 'thing' often carries, as in 'any-*thing*.' Spanish doesn't have this problem because the term 'cosa' is heavily skewed towards the material side. We definitely need a new word here: I will use 'mings' to stand for 'material things' in figures and tables, and when I need to restrict meaning to the material aspect. Then we have:

**Ideas	Mings	Links	Bonds**

Referred to us humans, think of it this way: - mind | body | memes | genes -. At the individual level we can use **mind** and **body** without much problem, noting that 'mind' refers only to the abstract aspects, what we might call '*mental states*.' These new concepts or alternatives are presented in Figure 13.

We talked about **genes** as the basic units of chemically coded information that define how our bodies are made, which are then passed on from generation to generation. A family or clan then is a group that is bonded by shared genes (common ancestry) and would be one of the earliest and most basic social units.

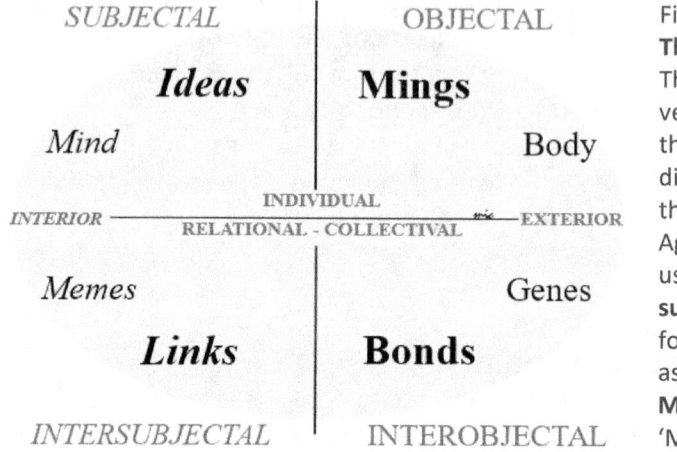

SUBJECTAL | OBJECTAL

Ideas | **Mings**

Mind | Body

INTERIOR — INDIVIDUAL — EXTERIOR
RELATIONAL - COLLECTIVAL

Memes | Genes

Links | **Bonds**

INTERSUBJECTAL | INTEROBJECTAL

Figure 13.
The domains and us.
The Michael Christie version of the items that compose the different domains in the human sphere. - Again, when useful, I use italics for the **subjectal** and block for the **objectal** aspects. – **Mings** is short for 'Material things.'

The term *'meme'* was proposed by the biologist Richard Dawkins as **"the basic unit of cultural transmission"** (Dawkins, 1976. *The Selfish Gene.*) This term might be unfamiliar to some readers. It echoes 'gene' obviously, and refers to the basic units that can be transmitted from one individual to another: *ideas*, *concepts*, or *thoughts*, and the likes. It can serve as a key notion for the *intersubjectal* at the biological and cultural levels. Just as 'gene' identifies the material base of the biological, *'meme'* identifies the abstract mental base of the cultural level. Since both imply the coding and transmission of information, the concepts are analogous.

The concept of the *meme* is useful only when we speak of the transmission (communication) and the evolution of ideas in complex socio-cultural levels. For example, sayings, slogans, theories, some aspects of folklore, etc. These memes can make up packages, as happens in political and religious constructs. But there are some aspects of the subjectal that are not memes (they are not 'inter'). We cannot speak of a transmission of pain, anxiety, or the joy a person feels. If I have a toothache, I can't transfer the toothache to someone else.

Nor is it practical to use *meme* for some aspects of group dynamics, such as the stages of development, or roles. Being a leader is a fact. The concept of leadership might count as a meme. Besides, we must remember that in the animal kingdom you get complex social systems that presumably have their *subjectal* counterparts, but only very basic levels of cultural abstractions or none at all. In fact, there is a whole scale of growing complexity going from schools of fish, through flocks of birds, colonies of ants and such, to elephant herds or wolf packs. There is a specific branch of science, sociobiology, dedicated to the study of these associations.

There is no clear boundary or limit to the complexity a meme can have but, if we understand them as *the basic unit*, the idea would be limited to notions you can hold in your head, like *"Have a good one..."*, which leaves a lot to your imagination, but most of us know the gist of what it stands for. The popular social media version is a little more limited. My daughter's idea is that *"a meme is a caricature or image with a brief text that condenses a general situation in an amusing way"* (see Chapter I.28, The Book of Richards).

Memes are born, spread through the population (of humans) by some means of communication, and with time may mutate, or die out (be forgotten completely). A collective of very basic memes might be a dictionary or an encyclopedia. When we slip into more complex structures made up of many of these units, a bundle of *memes* or **texts**, we would have different levels of a holarchy, but attempting to define categories or limits is not very useful here.

If we understand that the *subjectal* is composed of ideas, then the *intersubjectal* would be the exchange of these ideas, the conversations and the *memes* that travel within them. There does not seem to be another word in English, or in Spanish for that matter, that covers all the aspects of what we are considering here as the **intersubjectal**. In a rather loose sense, *meme* might work in that it refers to *ideas that are transmitted* between Subjects. If we exchange *ideas* with '*information*' then the concept can be applied to a wider spectrum of phenomena — the message carried by the growl of a predator or the song of a bird is also *intersubjectal*. Anyway, choose any wording that resonates with you.

Just remember these ideas, keeping in mind that they are only sketches that could be represented in different ways (Figure 14).

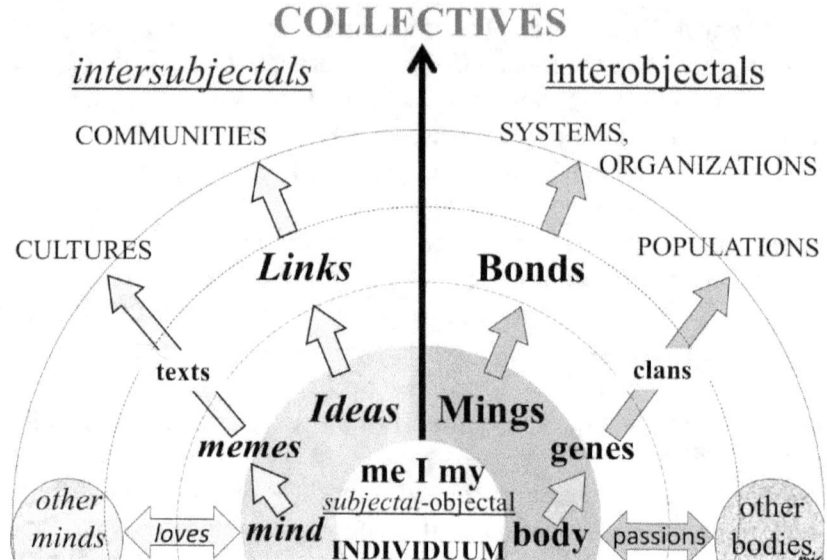

Figure 14. **The generation of collectives, as per Michael Christie.**
*Tricky to create a graphic image that transmits the fact that the **individual** aspect, the holon, gives rise to the successive tiers of the **collectival**. – The individuum is at the base. Collectives emanate from different combinations of individua. – **Mings** is short for 'Material things.'*

The domains are complimentary, existence is simultaneous

Classifications are useful to analyze and make sense of ideas, but we must remember that in practice these aspects are complimentary, none can exist without the others. As conscious beings we need our bodies to exist and operate, and at the same time it seems our bodies cannot function without that dynamic state we call life or consciousness. It's inconceivable to exist in nothingness, both physically and intellectually. We are sustained and nurtured by the material substrate that surrounds us, that space-time and its laws, which we call "our world." And we are also a product of all the social relationships that have accompanied us since our birth, the language we speak, the ideas we formulate. Even the very image we have of ourselves, our ego, is a mirror of the social world that surrounds us.

Besides, everything happens simultaneously. We can separate aspects to take a better look, isolate them from the ambient noise to study them, but the separation is illusory. Things are always embedded in the matrix. Just think of the domains as wheels or cogs that interact continuously, always. The issue is slippery. On the one hand, everything changes, and on the other, we feel we are still the same person.

One of the issues that intrigues us is the notion of space-time. According to Albert Einstein, space and time appear simultaneously, forming what we perceive as a single four-dimensional reality (three spatial dimensions plus time). In our everyday reality, two macroscopic material objects cannot occupy the same space at the same time. But the bigger question is: Why is time 'directional'?

Everything indicates that our universe is expanding. Yes, matter clusters into planets, galaxies, etc., but since the *Big Bang*, **on average**, things are drifting apart from one another. The known physical universe is getting bigger.

Because the effect is cumulative, the farther two bodies are initially, the faster they drift apart. As we move away from the galaxy, the speed steadily increases till it exceeds the speed of light. That point marks the outer limit of our known (and knowable?) universe because any radiation (data) from objects further away could never catch up with us, nor ours to them, but someone sitting half way would be able to see us both. How much lies beyond is anybody's guess.

In physics, **entropy** is a measure of the likelihood or stability of a state. The Second Law of Thermo-dynamics says that, overall, entropy always increases towards the equilibrium state. That is, if we leave things to their own design, they tend to break down or move to some more likely state of disorder. Thus, maintaining order consumes energy, and some processes and events are irreversible. If something shatters or we burn it, that cannot be undone. All this also contributes to the directionality of time.

Because all this happens simultaneously, each event has unique universal coordinates, which cannot be repeated. Most illustrations of the orbits of earth and other planets are ovals that end where they started, but in the real universe this is incorrect. Since the solar system is also moving in cosmic space, the orbits are more like spirals or the coils of a spring, never returning to the same cosmic spot.

Perhaps all this is what makes history unique, unrepeatable. The fact is that, somehow, the *'arrow of time'* is unbreakable, one of the basic Laws of *ah!* (But note that in some states of consciousness we may perceive time differently, as when past, present, and future are experienced as simultaneous).

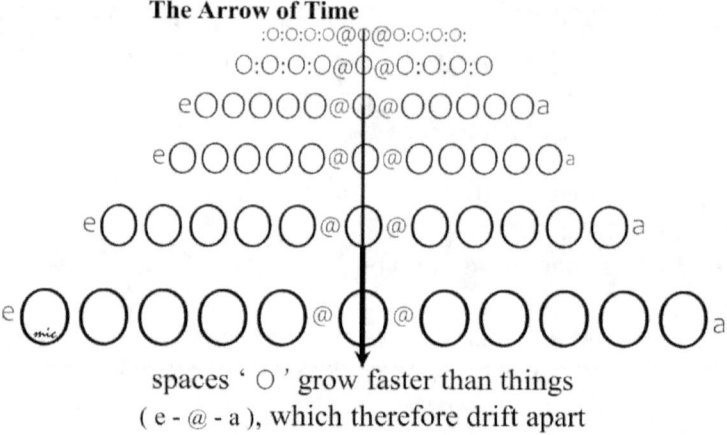

EXPANDING model of the EVOLUTION of the UNIVERSE

The Arrow of Time

spaces ' O ' grow faster than things
(e - @ - a), which therefore drift apart

Figure 15. **Sketch of the Expanding Universe.** – A model of the evolution of the Universe: large bodies (groups of galaxies or even larger clusters) are drifting apart because space between then grows continuously. Perhaps this contributes to what we perceive as 'the Arrow of Time.'

For more detail on many of these issues, see *Existential Physics* by Sabine Hossenfelder (2022).

===================== I =====================

Chapter I.13 –

Teaser – the subject and the Queen

Once Existence **simply *Was***. Natural, a land of dreams.

Its origin mattered not till someone asked, *"Do you know?"* The issue was pondered. *"Dreams anticipate,"* said one, *"it issues from dreams."* For a time, Magic ruled, and Shamans became Chiefs. And Dreams **simply *Were*** and all *Belonged*.

Such harmony, such perfection, *"How could this be?"* – *"It must be the work of only one, a master of masters. The Great Spirit created this world in a dream.*" The Word is out, we *are* by virtue of the Great One's Dream. Then Myth ruled, and Subjectivity became Queen. And the G. O. D. *simply Was* and people *Believed and Belonged*.

Praise the One, we are Her Subjects.

In time, Subjects again pondered, *"Where does the Word come from?"* The substance of different subjects was weighed. Spirit and Dreams were pondered, but found to carry no weight. By virtue of its mass Matter rose supreme. Logic ruled, Objectivity became King and evicted the Queen, dispossessing Subjectivity of all her properties. Disdain *belief and belonging*. Mere wives' tales, there is no *substance* in dreams! Only the King can speak of *any* subject! When asked to speak about the Queen he replied, *"The Queen is not a subject"* and we understood![7] Objectivity rules and dreamworlds *are not*. Only Matter *matters*. Know your own and own to be known. Now Matter *simply Is* and Objects *believe they Know* (or *belong*).

Praise *Knowing and Owning*.

And so it came to pass that ponderous proprietary **objects** ponder weightless **subjects** dispossessed of any properties.

Bemused I object, and subject the subject to your scrutiny. *'To ponder'* is a verb, so *objects* must be its subject and *subjects* its object. So then, *subjective* objects subject *objective* subjects to scrutiny? In order to subject an object, the subject must possess the object on which it acts. However, you cannot possess subjects that have no properties (belonging *is* a property), and only subjects can possess (verbs must have a subject). If subjects can be the objects of scrutiny, they must possess properties. So perhaps the Queen's subjects are objects that do have properties, and *Subjectivity* is a subject after all.

English is amazing.

The complexity it can produce with such an economy of words!

——————————— o ———————————

---

[7] Legend has it that once a famous writer, Oscar Wild, boasted in a London pub that he could talk about any subject. When asked to talk about The Queen he replied: *"The Queen is not a subject!"*

What you have to do with confusion is to be very patient and sort it out.
David Bohm, 1978.

Subject - Object and the use of subjective - objective

As mentioned earlier, our language frequently uses the same words for a host of meanings, the very essence of a pun. If the context is clear, this doesn't cause problems, but at times it can be confusing, even catastrophic. If we are ever to move out of the confusion we need to understand and redefine these overlapping terms, as I stated above. But I have a hunch that a mere statement is not enough. Since I believe the root of the problem lies in the use of language, let's start by reviewing the semantics. The problem with 'subjective/objective' is that each of these terms is currently used with at least two different meanings or implications.

Most words change their ending according to their function or meaning: parent – parental – parentally; critic – critical – critically. There are many exceptions, as in *the fast train runs fast*. English is a remarkably irregular language, so it's not easy to find clean examples, but hopefully you get the idea. Also note that adjectives can have many forms or endings. Two are of interest here: **-ive** and **-al**. These endings have different implications. The **-ive** ending means '*that executes …, that has a tendency to …, or is in the manner of*' …, and usually qualifies actions or processes (submissive, abusive, compulsive, creative, …). Instead, the **-al** ending means '*pertaining to …, relative to …, or that has the qualities of …*' and usually refers to the quality of 'things' (material, parental, legal, regal, …). So, when we want to refer to a domain, we should use the **-al** ending. Thus, the objec**tal** domain (rather than objec<u>tive</u> domain).

But what exactly do subject and object mean in this context?

The object – subject dilemma, used as nouns

It seems that Rene Descartes, the creator of the modern scientific method, used the term 'object' to designate ideas, those that allow us to make mental operations. In the sense we use the term today, Rene spoke of 'things.' Figuring out how this transmutation occurred is for historians, but we can see that the use of these terms has been confusing and ambiguous since the beginning.

In common usage we might say:

Joe says the <u>object</u> is valuable, but I have doubts. I think Joe is a rather shady <u>subject</u>.

In the preceding sentences the terms object and subject are used in their more usual sense, to refer to a material 'thing,' and to a person in his nonmaterial aspects. That is, when we use the word 'subject' in place of a person, we are not alluding to the physical person (the body, though he obviously has one), but rather to his character as a conscious being, an actor with free will. Instead, 'objects' are usually inanimate or unconscious. There is a gray area, when we speak of the parts (organs, bones, etc.) of a living person. Even though those elements are material, we feel it's not polite to depersonalize the patient. Still, doctors do this all the time: "*We have an exposed fracture in room 15.*" That the fracture is attached to a person is just a nuisance. The problem is that at times treating physical features as if they were conscious entities is also not appropriate. In some circumstances we play out physical roles that are independent of our spiritual nature. When too many people board the elevator, their moral or cultural standing is completely irrelevant, only their physical weight counts. Nowadays we perform linguistic juggling acts to speak of these issues without being offensive. The result is that modern discourse is often confusing or even contradictory. In a philosophical discussion like this one, at least, we need to be precise.

<u>Joe says</u> the object is valuable, but <u>I have doubts</u>. <u>I think</u> Joe is a rather shady subject.

The same sentence, with different underlining. These elements of the sentences question whether the statements are true or not. Any of the three statements might be accurate, '*objective*,' or they might be '*subjective*,' that is, ideas or prejudices that emanate from what we believe, what we think is happening or the other person wants us to believe. As these statements are contradictory, to decide which is what we need additional information.

I studied the nature of the object. It is a plastic imitation. My doubts are <u>objective</u>.
Joe's opinion is <u>subjective</u>. Is he trying to con us?

The same theme with new details: '*doubt*' and '*opinion*' are nouns referring to dynamic states or actions rather than material 'things,' so here we are using the term '*objective*' and '*subjective*' in a sort of adverbial form. In my view this is their correct, natural role. Restated:

> *My doubts about the object are justified (they are objective), so I can turn it into an affirmation- the object has no value! And this validates my opinion of Joe, he is not to be trusted.*

Confusion creeps in when we use these terms to qualify things, in the more typical adjectival form, as in "*Nature is objective; Culture is subjective.*" Nonsense, nature can be perfectly '*subjective*' and culture totally 'objective.' Well, yes…, but… no. The problem is that **you cannot use the adverbial declension as if it were adjectival** (as implied above) **without generating ambivalences or contradictions**. Perhaps the speaker has clear ideas about the issue, but the receiver must second guess in what sense he is using these terms. Getting back to their use as nouns, let's play a little.

> *The believer is a subject subjectively subjected to his subjectivity.*
> *Research focuses on objects to change the subject.*
> *The Queen rants about subjects that bore her subjects.*
> *In the middle of the talk, the subject suddenly changed the subject.*
> (Hint … the speaker ▲   …   the issue ▲ …)

The subject studies the nature of the object in order to change the subject. In this sense the subject is passive, an object, because in practice, the object informs the subject, which means the object is actually the 'actor,' *i.e.*, the grammatical *subject* of the interaction.

What? Confusing, isn't it. Instead, classic education, politics, and religion operate in the other direction. The subject informs objects with the intention of modifying those objects. Here the students, etc. are the grammatical 'objects' of the interaction.

Time-out! Time-out! as Richard Brodie might say.

Calling patients, volunteers, students, or parishioners 'subjects' is
Politically correct,
Grammatically incorrect (sometimes), and thus
Conceptually misleading.

Unfortunately, this glitch is so pervasive in modern usage that it will be difficult to change. Nonetheless, we need to start somewhere. As anticipated in Chapter I.3, the easiest solution is to capitalize these words when they stand for a person playing the role of 'Subject' or of 'Object.' This, I hope, will lessen the confusion. For instance, the sentences above can be rewritten:

The believer is a Subject subjectively subjected to his subjectivity.
Research focuses on objects to change the Subject.
(In this case the Researcher).
The Queen rants about subjects that bore her Subjects.
In the middle of his talk the Subject suddenly changed the subject.
(... the Speaker).
Also, note that the second 'subject' is the grammatical object of the sentence.
Very confusing.
So, *'hospital patients are the Objects of medical research'*
(not 'the subjects of' ...).

These issues might not have a universal solution that avoids all confusions, but at least it is important to pay attention to the grammatical role the words are playing, and to avoid these words in situations that are ambiguous or confusing.

As for the *subjective – objective* problem, a solution might be the use of other terms to designate these domains: abstract – concrete; mental – corporeal; ... – ...? There does not seem to be a clear solution. But to improve the situation we need to try new options, as proposed here and in Chapter I.3.

My recommendation is as follows:

Capitalize '*Subject*' and '*Object*' when referring to people,
Restrict '*subjective*' and '*objective*' to their adverbial uses, and
Use '*subjectal*' and '*objectal*' when applied in the adjectival sense.

These distinctions are not merely a scientific issue (*The Taboo of Subjectivity*). They are equally applicable to everyday life, in family relationships, etc. In the legal context, not to mention religion and politics, these problems appear all the time. The only hope we have of disentangling these areas of confusion is by improving the underlying terminology.

Let's leave this issue for a while. When we started, in the chapter on *The Book of Isaac...*, we considered the basic particles that make up the objectal domain. Then, sketchily, we 'constructed' elements, inorganic compounds, organic compounds, unicellular living organisms, and multicellular organisms. To get to the more complex levels that most interest us, we need to consider how organisms get integrated along the intermediate levels between the basic development of life and the evolution of culture. In the following six chapters we will always look first at these intermediate levels in nature, to then see how these structures influence or condition our daily life.

With these added tools we can then take a new look at aspects of the development of subjectivity and of culture, which I think is what is of real interest to most of us.

===================== I =====================

Chapter I.14 –

Life and Reproductive Strategies

We tend to value each individual dearly, in some societies more than others, but by and large everyone is granted a place in his or her society. God (or Nature) is not so caring. As we saw in the previous section, complex organisms deteriorate until eventually some function breaks down completely and we die. To keep going, all living beings must reproduce, have kids, lay eggs, or produce seeds. Reproduction is so critical that much of it is hardwired in us. Our inner urges compel us to take those actions that will lead to having offspring. Here we must make a distinction. Unicellular species have two ways they can reproduce. The simple way is to split or clone into two identical copies, each capable of going its own way and dividing asexually again and again indefinitely. The other is sexual reproduction (see below). Dividing into two might seem slow at first, but exponential growth accelerates very quickly. If the conditions are good, individual cells can reproduce every few hours, so a single initial individual can produce hundreds of copies per day and billions in a year.

Any microorganism living today must have an uninterrupted line of ancestors to the dawn of time. Still, they might not be truly identical. Every now and then small changes occur so that each line begins to take on a character of its own. This variation is the basis of adaptation, of adjusting to different environments and changing conditions.

But asexual reproduction has a limitation. Each line is isolated from any useful change or innovation that might have occurred in some other line. Some organisms learned to share their genetic information, to cross paths as it were. They 'invented' sexual reproduction. Initially they came together, fused, mixed up their genetic material and then split, but as cells got more complex this became risky and impractical. The more practical and popular solution was to have two copies of the whole genetic code and then produce special cells that carry only one copy, called germ cells or gametes, so when two gametes fuse, they now regain the set of two, but in a new combination. I won't bore you with the math, but this little change had enormous consequences. Everything speeded up, change could accumulate much faster and also spin off into different combinations and lines. It's difficult to convey a complex biological mechanism that occurs unseen at a microscopic level, so let me attempt a metaphor.

Imagine you buy a tool that comes with brief instructions. You use it for a time and realize one instruction is not quite right, so you jot down a correction. So long as your revised copy sits in your workshop you gain from the advantage and eventually your son might benefit, but that's it. Now a friend visits and complains the tool doesn't work properly, so you tell him of the correction. *Aha, so that was the problem, thanks!* He tries it and bingo, it works fine. After a time, he also realizes the tool has another application you and the manufacturer were not aware of, so he adds it to the instructions. As the news spreads, more people buy the tool because it has now become more useful and something that seemed to be a commercial failure suddenly takes off. Without this 'cross-fertilization,' progress can be painfully slow. That tends to happen to isolated communities, or those that close off outside influences by decree.

Sexual reproduction also solves other problems for complex multicellular organisms. When cells specialize to make different tissues (bone, muscle, brain, etc.), they deteriorate faster and some even lose the capacity to divide. To safeguard against this deterioration, all complex life forms keep special germ lines that remain in their undifferentiated state and produce the gametes for reproduction. It's a bit like the version stored in your hard drive. If your computer starts to fail you turn it off and reboot. Basically, it goes back to this original intact copy and starts afresh.

Another advantage is that it allows us to make many copies at a low cost, so they can be transported and scattered far and wide. This greatly improves the chances that at least some will survive.

A single weed, such as a plant of the European poison hemlock, may produce as many as 10,000 seeds, and then dies! Amongst animals, first prize goes to the Ocean Sunfish that can lay up to 300 MILLION eggs in one season. Nature can be quite lavish. This produces a sort of 'shotgun' strategy, millions of very small seeds or eggs so that a few may land in the right place and prosper. **High quantity, low quality**.

But that's not the only possible strategy. A coconut palm produces a much smaller number, but each 'seed' (the coconut) is quite large, and thus stands a much higher chance of producing seedlings that reach maturity. The extreme form of this strategy occurs in elephants and humans. An elephant has one calf every two or three years at most, so each calf is precious to the herd. They tend and defend babies dearly, just as we do. **High quality, low quantity**.

All this looks as though we have a lot of freedom to choose our strategies. Life as a whole does; we don't. This is one of the Laws of *ah!* Once you have committed to one strategy it's like a rut, you're sort of stuck in that strategy. Okay, you might have some flexibility. If the conditions are very good you might have a baby every year. Or you might skip several years if the conditions are bad. But mammals like us cannot have more than a few young at a time, no matter what! Conversely, a tree cannot suddenly decide to produce autonomous babies, only seeds.

==================== I ====================

Chapter I.15 –

The Book of Pierre – evolution by groping

Sexual reproduction is like a genetic blending machine. It ensures that new mutations spread across the population and meet-up with other variants that might allow it to work even better. With time, every possible combination is put to the test. Eventually the good ones prosper, and the old ones drop out. In '*The Phenomenon of Man,*' the Catholic Priest Pierre Teilhard de Chardin gives us his views on this process.

> "*By reckless self-reproduction life takes its precautions against mishap. It increases its chances of survival and at the same time multiplies its chances of progress.*"

> (In living beings) . . . "*we find the fundamental technique of groping, the specific and invincible weapon of all expanding multitudes. It would be a mistake to see it as mere chance. Groping is directed chance. It means pervading everything so as to try everything.*"

I particularly like this way of explaining evolution because it's easy to grasp and is in harmony with our own tendency to tinker, to try out a hundred solutions till we hit on one that works well (or at least well enough). One of the areas where this has been most obvious in recent times is the development of software: first we tried numerous programming languages, in the seventies there were a number of operating systems, then in the eighties (roughly) there was a profusion of word processor programs, and so on. In all these subareas 'consumer selection' weeded out most of this fumbling. Today we have only a few that proved more efficient, and the successive fusions and elaborations of these into ever more complex programs. An uninformed newcomer might easily jump to the conclusion that such marvelous complexity and efficiency was created instantaneously by some superhuman genius, a god of sorts.

Much the same can be said of the evolution of the hardware, cars, airplanes, cinema and virtually every other aspect of modern life. Take any end product. We know it was developed by successive small steps because we have, as a society, taken considerable pains to keep record of these developments in written accounts, blueprints, illustrations, photographs and even the physical examples in museums and other collections. But put yourself in the position of some naïve outsider, such as a Kalahari bushman, who suddenly comes up against some bewildering sophisticated modern contraption. What can he possibly make of it? The result is very well portrayed in the 1980 film *The Gods Must Be Crazy* filmed in Botswana. *N!xau*, a bushman who plays the central character *Xi*, finds an intact coke bottle dropped from a small aircraft and of course takes it to be a gift from the gods. Check it out, it's fun to watch.

According to Wikipedia, "despite the film having grossed over $100 million worldwide, N!xau reportedly earned less than $2,000 for his starring role. Before his death, Uys supplemented this with an additional $20,000 as well as a monthly stipend". If accurate, this little footnote highlights the magnitude of the systematic abuse of native communities by 'civilized' European 'Christians' and is a good example of people claiming to believe in one God but actually worshiping another ($$$).

========================== I ==========================

Chapter I.16 –

Relatedness – califragilistic...

How do we know all life descended from simple life forms? To give you an idea, I coined a long word, '*supercalifragilisticexpialidocious,*' that is a good stand-in for complex DNA chains. But first let me give you an example of one of these special long DNA chains, a gene that codes for the protein **Cytochrome C.** This protein is at the very root of the life process. It forms part of the structure that allows cells to breathe, basically, so it is a protein with a highly conserved sequence across a wide spectrum of plants, animals, and many unicellular organisms.

In genetic databases it is coded as Sapiens **Band 7p15.3** which is roughly short for 'The Library of Humans, Section 7p, Book 15, Chapter 3' and can be further defined as the string contained from script symbol (base-pair) 25118656 to 25125260. These location numbers actually vary some according to the coding system, etc., but you get the idea. As mentioned, this is roughly the address for the gene that produces **Cytochrome C**. In turn, the chemical sequences encoded in the gene would be analogous to packaged instructions in an industrial manual, which code for the manufacture this particular 104 amino-acids long protein. Because this protein has a highly conserved sequence across a wide spectrum of organisms, it is useful in the study of relatedness between a wide range of plants and animals. We don't have the space here to deal with something hundreds of letters long, but the word I just coined above might help us.

What? You don't believe I coined *supercalifragilisticexpialidocious*? How mean! Why are you so sure? You might think '*I just know,*' but that certainty comes from the word's uniqueness. The likelihood that I came up with exactly the same combination by chance is exceedingly small, almost impossible, right? OK, okay, sure, I borrowed it!

Google it. You'll always end up on some page about Disney's *Mary Poppins*. Why? Because it is a made-up word, and it's such a unique combination of letters that it is impossible to confuse with anything else. If you Google 'super' alone you'll get about 7,000,000,000 responses because super is an extremely common word.

But now just add 'ca' to super . . . *superca* . . and . . . bingo!

supercalifragilisticexpialidocious crops up right away.[8]

You only need '*supercalif*' to eliminate all the competition! Or even less for other parts of the word, like '*cexpia.*' These six letters are enough for an unequivocal result. Try other pieces of the word and most will take you to pages related to *supercalifragilisticexpialidocious*.

Yet, like '*super,*' a few other bits such as *istic, calif,* and *ocious* are not unique. They are also a part of other words. But this can be useful too, because it tells us something about the meaning and relationships of the words. Some, like calif and California, may not be related at all. But often, when the same string of letters appears in many different words, it tells us that it has the same root and similar function or meaning. Like '*istic*' which means *relating to, or characteristic of something,* as in *animistic, idealistic, realistic.*

This might seem like a silly exercise, but it is really useful to understand how we know the family tree of plants and animals. When two or more animals share the same or very similar strings of 'letters' in their proteins or genetic code (DNA) they must be related by common descent. If you only look at four or five letters that might be just coincidence, but when you get identical strings hundreds of letters long *coincidence* is out of the question. We can estimate the exact probability of a given string repeating itself independently and estimate just how similar or different sets of strings are to each other. For large sets the mathematics can get very complex but, as you just saw, the basic idea is easy to understand.

Back to Cytochrome C, a protein found in the cells of all animals and plants. It is made up of a string of over 100 'words' (amino-acids) and is essential for cellular breathing. The sequence of amino-acids in humans and chimpanzees is identical. Because it is such a long sequence, the probability that this 'coincidence' could happen by chance is essentially **zero**, in the order of $1/10^{99}$ or,

~**One** in 1,000, 000, 000, 000, 000, 000, 000, 000, 000, 000, 000, 000, 000, 000, 000, 000, 000, 000, 000, 000, 000, 000, 000, 000, 000, 000, 000, 000, 000, 000, 000, 000, 000, 000.

Does this prove evolution? Not directly, but it does prove relatedness. It's not a question of 'maybe' or 'perhaps.' Chimpanzees and bonobos <u>*are*</u>

---

[8] That's why search engines work so well, by the way.

our closest relatives, no questions about it. Monkeys differ in only one amino-acid, cows by about 10, hens by ~13, fish by ~23 and wheat by ~35. So, who do we share more features with? Mostly primates and other mammals obviously, less with birds, even less with fish and apparently much less with plants, right? All this based on only one protein. If you repeat the comparison using other proteins, the results are roughly the same and lead to similar conclusions. Now you tell me what mechanism might explain that relatedness.

=================== I ===================

Chapter I.17 –

There never was an Adam, never an Eve, and there never will be ...

The notion that we all descend from a single couple is so culturally pervasive and deeply ingrained that most people take it for granted. I suppose it sounds correct and is certainly easy to grasp, but that doesn't make it true. In fact, it is certainly false and should go the way of the Tooth Fairy and Santa Claus, at best a stepping stone on the path to growing up.

Getting the correct idea across requires that you look at 'us' in a somewhat different light. We feel unique, whole, made in one piece. But in fact, we are an ensemble of hundreds of separate parts, each of which has had a somewhat independent history. To use an example that plays an important role in our lives and in the history of our understanding of these issues, let me introduce you to mitochondria. Mitochondria are microscopic organic 'machines' that make up part of our own cells. Very active cells can have hundreds. In many respects they resemble bacteria, so much so that we believe they were originally free living but at some point, a long, long time ago, came into partnership with bigger cells, and then became dependent on them. But it's a two-way deal, they provide us with little power-plants and we provide them with the fuel and raw materials to make copies of themselves. They are also very peculiar in that only the mother's mitochondria are inherited. When fertilization occurs, the male's mitochondria are left out of the deal! No loss, because all males have clones of their mother's mitochondria.

Like bacteria, mitochondria have their own genetic material that reproduces independently of our nuclear genes. Very occasionally slight variations (mutations) do occur, so it is a useful tool to understand relatedness amongst populations of humans. After years of study scientists were able to reconstruct the sequence of changes and identify the 'common ancestor' to all humans living today. Rather unfortunately they and the press immediately began speaking of the 'mitochondrial Eve,' supposedly the first woman who gave rise to all other mitochondrial lines in existence today.

That interpretation contains two errors or fallacies. The first is the implication that mitochondria originated in that female. Actually, the history of mitochondria goes back to the dawn of time, so the first being that gave rise to mitochondria might have been some lowly slime that lived millions of years before dinosaurs. The specific variant carried by that woman could have been in circulation in prehistoric populations for eons.

The other fallacy is the implication that just because that piece came from her, all other *original parts* also came from her. This is impossible. Genetics simply does not work like that. Other parts of 'us' appeared at totally different times and were most likely passed down by many independent lines of animal and human precursors. It would be more realistic to think of it as a network that goes picking up useful bits and pieces as it goes along. Technically it is known as **reticular** inheritance. Each one of us is simply a sort of progress report, or a *test prototype* if you prefer. If we are successful enough to survive and have kids, they in turn are test-prototypes of some new combination of the genes provided by mom and dad. Eventually one or another of the existing variations might luck out and become fixed in all the population, at least till some new mutation appears and challenges the old one again.

You may be thinking something like *"No way!* That can't be". Move it closer to home. You surely remember when you were a kid some aunt or other saying *"Oh, look, she's just like her mother!"* or perhaps *"You know, you have your grandfather's eyes."* By the time you are a teenager you've been told that practically no part of you is 'original.' In fact, it seems like it took most of your extended family to provide the bits and pieces that make up 'you.' To a large extent, this popular wisdom is correct. Since you have four parents, eight great-grandparents, then sixteen and so on up your family tree, the bits and pieces that drifted through the reticulum till they came together to make 'you' could have come from almost anywhere in the human family tree (it takes only 30 generations to fan out to over a billion, *i.e.*, all humans living a century ago). In a nutshell, it works rather like an identikit. All the known types of eyes, of ears, of noses, of mouths and of all the other parts of our bodies are stored somewhere in the human gene pool (Figure 16). When you want to put together a person, you pick out a variant of each body part and put them together to make the ensemble. In practice we have no control over this process. It is more like a lottery, but that is pretty much how it works.

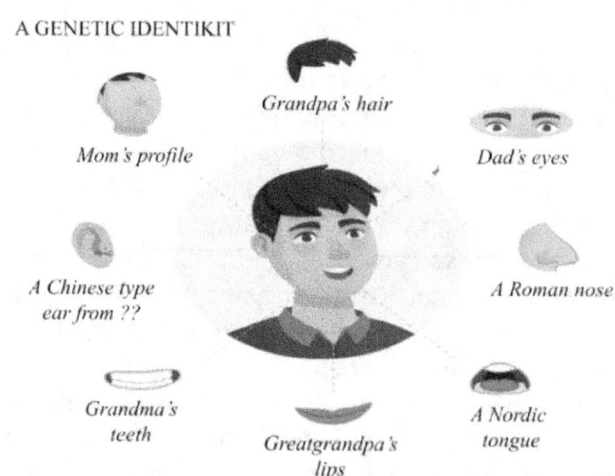

A GENETIC IDENTIKIT

Mom's profile

Grandpa's hair

Dad's eyes

A Chinese type ear from ??

A Roman nose

Grandma's teeth

Greatgrandpa's lips

A Nordic tongue

Figure 16. **Reticular heredity in a nutshell**. - The genetic identikit of the family history that ended up combining to make 'you.' The closer relatives are obvious, but they in turn inherited their features from their forebears, and they from earlier ones, till you get to some roman deacon who supplied Nero's nose, some Nordic elements and a lost gene that got to you from China, who knows by what tortuous route.

To a greater or lesser extent, we all have these sorts of genetic jumbles. Even the older ethnic groups, which are often considered 'pure,' are a mixture of all the prior influences that accumulated in their history and prehistory. Many of us even have Neanderthal and viral genes in our genomes.

The idea of Adam and Eve is a completely childish way to look at our history. It may be OK as a bedtime story for kids, but it is a dangerous idea in the minds of adults. Get rid of it and you will feel completely liberated of the responsibility of carrying **The Torch of Human Survival**. Today life has another eight billion copies to choose from and will eventually almost certainly favor some combination that doesn't even exist today. And don't worry too much about your personal variants. First, they make up a minimal part of the whole 'you,' and most are already scattered throughout the rest of humanity.

What we must ensure is that humanity survives with as much genetic and ethnic diversity as possible.

It's worth noting that this means virtually the exact opposite of what elites believe. Eugenics[9] and that sort of thinking stinks because it tends to **reduce** overall diversity, and we know for a fact that reduced genetic diversity is one of the conditions that leads lineages and even species to extinction. So, if some bluebloods want to drive themselves to an evolutionary dead-end that's fine, as long as they don't try to impose it on all the rest of us. We need to cherish and look after our ethnic diversities because it is the stuff of our future survival in an unpredictable and changing world.

This is so important that it needs to be emphasized. Elites of all kinds throughout history have always made the same mistake, thinking that just because they are successful today, they are superior and will continue to be successful forever. This assumption has little or no historical support. To begin with, these luminaries are the result of genetics *and* a peculiar blend of family and historic circumstances. Genius of any kind (political, financial, sports, scientific, etc.) tends to crop up in the most unexpected places. Think of many sports stars or of famous scientists. Cracks like Lionel Messi and Tiger Woods appear to come out of nowhere! As did Newton, Einstein, Mozart, and so, so many others.

Besides, we know of countless civilizations that thrived for a time, enthroned pharos, shahs, khans, tzars, Incas, emperors and a host of other 'chosen' elites, only to see them collapse and disintegrate without a trace of their luminaries left, aside from their tombs. In addition to the many genetic problems resulting from inbreeding, they seem to have a nasty tendency to get murdered by their in-group or pounded to oblivion by some envious out-group. To make matters worse, when living conditions change, what constitutes a genetic optimum also changes.

For instance, **which would be the ideal genetics for life on Mars?** Well, Mars has a very thin atmosphere, few life-supporting resources, high radiation levels, lower gravity than earth, it is colder, very arid, etc. So then,

---

[9] Eugenics is an ideology created in the US by a Mr. Galton and others that proposed the 'improvement' of the human race by means of reproductive control programs (as is done by animal breeders). It was later adopted as part of the Nazi ideology that gave rise to the holocaust in the Second World War.

which humans might be at least partly preadapted for such a living environment? To save on resources during the travel and initial colonization stage, very small persons (preferably pygmies); to reduce the effects of radiation, people with very melanic skin (deep 'blacks'); to reduce loss of heat and evaporation, people with short arms and legs (Inuit); to withstand very low pressure and oxygen levels, people from the Tibetan plateau or Andean Altiplano (Sherpas or Aymara); to withstand long periods of isolation in space, somewhat autistic nerds (Aspies); to work as teams in very confined bases, cooperative and tenacious folks with lowish levels of aggressiveness (women, mostly)[10] ...

Hmm, it seems the *perfect* profile for our ideal Martian colonist has little or no resemblance with the ethnic arrogances of the moment. Rather the opposite. **We will need a horde of antiheroines and antiheroes.**

===================== I =====================

Chapter I.18 –
Sex in Nature and the nature of Sex

Sex is perhaps the most tabooed subject of all, which is really surprising, a blatant contradiction if you consider that the first command in the Old Testament is to *"Go forth and multiply."* How would that work without sex? As mentioned, complex organisms cannot survive for long without reproducing. Since reproduction in higher animals and humans is the result of a sexual union, sex is a fundamental subject that is hard to avoid.

As usual, though, I think it is best to start with a broader perspective and take a quick look at sex in Nature. Nature exhibits an absolutely astounding diversity of sexual equipment, practices, and attitudes. Virtually anything we can conceive of has been tried out by Nature, with some plant or critter somewhere out there actually showing us how it's done. In fact, the 'standard' monogamous, loving, 'correct' way to go about sex is one of the rarest in Nature. Bisexual species do exist, of course, but most have harems; or maintain very brief sexual encounters and then each goes their own ways; a few species form stable couples each season but both males

---

[10] Women can surely be just as competitive as men, but they are less likely to resort to physical violence. An all-female crew would also save a lot of dead weight that can be safely replaced by a sperm bank.

and females cheat whenever they can; some species are hermaphrodites (male and female simultaneously); others start off as females that lay eggs for several seasons, but switch sex when they become the biggest and most dominant in their group (if the resident male is removed, the largest female changes sex and replaces it); still others eat their male partners after copulation (the extra protein helps them produce the eggs); different forms of prostitution are common (sex for food being the most common); homosexuality in exchange for food or shelter also occurs; in ostriches and their kin females lay their eggs and leave them for the male to incubate and care for the young, while the females go off with another male; a small number of reptiles have even managed to revert to 'asexual' reproduction, but strangely some of these all-female species must elicit and steal copulations with males of some related species so that the sperm initiates cell division in the ovum, even though there is no fertilization! Brood parasitism is post-sex (see next section), but it also reflects the huge variability God allows his critters to indulge in. The list goes on and on.

Going into the details of each is impossible here (you can find them on the web[11]), but one example may help. Some species practice a breeding system called '*lekking*,' which is a bit like a redlight district, but backwards. Males get together in traditional sexual arenas, called **leks**, and spend their days fighting for the best places, literally the center of the stage, and making elaborate displays to impress the females. Only the very top males get to mate, but it's actually the females who do the choosing. After copulation the females go off and do all the rest of the breeding cycle on their own, so the only contribution on the part of the males is their sperm. Males are thus freed of any 'responsibility' and can dedicate all their energy to adornment and display, which has produced some of the gaudiest and showiest species on the planet. The classic case is the European Capercaillie of the northern forest (Orr**lek** in Swedish), but they also include the Grouse and Sage-Grouse of the American prairies and in southern Europe the Great Bustard. In mammals the best known is the Uganda Kob, but it also occurs in other antelopes, in bats, plus a variety of smaller vertebrates and even in invertebrates.

Some anthropologists have tried to equate bars and nightclubs to leks,

---

[11] Lucy Cooke's (2022) *Bitch, on the female of the species* gives a fresh summary from the female perspective.

but this is a very poor comparison. They are meeting places no doubt, but all too often those strutting males end up caught in marriage, or get sued for child support, etc. I prefer comparing leks to sporting and cultural events (Olympiads, musical festivals, political and scientific conferences, etc.). Until quite recently these were almost exclusively male dominated events with all the characteristics and elements of a lek: *alpha* males strutting on stages, elaborate displays, fierce competition, female fan clubs, etc. No sex in public, of course, but you would be astronomically naïve if you thought that meant no sex at all. All these events have a variety of associated social gatherings, with plenty of room for the ladies to choose their mark. And some ladies seem to be irresistibly attracted to flashy *alpha*-males. But many of these events are too sporadic to consider them true leks. Besides, big get-togethers like carnivals and Mardi Gras have been free-for-alls since time immemorial. Instead, leks are definitely **not** free-for-alls! Only the *alphas* get the action. And, if they can, *alphas* will drive out and actively suppress sexual activity in all subordinate males at all costs. Knowing the propensity of human males towards sexual conquest and philandering, you can be sure that some guild somewhere has figured out a way to enjoy this sort of privilege with institutional impunity.

Now, if you are a 'creationist' all this poses a serious problem. Obviously, all these 'aberrant' sexual practices are the Creator's doing and responsibility, so you will have to concede that your God actually loves to play with sex. This in turn makes it difficult or impossible to seriously consider all the taboos as manifestations of *'God's will.'* Since different cultures have different taboos, and all taboos are easily broken, it seems rather naïve to consider them as God-given. They don't belong in the sphere of *ah!* at all. Any mature analyst will agree that most taboos are only valid in human spheres, and even here only locally at best. So, the more interesting question is, *why?* Why do priests so passionately insist in imposing these rules? What vested interest moves them to institutionalize mandates that clearly belong to the private sphere? How do *Sexocracies* arise and what keeps them going? I will return to this later.

Seriously, in our crowded world acts like walking naked down the street can hardly be considered a taboo anymore. These are basic social agreements imposed by law for a host of reasons that are way more basic than many taboos. I'm referring to those more superfluous encroachments into our private lives, our petty 'sins' that should be of no concern to anyone except ourselves and our partners (see Chapter II.67 on the use of guilt as an instrument for manipulation).

===================== I =====================

> Instincts are managed by understanding them,
> rather than by denying or repressing them.

Chapter I.19 –
Morals and ethics in Nature

Critical analysis of our social customs and beliefs can trigger strong emotions and reactions. So, let's first explore some neutral ground.

Centuries of fieldwork in the life-histories of plants and animals have revealed an amazing diversity of tricksters, liars, cheats, impostors, emulators, imitators, you name it! Sometimes both sides benefit, but more often one side reaps a benefit while the other gets duped, at times tragically (it ends up becoming someone else's dinner, for instance). Theoretical analysis of these interactions, in the form of mathematical models, has given us a pretty good idea of the conditions and limits required for different strategies to work. An example will help.

A wide variety of animals in different parts of the world imitate one another, or sometimes copy parts of plants, rocks or other features. A common reason is disguise. There are other interesting reasons for imitation or **mimicry**, as it is called. Two of these, Mullerian and Batesian mimicry will help us here. In nature if you want to stand out and attract attention you use bright colors that contrast with the background (advertising). If you are trying to pass unnoticed you wear dull colors that match the background (camouflage). So, if you are really good to eat you are probably better off camouflaged, especially if your kind is common and predators get into the habit of hunting your type. But what if you are foul tasting or outright poisonous? Well, in that case it turns out that advertising this is a good strategy. It separates you from the common edible critters around you. The more striking your colors, the faster predators learn to avoid your kind. Even more interestingly, it also benefits you to imitate the colors of other toxic critters living in your area. Soon all foul tasting and poisonous bugs in an area will have similar striking colors. The more the merrier because predators will learn faster and equally well, and the cost of occasional learning 'accidents' will be spread out amongst many. Since everybody involved is sending out an honest signal (*I'm toxic*), this is not cheating.

Now, once this system of communication between potential prey and their potential predators is well established, then it is open to some real cheating. Some species that are perfectly tasty and nutritious 'dress up' imitating the foul tasting/poisonous group of species. Predators that have learned to avoid the honest signals will fall for the ruse and also avoid these false ones, thus losing a perfectly good meal. The advantage to the imitator is obvious.

However, there are very specific conditions for this ruse to work.

The first condition is that the 'honest' signalers must pre-exist and be reasonably common in the community so that most of the young predators have a fair chance of encountering one or two real stinkers early in life and learn to avoid them.

Since even cheating has some cost, the second essential condition is that there must be some tangible advantage to cheating. If there is nothing to gain, as in the case of reptile reproduction described below, why bother?

The third condition is that cheats must be uncommon. If they become too common relative to their models the ruse breaks down because the young predators are equally likely to come across a tasty morsel as a foul one, so they won't learn. The signal is too confusing for the predator to make the connection.

There are many examples, some amazingly sophisticated, yet in most or all of them the three basic conditions must hold. All cheats, mimics, impostors exploit some preexisting honest system and all need to remain the exception to the rule for the ruse to work repeatedly.

Given these rules, it turns out some systems are much more vulnerable than others. Brood parasitism is a good example. Some bird species deposit their eggs in the nests of other species. These hosts then incubate them and feed the young parasites. In very specialized species they may even destroy the host's eggs or throw their young out of the nest, thus leaving only the parasitic young alive. The cost to the host is huge. Amongst birds this is relatively common and has appeared independently in several different families, the cuckoos being the best known. But this strategy is unknown in egg laying reptiles. The difference is simple enough. Most reptiles do not care for their young, so there would be no benefit to the potential brood parasite (the second rule). Recently a 'cuckoo' catfish has been discovered in Africa, parasitizing an unrelated type of brooding fish, the cichlids.

In mammals there is also no case of complete replacement of offspring by young of another species, even though there is considerable parental investment (pets excluded, we cuckold ourselves). Most likely this is because internal development of the fertilized egg(s), pregnancy, makes such a replacement virtually impossible. The closest analogue is adoption. Even though we adopt voluntarily, the biological reproductive effect is similar.

We do, however, speak of cuckoldry in allusion to the cuckoo's brood parasitic habits, but this is a bit misleading since it involves a somewhat different phenomenon; *i.e.*, when a female has extra-pair copulations with other males of the same species, obviously, and ends up having offspring fathered by males other than their regular mates ('husbands'). It might be better described as *sperm parasitism.* The logic from the female's point of view is complex and need not be examined here, but it is clear the cheating male gets a huge double benefit, and the cuckolded male pays a stiff double price: extra offspring at no cost, and no offspring at considerable cost of foster-parenting, respectively. *Cuckoldry is not a victimless crime.* So here only the male host is a victim, whereas in classic brood parasitism both male and female hosts are victims.

In general, differences in the systems can make them more or less susceptible to different types of scams, or not vulnerable at all.

Exposing these vulnerabilities is not an attack on the institution (the preexisting honest condition). In fact, if understood correctly it should help those involved to separate the chaff from the grain, so to speak. And this, in turn, can only serve to strengthen the genuine core elements of these institutions. If it turns out that some aspect of the institution you believed in is phony, well, what can I say? Perhaps you are lucky to have the tools to correct them, or to break away.

==================== I ====================

Chapter I.20 –
Putting these ideas in a historical framework

We have been reviewing the biological basis for some behaviors. Everything points to the fact that the social structures that we see today had their roots in this biology, or at least have been strongly influenced by these biological mandates. As we add more and more layers of history and culture, the relationship between the modern situation and its biological roots is ever harder to see, to the point that we cherish the illusion that we have 'overcome' our biology. Totally unrealistic. We are <u>always</u> rooted in that biology.

Just a sketch. Summing up several millennia of history is not easy, but for the purpose of this essay we only need to decide where to start and to understand some of the more general trends of the process. The details are better left to the historians. There are several excellent modern summaries: David Christian, 2011, *Maps of Time*...; Yuval N Harari, 2015, *Sapiens*...; Jim Baggott, 2015 *Origins*...; etc. Since we cannot travel in time or repeat historical events, it can be very difficult to understand and explain the whys of many situations, so it's often better to treat them as working hypotheses, or as mental experiments. Another way of getting a better perspective is to postulate the opposite of what the established dogma, cliché or belief says.

Let's take the hunter-gatherer stage as the beginning of 'our story.' A few tribes managed to survive until modern times, so we have a good idea of the rhythms of their lives, their social organization, their languages, and mythologies. Basically, it entailed family groups with a subsistence economy and very simple technology. Their language is usually quite sophisticated structurally, but their vocabulary is limited to what they know about their surrounding nature (climate, plants, animals, etc.) and their understanding about how nature works is very limited. The almost universal solution to the enigmas is to attribute their functioning to 'the gods.' At these levels, leadership and knowledge are personal, individual attributes. The group history and memory is kept alive by the elders, by oral tradition.

Simple communities usually start off with a fairly democratic attitude. Everyone has a say and there is little or no hierarchy. As communities get bigger some form of leadership creeps in. The notion that some lead and others follow becomes prevalent, which gives rise to the creation of power structures. At this early stage it seems there are two paths to acquire and maintain that power.

The two paths to power

On the one hand there is the more biological, materialistic path. The strongest and better able to handle weapons dominates. Dominant individuals acquire privileges. They can also make alliances with others and move from a personal standing to a social one. There is a whole chain of levels of complexity, based as much in the technological improvements of the weapons systems as in the advances in the military and administrative structures. Once social stratification appears, it tends to grow in complexity and stratification becomes progressively more rigid, till you reach the level of empires. The objective path based on material superiority has its drawbacks, no doubt. But it has one clear virtue: it is difficult or impossible to fake.

The other path is through knowledge and the manipulation of subjectivity. The first evidence of art, shamanism, and early forms of culture are extremely old, but for the greater part of prehistory all this could only be transmitted through oral tradition and the apprenticeship modality. It must have surely given rise to many local experiments. This situation changed radically with the appearance of writing, the great temples and the institutionalization of belief systems. The shaman becomes a priest, he appropriates their knowledge and captures it in the scriptures (and, as a rule, denies their 'pagan' shamanic origins). Priesthood also confers privileges. At times it seems to have subsisted in the shadow of military and ruling structures, but at others it acquired its own tempo and assume the role of governing. The basis of their power is through indoctrination and the manipulation of social ideology via the creation of intricate mythologies and the use of ever more elaborate rituals. The subjective path, in turn, may have its virtues. But it has one serious drawback: it is extremely easy to fake.

The notion that rulers or emperors either represent or are gods, combining both forms of power, was first invented in Sumer, and soon emulated in Egypt, but it seems to have cropped up independently in several places, like Japan, Mexico, and Peru, to name a few that presumably had no direct contact with the Sumerians and Egyptians.

Along the way several societies tried out forms of democracy, only to be overrun by military dictatorships and converted to empires (Greece, Rome). What seems unquestionable is that most of this happened spontaneously according to the conveniences of various groups and the mandates of our biology.

With time the dominant ideas have changed, but if you eliminate the external adornments a large part of history can be boiled down to swings between two postures or poles: democracies and dictatorships. Or, if you prefer, bottom-up *versus* top-down, ascending or descending.

All of this goes under the name of **politics**. Alongside politics, and sometimes overlapping it, are the developments in direct experience, understanding and belief. Curiously they show roughly the same dichotomy. Experience is bottom-up, beliefs are always top-down. To learn from experience, you must come into direct contact with the real world and let it inform you. To believe you must be told what you should believe in, receive the abstract conditioning from someone who claims authority on the matter. If you can verify what you are told by your own direct experience, then it is no longer a belief. Everyday understanding is somewhere in between, because it mixes direct experience with abstract concepts and explanations provided by our culture.

This is a very important issue. **As individuals, we seem to be hardwired for both options**. We learn from direct experience, but we are also quick to imitate others, to follow example, to believe what we are told. Learning from experience seems to be universal in the animal world. All animals learn to recognize their home turf, their foods, mates, and so on. Often, the general preference is hard-wired by instinct, but the specifics are learned. Paraphrasing, *"we like trees"* might be innate, whereas *"that oak-tree over there is my home"* is learned.

Learning from others, imitating, is also common in higher forms of life. Many songbirds learn their song patterns from their parents, apes learn how to make tools and build nests by watching adults. Imitation, however, is just a kick-off. The art must then be mastered through personal practice.

Belief systems seem to be very limited in Nature, if they exist at all. The only example I can think of is the identification of would-be threats, such as a predator. Reactions of fear, alarm-calling, scolding and mobbing shows young animals which neighbors might be dangerous, and this information can be passed down without the experience of a predation event. This makes perfect sense because naïve youngsters are much more vulnerable to predation than adults and trying to learn from experience in this case is not an option. It would be suicidal, fatal. All good, but here is the problem: once this tendency is hardwired into our system, it becomes vulnerable to error and to manipulation, as we saw in the case of mimicry.

Consider the plight of a biologist colleague of mine who has no problem handling dangerous wild animals but is terrified of cockroaches! I'm not kidding. Rationally he's perfectly aware that this is ridiculous, even embarrassing, but he can't control the sense of fear and revulsion. When I asked him about it, he told me he picked it up from his mother, who was totally petrified and revolted by them. When a child experiences this sort of reaction by an adult, the emotion can imprint permanently. Imprinting is a special kind of instantaneous learning that occurs in many animals for a brief period, for instance to cement recognition between mother and newborn. This connection is stored so deep down that we are often not even aware that it exists or how it got there. Mistaken association can be the root of many phobias, irrational fears that can be totally crippling. It's perfectly reasonable to be cautious of spiders (some are deadly), but it is totally silly to be terrified by a photograph of a spider (photos don't bite!).

For a large part of human history in a normal family environment, learning by imitation and believing what you are told must have been very adaptive. A quote from a Wikipedia review of the movie mentioned above, *The Gods Must Be Crazy,* might help:

> *The one characteristic which really makes the Bushmen different from all other races is that they have no sense of ownership at all. Where they live, there's nothing you can own. … They live in a gentle world, where nothing is as hard as rock, or steel or concrete.*
>
> *They must be the most contented people in the world. They have no crime, no punishment, no violence, no laws, no police, judges, rulers or bosses. They believe that the gods put only good and useful things on the earth for them to use.*
>
> *In this world of theirs, nothing is bad or evil. Even a poisonous snake is not bad. You just have to keep away from the sharp end. Actually, a snake is very good, it's delicious. And the skin makes a fine pouch.*

In that context, sticking to the tried and tested made total sense. It stands to reason that your parents and extended kin would be mindful of your interests. As long as you honored tradition and followed the example of your elders everything would be fine. But again, once this indirect learning device becomes ingrained in our biology, in us and in our societies, it becomes liable to corruption and manipulation.

As societies grew and social life became more complex the operational instructions contained in clan lore and traditions became increasingly mixed up with rules of governance laid down by clan elites. Nobody really knows the details of how and when this happened, but it is clear that it must have happened when you compare very simple hunter-gatherer societies with more complex ones. How did we get from Bushmen to the Old Testament? That is, from *"**gentleness and no rules**"* to *"**a lot of rules and no mercy**,"* as Joseph Campbell put it, referring to the Old Testament.

Several thousand years ago elites realized they could control people if they could get them to believe tribal lore early in life, better still if they could link rules to fear. Of course, *"because Dad says so"* will only carry you so far. Every kid eventually grows up and challenges Dad. *"Because Big Chief says so"* perhaps carries a little further, but even that has limits. A less vulnerable alternative was needed, and the role fell to the gods. Now, humans must have been aware of the supernatural a long, long time ago. Rock art depicting shamanic figures and stone layouts that experts believe indicate forms of ritual go back tens of thousands of years to the very dawn of civilizations.

Somewhere along the way clan history, survival instructions, rules of governance and the belief in the supernatural got inextricably mixed together into what we call 'our culture,' no questions asked.

==================== I ====================

Chapter I.21 –

The Book of Ken revised: deconstructing the 'classic' view

You are not allowed to question our beliefs. Not to mention *"our religion"* specifically! But alas, we can't seem to resist questioning. In time the apparently inextricable mix-up mentioned in the previous chapter began to unravel. The various components of 'culture' were elaborated socially and institutionalized into often competing ways to manage experience, knowledge, and belief. Nowadays we know them as **art**, **science** and **religion** (art in its wider sense: arts and crafts, martial arts, etc.) This roughly corresponds to the workings of **body**, **mind** and **soul**. Philosophers speak of more abstract equivalents: **esthetics**, **knowledge** and **ethics,** or *'lovely, true and good'* (though their opposites, *'ugly, false and bad'* would be just as accurate). Another twist was to consider **art** as the domain of Self, **science** as the domain of nature, and **morals** as the domain of religion or society. Also note that in some of his books Ken uses **culture** as the key notion for the intersubjectal domain, but in my view art, science and even religion are aspects of culture, so this seems to be in error and confusing. As mentioned, I prefer to reserve **culture** and **cultural** to designate **a level of complexity** that affects all domains. Though briefly, this gives a bit of historic perspective, and highlights some of the prevailing assumptions in current philosophy.

Now, bear in mind that there was a time when religions ruled supreme over all of these aspects. They censored art, imposed knowledge, and dictated morals. And when sectors of society began to rebel, they fought tooth and claw to suppress them. Eventually these ideas were instrumental in staking out territories between art, science and religion, and a sort of truce prevailed. But the underlying power-struggle continues, just a bit more subtly. Relinquishing power never comes easy!

As I mentioned earlier, Ken attempted to fit these ideas into his *"four quadrants"* model, but the lack of fit is obvious and reflects a problem. These classic ideas respond to the question: **What does it study or work with?** Thus, art relates to our senses, science deals with the external world, and religion plays out in the socio-cultural sphere.

It seems he had a hard time fitting this classic trio into his four-part model: **art** he assigned to the individual-subjectal, **religion** to the collective-subjectal, and **science** to cover the objectal sphere in both the individual and collectival domains. Presumably scientists would be delighted because they get half the cake, but when you try to represent this graphically the skew becomes more apparent. So, in some of his figures Ken represented them as a pie diagram with three equal slices (Figure 17). Unfortunately, this masks the problem.

Philosophers are thinkers rather than doers, so they tend to focus on their area of study rather than on the effects of what they are doing. We can develop a more useful model if we change the question to **What does it modify?** To answer this seemingly simple question we need to dismantle the whole classic edifice. Changing the question leads to very different groupings. Best to start from scratch.

Artistic sensibility may emanate from our senses and imagination (the subjectal), but all artistic creations are expressed in matter. Art is always an object of sorts (a sculpture, a painting, a photograph; even a piece of music or a dance are material expressions), which is why we speak of '*a piece of art*.' Of course, the *contemplation* of art, **esthetics**, is in the domain of the Subject, it is <u>subjectal</u>, but **art** itself is <u>objectal</u>.

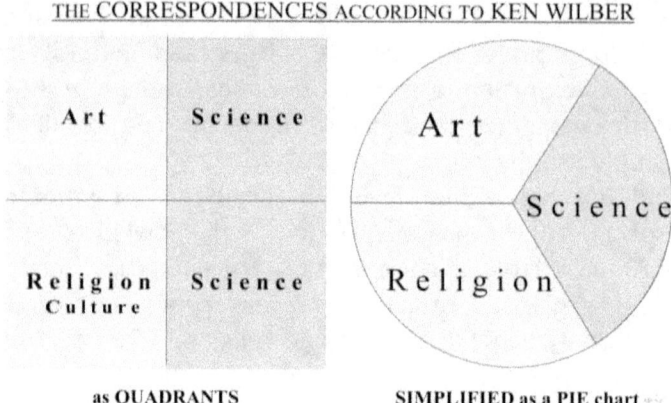

THE CORRESPONDENCES ACCORDING TO KEN WILBER

as QUADRANTS   SIMPLIFIED as a PIE chart

Figure 17. **Ken Wilber's original model.** – The placement of the major branches of human endeavors into "quadrants," and the simplified pie-chart, as per Ken's original versions. Note that politics does not appear.

Something similar occurs with what we collectively include under the term 'science,' but it is a little more complex. Even though experiments are performed on objects, the aim of these experiments is to change, to enlighten the Subject, the researcher. The same occurs with studies based on the observation of nature. And, at least initially, this always occurs at the level of the individual. The '*eureka*' moment is a personal experience. Therefore, this aspect of what we call 'science,' which I prefer to call **research,** is fundamentally individual-subjectal. This includes the empirical *eurekas*, the **in**-sights, gained by direct experience.

A better understanding of nature allows me to improve the methods I use to operate and manage that nature. If I learn to crack a nut with a stone, I can use the trick and benefit even if no one else knows about it. Sometimes this is called '*applied science,*' but I prefer to call it **technology**. At least until the industrial era, the aim of all technologies has been to create or modify material objects, or series of objects. Note that the creative arts fall within this definition just fine; hence we speak of *arts and crafts*. Now, you might think this is applicable to all the material side of reality, but my thesis postulates that technology (the classic type at least) is best considered as applying to the objectal-individual domain. The reason for this will become more evident as we move along.

Another essential aspect of the scientific method that differentiates science from religion is that to become truly **scientific** the discoveries and theories must go through a control process and verification by other researchers, usually specialists in the same subject, called *peer review*.

Once the novelty is communicated to the scientific community (published) any study or proposed explanation is open to this process of revision and any person can question the methods or the ideas. The fundamental element that makes this possible is a prerequisite that all the methodologies that were used in the study must be explicitly described in the publication. In short, describe how the researcher proceeded: *If you look in this manner you will see what we are describing.*

Descriptive reports might get by without too much scrutiny, but any significant novelty or change in the theoretical structure will surely trigger a lot of attention, and runs the risk of being torn to pieces if it is not well grounded and verified by independent testing. In the long run, it's NOT easy to get away with a lie. This constant testing methodology is what makes something scientific. The process is dialectical, Subject-Subject. Once a proposition passes all these checks, the knowledge gained gets incorporated into the scientific world view or what we refer to as **consensual science**. In short, the new knowledge and theories that make up **science** modify the intersubjectal domain.

The third central aspect of Ken's original cosmology is religion. Where should we place religion in this constellation? What does religion modify? As in the case of science, it seems clear that 'religion' is a composite concept. The main difficulty is that religion is often used as an instrument to govern, and therefore it overlaps extensively with politics. To cover the whole spectrum, we need to include politics. We cannot understand one without defining the other. These issues are so muddled, confusing, that I'll just state the result, my theory, and move on from there. Best start with the more tangible side.

Politics deals with the assignment of ownership and responsibilities. Its primary goal is to define who owns what, the interobjectal. The process, however, includes aspects from the other domains. Political insights, attitudes and beliefs are subjectal. Campaigning, lobbying, propaganda, and proselytism in general, all belong to the intersubjectal. We might include affiliation, but it too is a composite concept. All this leads to the construction of power structures. These include aspects that are material, objectal.

The term *religion* remits to our relationship with the divine. Insights, attitudes and beliefs are subjectal. Preaching, moralizing, lobbying, indoctrinating, and proselytism in general, all belong to the intersubjectal, as does faith, adoration, religious prejudice and hate. Religion based institutions are often used to govern. The use of religious notions to influence the assignment of responsibilities and material obligations (*e.g.*, tithes), political influence and action, and to justify political acts of violence, all move it into the very mundane interobjectal domain of politics. Again, all this involves power structures, and these include aspects that are material, objectal. Hence, as understood today, the concept and the practice of religion include aspects from all domains.

Clearly, religion and politics overlap extensively and neither can exist without a sociocultural substrate. This means that both religion and politics, as played out by humans, are aspects of the cultural level of organization, rather than domains in themselves. Still, to move ahead we need to disentangle and separate the parts and assign them to their proper domains (if possible).

Perhaps surprisingly, behavioral studies of social animals have revealed a host of actions that easily fall within the concept of politics: banding together, social hierarchies, forming alliances, battling over resources, staking out territories, even waging wars between neighboring clans. These societies show traces of incipient culture, but do not possess symbolic language. All this points to the primarily material nature of politics, the interobjectal.

On the other hand, it is impossible to conceive of modern religions without a sophisticated communication system via symbolic language, especially those religions that rely primarily on scriptures. Books may be material, but their meanings and the messages they convey are intersubjectal. However, their alleged primary source, "revelations," and the seat of all beliefs revolve around the (mystical) *in-sights* of a Subject, an individual, which brings us to a critical issue: you cannot find *ah!* in a book. The only place you can commune with the Divine is in your inner (*interior*) self. In current usage, the most appropriate word for this experience is *spirituality*.

Note, though, that in our embodied state spirituality requires some form of consciousness. This creates a bit of a circularity, because to the mystic conceptions spirit is what sustains consciousness, whereas to the materialist, consciousness is the basis for anything we might call spiritual. Either way, there should be little doubt that the connection between one and the other is mediated through our ***subjectal*** aspect or domain.

Most prominently, religions claim to be the keepers of faith. Faith, you may have noticed, is intrinsically *intersubjectal*. It is something that occurs between Subjects: "I believe in you." The same as love, worship, adoration, prejudice, hate. Belief is the backdrop that tends to *separate* the believer from the Subject of that belief, Deity, an experience which can and should be direct, interior, intimate.

Yet, because this direct relationship between Deity and you as an embodied soul very rarely occurs spontaneously, and in fact can be very difficult to achieve, this allows the possibility and even the need for instruction from those who have had these experiences spontaneously or have learnt from others before them, so as to learn the practices that facilitate the process. Again, because the numinous is not spontaneously evident for most of us, it seems we need to be told these other dimensions or realities exist and shown ways to perceive and relate to them. This opens the door to insert a wedge between the individual and the goal of his quest. It has given rise to a whole range of intermediaries or vicars that claim to mediate between Deity and the hopeful seeker (shamans, gurus, rabis, priests, lamas, etc.).

Before the advent of formalized religions, the role of the shaman or guru was to pass on his experience and knowledge to the apprentice, pupil, or initiate, so that the pupil could learn to access these other dimensions or worlds directly (I speak of 'dimensions' in plural, because virtually all spiritual cosmologies speak of tiers or layers of ever more subtle embedded 'realities'). This included the widespread use of psychoactive plants and the associated rituals. The practice of ingesting psychoactive plants or their extracts (psychedelics) was widespread in the ancient world and was an integral part of the rites of passage and similar ceremonies. Thus, most citizens had the opportunity to have **personal** contact with the otherworldly and the divine. This basic pupil-centered model continues to be honored in some religions, especially the oriental ones (Buddhism, in particular). This is the context in which *'re-ligio'* or **reunite** has its true meaning. To the extent that these teachings seek to afford the individual direct experience with the divine via the development of each person's own abilities and knowledge, the process is still in the domain of the Subject, and therefore **subjectal**.

With the development of religious institutions, the model changed into a priesthood-centered model. The clergy are the center. The faithful are there to serve the clergy (*to serve "God"*) and the stratagems of the church. Personal experience is replaced by faith in other people's experiences and what the clergy tell you to believe. Putting this wedge between the individual and his direct experience changes the nature of the interaction and diverts or distorts the original purpose of the practice. Rather than teach the person how to go within or create the conditions for this to happen on its own, the preacher now tells the person what he must think and feel, based on the dogmas imposed by the institution. As a rule, this includes some sort of commitment or affiliation to the religious institution. This creates the conditions to completely pervert the original meaning and purpose of the relationship.

Even so, the dynamics is mostly within the **intersubjectal** domain. As soon as teaching turns to preaching, there is a shift in the nature of the interaction, from the subjectal to the intersubjectal. Granted, you could argue that preaching is also intended to affect or modify the recipient, but it does so in a different way. The moment you include or appeal to faith, you inevitably include a third party in the relationship. Instead, the mystical experience is immediate, direct. There is no substitute for direct experience. Faith is mediated, indirect. This in turn allows for the infiltration or imposition of very mundane political agendas that are of little benefit to the believer or may even lead him completely astray.

I have extended this analysis to show how complex and multifaceted these notions are, and how easily they can be subverted. It should also help parcel them out and place the parts in their proper domains. But as we climb in the complexity ladder, the number of factors and possibilities escalates. One way to simplify is to take the opposites, the polarities. The subjectal domain harbors both direct experience and faith; in the intersubjectal we have teaching versus preaching; in the interobjectal both private and shared (communal) property, and so on. Based on the previous analysis, I propose rearranging the domains as follows:

Subjectal - (Individual)	Objectal - (Individual)
Contemplation – esthetics	Body practices
Observation – investigation	Material technologies
Inspiration – creativity	Arts and crafts
Inter-Subjectal	**Inter-Objectal**
Consensual science – education	Ecology - economy
Political ideologies – campaigns	Politics, government, legislation
Religious beliefs – preachings	Religious wealth, practices

Note that in this comparison I don't include the objectal. It partakes of these dynamics, of course, but for the most part in a passive support role. I will come back to these issues in Chapter I.24, but we need to move on.

This may be a good moment to mention the conditions that sustain authority and power. Three basic types have been proposed: authority conferred by **physical force** (the king and his armies); authority conferred by **knowledge** (elders, sages and philosophers); and authority conferred by **ethical and moral standing** (judges, lamas, saints). I would add a fourth, authority conferred by **material wealth** (money, resources, arms, etc.) Often physical force is referred to as 'power,' and wealth is subsumed as an aspect of power, but for the moment let's consider it separate. In real life situations there is a mix of these four aspects, but it is worth keeping the distinctions in mind because they rarely occur in perfect balance. In my opinion, true *power*[12] comes from that balance (Figure 18).

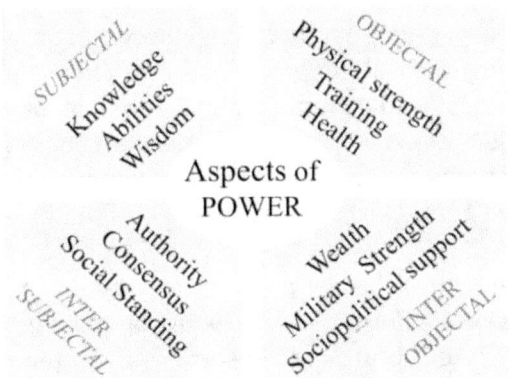

*Figure 18. **Aspects of Power.***
True empowerment develops when you cultivate all these aspects in a balanced way.

So then, what exactly does politics modify? It has been said that politics is an extension of war by peaceful means and war, above everything else, is a battle for conquest, control, and possession. We conquer, we claim, we own. Ownership is a specific kind of formalized bond that operates at the sociocultural level of organization. To better understand where owning fits in the context of the domains, first we need to clarify what we mean by and include under the term 'collectives.' What

---

[12] The Latin origin of the word 'power' is 'posse' - '*to be able to...*' - the ability or capacity to do things: "*you have the power to change things.*" This is a complex composite concept.

is the underlying difference between a plurality of unrelated things and a collective or a community?

====================== I ======================

Chapter I.22 –

What does 'collective' mean in different spheres?

If I got it right, Ken considers a collective to be either all or subsets of the members of a given level of organization in a holarchy. In this sense everything is part of some collective, but collectives vary greatly as to the level of organization and cohesiveness. But again, we seem to have problems with the use of language. Does 'collective' imply some form of bond or relationship or does it include random aggregates? What is the underlying difference between a series of unrelated things and a collective? Or a community? We need to clarify these terms and give them explicit meanings.

When we use the plural of any noun, say potatoes, we envision a bunch of objects, but there is no implication of order or relationship amongst them, beyond their likeness. Any number above one, in any combination, fits the term. Individual items are totally interchangeable. If I remove two out of five and replace it with a different two, I still have five. Following the terminology used by Enrique Pichon-Rivière I will call this sort of aggregate a **series**.

A simple series might be a bunch of leaves piled up by an eddy of wind. A simple example of a series in the human sphere would be a queue. Take a line at the bus stop or the ticket booth: people come and go, their number might rise and fall, fat ones, thin ones, old and young, it makes no difference. So long as you have people there, you have a queue. Even queues are not totally random, but they are close enough to get the idea.

Speaking of random, when we want to get a general descriptive idea of any series of things, the average individual, we try to get a 'random' sample. This ensures we are getting an unbiased cross-section of the whole population. Sometimes people refer to this as social, as in the phrase *the social distribution of neurosis,* or *social psychology* used in these contexts, but this is misleading. A more appropriate phrase for this type of study would be 'population (or statistical) individual psychology.'

At the other extreme we have highly structured aggregates, such as a sports team. All members know each other, each has a specific role to play, and interchangeability is very limited.

The problem with this sort of categorization is that something may look unrelated at one level but be linked at another. The people at the bus queue might look random, but they all belong to the same city, they are all Bostonians for instance, or those at the ticket booth are all fans of the same activity.

Aggregates come in an infinite variety of shades and numbers, and the edges between types are often difficult to define. We need to look at it from a different perspective. Not so much: *What does it look like?* Rather: **What holds it together?**

Let's start with the material side. If you look at Wilber's sequence of holons of the material – collectival (his lower right), the most basic stuff, atoms, make up the most basic collectives: galaxies, stars and planets. Nowadays these bodies contain much more than just atoms, but you could reduce everything to atomic dust and you'd still have a planet. We could add satellites and even flying golf balls. What holds these systems together? Well, one of *all's* basic laws, gravity, which is completely fascinating, because the existence of the billions of known galaxies, and stars with their planets and satellites can all be boiled down to just one principle. Even the behavior of more mundane mings like flying golf balls can be explained by gravity. Okay, granted, that's a bit of a simplification, but it's a useful starting point. The essential element that defines the range of collectives is not so much the stuff, as the **force** that holds that stuff together, or keeps it separate. Electromagnetism, friction and static, surface tension, chemical bonds (glue). Of course, in some cases we lapse from an aggregate or collective into some form of higher order holon. A pile of bricks, when glued together by mortar, becomes a wall.

These examples belong to the physical and chemical levels of organization. But what about biology? Biological systems also show a variety of underlying 'forces' that help shape the living world. In plants the groupings are often initially passive, a mere 'series.' A clump of trees in a prairie is clumped because that area has more moisture, for instance. But even in these cases the interaction between individuals will shape the clump, and will condition all the **community** of beings living in it. Tropism means something like *'the love of ____,'* so photo-tropism stands for *'the love of light'.* All green plants show it, which is why they all grow upwards, towards the natural source of light, the sun. Still, if you put your potted plant near a window with light coming at it only from one side, it will start growing sideways. But it is amongst animals where the play of active attractions and repulsions is more evident. Some display a marked attraction towards other members of their species, a **gregarious instinct**, which is enough to explain most herding and flocking behaviors. Very few basic rules can explain what looks like very complex behaviors. A flock of birds sitting on a power line might look huddled together but, if you look closer, they are not in physical contact. In fact, most likely they are very neatly spaced out at just about the exact same distance from the next one. They seem to defend and respect a personal space around each individual. Flock dynamics is a sort of dance between these two forces, one pulling them closer and the other marking a limit. Whether you know it or not, your life is largely governed by the same sort of forces: some are personal, like hunger, thirst or desire, and others are social, such as friendship, love, duty, hate, … Add the social rules, the taboos and similar notions, and we have a whole battery of intersubjectal forces that govern and at the same time suffice to explain the functioning of our primary communities.

However, the **intersubjetal** domain does not suffice to explain complex modern societies. In my opinion, complex social structures are held together by 'internal' forces similar to those described above, but ones that have been materialized in the form of contracts, rules and regulations, fundamentally, those that determine the owner-member relationships. This includes the formal assignment of roles and responsibilities, duties, affiliation and other forms of belongingness. Again, here we are moving from the **intersubjectal** to the **interobjectal**. That is, from folk's unwritten taboos, beliefs, and customs to the written laws, rules, statutes, contracts, etc. that are the modern way of materializing these relationships.

In a broad sense, the term *collective* covers any gathering of objects. This would include both random series and organized groups, which I will refer to generically as 'communities.' So then, how can we distinguish a pile of leaves mentioned earlier from a team? If you choose to be picky, even a pile of leaves is not totally random. A pile made by a whirlwind might show subtle differences from one made with a rake or a broom. But there is nothing in that pile of leaves that keeps them together. A strong gust of wind would scatter them in all directions. That's the problem, to explain the existence and the behavior of the aggregate you always have some external force or factor that produces the effect. Grains of sand may be clumped, but they are not linked. That's why sand runs or flows.

Unlike simple aggregates, communities even in their more ample sense, always have some internal thread that keeps them together or linked in some way. Let's go back to the previous examples. The leaf does not 'decide' to join the pile, it is taken by the wind. On the other hand, a flock of birds gathers because the individuals that make up the flock decided to join it. They are free to come and go at will. Instead, in the human example of the queue, the factor that brings them together is indirect, external to that circumstantial gathering. There was no decision to be with the other. Of course, being gregarious by nature, any circumstantial gathering of humans can rapidly turn into active interactions, but the factor or reason that gave rise to the situation was not to meet or to interact. Indeed, most of us hope that there is no queue at all. The same goes for commuter crowds in subway stations.

This difference between **external forces** and **internal forces** is what distinguishes a **series** from a **community** (or collectivity). In real life situations these forces interact, and may be complementary or in opposition, which is what produces the endless variety of groupings and associations that we observe around us. Here lies another problem with the use of the term 'collective' for the domain as a whole. If we include 'forces' as the feature underlying the domain, then it must cover repulsive forces as well. A typical example in animals is territorial defense, which produces an evenly scattered distribution of individuals over the landscape. Situations with no specific influences tend to produce random distributions with no discernible pattern.

It's worth mentioning that 'collective' is sometimes used as a synonym of 'series' in the sense given here, so we need to distinguish and limit these meanings. Words like dispersed, clumped, aggregated, random, etc., are all descriptive terms that do not imply intentionality, whereas 'collective' does carry that implication. Thus, we have several levels or degrees of association, a continuum. The least restrictive is what we might call a *category*, such as 'things.' The term could be applied to any plurality in any location or distribution, without the need for any sort of aggregate. But even in a loose category such as *birds*, all are linked by common descent, so it's a tricky issue. Then we have actual aggregates, and within these, clumped distributions (including some series) and true communities. From the perspective of the domain conception, I consider the term 'collective' is problematic because it implies some form of intentional aggregate. This excludes situations where the elements of a category are randomly distributed or scattered. This, I believe, is the advantage of using *'collectival'* for this dimension of reality, because it can encompass the whole spectrum of *'aggregatedness,'* including random arrangements, non-aggregates, and even hyperdispersed situations, where the elements are both scattered and evenly spaced out. These, then, become different conditions within the continuum, without any implicit contradiction. Collectival works for things, but is awkward when referring to forces or processes. In these contexts, *'relational'* is preferable (*i.e., individual – relational*).

Next, we need to look into the biological basis for social systems.

================ I ================

> *Individual selection promoted sin,*
> *while group selection promoted virtue.*
> Eduard O Wilson[13]

Chapter I.23 –

The mystery of altruism & the structure of social domains

This is a controversial issue that I would prefer to avoid, but I don't see how. In the chapter on 'Morals and Ethics in Nature' we saw that, in nature, 'cheating' in one way or another is quite frequent. In fact, it's quite obvious that if one side cheats and the other does not, the advantage to the cheater is huge, so much so that the 'others' always lose. Mathematical analysis of games of chance (cards, dice, roulettes, etc.) show that the slightest asymmetry that deviates from pure chance rapidly favors one of the players. It is the very basis of a whole cadre of scams and scammers (loaded dice, marked cards, and tricks of the sort). What works in games seems to be equally valid in everyday life.

This asymmetry is so evident that it has given rise to a long battle to explain its opposites, cooperation and altruism, both in practical and in theoretical terms. And in spite of it all, it seems we humans, (and to some extent other beings), have a tendency to be altruistic to some degree, on

---

[13] Eduard O Wilson, *The Meaning of Human Existence*, 2014, p. 33.

occasions even heroically, which poses a profound contradiction and a theoretical challenge. *How can something that at first sight is always detrimental to the individual that performs it be sustained over generations?* How and why does the 'altruistic' trait or tendency evolve?

Even defining altruism is difficult. As an attitude, we can think of altruism as a selfless concern for the wellbeing of others, but in more practical terms, as *an act that favors another person or group, but has no tangible benefit to the doer,* or has an incidental benefit that is clearly less than the cost or harm incurred.

Of course, between egoism and altruism there is a whole range of options, fundamentally including forms of cooperation. The issue is important because all the developments that we consider social and 'human' require some degree of sacrifice of personal interests in favor of the interests of the group.

In the usual everyday situations of our more intimate family and social life we are so accustomed to a constant *'give and take'* that we don't even pose it as a problem. But, as we drift from the intimacy of closed groups to more open social situations, the imbalances become more evident and the questions more pressing. Can a complex society be sustained if all its members are systematically 'egoistic'? How much egoism can a social system tolerate before it collapses?

The arguments have been particularly heated in relation to biological evolution, but also in the sphere of economics. The interpretation initially given to the notion of *'the fight for survival'* and *'natural selection'* proposed by Darwin is that this inevitably leads to a selfish position or stance. It became one of the pillars of the 'anti' movement, on the lines of *This theory is opposed to and destroys everything that is good in our societies,* and notions of the sort. A good part of the initial fieldwork and theoretical analyses supported Darwin's theses. In fact, I'd say they took them even further in that direction. Not only are individual organisms selfish, our very genes are selfish. Richard Dawkins, who proposed the notion of the *selfish gene,* is the most adamant exponent and defender of this view. But note a subtle distinction between being *'selfish'* and *'acting in one's own interest.'*

However, reality is always the nemesis of theories. Social behaviors and complex societies **exist**, in spite of the apparent primacy of selfish individual strategies (and of selfish genes). So, what's the trap? It has been one of the most difficult questions to find an answer to. And yet, it is fundamental because it affects the basis of all the institutional, moral, and political structure of modern societies.

Let's go back to the simpler systems found in nature. Well, 'simpler' is relative! As compared to your average insect, some of the more extreme cases, such as ant colonies or bee-hives, are truly complex societies, and at the same time complicated, involving thousands or even millions of individuals. But nature offers a whole range of examples, from the undifferentiated hordes of locusts and anonymous schools of fish to the very well-structured and lasting societies such as wolfpacks and elephant herds.

I believe it is correct to say there are five currents that oppose or counterbalance the strictly individualistic tendencies (or at least, five approaches to the issue).

1) **Family and kin selection** is based on the idea of shared genes. If I help my direct biological relatives (nepotism in the political jargon), I am helping myself (or at least, those genes shared by my relatives). This is fairly obvious as regards close relatives, especially offspring. The problem is that this effect gets diluted very quickly. With my siblings and my children, I share only half my genes, with my cousins or nephews and nieces only a quarter, and relatedness dilutes rapidly with more distant relatives.

2) **Reciprocal altruism.** *"Today for me, tomorrow for thee"* (or vice versa). I'll help you if you help me. In its origin at least, reciprocal altruism is a sort of psychological contract. It occurs in couples, for instance. There is always a notion of reciprocity. *"I will care for you because I know you will care for me."* But lack of continuity and cheating limits its application.

3) **Cooperation,** in its many forms, is distinct from reciprocal altruism because it usually occurs simultaneously. If we do this together, we can accomplish tasks neither of us could do alone, or obtain much better or faster results (as in the case of a hunting party, below). Everybody benefits to some degree, and the tradeoff between effort (costs) and benefits can be settled on the spot. Some form of cooperation underlies all forms of group selection (next).

4) **Selection at the level of groups and communities**. The idea here is that groups with individuals that cooperate are more successful than groups where nobody cooperates. This is fairly evident in sports teams, for instance. No team works without cooperation. Still, it's a constant pulling and pushing, as is evident from in-team bickering (...*pass the ball, you ...!*).

5) **'True' altruism** (the moral approach?). The good Samaritan that helps a stranger in distress; compassion and charity for the needy. Tax systems are, arguably, a form of investment in favor of communal infrastructure and essential services. Clearly a reciprocity. However, the portion of taxes that is dedicated to welfare edges into altruism, especially when that welfare is allotted to complete strangers in other communities or distant countries.

Yet, what might be obvious at the intuitive level can be very difficult to demonstrate under the prevailing theoretical framework, or some idea might only work under such restrictive conditions that it is seldom applicable to real-world situations.

It is *genetically* obvious that it benefits all organisms to invest effort and resources in their offspring, because if they don't their genetic line will disappear. Therefore, any gene that favors success in reproduction will be favored. That's why in general the care of offspring is not considered a form of altruism. But the limits of that 'investment' are not so obvious. If the effort to take a pregnancy to term at this time is likely to produce your death, perhaps it's not a good idea. Better wait for a more favorable moment. We already saw this issue in the chapter on **Life and reproductive strategies** (Chapter I.14). An intimately linked issue is the conflict between the parents' interests and those of each of their offspring. Under normal circumstances parents will spread their resources more or less evenly amongst their children. This is not *'the best'* as seen from the perspective of each child. Each one will likely prefer to be the only child, or at least the pampered one in the family. This can be seen in expressions of jealousy and fights between sibs. The counter side is that kids that are shortchanged can be particularly sensitive when parents show favoritism, a common source of indelible psychological traumas. Well, in short, family selection no doubt works[14], but it is a delicate balance, with frequent counteracting situations.

The second option has been called **reciprocal altruism**, but of course, if I do something with the expectation (or at least the illusion) that it will be reciprocated, perhaps it is not altruism, rather a form of trade or business. Still, the advantage of this idea is that it is applicable in a much wider range of situations than those based on familial relatedness. As mentioned, it is particularly relevant in the marital contract, in friendships and the like, but it is severely time constrained. The relationship must persist over time in order to allow for reciprocity, and it is very easy to cheat (accept favors but never return them).[15] A very interesting idea was proposed in the film *Pay it Forward*, a concept that to some degree underlies such conventions as traffic laws: "I let you pass on this intersection because another driver let me pass on the previous one. Since we may never meet again, return the favor to some driver you encounter in the future" (*i.e.*, *pay it forward*).

A duo or small group that gets together to go on a hunting venture can be perfectly justified and explained if this **cooperation** (teamwork) increases the chances of taking more or bigger prey in a proportion higher than the resulting need to share the catch. This has been well documented in social predators such as wolves and lions. When large prey is available, they hunt in large groups because it's the only way they can bring down these large animals. If they succeed there is a lot to go around (they fight over the carcass anyway, but still...). Instead, when no large prey is available each wolf or lion hunts alone, or at best in pairs. No doubt they would be more successful as a group, but one rabbit is not enough to share between six or eight wolves! **If there is no chance of sharing or reciprocity there is no cooperation**.

The fourth option, **group selection,** at the level of larger groups and even whole communities, is the one that has triggered more controversy as far as its theoretical basis is concerned. The original idea was proposed by Edward O Wilson as a result of his studies of colonial ants and other social insects (he is the promoter of 'sociobiology'). In its most extreme version, the individual sacrifices his life for the common good. Though he dies, his

---

[14] A more general formulation is the concept of *inclusive fitness,* but the subject is complex and its validity has been challenged, so I prefer to skip it.

[15] See Tess Wilkinson-Ryan, 2023. *Fool Proof. How Fear of Playing the Sucker shapes our Lives...*

social group prospers. Even though it has been proposed as an alternative to family-based selection, at first blush it seems this only makes sense if the individuals in question share a large part of their genetic makeup, an ethnic group or tribe, for instance. From a purely genetic perspective, he who sacrifices his life for totally unrelated strangers is a loser. But we must also bear in mind if the critical factor is in the origins or in the destiny. The allusion to ethnicity implies common origins, but I think evolution only 'cares' about common destinies - not so much where we come from, rather where we are headed... This is the essence of our emigration and colonization strategy. Even if the resulting groups are a complete ethnic mishmash, it often works! But in that case, we inevitably overlap with self-interest, cooperation, and family/kin selection of the descendants. The issue is undoubtedly complex.

Still, it is one of the fundamental questions you must ask, *'What is more important?'* Is it *'Where did my ancestors come from?'* Or better, *'Where will my descendent end up?'* In the *old world* it is often difficult to make this distinction, because origin and destination overlap almost completely. The issue becomes paramount in the *new worlds*, and the answer is pretty obvious. In the final analysis what matters is the future, much more than the past. Communities in the New World are a mix of all kinds of genetic backgrounds, which is fantastic. Outbreeding is known to have positive effects (geneticists call it *hybrid vigor*). Three or four generations and the inevitable crossbreeding will produce a whole range of racial hybrids, the ideal raw materials for natural selection...

Yes, okay, I know. It is not *politically correct* to speak about **us** in those terms. We humans are above natural selection, don't you think? No, I don't. This is one of the more generalized delusions that calm our *sapiens* pride, but that has not the slightest truth to it. Natural selection is like gravity: it is ALWAYS at work. Think it over a bit and you'll see I am right. It's the very basis of adaptation. Fortunately, in our hyper complex world the paths to adaptation are quite unpredictable (if they were predictable it would allow for planning). One of the most demolishing stumbling blocks of deterministic 'planifications' is that the effects or interactions between the multiple factors involved are **not** direct, linear. At times a lot of effort in one area can produce little effect, and at other times a change that seemed trivial can have a huge impact. It happens a lot with technological innovations, whose effects are often very difficult to predict. In other situations, the very changes produced by apparently desirable innovations have side effects that create new problems that demand new adjustments. This happens with new laws, which in practice are always **social experiments**. The usual scenario is that laws are enacted in response to some situation or event. Problems happen ... so we must legislate..., but the chosen solution is nonetheless an experiment... Sometimes it improves the situation, other times it does not.

This is one of the great indirect advantages of **cooperation**, because the group has a much higher operating and adaptive plasticity than the individual.

We tend to think of adaptation and selection in positive terms, but in the case of selection applied at the level of groups and communities the negative side is equally important. The errors, the arrogance and the stupidities performed by leadership can take entire communities or even nations to the brink, to ruin or to annihilation. One of the well-documented cases occurred in the most active cultural center of the civilization of their time. Occidental Christian self-centeredness makes us very unaware of the true origins of modern civilizations: India, China, Mongolia, the Middle East and the huge regions that lie in between, Central Asia, the very heart of that mega-continent called Eurasia. The land of the '-istans' (Afghanistan, Kazakhstan, Kyrgyzstan, Tajikistan, Turkmenistan and Uzbekistan). The greater part of Western Europe fits into these territories.

The area had been conquered by the Arabs and is still predominantly Muslim. Around the 1200's of our era the area was enjoying a cultural and scientific renaissance under the reign of the kingdom of Khwarazm, whose best-known exponent in Europe is Avicenna (Abu Ali Al-Husayn **Ibn Sina**)[16]. Everything was going splendidly till a large diplomatic delegation arrived from the East, from a kingdom as yet unknown to them. The governor of the city of Otrar, named Inalchug, had orders to retain the goods belonging to the caravan, but he had the decidedly bad idea of murdering everybody, diplomats as well as merchants. To make matters worse, he let one of the camel-boys escape, who managed to return to Mongolia and tell of all these events to his Khan, none other than *Chinggis Khan* (better known in the west as **Genghis Khan**). Grave error. This tremendous insult was more

---

[16] S Frederick Starr, 2013. *Lost Enlightenment: Central Asia's Golden Age, from the Arab conquest to Tamerlane.*

than enough to justify the Mongol invasion of all Central Asia. The retaliation was brutal, the governor and the nearly hundred thousand inhabitants of Otrar were annihilated, together with at least fifteen other prosperous cities of thousands of inhabitants, that were literally wiped off the map (Otrar, Samarkand, Bukhara, Khojent, Tirmidh, Nisa, Ghor, Balk, Bamiyan, Nishapur, Tus, Herat, Merv, Gurganj, etc.). But Genghis was a strategist. Those cities that capitulated without a fight he left in peace. Tirmidh and Khojent resisted and were devastated. In some cases, the authorities pretended to capitulate but then counterattacked, as did Nishapur, which was flattened *"so that it could be tilled with a plow."* Not even the dogs survived, literally.

What's the point of all this? We tend to think evolution works by rewarding the winners, but a large part of the process occurs not so much by rewards, as by penalties to the losers. Even though the example I chose is quite extreme, it serves to highlight a more general phenomenon. Those who make bad decisions end up being excluded. If these bad decisions are made by heads of governments, this exclusion drags and affects the whole society. In many cases it's not so much '*the survival of the fittest*' as '*the failure of the inept.*' This is particularly relevant to the selection of groups and communities. Inefficient societies slowly lose ground till, in the long run, they lose the whole championship. Of course, local politicians will always put the blame on the winners, but the root of the problems are almost always in their own bad decisions.

At this point it's worth pointing out that all the great nations, kingdoms and empires of the last millennia were built on the basis of very strong ethnic cohesiveness. A certain group succeeded in creating a prosperous and tightly knit society that slowly gained ground and territories based on strict military discipline and an unbreakable commitment of its citizens to 'the common good.' '*Honor, loyalty, discipline, dedication, service,*' and vows of the sort. For some reason, after a century or a millennium, that structure seems to weaken and the initial supremacy of the group slowly dwindles, till some other group, often unknown till then, starts gaining ground and ends up taking over leadership. A number of external reasons have been postulated to explain these cycles (climate change, catastrophes, epidemics, etc.) but, as the process seems to repeat systematically, in my opinion the cycle often occurs due to an evolution **within** the societies themselves, that lead to internal failures of the social strategies. In these cases, the external context only serves to precipitate the actual downfall.

Everything points to the idea that social dynamics are a mix of genetic predispositions and social conditionings. All modern societies are 'newborn offspring' of hunter-gatherer societies (at least in terms of genetic evolution). They in turn were made up of small family groups with a high degree of social bonding and of genetic relatedness, relatively 'closed' groups. In this context, survival is an immediate cooperative effort both in procuring food as in the defense of the group. Fine, but how did they think and feel? What was their valuation scale? Hard to know for sure, but there are hints, both in groups that have conserved ancient structures as in some variants of neurodiversity and of the current neuro-divergences. Believing in the wisdom of the elders, for instance. After all, they were the *living memory* of the group, of their survival strategies and their social identity. Today this has ceased to be essential, but we still retain the predisposition to being *credulous*. We changed our gurus, but we still have gurus.

Still, the critical issue has to do with the subject of the chapter. Societies that gave rise to empires were based on high degrees of cooperation, of service to the community, of reciprocity, honesty, ethnic and cultural identity, 'tribalism' if you wish. In addition to grit, courage, and combativity, indispensable for a hunter gatherer lifestyle and for the constant warmongering between tribes. In these societies change was always kicked off by the adoption of cattle-herding systems and especially by agriculture. The increase in resources and predictability that these changes ensured allowed for a considerable increase in population and the complexification of social hierarchies. It becomes possible to save and accumulate wealth, weapons and so on. All these elements are essential in the construction of kingdoms and empires.

However, the passage from dispersed clans to tribes and on to nations has other effects. The growth in populations dilutes the relatedness within the clans, and weakens the ever more distant cooperation networks. The brave and the loyal die in the constant wars. The population that remains is increasingly biased towards the cowards, the handicapped and the cheats. In truth it does not matter much if these changes have a genetic basis or are purely cultural, though in all likelihood it is a combination. The cumulative effect is the same. The empire that was built on the bases of loyalty and cooperation succumbs to treason and corruption. The most significant notion in all this is that the very conditions created by the intelligences that built the empires may generate the conditions that destroy them. Empires can become the victims of their own success.

Returning to **altruism** for a moment, some of us definitely have the 'gene' for compassion and altruism. Feeling empathy for the distress and suffering of others seems to be part of human nature. In the context of family, extended social ingroups and even within local communities, this makes perfect sense. Charity should start close to home. As we drift away from these local contexts, the issues become iffier because any form of aid in these cases inevitably involves an increasing number of anonymous intermediaries over whom the donor has no control, which opens the door to discretional distributions and outright scams. The institutionalized version means allotting tax moneys to welfare. Welfare is also a complex issue, undoubtedly necessary and justified in many well-defined local or regional situations, as in emergencies and catastrophes. When that welfare is allotted to complete strangers in distant communities or countries, the tractability dwindles and it is difficult to avoid the aid being taken as a 'political' statement or intrusion, especially when the 'catastrophe' in question is the result of internal wars. Here it is important to distinguish aid in kind (goods) from aid in cash. Both can be misused, but it is difficult to buy arms, drugs, etc. with packaged food, clothes and similar goods. When the allotment is too discretional, sloppy or ends in the hands of the corrupt rather than the needy, from the taxpayer's point of view it's just another scam. This is particularly infuriating when the aid is channeled through governments or non-government organization that are known to be totally corrupt and abusive, even partial to acts of terrorism. You may be altruistic. Unfortunately, there is no guarantee that the middlemen share your vision and will honor your intentions. Actually, this problem affects all levels of delegated power.

Let's look at the vice of corruption in more general terms. Societies based on cooperation (basically all of them) work to the extent that they find ways to limit individual aspirations so that these don't ruin or upset social commitments. We assume that the governing delegates work in favor of the interests of the community, for which they earn a salary or some form of legal remuneration. In small societies personal relationships are more or less direct and the system works passably well. But as societies grow, the links between the governing elites and their people become ever more tenuous. This is particularly bad with very centralized governments. Two hundred years ago centralized democracies based on the use of representatives were inevitable due to the great distances and the inadequacy of communications. Today they are obsolete. The representative that spends months or even years in the Capital finds himself ever more separated from his constituents and becomes ever more 'cosmopolitan,' with all the temptations and vices the capital city has to offer. It's no surprise that he ends up betraying his constituents in exchange of some privilege or other, and also becomes ever more prone or vulnerable to bribery and extortion. The problem is mathematical. The damage to society is not so much the amount of the bribe, which is often meager in relation to the concessions and benefits the traitor gives away in exchange. Any society can withstand a bad deal now and then. No society can withstand 'bad deals' systematically. Something breaks. But I am getting ahead of myself.

With these ideas in mind, let's return to the emergence of modernity.

===================== I =====================

Chapter I.24 –

How did they parcel out the cake? The birth of modernity

Religion dominated the western world for much of history, but ideas began to change a few centuries ago when philosophers started to identify and separate different roles. Art, science, religion, politics and other lesser roles took separate paths. Today this may seem to us a trivial change, but it had such a profound impact that many consider this marked the beginnings of 'modernity.'

In Chapter I.21, I presented an analysis of the main conceptual divisions that gave rise to modernity, defining and differentiating the roles that had been dominated by priests until that time. Most consider that the three most important domains are art, science and religion, so they are often called '*the big three*.' As we saw, Wilber tried to retain this division and afforded it considerable weight, but at the expense of forcing the fit. What is my view on the Big Three? Earlier I analyzed 'art' and 'science' and found they are composite concepts whose parts operate on different domains. In short, at the time it was a step forward, but it is also a misleading model. We need to get beyond it.

The conception I presented in Chapter I.21 is different from the classical view and from the treatment Wilber gives the objectal-collectival domain (the interobjectal, systems theories, etc.). Given that ensembles are the result of external and internal forces described in Chapter I.22, we would need to replace the holarchy of things with a holarchy of relational forces.[17]

Nowadays almost every aspect of wealth and responsibilities is conditioned by a host of written rules and regulations. *"It's the law,"* the laws of men. However, the fundamental point is that the *inter-objectal domain* is in no way an inert depersonalized **Its**, as Ken postulated in his writings. It is very much alive and kicking and has a very definite internal representation in us, which has little to do with systems theories and such. Ken uses the term *social autopoiesis*, but I must confess it rings few bells in me. Autopoiesis means something like *self-regulating*. Of course, societies have cultural mechanisms that can be understood as self-regulators of those societies, but then so does biology and so does inert nature. Instinct self-regulates flocking behavior. Gravity self-regulates the orbit of planets. Social regulation is not just a question of 'systems.' It involves a host of very deep biological responses. Our everyday relationship to our belongings, whatever they may be, can be quite passionate. If you don't believe me, just imagine snatching a lady's handbag, or watching some stranger driving off with your car. The inter-objectal is not as much a simple 'its' as it is an **'our'** or a **'my'** issue. At the personal level, it refers to our *attachments*. At a social level, it refers to the laws, deeds, contracts and other materialized instruments that regulate ownership and belonging.

Now we are better equipped to analyze politics and religion. The term *politics* derives from the Greek word *'polis,'* meaning city, so politics refers to the affairs of a city state, and by extension, the affairs of state in general. The etymology of 'religion' is less clear. It may have its roots in the Latin term *'ligare,'* to tie, so *re-ligare* would mean 're-tie' or 're-unite' (with the Divine, implicitly). To see what these activities modify we need to separate the individual, the practitioner or believer, from the social operator (politician or preacher).

One important aim of both political and religious operators,

---

[17] This may correspond to one of Wilber's 'zones,' but I'm not sure we are referring to the same thing. If we reorganize the domains as I propose, the whole idea of Ken's *zones* will likely need a revision, so I'll just press on and see where it leads.

proselytism, is to influence the individual across the population: preach, indoctrinate, convince, manipulate, lie, coerce, ... whatever it takes to influence the way people perceive and respond. However, the political approach refers primarily to our material reality, wealth, power and so on. Instead, religion allegedly refers to our spiritual reality, the subjectal domain. Both belong to the social level of organization, but religion is much more dependent on culture than politics is.

So, in essence, what does politics seek to modify? Like science, politics is a composite term. Even so, the correct answer, I believe, is that it is designed to operate on and modify the inter-objectal domain. Informally, if science and technology tell us how to bake the cake, **politics tries to determine or impose who pays for it and who gets to eat it**. Historically this was achieved by raw physical power (brute force). The strongest army conquered, usually killed all competing males, raped, enslaved, and pilfered; in short, took all the *spoils of war*. Establishing property claims has always been an important issue: cowboys staked their claims by branding wild broncos and steers; empires by planting their flags.

But war is costly, even for the winner. As social organization progressed, novel forms of commerce and ownership cropped up, and the concept of private property started replacing raw power. A nobleman's title and a land-deed are much safer and easier to hang on to. Besides, they can be passed on to their descendants, even if they are weaklings or morons.

It has been a historical process, slow at times, but that has gained ground. The laws and regulations tend to be ever more secular. Still, some vices are passed down. Taboo is replaced by useless administrative bureaucracy that is not complied with, but that serves to hinder the competitor and to extricate bribes.

Fast forward. If you pay attention, a very significant part of today's social institutions and conventions are dedicated to the assignment and maintenance of ownership and belongingness. Attorneys, scribes, escrow offices, land tenure systems, material exchange (commerce), police forces, banks, patents, franchises, copyrights and revenues, taxation systems, even international borders and border patrols, and many more dedicate all or much of their time and effort to this sacred chore. Many of these activities have no other purpose than to define, modify, and control our inter-objectal relationships: what belongs to whom, or who owns what, if you prefer. This, it is worth stressing, includes our rights and responsibilities. The inclusion of rights and responsibilities might not be obvious, because to a large extent they seem to be 'intangible,' but think of contract laws, where the fulfilment of a responsibility is rewarded with a salary, or of monetary compensations for some violation of your rights. Once established by law, these things either have direct material (economic) value, or can be translated to one by a judge or an insurance company, for instance.

Considering the fundamental role these ties have in the structure and dynamics of modern societies and even in our everyday life, I was surprised to find little mention of any form of 'ownership' in developmental models I have reviewed or in Wilber's books. Perhaps I missed it. (Ken does refer to *the shadow* and the 'disowned' self, which is important, but has little to do with material assets or social responsibility).

We definitely have an internal signaling system for these issues. For starters, we 'belong' to the earth and feel it as our weight, literally. Love and affection make us '*gravitate*' to our family and home. More generally, our perception of ownership varies with both age (developmental stage) and cultural background. Small children can be quite ruthless when it comes to deciding who plays with which toy. Some societies stress individual rights, others tend to be more in favor of communal approaches, which is reflected in many ways. Inheritance laws, for instance, may grant total freedom as to how you dispose of your assets (you could give all to charity or to your cat). Others impose restrictions, such as considering your spouse and kids as obligate heirs.

Again, the question of responsibility might be less obvious. It operates at several levels. On the one hand, most remunerated activities are regulated as to what sort of service you can or cannot provide, what training you need to be a provider, who is authorized when and where, and so on. We invest great effort to **own** the corresponding license. Another aspect is related to what happens if you screw up, or do something which is illegal, or somebody gets hurt, etc. In those cases, the critical issue is defining and proving who is responsible, because that determines who pays the bill. Which is why suddenly everybody is desperately trying to **dis-own** whatever is at stake.

And then there is the question of moral responsibility. Although it clearly intersects with the interobjectal, moral responsibility is usually an unwritten aspect of social lore, linked to things like altruism, and is best treated as intersubjectal. For the same reason, we can provisionally place religious preaching and beliefs in the intersubjectal domain.

As I proposed in Chapter I.21, we can summarize these ideas the following way:

Subjectal - (Individual)	Objectal - (Individual)
Contemplation – esthetics	Body practices
Observation – investigation	Material technologies
Inspiration – creativity	Arts and crafts
Inter-Subjectal	**Inter-Objectal**
Consensual science – education	Ecology - economy
Political ideologies – campaigns	Politics, government, legislation
Religious beliefs – preachings	Religious wealth, practices

We could include more items, but this list covers the more important aspects considered here. This is not the place for an exhaustive analysis, but hopefully these examples convey the basic ideas.

Going back to the more conceptual version of the domains, and limiting it to the human level, we can reformulate them as presented in Figure 19.

Now, we need to make some distinctions here. Even very old societies had unwritten lore about these issues. Lore, however, fits best in the inter-subjectal domain. In turn, the inter-subjectal is influenced by science, religion, and politics, all of which make up what we might call **society's worldview or cosmology**. Since the three compete for the same domain, this approach makes much more sense when it comes to understanding the vicious battles that have dominated the interactions between politics, religion and science. However, there is a very marked difference between science and the other two. Scientists may patent their ideas and technologies, but

As a **method**, SCIENCE has no bearing on issues of **property and belonging**.

If you need to resolve or dispute a property-related claim, you might call an attorney, or appeal to a judge, never to a scientist. True, you might need an expert to resolve some technical issue, but the final decision is in the hands of the judge.

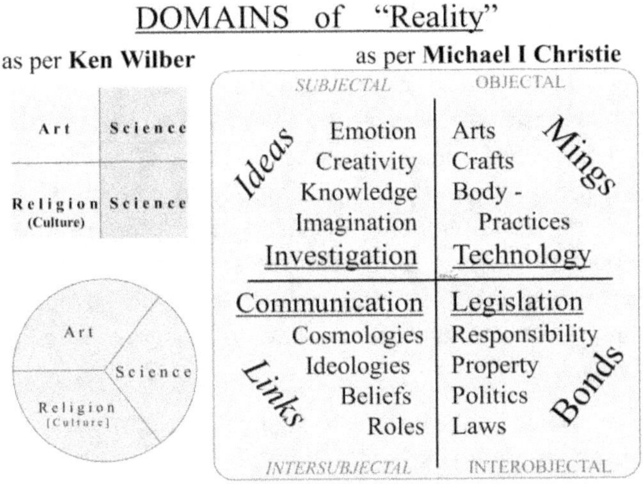

DOMAINS of "Reality"

as per **Ken Wilber**   as per **Michael I Christie**

Figure 19. **The new formulation of the domains proposed by Michael Christie.** – *The content of the domains as proposed here, compared to the original proposed by Ken Wilber in his two versions. – The underlined terms in each domain are, perhaps, the innovations that best define our modern cultural level of organization. – **Mings** is short for 'Material things.'*

On the other hand, religious and political leaders have feuded over these issues for millennia, often tearing each other apart, or dragging whole communities to war. Until recently the 'church' was the richest corporation in all the western world, and religious institutions still hold title to huge fortunes. It took powerful kingdoms to begin to debunk the Catholic church's grip on Europe, and to decouple the church from government and state. Of course, since controlling the masses at home, conquering new lands and hoarding riches was in the interest of both parties, they have made alliances and cooperated as often as they have squabbled. All too often, the sword in one hand, the *holy book* in the other.

But what are the clergy actually doing? What 'god' are they really worshiping? To answer these questions, we need to look at another issue, the focus and style of religious practices and spiritual paths.

===================== I =====================

Chapter I.25 –

Four Spiritualities – Four Gods – Four Yogas

Different spiritual paths and religions share a range of features, but I think it is fair to say that each has its primary focus, a special flavor or color. These, in turn, seem to emanate from basic differences in the way we relate to the world around us, our personalities.

This issue was formally studied by Christian Minister Peter Richardson in his book *Four Spiritualities: Expressions of Self, Expression of Spirit* (1996). In an effort to understand his congregation, he studied the Jungian '*Types*' concept of personality and proposed that there are four basic styles or roads. He described these four styles, referring to the different paths as 'journeys.' He also pointed out the similarities of these approaches with some major religions and the personalities of their creators, and then to the types of yogas.

- the Journey of Works – Moses – Judaism – (Karma Yoga)
- the Journey of Devotion – Mohammed – Islam – (Bhakti Yoga)
- the Journey of Unity – Buddha – Buddhism – (Jnana Yoga)
- the Journey of Harmony – Jesus – A bit of each – (Raja Yoga)

Of course, being a Christian minister may have biased his choices. But the general idea that one size does not fit all is still valid. You should be free to choose what resonates with you, without some self-centered rabbi, priest, or mullah condemning you to eternal damnation just because you didn't happen to choose *their* version of dogma.

Richardson himself recognizes that the only other tradition that postulates something similar is Yoga. Hinduism has long recognized that people have different ways of 'knowing' and of worshiping their deities. Over time they developed different practices for each of those modalities, the Four Paths of Yoga. In a nutshell:

– Karma Yoga	– action	– life practices	– Serve
– Bhakti Yoga	– devotion	– adore, venerate	– Love
– Jnana Yoga	– wisdom	– explore, know	– Meditate
– Raja Yoga	– integration	– think, decide, do	– Realize

A modern exponent who is well known in the West is Swami Sivananda. His approach to yoga was to combine the four main paths mentioned above, along with various sub-yogas such as kirtan and hatha yoga. In his own words, "One-sided development is not commendable. Religion and Yoga must educate and develop the whole person - **their heart, intellect and hand**." Ramiro A Calle speaks of the harmonic integration of the **bio-psycho-social** aspects of the individual. These paths are usually seen by others as different and separate, suited to different people addressing their individual temperaments or approaches to life. There is consensus that all the paths lead ultimately to the same destination - to union with Brahman or God. Swami Sivananda, however, saw a need for balance in every individual's spiritual development. He maintained that though the seeker would naturally gravitate toward one path, the lessons of each of the paths need to be integrated by every seeker if true wisdom is to be attained. Thus, he did not see them as different paths but as methods to be used in concert for the one destination. A similar idea is expressed in Wilber's *Integral Spirituality* approach.

But I must point out that though these schools speak of four paths or journeys, in practice they are only considering three basic ones and a fourth that is a combination of the other three. Terminology varies but, as mentioned above, all refer to three basic approaches. That is, the corporeal aspect (deeds, hand, bio-), the mental (thought, intellect, psycho-), and the relational (word, the heart, -social).

It is also worth pointing out that although these schools don't express it explicitly, in most cases there seem to be two alternative **opposing ways or paths.** You can attain spiritual mastery by *denial* or by *exaltation*. Take the huge variety of physical approaches ('works'). On the one hand you have those that consider forms of physical punishment and abstinence as the path to enlightenment: fakirs, flagellants, hermits and the like. But then there are those that consider cultivation of the body to be the correct way: martial arts, dance, bodybuilding, sports, music, all require extreme discipline and concentration that molds the body and tempers the soul. Same with food and drink: fasting or feasting. Even sex can be approached by abstaining (celibacy) or by indulging expertly (kundalini, the Kamasutra, Gnostics, etc.) Implicitly, what doesn't seem to be of any value is to be sloppy and mindless about everything.

The notion of the different paths that we just saw above can be matched to the concept of the four domains fairly well, but there's a problem. Even taking into account the different ways, something is missing. We can assign the four paths the following way:

Jnana Yoga, Unity, meditating – knowing, would be
Individual Subjectal.
Karma Yoga, body-oriented practices - martial arts, etc. - are
Individual Objectal.
Bhakti Yoga, devotion, fits the communing and loving, the
Inter Subjectal.
Raja Yoga, the path of Harmony,
would then be a **Combination** of the other three

All refer to three domains of reality and their combinations, but either omit or are unaware of the fourth domain, the interobjectal. If you consider the COMBINED forms as a different path, then there should be five options.

Thus, this leaves the Interobjectal domain 'vacant' (my version of I-O.), so vacant that it does not even have a name. Let's see it in the form of a figure (Figure 20).

What, then, are the Paths of the Interobjectal domain? I propose it has to do with the way we relate to material possessions, having and owning, giving and receiving, perhaps to include some aspects of belonging (affiliation). From the more conceptual perspective we have been following and just to be clear, keep in mind that neither '**doing**,' nor '**knowing**,' nor '**worshipping**' is a substitute for '**owning**.' For instance, you can 'do' all your life and own nothing, or you can own lots even if you did nothing. A balanced life should include a balanced relationship with 'owning.'

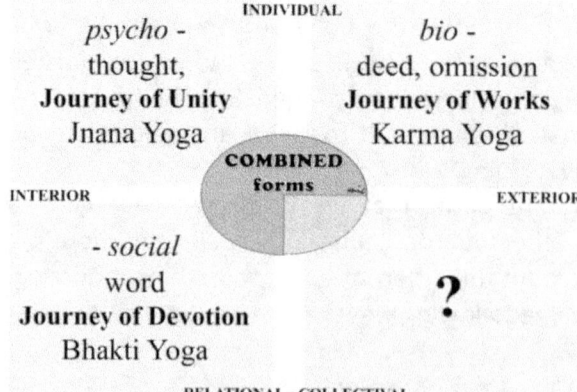

INDIVIDUAL

psycho -
thought,
Journey of Unity
Jnana Yoga

bio -
deed, omission
Journey of Works
Karma Yoga

COMBINED forms

INTERIOR

EXTERIOR

- social
word
Journey of Devotion
Bhakti Yoga

?

RELATIONAL - COLLECTIVAL

Figure 20. **The styles of spiritual paths.** – The placement of the dominant aspects of the religious paths and spiritual practices according to the different 'schools.' – All refer to three domains of reality and combinations, but omit or are unaware of the fourth domain.

As with the other approaches, the Path of Possessions is a two-way path. Like any other aspect of existence, you can cultivate it by learning to renounce, to give. Or you can cultivate it by learning to possess, to have, even to save. Though few call it a religion, it does have a goddess, *Fortuna,* and there are many temples that preach this practice. The Ivy League schools of business, for example, are not much different from your average church, except that you go there to hear sermons on how to make and keep money and wealth, to learn the difference between the haves and the have-nots, and so on. Still, these are rather superficial approaches, technical or operational. If you wish to go deeper, you need to attend the schools of law, because the defining bonds of who-owns-what are established and maintained by the instruments elaborated in the **temples of the law.** The laws of men, that is. For centuries this was inextricably bound to and dominated by religious leaders, which again puts the church right back into politics.

But there is yet another level to this domain: one that has more to do with the personal, spiritual approach towards life in general and the inter-objectal in particular. If we pay close attention, it turns out it has a long history, but I only know of one popular version that presents an integral 'practice' explicitly: **The Secret**, by Rhonda Byrne. Now, you might complain that it doesn't work, or that it does, for that matter. But that's not my point. The real issue is that this is pretty much the first attempt to change popular perception on ownership and wealth **in favor of the believer**, first and foremost by accepting that wishing to have things and striving to achieve them is OK, including material things. Even more important is the notion that the way you think, and what you wish for, affects the way your life plays out.

Just in case you are not familiar with *The Secret*, the basic idea is that the outside world you live in ('the universe') is responsive to, and therefore a reflection of, your inner world. It refers to the process of thought and creativity, the notion that your thoughts 'create' the conditions you inhabit. This need not be the same as 'wishful thinking' or magic. The way you perceive yourself and those around you has a direct effect on how you act and how you relate to them, and this in turn affects the outcomes. Something similar happens with the notion of the shadow and what we call *projection*, which we will see later. If your parents and everyone around you believed that education had to be beaten into you, you'd be hard put to see that there are other ways. Your world will be violent. This in turn will affect the way you relate to your spouse, your kids and even your pets. At least, until someone shows you less cruel and more effective ways. If you change your attitude, the people around you will have to accommodate. Perhaps your current company will resist the change and you may feel you need to change your social surroundings, but either way your life will change.

A related aspect is the need to take the time to perceive and explicitly state what you wish for. If you have clear goals and if you are correctly focused, the *cosmic genie* will help by providing the necessary opportunities and synchronicities. According to this vision and equally important is the notion that underlying all this is one of the Laws of *ah!* As in the classic tale of the *One thousand and one Arabian Nights*, the cosmic genie always says the same: '*Your wish is my command.*' I don't dare say if the idea of the genie has any real basis or not, but at least it's a useful metaphor. These opportunities probably occur all the time to most of us, but most people are not tuned in, or explicitly aware of where they wish to get to, so we let them slip by without even noticing them as opportunities.

I see it closer to the notion of a *self-fulfilling prophesy*, which means that if the preacher or the politician convinced you that being poor is the correct way to 'heaven,' you will no doubt be poor (or at least poorer than you might have been). Of course, giving your worldly belongings to church and preacher sure as hell helps you attain your *sacred goal* of poverty as soon as possible. It also helps the reverend attain **his** goals. Since he's at the receiving end, clearly his goals are not the ones he preaches. An institutionalized version is the notion of the tithe: giving 10% of your crops or earnings to the church. The impact on the poorer sectors was terrible. Societies were decimated. Of course, it was no different than excessive taxation in today's world. In the historic period in which virtually all current religions came into being, the dominant socioeconomic structure and form of government was by way of kings, their kingdoms, and the ruling elites. There was an established order, a 'naturalized' social structure.

Many of the swings of recent history have been due to changing views on this issue. The protestant reform that rocked Europe starting in the 1500s was in part a reaction against an abusive Roman Catholic church. But it was not till Karl Marx and his *opus magnus Das Kapital,* where he reviews the impact of the material conditions of existence, that the issue was elaborated in detail. This explicit analysis of the workings of the interobjectal domain at the social level of organization unleashed one of the most dramatic ruptures in recent history, the surge of communism. This movement seemed to change the polarity, but was not successful in changing the underlying structures.

The central issue is that imposing the laws that determine who-owns-what at the material level is interobjectal, a political action, even when it is influenced by moral precepts claimed by some religion. The compulsory imposition of affiliation is also political.

================== I ==================

Chapter I.26 –

The shadow and our 'split' personalities

One of the most significant discoveries of the 20th century is the recognition and exploration of our subconscious inner worlds. We humans tend to be blissfully unaware of a process that occurs as we grow up. We tend to bury, repress or 'forget' painful and stressful situations as a form of self-defense. Technically we say that we 'disown' any material that is too threatening or painful. Actually, there are two or three ways to do this. The most obvious would be to simply 'forget' the event, but experience shows we forget events that we find boring or of little value. We never seem to forget events that carry a high emotional charge. Since we can't forget bad experiences, we bury them under layers of excuses or piles of activities that distract us, or we repress them with considerable expenditure of energy, till they lose their emotional impact and the memories no longer bother us consciously. But they are still lurking under the surface, unbeknown to us.

Or, if some aspects of our desires or actions are in conflict with what we consider appropriate, good, moral and so on, we can '*project*' those discomforting feelings onto someone else: "*I'm not nasty, she's the nasty one*"; "*my son never lies, the girl must be lying*"; "*our religion is the only true religion, they're all heathens*"; "*we're the good guys, they are the bad guys.*" The list is never-ending. This process can equally apply to positive aspects that we think or have been told are undesirable. "*He's sooo polite it hurts.*"

The whole bundle of these buried or projected aspects of our personalities is called '**the shadow.**' Now, if someone is accused in a '*who done it*' situation, it might seem natural to try and weasel out and even lie a bit if necessary. But in that case the person is actually conscious of what's going on and knows when he's telling a lie. He retains power over the situation and the capacity to make a conscious decision.

The problem with *the shadow* is that the person has lost contact with the issue, without even being aware of it. He has therefore lost his power over the issue, and cannot make conscious decisions. His submerged fears and prejudices decide for him, so to speak, even when the decision is actually to his own detriment, or they may show up as symptoms of a physical or mental disorder. Granted, a bad decision might be protecting him from an even worse fear, but if the fear is irrational, then he's paying a high price for nothing!

Unfortunately, moralistic religions that rely on guilt often make matters worse. By moralistic I refer to the polarized dualistic view: Good against Evil; You are either a believer or you are a sinner; God and the Devil; etc. … Think of them as *mutually excluding or opposing dualisms*. The conflicting emotions and guilt these oppositions elicit cause many of the traumas that make up the shadow.

As we saw in Chapter I.11, *The Book of Pichon*, in everyday life these oppositions change continuously according to circumstance. Getting stuck in a single polarity seriously limits the opportunities for resolution and represents a sign of poor mental health. At the social level it's also an obstacle and gives rise to that political ploy of keeping the country divided. *Divide and reign*. Besides, converting something into the social focus always has the simultaneous effect of sending other issues to the shadows. If the dominating oppositions change according to circumstances, as you would normally expect, societies don't polarize, or at least not as much.

As mentioned, the emphasis on sin and damnation actually helps create the shadow, especially when those taboos are directed to aspects of our biology that are impossible to avoid. Sex is a fact of life, so if you have been persistently told that anything to do with sex is 'bad' you've got a serious problem, a double bind. Either you break those taboos and become a 'sinner' or you repress all your sexual urges and end up with a split personality. Both options are unhealthy. Either way you are condemned. This is a double bind because it's a trap, there is no healthy way out for the believer.

Directly linked to this is the religious obsession with putting the blame on someone else, including 'the devil.' *"It's not our fault, it's Satan's doing."* Having an external enemy to dump all your subconscious garbage onto is undoubtedly very appealing and is probably one of the reasons why some of these sects are so popular. Unfortunately, this kind of thinking exacerbates the alienation, the pathology. It is maliciously lame when it is used to get delinquent priests and preachers off the hook. First and foremost, if someone is pigshitting you with this sort of excuse for his crimes or abuses, call a help line or go directly to see an attorney.

But I am more interested in your personal relationship to these issues. Let's be specific: pathology and delinquency are both real, they exist. This is not a perfect world, granted. The snag is that blaming everyone else for your problems actually **weakens you**. You are explicitly saying you are blameless, but at the same time admitting that you are powerless. This may bring you temporary relief, but it seriously limits your capacity to understand your own contributions to your problems, and to find ways to solve them.

We tend to think of health as all or nothing, you are either healthy or you are ill. While this is relatively true for physical diseases, it is not useful for mental health. Mental health seems to be more like a continuum, with the scars of life producing differing degrees of handicap. From the flow of health at one end, through increasing degrees of difficulty to conditions of outright pathology. Some lucky souls seem to be relatively free from troubling fears, crippling inhibitions and anxieties, useless taboos, anger, hate, addictions and so on. For many of us these problems pretty much dominate and greatly impoverish our lives. Often these misconceptions, fears, or blocks are buried so deep in our subconscious that it would be very difficult for us to deal with them without expert help and support. But deal with them we must.

More often than not, going to see your preacher will not help, in part because preachers are not qualified to deal with mental health problems and psychological difficulties, but also because their mindset is often part of the problem. Today we are very fortunate because we have at our disposal a multitude of therapies and practices that are designed to help you work through these difficult emotions.

Here is not the place to go into a lengthy discussion, but a simple exercise might help get the idea. We've all faced situations where someone has insulted us, or where we felt compelled to insult someone else. Going back to analyze those situations is not practical because they are emotionally loaded. Best try this with people you don't know personally. Sit at a coffee-shop or a park bench, anywhere with passerby traffic. Discreetly, as folks walk by, see what each person triggers in you, notions like: *'this guy looks like a total jerk,' 'what a nerd,' 'she looks cute but very shy,' 'this guy has good vibes,'* and so on. In fact, jot down two impressions, the best one and the worst one for each of several folks taken at random, but representing different ages and styles. Done? OK, now let the dust settle for a while. Take your two lists and underline the qualifiers (in the above: *jerk - nerd – cute - shy - good vibes*).

As you go through the list, pay attention to how each statement 'sits' with you. Read the list out loud, preceding each qualifier with *'I am… or I have…'* (- *I am a jerk - I am a nerd – I am cute – I am shy - I have good vibes* - etc.). What most people find is that practically all the 'insults' and all the 'praises' have some degree of emotional charge for them. Curiously, we often find certain praises as uncomfortable as insults. A few might be neutral, but the most common outcome is that we project onto others tags that are significant to us. The world *out there* acts as a mirror of our world *in here*. The explanation is simple enough. You don't really know any of these people, so whatever you hang on them is your **subjective** perception and projection, and that is mostly a reflection of your inner world, rather than an accurate reading of the person you insulted or praised. That's why I used *subjective*, because the qualifiers you use have to do with you, the Subject, rather than emanating from the outside world, the Objects of the comments.

Now, you are sure to pin the insult on the most likely candidate you have at hand. It's unlikely you would pin something like *'fat slob'* on a thin guy. For sure it will go to the chubbiest person in sight, but it is still your choice of insult. The same candidate might evoke a totally different insult from someone else (*sloppy, greedy, lazy, …* who knows?).

Tav Sparks extended this idea to what he called *Movie Yoga*. As you watch any movie, even a very bad one, pay attention to what emotions it triggers in you, what movies attract you, what roles make you very uncomfortable. Some aspects most people are usually aware of (he likes action films, she prefers romance), but it's the ones that surprise us, that strum a chord we did not expect, that are the most informative and useful. *Oh my! That's shocking.* What each movie triggers in you personally, is information about your *shadow*, and getting to know your *shadow* will help you make better decisions and lead a richer life.

It must be stressed that sometimes these experiences can expose very sensitive, sore and difficult issues that you had completely buried. Some may be so overwhelming that you may need expert help to work through them. But trust me on this one, facing these issues may be difficult, but once you have faced them you will feel much stronger, self-empowered.

There is an intimate connection between mental health and spiritual awareness. Before you can have a healthy relationship with the divine, you need to have a healthy relationship with yourself. For instance, dependency problems often lead people to very manipulative sects. Some of the most horrific collective tragedies in history were perpetrated by people that claimed to be moral leaders of their day, but that must have had very twisted personalities. The appalling excesses of the 'holy' Inquisition were more the work of sadists than of saints, pure pathology, as were the paranoia and mass hysteria that led to the burning of thousands of 'witches,' most without the slightest incriminating evidence beyond false accusations and hearsay. An unbalanced, distorted mind will project those distortions on the surroundings and see 'demons' wherever it chooses. As the saying goes: *Hurt people hurt people.*

==================== I ====================

Chapter I.27 –

The inter-subjectal and postmodernity

Being forced to **write** about 'reality' is a bummer. No matter how eloquent you might be, language is linear, flat. We are trying to deal with things and events that occur simultaneously in four or more dimensions with an instrument that barely handles two. And, as we delve deeper, this limitation only worsens. It is so important that it deserves consideration in and of itself.

We saw that modernity emerged as knowledge broke free from the dogmas imposed by religion, replacing them with a scientific empiricism, but it retained the notion that truths were 'absolute.' With time this somewhat rigid vision yielded to relativism – from the linear to the relative – "*But that's relative*" – Well ..., yes, precisely!

We talked about the subject-object dilemma and how the use of language can bias the conversation. Also, about our '*shadows,*' underlying forces that can distort our perceptions of people and situations, and how these biases can make us vulnerable to error and manipulation. These notions are important, but in our hyper-cultural world there is an even deeper problem, language itself and the construction of meaning. These issues belong to the inter-subjectal domain.

Most of us assume that language is a direct and correct reflection of the outside world. For simple everyday dealings in a specific context this is mostly so. If you ask for a pastrami sandwich in the US, chances are you'll get what you were imagining. But if you change country, language or epoch, then there is no telling what may happen. For instance, embarrassed and 'embarazado' in Spanish clearly come from the same root. Men can be embarrassed. But men can't be *'embarazados'* because in South America it means 'pregnant.' Meaning has drifted. The similarity of meaning is more evident in another declension, *'embarazozo,'* which does mean 'embarrassing' as used in English. No doubt, under some circumstances getting pregnant could be very embarrassing, but the Latin root of both words meant something like hampered, obstructed or encumbered. Even within a language, the same word can refer to different items from country to country, or the same item will be called by different names. As in biological evolution, isolation allows languages to drift apart.

The critical issue is that *meaning is not a natural intrinsic property, a given*. **It is a social construct**, a convention created and developed by each society over a period of time. We can understand each other because we come to a communal agreement as to what convention to use, how the coding system works and what words and symbols stand for.

To make matters worse, often the actual meaning depends on the context or the subject: -*"The man in trunks put her trunk in the trunk of his car, and then crashed into a trunk."* – That sounded rather redundant. Again... "The man in *shorts* put her *suitcase* in the *boot* of his car, and then crashed into a *tree."*
Or perhaps: *"The future of the subject is subject to revision."*
 "My objective is to be objective in the study of objective reality."

All of this basically means that meaning depends on context and perspective. Every aspect of modern culture is plagued by these sorts of ambiguities. What is a CD? For many of us of a certain age it meant *'Compact Disk,'* right? For a finance officer it might be a *'Certificate of*

Deposit.' On a license plate in South America, it stands for *'Cuerpo Diplomático,'* and so on.

Science, legal documents, ontologies, and others try to reduce this problem by giving precise definitions of what each term means in their particular context. Comedy, advertising, religion and politics often do the opposite. Jokes and puns play on these linguistic traps and double meanings. Advertising uses the implied associations to make you believe something that's not really there.

In the bigger picture, you need to be aware that anything that comes in the form of language, speech, a book or brochure, ad or movie is based mostly on social constructs and thus cannot be taken literally, at face value, as an absolute fact. Technically it has been called **'the myth of the given,'** amongst other names. What appears to us to be a direct appraisal of 'reality' is actually a mental construct that is strongly influenced by the construction of language itself and by our preexisting conceptions and world views - what we believe we know. There are ways of getting closer to 'the truth,' but it's not a given, not something automatic.

You always need to be mindful of context and keep a critical eye on perspective. Who's talking? What is he trying to achieve? Does he have any conflict of interests? If he's peddling this or that idea, where does it lead me? And what's in it for him? This is especially true for commerce, politics, religion and other aspects of culture.

I worked for several years coordinating workshops and meetings with a social psychologist who was very much into this sort of analysis and, I must say, in a social context such as mediation or consensus building it is very powerful.

But it is also a pitfall when you try to push the idea too far, and again it has to do with the ambiguous use of 'subjective' and 'intersubjective.' If you designate everything cultural as 'subjective' and for you the word carries the usual scientific notion that anything 'subjective' is illusory, false, phony, undesirable, then by extension everything cultural (and therefore pretty much 'everything' period, to a humanist) is illusory or determined by culture. But, again, if you substitute the **-ive** ending with the **-al** ending proposed here, with ***subjectal*** and ***inter-subjectal***, then you discover that inter-subjectal is as real as 'material,' just on a different domain. As a meta-concept, an *'illusion'* is just one more **real** condition of the subjectal domain, just like any other idea.

Politics and religion use the common perception that '*that's just the way things are*' to naturalize ideas (memes) that suit their purposes. We need to learn to question the basis for these statements.

=================== I ===================

Chapter I.28 –

The Book of Richards

As mentioned in Chapter I.11, communication is not free of dangers. Once you replace the real object with any form of symbol, it is easy to get confused or to confuse others, even to cheat. Recall the example of demanding stag horns and expensive status symbols, such as owning a privet jet or a fancy yacht to outdo the competition! It's important to pay close attention to the rules of communication, but before getting into that we need to talk some more about the domains.

The general principle proposed by Ken is that any item or structure we can identify in the 'real' material world must have a subjectal counterpart or equivalent. And that all we can identify at a personal (individual) level must also have an equivalent collectival manifestation. This seems to be a useful concept, but it's easy to get lost in the details. We need to skip some and move forward a little.

Since the only access we have to the subjectal is through our own *interior* perception, let's take a quick look at the correspondence between diverse animal bodies and what they *are* capable of doing. All living beings, even single cells, have the capacity to perceive simple stimuli, like heat or light, and react to them. Once you acquire neurons, the cells that make up the nervous system, you can manage more complex responses, like reflexes: a stimulus here produces a reaction over there. If we move on to neuronal networks, then you can integrate even more complex and longer chains of actions, like instincts. And at the same time, incorporate more refined controls of your reactions, like emotions (fear, anger, etc.). Perhaps we don't know what a dog feels when it shows fear or aggression, but we can certainly recognize the postures and attitudes and relate them to our own known emotions. All these abilities correspond to increasingly complex nervous systems and to ever larger brains. Keep in mind that the new layers do not eliminate the previous ones. The fact that we can think does not mean we lose the capacity to feel. What does happen is that thoughts can block or modify an emotional response, a feat that a dog might have trouble mastering.

Many studies have demonstrated that, as we grow, each one of us goes through the same stages that mimic or repeat the stages I have just sketched for animals and goes beyond, of course. Babies can be very 'robotic,' driven by instincts. Small children see the world as magical. For instance, they tend to believe their thoughts might become real. Eventually we move out of that phase and move into a mythical one, in which all is literal, we feel the stories they tell us are true, life is white or black, we are good, and the other guys are bad, and so on. Some people seem to remain stuck at this stage and never get beyond it, but nowadays most people go beyond this limited worldview, and realize things are much more complex and relative. Good things can have bad secondary effects, or things that are bad for us may be good for someone else. All this corresponds to the development of the subjectal. A fundamental insight of postmodernity is that all these developmental structures are strongly influenced by the social setting that surrounds the individual as he grows up. Eventually we adopt and stick to a belief system, a worldview, a moral code, etc.

The greater part of this development is not conscious. We simply 'absorb' it from our families and the social medium in which we live, sometimes with the additions and manipulations of the school system and the religious influences (Sunday school, sermons, and the like). Perhaps during high school, if we are lucky, some of these ideals will be analyzed with a more critical approach, but most times we just go on with our lives and assume that everything we were told is literally true. Chances are **a fair part might be true**, or at least useful; **another chunk is useless obsolete deadweight**; and **the last third is designed to manipulate your life** for the benefit of others. It would be very recommendable that you learn to recognize the differences before these parasitic ideas damage or ruin your life completely.

As we saw earlier, the term '**meme**' was proposed in 1976 by biologist Richard Dawkins in his book *The Selfish Gene*, who defined the meme as *the basic unit of cultural transmission*. It refers to an idea, concept, mental image, or similar notion, a unit of thought, typical of the intersubjectal cultural level, just as 'gene' belongs to the biological 'material' level. Since both refer to the coding and transfer of information the concepts are analogous.

Even though Richard Dawkins coined the term 'meme' and defined the idea of the *viruses of the mind* in 1991,[18] it was his namesake, Richard Brodie, who popularized the idea and developed the concept of 'memetics' in his book by same name *'Viruses of the Mind, the New Science of Memetics.'* Worth reading.

Unfortunately, the current usage has drifted, and the idea has been somewhat trivialized in social media. Still, the study of memetics is fundamental because memes govern our lives at many levels, at times innocuously, but often with huge impacts and consequences that affect the quality of our lives, our prosperity (or not), etc.

In the sense proposed by Brodie, it is more useful to think of memes as **subliminal messages that affect our behavior without us noticing it**. This is what makes them akin to computer viruses.

As we saw in Chapter I.12, memes are the *'basic unit'* of cultural transmission, so they are limited to notions you can hold in your head. As it is used today on the web, we can stick to the definition we saw before: **an image, with a short text or none, that condenses a general situation in an amusing way**. The *'amusing way'* part is important because it's what promotes the meme's dispersal. Though it could also appeal to fear, greed, or any other of our emotional buttons.

But the most important aspect of the meme concept is that **memes tend to acquire a life of their own**. If the meme produces alarm or if it's catchy or amusing, then it's more likely that it will get replicated and spread, become 'viral.' Whether it is useful or damaging is irrelevant to the life of a meme.

At this point it might help to give examples, but it's a little tricky because many of the most popular and juicy ones relate to real political or religious situations. As the saying goes, *'tell of the sin, but not of the sinner'* (a meme), so better we speak of hypothetical cases referred to an imaginary country we'll call Sucker-land.[19] *If the shoe fits, then wear it!* (Another meme, of course).

An example of a political meme used in populist Sucker-land is that

---

[18] See conference and paper by Richard Dawkins: *"Viruses of the Mind"*, 1991/ 92.
[19] We could use *'dummy-, fools-, idiot-, nerd-land,* or any number of related expressions. Yet, *'sucker'* seems appropriate because it's the counterpart of *'conman,'* and it is a flexible term that can be applied to attitudes or situations, rather than implying a constitutional problem. Even the smartest get suckered now and then.

'*the people are never wrong*' (which is a euphemism meaning '*if you vote for us populists, you won't be wrong*'). But it turns out that at the beginning of the 20th century our hypothetical land was one of the richest countries in the world (as rich as Germany or France, let's say) and that after many decades of governments chosen by '*the people*' their economy has fallen to third-world levels, and they stumble from one economic crisis to the next. In such a scenario believing that '*the people are never wrong*' doesn't seem very realistic. In fact, '*the people*' seem to be getting it wrong systematically.

Perhaps it has to do with other memes. A few decades ago, another one cropped up that for some reason seems to have stuck. After some years of governance by a political party with some fame of being honest but incompetent, the underhand slogan of their opposition became "*we steal, but we get things done*". What is surprising is not that some shady politician should have coined the phrase. Amazingly, much of Sucker-land accepted the idea without much protest: '*Yes, of course, they are crooks, but at least they get things done!*' That, and giving politicians license to steal at will is about the same. The progression might run something like this. The oldest scandal that comes to mind occurred several decades ago and involved the first lady issuing a shady check for a million local pesos. A couple of decades later the 'lady' in office was accused of stealing 200 million dollars (and served time). A decade or so later the accusation (unverified but credible) was for 2000 million. The latest scandal is rumored at 20 billion! ***Peanuts!*** After all, they steal but they get things done, don't they? Unbelievable. Greed has no limit. Maybe that's why they call themselves *suckers*. Guys, reformulate, '*they may get the job done, **but they steal**!*'

These memes may **seem** innocent, even amusing, but they slowly get us used to these ideas so that they become more acceptable (or less so, depending). If everybody says "*they steal, but they get things done,*" then it must be OK, don't you think? **No**, I don't think so. Definitely NOT, **it's a terrible idea**.

In a nutshell, **these memes can undermine our ability for critical analysis and our good judgment.**

==================== I ====================

I ludere, ergo sum.

Chapter I.29 –

We widened the horizon of everyday reality, but *how far*?

We have attempted to expand the horizon accepting that the subjectal is as real as the material, including and giving entity to such notions as our illusions, our 'subjective' side. In other words, the *subjectal* is as much a part of this reality as atoms or gravity. In fact, they are two inseparable aspects of a single 'thing.' But the limits of these conceptions are still a little fuzzy for us. So many centuries of battles between subjectivists (*delusionals*) and objectivists (*materialists*) have polarized the opinions to such an extent that they are postulated as opposing, excluding, or alternative positions.

One of the areas where the evolution of this battle is most evident is in medical practices. For a shaman, body and soul were inseparable, to such a degree that they often had trouble distinguishing the effects of their rituals from the effects of their concoctions. After the incorporation of the *scientific method,* the practices were critically studied and the conclusion was reached that the rituals were a *subjective* complication that only hampered the diagnostic process and the cure. This may have been initially correct. At first this change of approach gave spectacular results, to such an extent that almost all subjectal aspects were removed from the theories about disease and from the healing practices. Paraphrasing, *only doctors know, witchdoctors and shamans are all charlatans.*

But there are symptoms that reveal the error (and the resulting hypocrisy). The historical fact is that modern medicine was born of European shamanism (medicine men, witchdoctors, and the likes) and a very important part of the modern pharmacopeia derives directly from the purified essences of medicinal plants used by shamans, alchemists, grandma's teas, and all the cultural baggage that humans have been accumulating all over the planet for millennia. When it became evident just how lucrative the industry really was, the pharmaceutical companies sent anthropologists and botanists to all the indigenous communities that still kept their traditions, with the express purpose of stealing their precious knowhow on this issue. The tragic aspect of this story (aside from the generalized ingratitude to the shamans, most of whom never received a cent for their contributions) is that all their accompanying subjectal knowhow on the management and cure of disease was discarded wholesale. And it's not that they didn't realize. It's just that for the interests of the pharmaceutical industry, this was a non-profitable aspect that might even compete with their own goals. Why am I so sure? Because of the industry's acknowledgement of the *placebo effect*. To test if a new drug is effective, the laboratories are forced to use an experimental protocol called '*double blind*' because it has been undeniably shown that both the (subjective) *expectations* of the patients and the attitudes of the doctors **alter the results**. To avoid these subjective effects, neither the experimenters nor the patients can know who is receiving the active drug and who gets the substitutes. All is well as far as testing the effectiveness of new drugs, but that does not justify discrediting all other approaches that claim to treat illness precisely via the management of that subjectivity that is so bothersome to pharmacological laboratories. If they are forced to spend millions performing these special tests, it must be for good reason.

To be fair, we have to recognize that at the time this controversy gained prevalence, most of the ailments affecting humanity were pretty severe and crude, the product of accidents, malnutrition, parasitosis, and other infections, all ills that respond better to materialistic medicine and practices than to subjective rituals of any sort. But as the physical impact of these pathologies have been treated and resolved, we begin to see ever more subtle pathologies, some of which do in fact respond to the **subjetal** model of disease and treatment. In other words, if someone broke his arm, go directly to the emergency room for an x-ray and a plaster. But if he suffers from fractures with any frequency, this mandates more detailed tests to see if he has a calcium deficiency or some other metabolic dysfunction affecting the bones. And if all these tests run negative, it's fitting to ask what attitudinal problems might be contributing to his accident proneness. And if even here we find no answers, we might probe into even more subtle layers[20].

Here is the issue. If we recognize the existence of psychosomatic illnesses, the placebo effect and a whole slew of 'subjective' factors that affect the results of therapies, we are in effect recognizing that the shamans were correct in their use of ritual practices, at least in part. Keep

---

[20] For instance, see **Heal**, a recent documentary about complementary approaches to health and healing.

in mind that one of the key factors for the placebo effect to work is that the patient must be convinced the treatment works, a condition that was undeniably operative in the case for the more venerated and feared shamans and medicine men, especially in the very superstitious communities of yore. Tricky because, if this is true, any cultural change in the popular imagery will change the results. It becomes a circular argument, a self-fulfilling prophecy either way. Unfortunately, it's very possible that in the battle against 'superstition' we have also lost a very powerful tool. Well, not completely. Religions and their priests took it upon themselves to capitalize and perfect this side of shamanic ritual practices to further their own goals. What if we strive for a healthy equilibrium?

There is no reason for these approaches to be 'alternative,' reciprocally excluding. They are better thought of as **complementary,** the mind-body connection. In fact, they **must** be complementary. But this binodal model of a complementary objectal-subjectal approach also has its limits. I am in no way suggesting that any 'alternative therapy' is effective. If we postulate all these variants as possibly complementary, then they can be studied with equal rigor using tests analogous to 'double blind' methods to see which interventions are effective in which cases and under what conditions. Only then will we know which work and which are truly inoperative or phony.

Modern medicine works well for the majority of the physical manifestations of disease. Denying that merit is a silly and dangerous superstition. Denying that the subjectal domain has a significant impact on health and disease is equally unfortunate. The conditions of the environment, the emotional support, the expectations about treatment and healing, the very desire to live and many other aspects all contribute to the outcome of a treatment. At present there is more than enough evidence and the processes are not in contradiction with what we know about physics and biology. Postulating that there is an intimate relationship between the physical condition of the patient and their beliefs and mental attitudes has sufficient support to require that doctors give the issue the credit and attention it deserves.

The plot thickens and the evidence thins when the 'alternatives' become more esoteric. For instance, the curses, witchcraft, hexes, even the prayer chains. Of course, there are preachers of a variety of denominations that will swear that in their congregation there have been a number of 'miraculous' cures, and will put on a show in the form of *testimonials* as proof. But here we are drifting from the subjectal but tangible to the illusory (or perhaps esoteric?).

True that illusion is also a subjectal state, a conjunction of energies if you wish. But we need to make a distinction between an illusion and the use of deliberate delusion to commit plain fraud, such as peddling some cure with false claims that generate false expectations. The validity of the 'treatments' at a distance is still doubtful, especially when the recipients are not even aware of the efforts being made on their behalf. If you think about it, this is truly fortunate because, if the curses of many would really affect their intended 'victims,' more than one politician would be in serious trouble.

Now, before some of you start screaming that I know nothing of samsara, and the '*illusory*' nature of this reality, let me say that whereas this may or may not be true at another level, it has nothing to do with being 'subjective' in the mundane sense we are talking about here.

Real problems appear when you start postulating that all of this is 'illusory' in the absolute sense, because then you must postulate the existence of a self-sustaining parallel reality that gives rise to the illusion. This, of course, is what religions and most forms of spirituality actually postulate. It seems to be as difficult to prove as it is to disprove.

But going back to the other idea that everything in this social universe is illusory, let's review the notion of *the myth of the given*. Some humanists tend to think the only sphere where life communicates meaning is through our cultural constructs. There is nothing ambiguous or metaphorical about a slap in the face. Likewise, a lion's roar also communicates a fairly literal meaning, something like "*I am big and ferocious and this is my territory, keep out.*" And the neighbors understand the message quite clearly.

Those who have had the good fortune to meet an angry grizzly bear at close range and lived to talk about it, describe the growl as terrifying. The animal is upon you in a flash (they can move at surprising speed) and all your academic fantasies about the myth of the given, the illusory nature of reality and so on fly out the window. Those who actually got caught coincide that you scream like a baby, shit in your pants, and curl up like a fetus in self-defense, all of this mostly automatically (your body reacts without you even 'thinking'). The experience feels devastatingly real, nothing *illusory* about it.

Now, some will try to convince you that the bear is illusory, and that you made up this illusion in your mind. But this misses an important point. The bear is totally convinced she is real, and that you are a very real threat to her (rather than an 'illusory' threat). I defy you to convince her otherwise! Actually, to a point you can. Playing 'dead' is said to be the only strategy that might work if the grizzly is just being defensive. But the point is that if existence is an experiment in consciousness, as many now believe, then the bear is also living her version of the experience. No doubt an acorn is deluded into believing it is an oak, and an atom is conned into thinking it is an atom, but they play out their intended roles anyway. Even if you suppose only humans have spirit and all of these props are just the constructs of Spirit so that it can afford itself novel experiences in consciousness, Spirit seems to be playing the same trick simultaneously for eight billion versions of itself, the majority of whom are just as deluded into believing their existence is real as the bear was.

In my opinion, all of this means that nature, or the illusion, that we perceive is real in itself, or is an integral aspect of that bigger reality that we call *the Divine Comedy*, or *the Cosmic Game*. You cannot say that *the illusion* is nothing, a no-thing. - '*I play at illusion, therefore I am*' - If that is a given, which it must be one way or another, then the scientific method is the best way we know to understand how this 'illusion' is constructed and how it works, at least in its mundane material and subjectal aspects.

===================== I =====================

Chapter I.30 –

Intention, action, interaction

So far, we have dealt mostly with things. However, we live in a very active and lively reality. The cosmos is dynamic, in perpetual motion, a feature that seems to be woven into the very fabric of existence. In Chapter I.22 we took a brief look at the ways different forces affect the structure of reality. Gravity is amongst the most basic. It seems to act on us, propelling us towards the earth. Yet, gravity is actually an interaction: it pulls us and we pull it. Of course, the difference in mass is so huge and the effect so minute it is impossible to notice. But when the objects are of a more even size, like the earth and the moon, the two-way effect is more obvious. The moon's motion has a direct effect on the earth, most easily seen in the ebb and flow of the tides.

These forces underlie and produce movement, and all movement seems to require and consume energy. We all know about energy: what we need it for and what it can do. Energy is defined as the capacity to do work. Modern science has laid out much of how energy flows, transforms, and what it does. But all this tells us what it does, not what it is. It seems to be one of the great mysteries of existence.

By definition, any activity is *inter-* something. To avoid this problem, it seems appropriate to leave the actor out of the count, a concept similar to the 'degrees of freedom' in statistics, *i.e.*, the number of independent variables. The observer/ actor is not independent, in the sense that there cannot be an observation or action without a subject for the verb. This is implied by language when we refer to most simple activities as 'actions,' rather than 'interactions.' According to physics, this is not strictly true, because every action produces a reaction of some kind, like two billiard balls bouncing off each other. But it serves as a practical shorthand. Chains of actions, such as running, are better referred to as *activities*.

Still, there is a difference between those 'passive' types of interactions and some human equivalents, and it has to do with intention. A door slammed by the wind is in a different category to a door slammed by an angry customer. We assume the wind has no intention and therefore the event has no special meaning, whereas the door slammed by an angry customer is definitely intentional and is *loaded* with meaning.

In the human sphere we usually talk of actions when it entails a Subject and a passive object, as when holding a book. That 'object' can also be a human body, as in a massage or a haircut. When the 'object' reacts and responds to the actions we speak of *interactions*. This is directly relevant to understanding the subjectal domain. When talking about a person, his inner world, psychologist speak of the manner of relating of the person with his environment as Subject-object relations, even if the 'object' is a family member or friend. Instead, social psychology deems these exchanges to be interactions, where both parties are considered *Subjects* in a Subject-Subject relationship.

===================== I =====================

Chapter I.31 –
Book I, in a nutshell...

We started this journey by analyzing the different aspects of reality and redefining Ken Wilber's ideas into a new model. 'Reality' for sure can be infinitely diverse and changing, but we managed to arrive at a relatively simple conceptual framework that is useful to help us organize our ideas about this diversity. On the one hand we have the material aspect, the **objects**, and their natural tendency to form **unions** with other similar objects to create groupings, thus moving from the **individual** to the **collectival**. At the same time, we recognize in ourselves that this **objectal** material reality has an 'interior' aspect that allows us to perceive ourselves and perceive things as **Subjects**. This **subjectal** reality has manifestations at the individual level and **links** that give rise to certain collectives. Also, the apparently interminable multiplicity of things and their combinations can be organized if we recognize that they have differing degrees of **complexity**, so that each unit at a given level constitutes a whole, a **holon**, and at the same time is a part of a larger order, in other words, a 'whole/part.' Starting with the more basic components of matter, the atoms and subatomic particles, we find that this layer is the most numerous, virtually infinite, and that the successive 'layers' of growing complexity are at the same time less numerous, forming natural **holarchies**.

An example of a holarchy might be: ...house, block, neighborhood, district, town, city, ... Or a hypothetical social scale summarized in Table 4.

Holon	individual	family	clan	pueblo	tribe	ethnic lot	nation
Group of:	1	10	100	1 000	10 000	100 000	1 000 000
Quantity	1 000 000	100 000	10 000	1 000	100	10	1

Table 4. A very sketchy example of a holarchy in the social domain, showing the number of individuals that make up each level, and the abundance of each type of grouping in the land.

We have the illusion that we are privy to our free will, that we are intelligent beings capable of choosing our destinies, but in practice this is only true within certain limits imposed by the structure that we have just sketched and by the laws that govern it. These laws I have called *The Laws of ah!* You can think of them as the laws of nature or as divine laws, it makes no difference. In the ultimate analyses Nature and Divinity become indistinguishable. And yet, these options give rise to two apparently different conceptions on the issue. The 'naturalistic' approach considers that the whole universe is constructed from the 'bottom up' (or from the material elemental level towards the cultural complexity of humans). The alternative is to consider that everything emanates from the divinity, which is to say that the cosmos is constructed 'top down.' As nobody has managed to provide irrefutable proof that divinity exists, nor for that matter, that divinity does NOT exist, we can only assume that both options are possible and, for the moment at least, equally probable. Even worse, it could be that 'reality' is actually a combination of both options.

What is undeniable is that to live and evolve in this world it is best to understand it as well as possible. Unfortunately, this depends greatly on the point of view that you adopt. If you consider that everything emanates from a top-down divine source, you will see the world in a very different light than those who consider it the result of self-regulated bottom-up natural processes. Even assuming that the first option is true or likely, there is the very real danger of abuse of authority on the part of those who claim to know *The Will of the Divine.* It is too easy to claim that some 'commandment' or other 'emanates' from the will of Divinity, when in truth it is merely a matter of human convenience or even a ploy to take advantage of the naïve. With this risk in mind, it's indispensable to have independent guidelines to evaluate these claims and to have tools to place them in their proper perspective and place. At the very least, learn to see which laws are of universal significance, which are norms pertaining to the human sphere, and which are merely the conventions and mandates of your particular society.

There is a further catch to all this godly top-down business. Our analysis clearly shows that the universe is constructed bottom-up. It is impossible otherwise. In fact, the Bible says so quite clearly. The order of creation in Genesis follows the same sequence almost to the letter. Since increasing complexity always goes hand in hand with increasing degrees of freedom, it seems clear that God intended to give his creations increasing liberty and free will. Why in heaven would he then change his mind and impose a whole bunch of arbitrary restrictions? Hard to take seriously.

Okay, so now we have a general idea of the structuring of our world and the universe. Because we need to use language, this worldview is surely still limited and distorted by our social preconceptions, but nonetheless it is the best approximation we can imagine for the moment, a sort of working model to help us move on. All of this rant is fine, but not very practical when you need to make a quick decision. It's a bit like the *theory of ballistics* for any ball player. If he has to get his calculator to estimate the trajectory before he kicks the ball, he's not going to get very far as a player.

It becomes easier to make informed decisions if you take note of a general trend in the structure that we have outlined, a progressive shift in the partitioning between the obligate and the optional, between the Laws of *ah!* and the rules of men. To a large extent it depends on the level of organization that we have been considering. Broadly speaking, we have seen that complexity increases, starting with a set of very basic premises that establish *the rules of the game*, the **ahxioms**, going through the physical, chemical, biological and social levels, till we get to the cultural level of organization, the most complex we are aware of. If we accept the premise that the *subjectal* is an inseparable aspect of reality together with the objectal (material) domain, then there must be a whole parallel sequence of developmental stages in the *subjectal* that matches the material aspects. Unfortunately, it is difficult to perceive and demonstrate because we only have a perception of the *subjectal* as a manifestation of our own interior world. For the lower levels of complexity, we can only infer its existence, which is relatively feasible for higher animals, but it becomes progressively harder to imagine as we move to lower animals, plants or to 'inanimate' objects. Now we come to an important break between strict materialism and the more flexible 'naturalism' that I am proposing here. In my opinion strict materialism is no longer viable, it's dead. The old 'scientific' polarity between objectivity and subjectivity is false, at least in the simplistic terms it was originally postulated. But this is not proof that divinity exists, only that this 'reality' we perceive is infinitely more complex than we had previously imagined.

Since my definition of an *ahxiom* means it is 'fixed,' a given, part of *ah!*'s implicate or enfolded order (sensu Bohm), we can assume *ahxioms* are "99%" predetermined features of *ah!* - (Figure 21).

The other extreme, such as "*what color you pick to paint your nails today*" is largely your choice, but with some limitations. Your available varnish colors impose an **objective** limitation, the colors dictated by current fashion induce a **subjective** limitation.

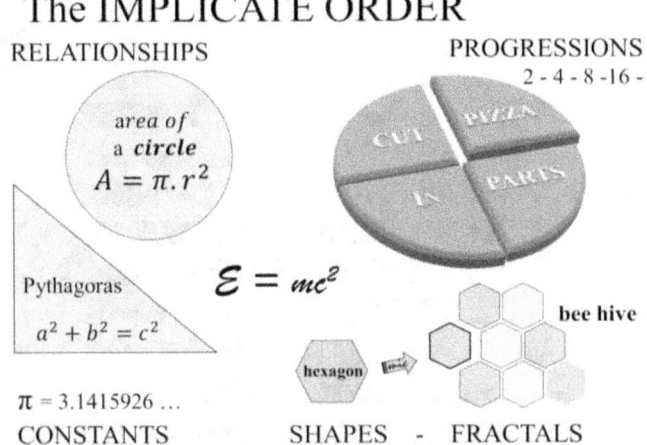

Figure 21. **The true Laws of *ah!*** – The figure shows some of the ahxioms: the relationships, features, progressions, and similar patterns that underlie our reality, the 'implicate or enfolded order*.' All levels of the manifested cosmos must conform to these constraints. We could also include here the 26 cosmological constants, such as the speed of light. - *David Bohm's Implicate - explicate or enfolded - unfolded Idea.

Now we have a sort of scale or ruler on which to place any situation we encounter. We could use decreasing influence of *ah!* or an increasing influence and liberty of humans:

ahxioms > physics > chemistry > organic > biology > society > culture > politics > art
ah!   ← more predetermined ← | → more flexible   →   us

The exact placement along the scale might vary a little according to the criterion, but the position in the sequence does not for the simple reason that each level is built on the previous one. Also, note that the percent idea (see below) is just illustrative and refers to the variability **within** each level. For instance, at the cultural level you can choose your language, but once you made the choice, the rules of grammar, the lexicon and other details are mostly preset for you.

Perhaps it is clearer if we represent it as a surface, rather than a line:

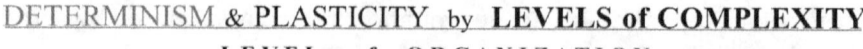

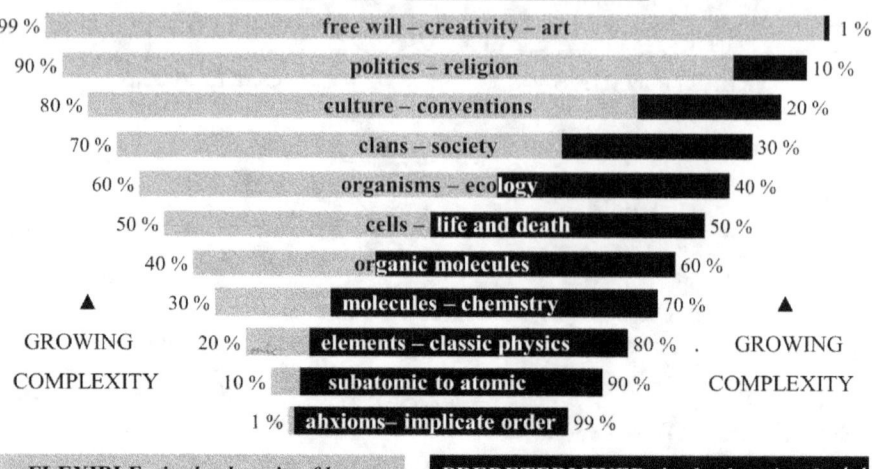

Figure 22. **The Complexity Ladder.** *Relationship between determinism and plasticity as a function of **levels of complexity**. The order follows the order of 'construction,' with the most basic at the bottom. The percentages, which are not factual, refer to the relative weight within each level, but always constrained by the restrictions of the lower levels.*

In Figure 22 each bar represents a level of organization, and each 'step' up marks an exponential increase in complexity. That is, each level is at least ten times as complex as the previous lower one. But don't forget that when we speak of any level, it includes all the levels below it and is therefore constrained by many of the restrictions and limitations of these lower levels. When we say 'culture,' we are automatically including the social, ecological, biological, chemical, and physical levels that sustain it.

This is a better approximation. In some respects, though, it may be misleading. Each level has more freedom, but it continues to be rooted and constrained by the lower levels. Organisms can get on with their lives, but they are still subject to gravity, and to all the other underlying restrictions. Besides, the more basic levels are less complex but **much** more extensive, with those laws applying all over the universe. Instead, the more complex levels are only valid in increasingly more limited spheres. The living entities with a politico-religious level of organization constitute an infinitesimal part of this universe.

An even more refined model might be a 3-D dialectic spiral that highlights the interactions of the four domains, reflecting the growing complexity and interconnectedness, but the page has its limitations. Hopefully I managed to convey the general idea.

The dividing lines between biological, social, and cultural are often fuzzy. Birth is biological, family is social, fashion is cultural. Easy. But how about language? Meaning and the language you chose to speak is cultural; speaking some language or other is social; but the predisposition and ability to learn languages is biological, as is the range of tones, speed, and so on (or at least, biologically constrained). To a greater or lesser extent, all real situations contain all the levels at the same time. Separating what part lies where takes a bit of practice.

On a more practical note, how can this help us navigate our everyday lives? A rule of thumb is that increasing complexity goes along with increasing freedom from the Laws of *ah!* Flexibility and freedom of action (*'free will'*) progressively increase. A couple of examples might help.

Recall the oft repeated maxim: *Nothing is certain, except death and taxes!* Politicians love it, after all, taxes are the very blood they live off. The implication of the meme is that **taxes are as unavoidable as death**! What? That's nonsense! The implication masks a fallacy that becomes evident if you place each part in the scale. That death is a rigid inescapable **biological** Law of the Cosmic Game valid globally is unquestionable, part of that 50% we cannot choose. But taxes? Taxes instead are man-made rules of the political level (a bit to the social, perhaps), and represent very superficial human rules, valid only within very local areas. They vary from place to place, in other countries almost everyone cheats on their taxes, all the time! In a few societies they don't even have taxes! They are trying to make you believe that taxes are 'unavoidable,' but from a global perspective that's nonsense.

Near the flexible end of the imperative scale come the cultural dictates and taboos, those acts that you can choose to do or not to do, **the rules of men**. Don't forget, 'rules' come from rulers, not gods. The same goes for most of the religious taboos. Look over the *Commandments* and ask yourself what level they might apply to. Let's go over part of the list from the Old Testament and see to which level they correspond (Table 5, following the sequence in Figure 22).

Table 5. The *Commandments* on the imperative Scale of *ah!* - from most deterministic at the bottom to least deterministic in the upper tiers (as in Figure 22), with the levels showing the **greatest freedom** at the top. Note the contradiction in the hierarchical order between the *Commandments* and the cosmic *Laws of ah!*

		Don't worship other gods but Me – political.
		Don't make or adore idols of any kind – political.
↑ ↑ ↑		*Keep the sabbath as a sacred day* – limited to Jewish culture.
GREATER FREEDOM		*Don't use the name of God in vain* – which name? – cultural.
	Don't give false testimony – cultural, (In politics it's the norm).	
	Don't desire your neighbor's wife – social, plastic, culturally conditioned.	
	Respect your father and mother – (till adolescence), social – conditioned.	
	Don't envy your neighbors' wealth, house or belongings – social – conditioned.	
	Don't commit adultery – social, biologically and culturally repressed.	
	Thou shalt not steal – social, plastic, culturally conditioned.	
	Thou shalt not kill – life and death, basic biological, but politically manipulated.	
[multicellular and organismal biology level: skeletal list of things created]		
[unicellular biology level: no mention]		
[organic chemistry laws: no mention]		**MORE DETERMINISTIC**
[basic chemical laws: no mention]		↓ ↓ ↓
[physical laws: no mention]		
[implicate order: perhaps implied, but no specific mention in the sacred books]		

You might question the placement of '*Don't worship other gods but Me*' in Table 5 – which seems to be almost axiomatic, but there's a catch. If God is truly infinite, 'other gods' is delusional because all possible manifestations **are** God. Thus, the commandment only makes sense as a political statement.

As you can see in Table 5, most if not all religious rules and taboos are of a very superficial political or cultural nature, totally relative to the place and time you chose to look at. Some edge into more basic social rules and conventions for better living (see box below), but they are still entirely within the human sphere. Many are not even relevant at a social level. '*Don't spill your seed*' (*don't masturbate*) is not only very dubious from the biological and medical perspective, it's entirely private, personal (assuming discretion and privacy, of course). It only serves to generate guilt.

The contradiction in the hierarchical order between the *Commandments* and the cosmic *Laws of ah!* is in no way 'ideological' or whimsical. It derives from the basic structure of the cosmos: politics and religion appear and can only exist in the upper layers of the complexity scale, and are therefore the least restricted and potentially most diverse structures we are aware of.

An important note on **conventions**. Rules in our societies are clearly 'cultural' in that they are optional and change from one society to another. But at the same time, they are an integral part of the very structure of each society. It is physically possible to drive on the right side of the road. It is also possible to drive on the wrong side. Right or wrong is not determined by some intrinsic property of the terrain or of the art of driving. They are only valid according to their fit to a socially determined convention. Objectively speaking, we are free to drive on either side, crisscross or zigzag, whatever strikes our fancy! **BUT**, once that society commits to a given choice, the only way the system will work is for everybody to follow the rule. Once adopted, **social conventions are much more basic than social taboos**. Note also that I used 'right side' and 'wrong side,' precisely because that rule is 'subjective,' top down. In England or Japan, the 'right side' is the left and the 'wrong one' is the right.

================== I ==================

Chapter I.32 –

Changes of state, decoupling of scales, theoretical ladders and free will

We've covered quite a lot of ground, from simple individual stuff to the very numerous and the very complex. Many of those levels and the mings they contain are familiar to us and we have an intuitive knowledge of how they function. Water is liquid at room temperature; if we put it in the freezer, we get ice; on the stove it will begin to bubble, then boil and turn into steam, vaporize. Though these changes of state are quite familiar to us, the rules that govern them may be less obvious. Also, it's still pure H_2O, but the material properties of these states are quite different. Water is our quintessential liquid. As solid ice it behaves more like a rock, and as a vapor much like a gas. Yet, according to physics, all these properties and behaviors can be explained by the molecular structure of water, and that in turn is determined by the subatomic properties and the interactions of its constituent atoms.

The important thing is that the deeper levels, the microstates, determine the emergent properties of the aggregated levels, the macrostates. But the converse is not valid: we cannot deduce the subatomic laws from the properties of water. What we see at the emergent levels is a sort of average behavior of multitudes of molecules acting together, not the particulate nature of the atoms they contain. The laws that govern the behavior of fluids and of gases are of a different order, yet useful as practical approximations to understand and operate on nature. This is achieved by ignoring a lot of the underlying detail and mathematically 'averaging' over large quantities. The whole is still the sum of its parts, no more, no less. As posited earlier, material things are made up of smaller mings, holons inside holons. As far as we know, no complex system made up of matter is in conflict with the physics of elementary particles. Thus, according to the materialistic perspective:

> "*For all we currently know the future is fixed, except for occasional quantum events that we cannot influence*" (Sabine Hossenfelder, *Existential Physics*, 2022).

Random events, however, just lead to lower predictability, but low predictability is not a synonym of free will. Now and then, there is an unexpected change in 'direction,' but the trajectory of the new course is again deterministic. Still, I have difficulty with physicists' notion of "occasional" quantum events. What do they mean by *occasional*, let's say in terms of my body's 10^{27} atoms? Once a day, or once in a lifetime? How many of those random events are likely to occur at a junction that might make a difference at a macroscopic scale and have an impact on my daily rhythms or my decisions?

However, physicists also say that beyond a few atoms at a time, or simple compounds, the actual mathematics needed to compute the deterministic flow of events are so complex that no computer available today can perform the calculations. Doing so for huge systems like whole ecosystems or world political events is likely to remain out of reach forever simply because you'd need a computer chip for every atom in the system and would soon need another planet's worth of chips to do the calculations for all that is going on in this one. Thus, there seems to be a rather big breach between '*theoretically deterministic*' and knowable or predictable in practice. This breach gets worse as we step up the ladder of complexity because each jump entails what is called a '*decoupling of scales*' similar to the jump from atoms to macroscopic water. This, in turn, gives rise to a 'theoretical ladder,' on the lines of the complexity ladder in Figure 22 (Chapter I.31). Since the climb from the simplest level, 'atomic and subatomic,' to the most complex level, 'free will – creativity – art,' has six or eight of these jumps, the deterministic thread becomes tenuous indeed. Unfortunately, nobody understands just why this *decoupling of scales* occurs, so we are not sure if this allows for some escape from strict determinism or not*. What is certain is that the number of possible combinations and discernible outcomes increases exponentially.

---

*One factor is the loss of degrees of freedom as we ascend the complexity ladder. Parameters that are fine tuned to many decimal places can only be achieved over very large numbers of 'free-floating' basic holons. As they bind together to form more complex units, atomized randomness is restricted and the number of holons inevitably decreases. The theoretical sex ratio might be 50-50, but this is rarely exact in small groups, or in species that have few offspring. Small *rounding off* errors can accumulate and produce significant drifts in values, and once you've rounded off you cannot recover the original precision. This loss matches the gain in agency as holons complexify.

At the other extreme, a popular idea is that in an infinite cosmos *"anything that can happen, will happen"* (in some parallel reality or universe, perhaps). It has been proposed to explain the 'fine tuning' of our universe for the emergence of life: simply put, we exist because ours is the one that hit the jackpot. However, according to Sabine (*op. cit.*), the idea of parallel universes has little practical application or predictive value in standard physics. The more speculative version suggests that for every decision we make, parallel universes appear that play out the other alternatives (the roads not taken), and then again and again for all options and decisions. My hunch is that this quickly becomes impossible because an increase in substrates (universes) produces an exponential increase of options, which thus grow faster than substrates (as with numbers: for each digit you add, there are 10 options, so 'options' grows ten times faster than 'digits'). It makes for great sci-fi, but the practical implications of these speculations to our reality seem very low. Most likely, our planetary and personal histories are unique.

Now, the notion that all outcomes can be predicted from the initial conditions and the fundamental evolution laws (the physical ones, not

Darwin's), is what bothers a lot of people, because it "reduces" humanity, free will and everything else to this mechanistic principle. But the very complexity of our world seems to work against straightforward determinism. There is no practical limit to the number of possibilities. What is seriously **reductionistic** is claiming that there is only one "true" religion or political system. At the socio-cultural level of organization, the possibilities are inconceivably numerous, so there is no telling how many viable and equally valid political and religious options are out there.

Random quantum events, errors, cumulative uncertainty, noise, all contribute to give us the *feeling* that our world is not, cannot be, entirely deterministic. Since this seems to be contrary to the fundamental laws of physics, perhaps we can negotiate a truce. The fundamental laws of physics stake out boundaries we cannot cross, for sure, but within these, complex systems can enjoy a certain degree of plasticity and unpredictability that at least makes life intriguing and enjoyable (or terrifying).

This flexibility, however, is quite a stretch below the human illusion that we have "free will." Even without invoking the fundamental laws of physics, the truth is that our choices and behaviors are much more constrained by circumstances, past experience and cultural conditioning than most people would care to acknowledge. In fact, this is so obvious that it's hard to imagine situations in which you would be able to display 'free will' with complete freedom. You would need to find situations that were not physically or culturally predetermined or heavily loaded in one direction. Part of the limitation with these speculations is that the problem is often postulated as a binary decision. Will you, or won't you? Yes, or no? This is not very realistic. I can always decide the whole issue is irrelevant, and go fishing instead. Or clobber the researcher on the head for asking stupid questions. Would that be predictable? And even if it is predictable, would it represent an act of free will? Perhaps free will appears when we are confronted by a range of similar options, as on a dinner menu.

We can turn the issue around. Entities that have no internal force or purpose that can drive them in some way cannot have free will. Their futures will always be subject to whatever external forces act on them, like autumn leaves in the wind. Internal consciousness and the capacity to act on it is thus a requisite for free will. Even so, the notion of free will is not applicable to situations that are physically or biologically impossible, like unassisted flying for a human. Another condition is physical freedom.

Entities or organisms that are physically bound by 'chains,' imprisoned or immobilized, clearly are not free to exercise their will. Likewise, situations that have only one possible outcome, like aging, are not really amenable to our 'free will' either (maybe a little, we can choose ways to age faster or slower, but that's about it). Okay, now assume a situation where none of these restrictions apply: we are sentient beings with willpower, free to exercise that will, and now we are faced with problems or choices that have several possible outcomes or solutions, both physically and biologically. Will we be free to choose? That depends. If we have been culturally conditioned in favor a certain course of action, or against other options, then our decision or 'choice' will be constrained by these conditionings. Even if the option *'feels'* good because it is internally consistent with our sense of self, duty, convenience or whatever parameter is important to us, our decisions are still clearly conditioned by all the prior indoctrination, and therefore not 'free' at all. Or consider this situation: you are driving, in a hurry, and see two empty adjacent parking spaces. Parking in the middle saves you a few seconds, but you would block one of the spaces needlessly. What would **you** choose to do?

Okay, maybe we were lucky to be born to very evolved parents who made every effort to give us an education that prepared us to operate in the world with a battery of abilities and tools to solve most of life's practical problems. They also took care to avoid prejudices, taboos, religious mandates, political doctrines, and even social mandates beyond the basic rules of civility needed to live in a social setting. They even taught us mindfulness techniques and ways to recognize hidden agendas and manipulation attempts by others around us. In this perfect world, what would our choices be and, if they are deterministic, what would determine them? Our underlying biological drives? Convenience? Whim? An urge to make the best of everything? Tricky, because picking the best option available to us is totally predictable, so to what extent would it be 'free'? Perhaps the notion of free will is a little overrated.

However, this is not to say that we can dispense with freedom. Though it may be difficult to define what freedom means, we have no problem understanding its opposite. Being forced to comply with another person's mandates and whims is no fun at all. Yet, we are often incredibly prone to act in ways that conflicts with our convictions, our desires, or even our self-interest, just to please others or to avoid being rude or confrontational. Tough choices. Not easy to find a clear solution.

The one area where we find germs of 'free will' is what we call *creativity,* whether it is expressed as art, imagination, inventiveness, or simply as creative living. When people come up with something completely novel, an invention, a new process, new artistic styles and so on, the idea that these innovations nonetheless are determined by the cumulative effects of the underlying physics, biology, and culture seems like a contradiction, because the very definition of creativity is breaking away from all preexisting conceptions, thinking out of the box, and so on. Perhaps this is why many artists feel they connect with some underlying pool of greater wisdom, their muse or even *the Great Creator,* who acts *'through'* them (*e.g.,* Julia Cameron, *The Artist's Way*). This echoes the notion that the *pregnant void – ah! –* is the source of all creativity and, therefore, of all things created. According to this view, *ah!* has never stopped creating, but now just does so *through* the living, us.

If creativity is the very essence of divinity, dogma must be its antonym. Indoctrination of any sort makes people mindless, obedient, and predictable, but at the expense of spontaneity and autonomy, clear restrictions of their freedom and their ability to be creative. You can't be forced to be creative nor can you somehow do it willfully, but creativity can certainly be cultivated. This entails more a process of *letting go* of your mental hackles than of *doing* something in particular, as in the popular wisdom "I need to *sleep on it.*" When it comes to creativity, our untethered subconscious mind is much better at it than our rational mind. A flexible and unbiased education helps because it makes people more autonomous and capable, with less loss of spontaneity. Most likely you had no say in your upbringing, but even so you can learn to be mindful of your choices and more creative as of now.

It's time to explore the wider world, keeping these ideas in mind.

==================== I ====================

Chapter I.33 –

Epilogue and Prologue – So then, what is a religion?

In the preceding pages we have slowly placed a number of aspects that were formerly considered religious terrain, assigning them to other more modern categories, such as art, science, justice and politics. There is no question that in simpler communities the religious apparatus served many of these functions plus other administrative duties, such as health regulations and keeping civil registry (births, marriages, deaths, etc.). In Western societies nowadays the majority of these functions and social conventions are regulated by laws that fall within the sphere of what we encompass under the concept of 'government.' If we strip religion of all these sidelines, where does religion *per se* lie?

To give an example, Roderick N. Smart has given us a rather descriptive definition that includes seven or eight basic points. Religions are based on: a religious doctrine and philosophy; a narrative and its mythology; an ethical and legal content; a religious institution; rituals and ceremonies; an experiential and emotional aspect; and a 'sacred' set of objects and places that have special significance to that religion. This interpretation is interesting because it clearly includes aspects from the four domains, which supports my thesis that the phenomenon of organized religions cannot be ascribed to a single domain. In this sense it is better understood as one of the many expressions that correspond to the cultural level of organization.

Still, Roderick's definition is not useful to our discussion here. These are descriptive definitions that give us little help to understand the religious process, its aims. The Brazilian, Luiz DeRose puts the emphasis on faith: in theological terms, what characterizes a Religion is the **dogma of faith.** According to DeRose, if it doesn't have a *dogma of faith,* it cannot be a religion.

This at least simplifies the issue for us. We belong to or profess a given religion if we believe in their version of faith, or if we put our faith in their version of the story. This is more useful because from this perspective it is easier to understand some of the obsessions of several organized religions, above all the obsession with preaching. To capture followers, you first have to convince them that your proposal is better than other options (or better yet, hide those alternatives from them). Then you can make up a whole slew of supports towards that end (a mythology, appropriate 'scriptures,' pamphlets, temples, rites of admission and initiation, a liturgy, etc.) In other words, a whole battery of instruments that give the believer a sense of purpose and belongingness. And a compulsory brain-washing as to the *'dreadful consequences'* of abandoning their commitment to this particular faith. Love at gunpoint is not love at all, it's control.

Aside from the ironic tone, the preceding description falls close to what several of the mainstream religions of our day are actually doing. But this still does not allow us to separate religion from politics. What does politics do? Modern politics is based on promoting 'faith' in a given ideology, a 'dogma of faith' of sorts, and affiliation to a political party, through speeches and political propaganda (pamphlets, etc.) and periodic reaffirmations from the 'faithful' (constituency rallies, elections, etc.) If you strip them of the frills, both the instruments and the goals of religion and of politics seem to be virtually identical. Besides, both start off on the premise that *their* version is better, or more convenient, than everybody else's. In this sense both are inescapably 'subjective,' '*top down,*' which makes them very vulnerable to all sorts of authoritarian abuses. The meta process is indistinguishable. What does religion modify? And what does politics modify? If we pay attention to the methods, both strive to modify what people believe, our worldviews, in an attempt to induce us to do specific acts in favor of the institutions they represent (becoming a member, donating, voting a given way, fighting for 'the cause,' etc.). And yet, we feel they are not entirely the same. So then, where lies the difference?

All this has been a horrible muddle from the very beginning. Let's start from scratch.

Try as we may, it seems virtually impossible to make a clear distinction between organized religion and politics because, for much of history, religion has been the effective governing agent, law maker, tax collector, judge, administrator, and executer of virtually every other function of what we now call government, including the control of the armed forces. Thus, religion has been and still is the hegemonic ruling force in many countries and even large regions of the world. Under these basically dictatorial regimes, there in nothing equivalent to what we now understand as free politics. You can't argue or negotiate with dogma. Which is not to say that most of the actions involved in the preceding list are not 'political' in nature, by modern standards. The political nature becomes even more obvious when you consider the internal dealings and conflicts *within* the ruling religious elites, and their murderous attitude towards other faiths. Thus, in the context of today's world, religion is just another form of doing politics, and a rather devious one at that. This is especially so from the point of view of a materialist.

In theory at least, religion is also the door and vehicle to spirituality.

However, I find it impossible to concede that justifying acts of terrorism, mutilating and subjugating women, promoting war, or murdering people in the name of any god is a 'spiritual' act. As mentioned, these are better understood as crass and brutal political acts. We should not be fooled by attempts to hide these acts under the umbrella of 'religion.' For Islam in particular, there seems to be no separation between the *faith* and their political mandate to overrule the world by any means, including violent strategies such as jihad.

Tragically, these devious politicized stratagems degrade all of 'religion' to the level of mundane politics, leaving the genuine believer and practitioner stranded, caught between a rock and a hard place. We need a separate term for what most western believers in the Divine seek in a spiritual guide, a church or a community institution. The simplest is to use *spirituality* and *reunion* to designate the properties and the processes that foster a direct **personal** experience, practical ways to perceive and reunite with the numinous nature of existence.

In view of these difficulties, I will postpone the discussion of the spiritual domains to Book III, and for the moment limit the discussion about *religion* to its institutional aspect from a global perspective. Even if you live in a country that is committed to religious freedom, you must keep in mind that other countries and cultures are definitely not. The danger is that they can abuse our freedom to infiltrate their tyranny.

We will come back to these issues, but we need to return to the question of growing complexity that we have been reviewing. It is rather like using basic squiggles to construct ever more complex and sophisticated **arabesques** (or *fractals*, if you prefer). But to adopt a new structure free of the distortions of the old, first we need to 'deconstruct' these failing structures, clear the terrain. At the very least, we need to become aware that these failings exist.

=================== I ===================

Book II

ARABESQUES

Book II

ARABESQUES

As we add layer upon layer of complexity it becomes ever more difficult to keep a clear linear sequence of issues. Diversity increases steadily and with it, the number and manner of possible combinations and outcomes skyrockets.

As everything is related to everything else, the links and relationships crisscross to such an extent that attempting to tie them into a single bundle would be confusing. It's impossible to speak about two or more dimensions at once and, at the same time, it's difficult to talk about one issue without involving other aspects. We can consider different 'blocks' separately, reshuffle issues, ideas and suggestions, each one seen from different perspectives. But alas, to do this we need to choose subjects and neglect many others. What we choose to bring to the light and what we choose to ignore or hide is a *subjective* choice. This is a constant problem in the political and religious discourse, so here we will attempt to do the opposite, skip the usual and see if we can shed some light on what politicians and clergy prefer to omit or keep hidden. As an organizing umbrella I follow the groupings dictated by the domains. To make it easier, I have tried to make each issue or section stand alone. It might also help to review the essentials of my model in Figures 13 and 19.

Repeat of Figure 13, (p. 57)   Repeat of Figure 19, (p. 114).

SUBJECTAL	OBJECTAL
Ideas	**Mings**
Mind	Body

INTERIOR ——— INDIVIDUAL ———— EXTERIOR
RELATIONAL - COLLECTIVAL

Memes	Genes
Links	**Bonds**
INTERSUBJECTAL	INTEROBJECTAL

Mings is short for 'Material things'

Growing numbers and complexity in material systems

In Chapter I.22 we took a brief look at the issue of growing numbers of items, and the different types of aggregates they form. Some were clumped but the individual elements remained independent of each other (*e.g.*, piles of leaves and sand dunes). Others showed different degrees of cohesion, forming a variety of collectives and organizations. We mentioned the growing internal complexity of living beings. Manmade objects can also evolve into extremely complicated structures and machines. A modern car might have around 30,000 parts, whereas a commercial airplane such as a Boeing 747 can have about 6,000,000 parts that, once assembled, can be operated as a coordinated whole! Yet, going into the details of this type of structural complexity is not very useful here. A person or thing can be very complex inside, but when we encompass it as an *individual* item, that unit is the simplest entity we know. The notion of holarchies allows us to conceptually handle very complex beings and machines belonging to different levels of organization with economy.

Better we look at the different ways systems can interact as we go from individuals to multitudes.

===================== II =====================

Book II – Types of complexity

Chapter II.34 –

Complex minded ... between the simple and the chaotic

Interesting issues appear in dynamic systems involving many items and different types of interactions. We've talked about the individual and the collectival. As more individuals or items are added, a variety of groups and systems materialize that we can order and classify in several ways based on three primary variables.

First, we have the **number of items**, which take us from **simple to complicated**. Putting three or four items in order by their size is easy. If we have 300 it's harder, it requires concentration and there are several ways you could tackle it. But the **organizing criterion** is the same, just as simple. There are many collectives and processes that fit this category: strings or piles of things, aggregates, dictionaries, catalogs, any race, a marathon with thousands of runners, even agricultural processes and production sequences in factories, and many more. Some may give the impression of being complex on account of the number of participating items or steps, but their structure is simple. In the case of processes, we say they are '**linear**,' which is why we speak of '*production lines*.' We work on them because they are necessary, but we soon get bored.

Things change dramatically when we go from 'chains' of items to interaction networks, the different ways in which these items can be linked. Here we must make an important distinction. Series of inanimate mings interact, but these interactions are 'mechanical,' motivated by external forces, and as a rule relatively simple, linear. More complex webs appear when individuals are autonomous, have their own power, and this takes us to living beings. Us.

We love to interact. Almost all team sports fit into this category. We rapidly go from complicated to complex. We talked repeatedly about complexity, but it's not easy to get a true feeling for what it means, what it implies in the dynamics of organizations, for instance. Unfortunately, one of the few ways to make it evident, in a book at least, is with numbers, mathematics.

In complicated situations the rules are simple and there are few variations. A marathon can have thousands of participants, but there is little or no interaction between them. The process is linear and mostly independent. In fact, you could very well run it on your own as Pheidippides did. The same happens with a production line. You might produce millions of copies, but each one follows **exactly** the same process. The process can be broken down to a string of **sequential steps**, each of which is relatively simple and leads to the next step. That is why we speak of a **cascade** process. You might be able to change the order of some steps, but the options that work well are very limited, which is what leads to the notion of a **critical path.** In some cases, there might be several equivalent solutions, so we need to choose one that then becomes the accepted **social convention.** The three colors of traffic lights, for instance. The best option gives rise to a 'simple' or 'clear' method or context.

Instead, any team game has more elaborate rules and the process is the result of a web or network of **simultaneous** interactions. You cannot play on your own. The essence of the complex appears when you add shifting and crossing links and interactions. The number of possibilities skyrockets. Instead of four or five, we jump to thousands or millions. **You**

cannot reduce it to simple, and the number of forms the process can evolve in is often virtually infinite. You can posit some general rules, strategies, but the specific development of each game is unique, unrepeatable. That is why they entertain us! The fundamental nature of the complex is that it cannot be approached in a simple fashion. What you can do is to divide the issue into smaller parts that are easier to understand and resolve, but the global interactions of the system in the real world will never cease to be complex (or complicated).

There is an additional variable that to some extent overlaps with the other two, the degree of **order** or **disorder** (Figure 23). In physics this variable is called 'entropy.' Obviously, any system has some degree of order, but within this framework there is flexibility. Besides, one aspect of order is independent of both numbers and links. We could call it 'disposition,' how we decide things *should* be organized. In some cases, almost any deviation from the norm is considered 'disorder' in the negative sense (as in *'mental disorders'*). This is the more prevalent and accepted social conception, I might even say imposed by conventions and taboos. Unfortunately, this generalization is counterproductive in many cases and situations.

As living beings, we **need** a bit of order (it seems the gods don't care). That's why it is important to stress the issue of playing by the rules, the social conventions, as an organizing factor. Sports are fun if they follow certain rules. If there are too many breaches (too much cheating or foul play), the game starts to get stuck, derails, and often ends in a free-for-all battle, chaos. Totally predictable situations are a bore, a certain degree of uncertainty and mystery is fun, total chaos is terrifying. Each person has their own degree of tolerance, but the general trend is quite universal. Besides, we need diversity, a change of vibes. When the weekend arrives, the workman who spent all week stuck in a monotonous production line needs to **'plug in,'** go out, have fun, interact with people, noise, even a bit of chaos. Instead, those who have very demanding jobs with high degrees of interactions and stress seek to rest, quiet surroundings with soothing music, time out in nature, all ways to **'unplug.'** But always within our comfort zone, what we are familiar with.

In a nutshell, simple gives rise to **best practices**, complicated requires **good practices** and complex systems or situations require **emergent practices** that include the steps needed to solve shifting problems (optimal solutions change continuously). I have lingered on these issues because they are very important in the understanding and management of organizations, politics, and religion.

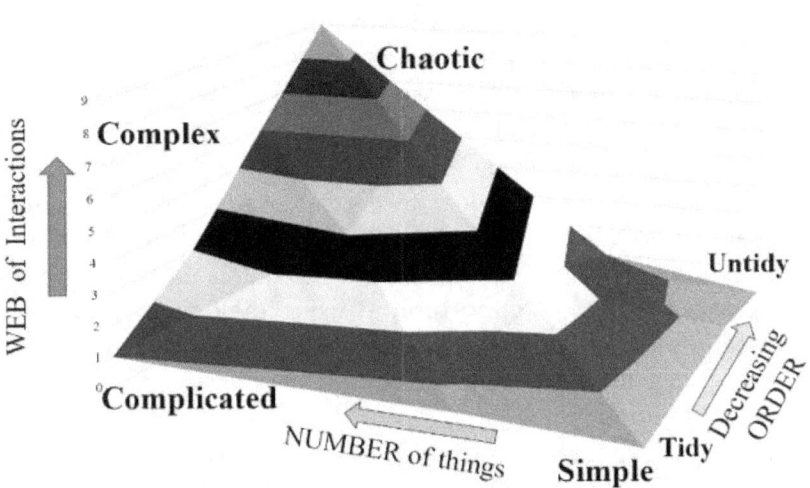

Figure 23. **The structuring of complexity**. – *Relationships between the number of elements, underlying **complicatedness**, the number of interactions, producing **complexity**, and the degree of **order**. – Simple can have several individuals, but little interaction, or just linear (no crossed links). Complex systems have many individuals and interaction networks with many levels. They have a degree of order, but as interactions intensify, they tend to disarray and eventually become chaotic. – Simple collectives have few restrictions and are abundant (gray base). Complex ones are progressively rarer. At a macroscopic scale, true chaos is very rare.*

Most of the dogmas that affect our world today were conceived at a time when the understanding of these processes was very sketchy or nonexistent. Often the interpretations were incomplete or biased. Besides, those societies were based on relatively simple productive systems. In these situations, the pyramidal power structure and their tendency to rule based on command and control worked passably well. But the modern world has become increasingly complex, particularly in the commercial and political spheres. Good practices are not enough. Complexity requires a different strategy.

The change is simpler than it looks, but it is so contrary to the top-down mentality that most of the top management either don't understand it or don't dare try it. Think of it as a soccer team in the middle of a very tight game. Good players know how to play as a team, but they are also totally autonomous and creative. Nobody in their right mind would consider telling some ace player what to do minute by minute, or exactly when to kick the ball. He knows that better than anybody. Coaches might create optimal conditions, supervise, and give general instructions, but once in the game each player makes his own decisions on the go and any combination play is decided by the players themselves, instant by instant. True, they had many opportunities to plan their strategies and to practice those strategies as a team, they have played together many times and they know each other's strengths, weak points, and quirks. **But they are <u>always</u> free to make the best of opportunities using their own creativity**. Self-organization is not anarchy. This form of leadership seems like the antithesis of '*command and control*,' but it is the only one that is successful in complex situations.

It is worth saying that this is even more so in crisis situations, such as fires, floods, and other natural catastrophes. That is, when an external force disrupts the provisions of normal social order. In these cases of relative 'chaos' there is no time for discussions, one must act, and quickly. But to do so effectively you have to know, be prepared, something politicians usually don't have and are not. The ideal is to have specially trained teams for these emergencies (firefighters, first responders, etc.). Here prior training, coordination, equipment, and so on are decisive. What does not help is political interference.

But then, how do you handle chaotic situations? What is the method? Chaotic situations are even more unpredictable than complex ones. They frequently make us face unprecedented situations. They are similar to complex systems, except that the outcomes are much less or not at all predictable, which requires a special strategy that functions via decentralizing management and delegating the job to local autonomous teams that tackle the crisis by sectors and are free to adjust their actions to meet the immediate challenges of each situation. The crisis affords little time to consult with the boss. Those who are at the front line must find special solutions at every instant, which is why this form is referred to as *novel practices*. Almost any outside attempt to control or orchestrate the details of the ongoing process only hampers the responders.

This type of model has been studied by several schools that attempt to understand and manage the different levels of complexity. The four 'practices' model that I have just mentioned was developed by Dave Snowden, a Welsh systems analyst who worked for IBM. The graphic version of his conceptual scheme, which he called 'cynefin' (Welsh for habitat or living place, apparently), with its four aspects looks rather like the figures used here, but it has little to do with the 'domains' we have been considering. It's more like one cycle of complexification, one turn of the spiral, as in the Spiral Dynamics developmental model based on Clare Graves' research (see Chapter III.86), and other cyclic and recurring models. In human social dynamics it can be difficult to perceive.

Let's try with a more visual example. You are in a great bay peacefully floating on a mat while a mild breeze rocks you softly. This is a **simple** scenario, you don't need to do anything, just float. A while later the breeze picks up and turns into a steady wind, and a constant chain of waves begin to enter the bay growing slowly but steadily in strength. Soon it becomes difficult to stay on your mat, but you could surf! Better go get your board. You return to the sea and spend some time surfing happily. The situation slipped from simple to **complicated**, but it is still easy to handle. With a bit of practice, you can master surfing perfectly. At some point you lose track and suddenly you find yourself amid those rocks that had seemed far off. The waves are breaking erratically on the rocks and the place is full of snags and whirlpools. You need all your concentration and skill to get out of the trap. You moved from complicated to **complex**. Suddenly, without warning, you are caught in a gigantic wave that passes over you and drags you towards the shore. As it gets closer to shore, it rises and starts to break. You are being tumbled along, you have no idea which side is up or down, everything jumbles, you hit trees, stuff shatters around you and the water that was clear minutes before is now a horrible mess of drift and debris that lacerates you all over. You are terrified, nothing you can do helps. Soon you realize that you are in the midst of **chaos,** and you surrender to your inevitable fate. The parable alludes to the tsunami that hit the Indian Ocean in 2004, in which close to 230,000 people lost their lives. But there were also some who providentially escaped the tragedy. Here we have the four phases of the cycle of growing complexity and disorder described by

Snowden. As applied to politics, revolution is the condition closest to chaos and therefore the outcomes are erratic, impossible to predict. Bad omen. They hardly ever end where their wishful puppets had thought or intended.

Now, if you happened to be on the shore on that fateful day all ended in total **chaos** impossible to overcome or even to comprehend. Only chance or providence might have decided your fate. For its victims caught in the tumble this chaos must have seemed like the end of days, a sort of Armageddon, but this is only a problem of scale. If instead of being in the water, you had been in a light aircraft or high up on some overlook close to shore your perception would have been totally different. You would have seen a perfectly arched and uniform gigantic wave advancing at 700 kilometers per hour, expanding along hundreds of kilometers of ocean, to break and crash against the shorelines with the same elegance and power of the waves we are used to seeing, only bigger. A giant on his huge surfboard might have surfed the wave with great enthusiasm and glee. Perhaps that's why chaos doesn't seem to affect the gods.

It is as if these stages were like steps in a circular staircase with each cycle ending where it started but one stage higher, so that the stages repeat themselves but amplified and transmuted into something else.

The myth of '*multitasking*'

We all have the illusion that we can handle complexity, especially those very conceited politicians, but it's a false illusion (a delusion). It has to do with our very limited capacity for multitasking. Basically, multitasking refers to doing two or more activities at the same time. At its simplest, it seems to allow us to be doing one task without losing sight of what's going on somewhere else.

But one challenge is keeping track of several items at once, and another is actually **doing** them, especially if that *doing* involves our eyesight. We simply cannot look in two directions at the same time. Some critters can, we can't. The change of focus from one chore to another produces a significant delay in the execution. The best modern example is texting while driving. If you are going at 40 or 50 miles-per-hour, looking at your cell phone even for an instant is asking for trouble. The chances of provoking an accident escalate exponentially. In fact, driving in the midst of urban traffic is an excellent example of a **complex activity** that requires constant adjustments. The somewhat robotic education that was ideal for a production-line workforce is **not** appropriate for the modern world.

A sideline is called for. It's quite common to say that traffic here or there is 'chaotic.' This is a conceptual error. In some places traffic might be a little more disorderly than in others, but never chaotic. The classic case of chaos is the behavior of atoms in the gaseous state. Because they are highly charged with energy, the atoms are propelled in some direction, but as there are so many, they bump into each other and change directions continuously. It's a bit like billiard balls hit by a player with very bad aim, they scatter randomly in all directions! That's chaotic. The fact that millions of vehicles can circulate in a big city **without** bumping into each other is not in the least chaotic. In fact, **it is a miracle of dynamic order that can only be achieved because each 'atom'** (vehicle) **is intelligent and autonomous and is free to correct its trajectory at every instant**.

This is the Achilles' heel of state interventionism and the rigidities imposed by some labor legislation. Top-down *'command and control'* is almost inevitably linear. The world is no longer a production line. It has become a complex dynamic system where each of the players are adjusting their behavior continuously. Imposing many arbitrary rules on a complex system is a sentence for failure. Truly, the economic downfall of the more rigid communist regimes is a good example, but it also explains the migration of leading corporations of the 'first world' to countries with less restrictions. If your politicians insist on telling you **how** to run your business just say no, be it with your vote, protests, legal actions or whatever innovative alternative you can come up with.

Playing as a team...

We breathe, drink, eat, go potty, and sleep with no need for instruction manuals. Everyday chores don't require help from external experts. We are experts.

For more complicated tasks we can learn by trial and error, but it is easier with a teacher. If not, it's useful to have a 'recipe' as a guide. *Gather these ingredients, do this or that, and you will obtain this result or product.* The whole process is mostly mechanical, almost robotic, ideal for mass production. In times past trades and skills were learnt by practicing and you had to memorize the details of each method. Later we developed formal schools and instruction manuals. This is the model that prevailed during the 20th century, just enough to enable workers for factories and similar trades.

The methods were developed by some expert, the apprentice only needed to follow the instructions. No doubt you know about these situations, you've seen them at school for years and maybe even at work. The feeling I get from the youth today is that this is of little use to them or, at best, it's not enough.

And they are right. Many educators continue with this line on account of their vocation, a commitment of service to their students. But they are nonetheless stuck in obsolete paradigms. Besides, we are still influenced by the idea of 'universal education,' which is fine as far as the possibility of access to education, but it's a disaster when it's used to justify the imposition of foreign or outmoded models of culture. Like learning about how to murder your brother or how many mistresses Abraham had, or what some tribal king did thousands of years ago. Much of this is totally useless in todays' world. It just clutters the mind.

There are no rigid formulas for living in the modern world, especially in this phase of accelerated change. We need an organic education that promotes active adaptation to these new realities. More than the information, we need to learn how to save and store it, and how to retrieve it. The '*material conditions of existence*' are increasingly less material, more fluid and changing. Paradoxically, the more globalized and impersonal the world becomes, the greater the importance of working in multidisciplinary teams. **It's more important to know what you're good at and what makes you special**, than to know the details of some antiquated formula imposed by the educational system.

===================== II =====================

Book II – Mings
Scales – Complexity – Reproduction

Chapter II.35 –

From our surroundings to our cosmic neighborhood

Complexity is born of a multiplicity and diversification of things, of individual items. We must somehow move from single mings, or a few mings, to the different environmental, national, global and even cosmic levels of these mings. It's clear that many folks are not fond of numbers, especially big numbers (except, perhaps, for numbers in their bank accounts), but it is impossible to understand the modern world without including the numerical factor. For some reason, mathematics is the primary language of the cosmos. Rather than "the word", as preachers would like us to believe, over most of the cosmos **numbers rule**. Words are confined to an extremely thin sliver of our universe.

To begin with, we are already a bunch! More than 8 000 000 000 - (eight billion). How we managed to be so many is an issue in and of itself. We can't just keep looking the other way without evaluating the impacts and making responsible projections for the future. Since those numbers arise from the sum of personal decisions, yours and mine, it's worth giving them a few paragraphs.

Another issue that derives from these numbers is complexity itself, and the myth of the 'soft sciences' (sociology, psychology, etc.). A necessary step in the development of knowledge is to simplify complex problems to levels that can be handled by the practical and conceptual tools available to us. This is the stage that has dominated virtually all the sciences over the last centuries. It hasn't been more than the last few decades that we began to move from dissecting and analyzing individual things to attempting to understand groups and communities as integrated systems. The sciences that study collectives are not 'soft,' they are complex.

And then there is the practical issue of globalization. Numbers rapidly escalate beyond what our primitive minds can grasp. You need special training, education, to even begin to understand and manage these numbers. Here all we can do is put them on the table, make them evident.

Where do all these things come from? We can simplify it to three levels. The greater part of what makes up the physical base of the universe, the solar system and the planets was included in the original package or evolved within it. It can transform and regroup, but it cannot multiply, at least in the timescales we deal with. What we have available on Earth are apparently abundant resources, but limited, finite. We can exhaust them.

Then we have the biological level that takes up these resources and transforms them in order to live and multiply. Last is the cultural level that also uses those basic resources and transforms them to make 'useful' things. Modern technology has the capacity to make almost limitless numbers of trivial things, but also very complex mechanisms and machines.

Very well, now that it's clear that all these things exist, we can put them aside and move on to more interesting issues. Here you have a few estimated numbers to warm up with:

Humans on planet Earth:	8 000 000 000
Stars in the Milky Way (our galaxy):	100 000 000 000
GNP of Spain in 2019 in Euros:	1 244 000 000 000
Number of cells in the human body:	20 000 000 000 000
Meters traveled by light in a year:	9 460 700 000 000 000
Grains of sand on planet Earth:	375 000 000 000 000 000 000
Stars in the observable universe:	1 000 000 000 000 000 000 000

And what about our knowledge of these things? Over a decade ago the English version of Wikipedia had in storage about **2.9 billion words** (Figure 24). By mid-2024, it was up to 4.9 billion words.

And of our own creativity? Estimates indicate that just the printed materials stored in the United States Library of Congress fill close to **1,350 kilometers** of shelf space! (about 845 miles), and include over 125 million catalogued items (books, manuscripts, maps, prints, photos, etc.)

*Figure 24. **Accumulated human knowledge**. – Library style image that reflects the size of a printed version of Wikipedia in August of 2010, using volumes of Encyclopedia Britannica as 'units.'*

Incredibly small

At the other end of the continuum, we find numbers get inconceivably small. Is *incredibly small* equal to meaningless? Not at all. Incredibly small goes hand in hand with incredibly fast. In our everyday life we say *'in the blink of an eye'* to indicate something is fast. But many critters are a lot faster. Hummingbirds can breathe faster than we can blink, but it's the wings that beat all records: 70 beats a second, less than 15 milliseconds each. That's what produces the hum.

Our brains are a mass of tissue containing some hundred billion neurons (86,000,000,000), and each of these in turn has several thousand connections to other neurons. That puts our neuronal network in the order of 260 trillion connections. And they are fast. Our retinas, the membranes at the back of our eyes, have over 100 million sensitive cells that send about ten million pulses a second to our brain, at speeds near 460 kilometers per hour (270 mph). *In the blink of a neuron*, perhaps?

But that's still slow compared to modern technology. If you google 'man' you get about 15,820,000,000 index hints in 470 milliseconds. Thus, the search engine is optimized to perform these tasks at incredible speeds. And your query traveled from your location to the data base and back in less than a blink. Why is all this important here? Well, because your whole conception of how fast things can occur is totally biased by the fact that you are a rather clumsy human. This is also true of any other dimension you chose to look at. This fantastic speed of transmission and recovery is what allow3 for almost instantaneous communications, even across continents.

Without training, our rational minds simply cannot imagine or understand these numbers. We are also incapable of imagining or understanding anything that approaches infinity. We have just as much difficulty trying to grasp and understand *'incredibly small,'* as we do with infinitely large. But our imagination has no difficulty dealing with worlds within worlds. Dr. Seuss captured this idea in his delightful book *Horton Hears a Who*. Another notable fun effort is the multilayered drawing titled 'Silhoulettes' (sic) by graphic artist Bobby Chiu. Just think how many worlds within worlds might fit between us and the smallest known particle, the neutrino, at 37 orders of magnitude smaller than a quart carton of milk : (10^{-37} kilograms), or: **1.**000000000 000000000 000000000 000000000 ●

                  (where **1** represents the quart and the ● the neutrino)

As numbers become ever smaller, or ever bigger, our understanding begins to lose grounding in our everyday perception of material reality. Comparing the masses of the smallest thing, the neutrino, to the known material universe is staggering, in the range of 90 orders of magnitude (10^{90}; Figure 25).

🌀00000000 000000000 000000000 000000000 00000000▲ 000000000 1.000000000 000000000 000000000 000000000 ●

Universe   **Pyramid**   ⸕   **neutrino**

*Figure 25. **Our universe scaled by mass**. – On this scale, the Universe is to the Great Pyramid as the Great Pyramid is to the neutrino.*

==================== II ====================

Chapter II.36 –
Can you think like a Roman?

One aspect we find difficult to grasp is that modern life is heavily dependent on very sophisticated handling of mathematics. Most ancients were limited by their very sketchy math and a writing system that was not good for handling large numbers and complex operations. For instance, the roman numbering system was totally cumbersome. It only has symbols for a few digits: I is 1 -; V is 5 -; X is 10 -; L is worth 50 -; and the C is 100 -; etc. In-between numbers were built by combining these primary ones (I, II, III, IV, V, VI, VII, VIII, IX, X, XI, XII, ...). Now, try expressing large numbers or doing complex commercial or financial operation with this system and you will see just how difficult it is, close to impossible.

Today we use the numerals and numbering system developed by the Hindus (often referred to as 'Arabic,' but the Arabs borrowed them from the Hindus). Even though the Roman numerals went out of fashion, the general idea is still with us: it's the basis of our coin and bill numbering system.

With the Roman system in mind, it's worth going back to genetics for a moment. Many biological attributes have continuous distributions across a population. Before the development of modern genetics, the prevailing idea was that inheritance involved the mixing or 'blending' of these parental traits, a bit like a cocktail. Hence the notion of *'mixed blood.'* If you crossed a big horse with a small horse, you'd expect to get a medium sized horse. Since this tends to take everyone to the population average, the problem with this idea is to explain how you got the big horse and the small horse in the first place. For most of our history, the universal answer was 'creation.' Whenever you got stuck in a dead end of this sort, you just invoked some god or other who *created* the big one and the small one. This apparent deadlock was resolved when Gregor Mendel demonstrated that inheritance was particulate. Inheritance then becomes closer to flipping a coin: you either get a head or a tail. Genetics works a little different from our coin system, but it's easy to see that by adding different combinations of a few discrete numbers we can generate a whole range of values (see box below). What started as discrete units results in a trait that varies continuously across a population. Today it is clear that many biological attributes result from the additive effect of many genes. As I will explain in Chapter II.59, average individuals are the most common. Extremes are rare, but by this random additive mechanism they are actually expected in low frequencies.

> Some genes have variants called alleles that can confer different values or points to a trait. Since every individual has two copies of each gene, this is equivalent to flipping two coins of each kind simultaneously. If 'heads' adds zero, and 'tails' adds one point, then any individual can have 0, 1 or 2 points contributed by that gene. If you have several variable genes that can contribute a few points each, the resulting individuals can display a wide range of values. These groups of genes are like our currency. With a few pennies, nickels, dimes and quarters you can generate any number from zero to 100. Add a little fuzz due to different environmental conditions, and what started as a series of discrete units develops into a continuous trait.

Most folks are not fond of mathematics, but it's difficult to understand our world without it. And it is becoming ever harder to operate in today's world without a basic understanding.

In general, it is important to bear in mind that we have great difficulty imagining how the ancients saw their world, how they understood their stories, their fables, and their beliefs. Any interpretation of the world and the scriptures of ages past requires a huge amount of speculation. What you are told is the modern interpretation of something that is impossible to recreate. Only a child brought up in the old ways, without any contact with the modern world, might perhaps 'think' like an ancient.

==================== II ====================

Chapter II.37 –

Human population yesterday, today, tomorrow –
The delusion of escaping to Mars

Ninety percent of what makes you 'you' as an individual being is not your genes *per se*, but rather the particular combination of genes and circumstances. The probability that your particular combination will occur again in the general population is virtually ZERO. Even the probability of another EXACT 'you' appearing spontaneously in your own family line is exceedingly small. This day and age the obsession with having lots of kids is based on a cultural myth and on completely outdated instincts. Even in the off chance that the genetics repeats, the circumstances will not.

But this is not what the majority believe. Geneticists, scientists, economists, bible fanatics, preachers, politicians, you name it. All seem to buy into the idea that the only way to go is to reproduce, reproduce, reproduce. Quantity, growth, more quantity! Screw quality.

Granted, the tyranny of our instincts tells us sex is fun, fun, fun. Our genes do their utmost to lure us into having kids, even when we might have preferred not to. In the old days a high reproductive rate was a sign of prosperity, both at a personal level and as a military, economic, and therefore political asset. Military because a large component of military force was in the numbers of soldiers. Economic because in the preindustrial age, development and wealth were heavily dependent on the labor force. Even today population growth is seen as one of the drivers of economic growth. This notion must have been evident to the early rulers and got duly incorporated into the social and religious mandates.

However, most of those conditions are no longer valid and they are likely to become even less relevant in the future. Too many things have changed. Population density has changed, the resource base has changed, production and military technology has changed, medicine has changed, religions are changing, politics . . ., even biology is changing. Virtually everything relevant to the old rules that governed human reproduction has changed, including accountability. But all of this has happened so fast in biological terms that our basic impulses are completely out of sync.

This ties in with the basic feeling and notion that we survive through our descendants, valid perhaps at small scales. But think of it in a wider context. Even the richest of the rich of times past: pharos, kings, emperors, czars, popes, khans, Incas, including tycoons who remained nameless by keeping a low profile... After just a few hundred years what is left of them? In most cases, little more than their memories. Granted, every now and then a noble family line has had the wit and good fortune to survive through it all. A name here, some nameless descendent over there... Even then, consider the odds. Sexual reproduction is a discount machine. Say an average of four generations per century, so King So-and-so had several kids with the queen, but by primogeniture only the eldest son inherits anything significant. Only half of the son's genes came from the father. The son out-marries and the cycle repeats another three times. The grandson has 25% of So-and-so's genes ('blood'), then 12.5%. Before a century is out only about 6% of the original 'blood' remains in his heir (some more might be scattered among other less noble sidelines). That in the lucky event that there were no premature deaths, infertile dead ends, assassinations, adoptions, cuckoldry and any of the many other contingencies that can befall a 'noble' family-line. But let's concede an optimistic 10% per century, so 200 years later any living descendant would be lucky to have 1% of the original and personal great-g-g-g-g-g-g-grandfather's genes left standing! The only salvation might be strict inbreeding, but there the risks of total catastrophe are important.

Resign yourself, your personal genetic bundle won't outlive you for long.

Does that mean everybody 'fizzles out'? Well, as distinct genetic limited editions, YES. But take heart, the same process that scattered the inimitable 'you' has scattered bits and pieces of 'you' all over the place, if only you could trace them. A sample of your 25,000 or so 'pieces' (genes) will live on in hundreds of re-combinations, perhaps to regroup every now and then in that eternal crisscrossing of genetic trajectories to make a semblance of you in some other place and time, only to disperse again in the blink of history's eye. Trust me on this one, even if all the members of your parent's families got together and started having kids in all possible combinations, the chance of them hitting EXACTLY the same combination of genes that made you is vanishingly small. And that's not even taking the possibility of new mutations into account.

Besides, the relative value of genetic exclusivities has been changing over time. Suppose we start with the last population bottle-neck about 100,000 years ago, when the total human population is thought to have been as low as 8,000 or less. Had you been one of them, the chance that some of your genes lived on to populate the earth were quite high, particularly if you managed to have lots of kids! Even so, many of the variants that were present at the time would 'drop out' just by chance, accidents and fluctuations.

Now fast-forward some 80,000 years and about 3,000+ generations, to when the population was around 8,000,000 scattered over much of the globe. The value of your personal contribution to the next generation has now dwindled by a factor of around 1,000, even if you have a bunch of kids. There are many more copies of all types, but also an accumulation of more variations (mutations), so the average number of copies per variant is higher but their proportion in the population is often lower.

Fast-forward again to here and now, to a population of about

8,000,000,000 humans. With about a thousand times more people, the probability of your personal genes contributing to the future of humanity are becoming vanishingly small. Even if you were the lucky bearer of a wonderful new mutation, the chance of it making it into the distant future is very small. The probability that **all** your genetic makeup will survive to the distant future is virtually **zero**.

This rather crude fact is not obvious to many people, perhaps to a majority. We are still under the delusion of the Adam-and-Eve-myth effect, the notion that we are all descended from a single couple. And of course, being incorrigibly narcissistic, we are all under the wishful delusion that WE might be the next Adam or the next Eve to the humanity of the future. Simply put, that's a total misconception. It is NOT how life works.

Yes, there is some point in time and place where some new trait is 'born' (appears, mutates, is created or invented, it makes no difference). But from then on, its trajectory is largely independent of all or most of the rest of the genome of the lucky body that received the gift of the useful novelty.

Sexual reproduction has been so successful precisely because it produces genetic mixing and re-combination of all the genetic variants in the population, so that beneficial mutations that occurred in different individuals who may have lived centuries or even millennia apart will eventually cross paths in some new combination. In a few generations everything gets reshuffled. When a new variant finally emerges triumphant hundreds or thousands of generations later it most likely does so in the company of a totally jumbled recombination of old and new variants of all the other genes that have come together from all over the geographic distribution of the species. Over long periods of time gene-mixing knows few boundaries. In modern humans, none.

Perhaps it's worth clarifying a little. The differentiation of races and species is largely due to genetic isolation between populations. This is why there are so many different species between one continent and the next and so many unique species on islands. On the same continent you only see changes in species or races where there is some important natural barrier such as a mountain range, or a very marked change in the ecology (from jungles to deserts, for instance). For us humans, civilization has completely erased all these barriers. There are virtually no 'pure' ethnic groups left anywhere on earth. We can still recognize ethnicity because these changes are relatively new in evolutionary terms but, if current ethnic mixing trends persist, in a few centuries those differences will get inexorably erased.

Besides, the greater part of the human genome is fixed, which means that all humans alive today have identical copies. So, if you want to flatter yourself that the future of humanity lies in your personal set of copies, be my guest! Sadly, however, *'the future of humanity'* doesn't give a hoot about what happens to your personal copies. It has no less than 7,999,999,999 alternative copies to choose from! Considering the almost limitless number of contingencies any given gene-line has to negotiate, that's probably just as well.[21]

So, relax, sober up and accept it. Even with considerable luck, the chance that some molecule of your unique personal edition will contribute to some distant *'future of humanity'* is about as high as the chance of winning the lottery several times in a row!

Besides, we come from a period in history in which, if you had no future in your country of origin, there was always the possibility of emigrating, of colonizing new lands. ***That era is finished!*** Every day it becomes more difficult to emigrate to another country. But the illusion persists in popular imagination, kept alive by the fantasy of colonizing other planets, other worlds. Mars seems the most accessible, a stepping stone to other worlds. This is easy in the domain of imagination and virtual reality, where we can violate all the basic Laws of *ah!* However, in practical physical, material reality even Mars is currently virtually impossible. No person already born that reads these lines is likely to see it, let alone live it. Your future and the future of every person you know is here, on Planet Earth, the only viable livable place we have access to. **And here is where we will stay!** We damn well better look after it, each in their place, because there's nowhere else to go.

================== II ==================

---

[21] We speak of 'bloodlines,' 'pure blood,' and the likes, but this reflects an incorrect understanding of our biology and the mechanisms of heredity. 'Blood' is a consequence of heredity, not its cause.

Chapter II.38 –

Grasping the scale of mings (material things)

To see an atom in a dot like this • with the naked eye you would need to magnify the dot to the size of a football field. To see the nucleus of an atom the dot has to have the diameter of the earth, and to see a quark you need the dot to be a circle 20 times beyond the orbit of the moon.

Our current estimate of our event horizon, the maximum distance from which light emitted now can ever reach us, or ours them, is about 16 billion light-years. Which means, if we express it in units that we humans can normally relate to, it is on the order of 10^{26} meters (16,000,000,000 light years x 9,460,800,000,000,000 meters light travels in a year = 151, 372,800, 000,000, 000,000, 000,000 meters). Not that I expect that to mean anything to you, I just want to push you out of your comfort zone. Even astronomers struggle with these numbers.

The outer limit of what we can see or detect with instruments from events in the past is called the 'observable universe.' The observable universe is currently estimated to have a radius of 46.6 billion light years. This doesn't mean the universe ends there, only that we cannot see further.

Now, we can argue for ages about the reliability or the veracity of these numbers. It's definitely close to impossible to grasp what these numbers really mean in terms of our conventional experience. Suppose you put all of the human race standing head to foot in one fantastically long 'string.' That would cover about 10,000,000,000 meters, so you would need to repeat that string well over 10,000, 000,000, 000,000 times to get to the edge of the universe. Even if the calculations are wrong by many orders of magnitude, that still leaves over a billion times the number of humans. The numbers are truly staggering, astronomical.

Unaided, the range of human perception is very limited indeed, both in space and in time. It's no wonder then that even the most erudite kings and scholars alive two to three thousand year ago could not see any further than their immediate surroundings. Just because *they* were handicapped, does that mean we have to be condemned to be equally short-sighted for the rest of time? And on top of that, must we transmit the same shortsightedness to our children? It's time to move on.

===================== II =====================

Chapter II.39 –

Quantity, and more quantity, to hell with quality! –

(r and K strategies).

One of the problems created by Darwinian theory and the idea of the selfish gene is the myth that all-out reproduction is the best strategy. I'd even say, the only strategy. In reality, this is true under a very limited number of conditions. As a result, very few species practice the extreme option of putting all their available energy into one humongous reproductive effort and then drop dead, literally. Pacific salmon is one of the most studied and widely known. Fry (baby fish) hatch in some mountain stream and then migrate out to sea where they grow up. After a few years they return to the same stream to spawn and then die. Many, many offspring with as little energy for each as possible. **Quantity** over Quality, and, often, a <u>short</u> lifespan.

Biologists recognize that under most circumstances this all-out reproduction is not the best strategy. If conditions are unpredictable and the chance of this generation of offspring surviving to maturity is very small, a wipe-out, then you are better off staying alive as an adult and having another chance in some future season when the conditions might be better.

Also, if survival is difficult or competition is high, then you would do well to have fewer offspring but give each a better start in life. If they are likely to die *en masse*, what's the point of wasting effort in quantity? This delicate balance between quantity and quality is what produces the variety of reproductive strategies of most of the species you are familiar with. Different equilibrium points between **quantity and quality**, and correlated differences in longevity.

At the other end of the continuum lie the extreme cases, including us, who put a huge amount of effort into a very small number of offspring! **Quality** over Quantity, and a <u>long</u> lifespan. Quality is often coupled with **longevity**. That's what makes us human, what sustains our unique brain, culture, civilization, even our religions.

But even in us there is a built-in security buffer. We have the capacity to produce quite a number of offspring in order to compensate for high losses when they occur. The tragedy is that this mechanism does not automatically switch-off when the conditions are good and mortality is very low, as has been the case over the last decades, even centuries, due to better diet, medical care and living conditions in general.

If by '*Be fruitful, and multiply, ...*' God intended to mean quantity over quality, we would have been created rabbits, or locusts or nematodes, anything but humans. Of the several-million known species alive in the world today, only a handful share such extreme specialization in this regard: our cousins the apes, elephants, condors, orcas, and a few others. That the strategy can be very successful is unquestionable, we are living proof (if we don't push ourselves to extinction, that is).

Unfortunately, it seems to displease most, especially men, who seem to have a boundless lust for harems, fantasies of countless virgins and the likes. Of course, this bias is quite understandable. Men have the fun, and don't carry the burdens (pregnancy, giving birth, etc.) The pinnacle of this tendency is lekking and cuckolding, where you can have constant fun (if you are amongst those very, very, very few who make it at all), without having to bother with an iota of the burden, which you hopefully dumped on some unsuspecting victim or other. Few can afford the luxury, but having a steady job that gives you freedom during most of the week when other guys are working helps.

Still, given the current state of the world, and the rather dismal prospect of a future if things continue to snowball in the direction they are now going, it's becoming a compelling, if obnoxious, mandate for those of us who can do the math to dampen the ardor, or at least to forcibly **decouple** sex from reproduction. Just enjoy recreational sex, as it's now called, without strapping your partner and society with the burden of more children. Having fun is one thing, obliterating the planet is something else.

Regrettably, over much of the west at least, this means directly confronting a horde of self-serving egos with lots of power and/or money who choose to do as they please, regardless of the consequences. Actually, that might not be so devastating if it weren't for their almost morbid need to pad their odds and cover up their tracks by inducing everyone else into the same demented stampede. Arguing for quantity if you are stinking rich and can afford to foot the bill might be OK. For those who haven't a dime and have every intention to dump the outcome of their irresponsibility so that others foot the bill (single mothers, naïve cuckolded husbands, equally naïve congregations and charitable organization, governments, ...) or those who are sociopathic enough to willfully generate progeny that will almost certainly lead miserable lives or starve, then it's definitely NOT OK at all.

The epitome of deceitfulness goes to those who use institutionalized cover, dogmatic manipulation and insider information to either coerce, abuse or confabulate with potential cuckoldresses with the deliberate intent of fathering little bastards that are then dumped on unsuspecting parishioners and the community at large. Institutionalized cuckoldry is not a victimless sin. It's more like an organized paternity crime against legitimate fatherhood and should be treated as such.

It's a historical fact that countries that suffered human population crashes, either by accident (cataclysms, epidemics, even war) or imposed severe restrictions on population growth, have subsequently enjoyed periods of relative prosperity. It soon helps balance available resources to population survival needs, and in the mid- to long-term it allows for economic growth to 'catch up' with population needs and demands.

If we already know this, and can predict the outcome of current situations with a high degree of reliability, please tell me wherein lies the logic and the religious compassion to allow, even foment, unchecked population growth in situations that are glaringly headed to catastrophic famines and social collapse? Just because some self-serving sons of cuckoldresses claim that using contraceptives is immoral? Whereas condemning thousands of as yet unborn defenseless kids to death by spontaneous abortion or starvation is moral? (Severe malnutrition leads to spontaneous abortion). This is unforgivable hypocrisy.

———————— o ————————

The Charge of the Blight Brigade[22]

1   *Start a siege, half a siege,*
        Such a siege on world.
     All in the valley of wealth
        Strode the six hundred
     "Go forth and multiply", He bade
        "Forward, the Light Brigade!
     Charge for the nuns!" they said.
     Into the valleys of Earth
        Strode the new million

---

[22] My adaptation of Alfred Tennyson's *The Charge of the Light Brigade*, 2016.

2   "Forward, the Might Brigade!"
     Is there a man dismayed?
     Not though the Holier knows
       Someone had blundered.
     Ours not to make reply,
     Ours not to reason why,
     Ours but to do and die.
     Into the valley of Dearth
       Strode the six million.

3   Famine to right of us,
        Famine to left of us,
        Famine in front of us,
          Harrowed and hungered
        Stormed by pest' and pall,
        Boldly we stride, come all
        Into the jaws of Death,
        Into the mouth of Hell
          Stride the six billion.

4   Flash, all our hatchets flare,
        Flash, as they turn in air,
        Hacking our forests bare,
        Charging calamity, while
          All the world slumbers.
        Plunged in the flattery-smoke
        Right thru our *spine* we broke;
        Outback and Ocean
        Reel from the hatchet's stroke,
          Battered and plundered.
        Then we'll turn back, but not
          Not the eight billion.

5   Famine to right of us,
       Famine to left of us,
       Famine behind us
          Harrowed and hungered
       Stormed by pestilence and pall,

While haves and have nots fall,
We that had bred so well,
Limp thru the jaws of Death
Back from the mouth of Hell,
All that is left of men,
    Left of eight billion.

6   When will our sorrow fade?
        O the rash charge we made!
          All those left, will ponder.
        Horror, the charge we made.
        Horror, the Blight Brigade
          Ignoble eight billion!

================== II ==================

Chapter II.40 –

The tyranny of 'normality'

*That's **not** normal!* Surely you have either said or heard it sometime. When it's about your health, it might be a sign of genuine concern. But when it is aimed at character or at some quirk of behavior it always comes with an overtone of **disqualification**. Not long ago, in the West at least, left-handed kids were forced to write with their right hand because being left-handed was 'not normal.' Admittedly, left-handedness is *infrequent*, but saying left-handedness is '*abnormal*' is something else.

In today's world it's almost impossible to define normality. Who dictates this 'normality'? On the basis of what criterion? Unless you define the 45 normal ranges for the 45 different possible categories of people: male or female? – child, adolescent, adult or elderly? – right-handed or left-handed? – introverted or extroverted? – We already have 32 combinations. Add the neurodivergent (Asperger, autistics, bipolars, hyper-actives, hyper-sensitives, obsessive-compulsives, …) and all the variants of *typical* neuros (addicts, agoraphobics, anorexics, bulimics, child abusers, compulsive gamblers, depressives, hypochondriacs, megalomaniacs, narcissists, neurotics, nymphomaniacs, posttraumatic stressed, psychopaths, suicidals, rapists, …). As far as 'normal' is concerned, it would be hard to find a single candidate. How many of these presumed 'abnormalities' are simply personality variants that have been demonized because they don't fit the social expectations of the place or the times? Granted, when they become a serious impediment to the survival of the sufferer or a threat to others, they can be really problematic, true dysfunctions. But all too often the person suffers more on account of **the stigma of being different** than from the 'condition' *per se*. They only become problematic to the extent that society stigmatizes and ostracizes them. And we didn't even get into the juicier variants: asexuals, bisexuals, females, homosexuals, lesbians, males, transgender, and several other categories you've never even heard of. So then, which would be the normal features of a *lefthanded introverted transsexual teenager*?

Leftovers of a simplistic and primitive mentality that still thinks the world is either black or white ... Oh, yes, sorry, **I forgot**: *black, Polynesian, pygmy, red, white, yellow,* ... Forget it! We humans are very complex, so complex that every human being on the planet is unique in some respect. In fact, we are the most complex critters that we know of! And, like everything else, the more complex, the more heterogeneous and diverse. It doesn't matter which **slot** you belong to, or which you believe is the 'normal' one. This may seem so in your microcosmos, but for the rest of the world it's just a sign of a confused and self-centered mind.

Respect our differences!

================== II ==================

Chapter II.41 –

Masters of Creation

"Go forth and multiply, fill the Earth" (Genesis, many variations).

Let's face it, from the original statement supposedly made to Adam and Eve ages ago when humans were just TWO, to the current 8,000,000,000 we have come a long way to fulfilling the commandment!

Perhaps enough? Anybody know what God intended once the Earth *filled*? (with humans, that is).

At the time most of these Bible stories first appeared some three thousand years ago, the global human population is estimated to have been around 80 to 100 million. Large tracts of land, like Madagascar and many oceanic islands, were still free of humans, or very thinly populated. For instance, at the time England had a population of 100 to 200 thousand, but just a few thousands at the end of the Ice Age. Now it has 65 million, an increase of over 1000 times in about 10,000 years.

The UN tells us we are now over eight billion (8,000,000,000+). We can argue if this is what God had in mind with *'fill the Earth,'* or if we still have some way to go. But you have to admit, we are at least a billion times closer, no doubt close enough to start thinking about what will happen when we get there. Surely you don't think God meant for us to trample and bulldoze the Earth to oblivion, a sort of Holocaust of Nature. After all, it is **His** Creation, isn't it? He seems to have been rather proud of it!

Of course, I have some ideas about what needs to be done. I love nature and, like many others, feel closest to divinity when I am surrounded by pristine Nature. But that might be a personal bias. Even allowing for this, I am certain religious leaders need to re-think their stance on several related issues. What does it mean to be '***Masters of Creation***'? Unlimited power? *Cart blanche* for ruthless rape of any and all available resources? Deliberate creation of extreme poverty and miserable living conditions that come with mindless population growth? Endless obsession for quantity over quality? Just because you want to make us believe that using contraception is a bigger sin than starving millions? How about you, your family and friends starving? God may be infinite, but the Earth He gave us is **finite**. It will not, it cannot, stretch forever.

'The more the merrier' sounds fun to a member of an affluent society. It sounds dismal if you are living in an already overcrowded refugee camp!

Religious leaders, all leaders in fact, cannot continue peddling notions that were valid hundreds or even thousands of years ago as if nothing had changed. And their congregations have to see to it that at least part of their contributions is used to turn the tide (the tsunami of human overpopulation overrunning the planet, that is).

The Catholic church has been, perhaps, the most stubborn actor in its crusade against contraception and abortion. Granted, abortion is a complex and delicate issue, but contraception is not. Virtually every tribe that has been studied has used some form of population control, even infanticide as a last resort which, one would imagine, is much worse than abortion, and orders of magnitude more problematic than contraception. Starvation has been a dismal alternative regulating factor in many marginal habitats such as the arctic and in extremely poor 'modern' countries. No matter how I look at it, I just cannot see how contraception becomes a sin, **whereas**

willfully condemning thousands of people to poverty and starvation is not! You have to be a pretty selfish son of a cuckoldress to inflict that kind tragic destiny on thousands or millions of people, just to feel good about yourself and ensure your own 'salvation.'

Unfortunately, it's not just religions that fuel the furnace of overpopulation. Politicians, particularly those inclined to 'populist' ideologies, also root for 'population growth,' perhaps in the hope that an increase in poverty-stricken underdogs might give them more votes. Some equate population growth with economic growth. Dangerous ideas!

Even worse, some popularizers can compound the problem. One of them has promoted the erroneous and particularly virulent misconception that the best, in fact the only, reproductive strategy is to have as many offspring as you can. Only quantity matters to DNA, not quality. Tragically, this is a blatant misconception, and a very dangerous meme to be spreading around unqualified. Sometimes these ideas are peddled to help sell a book or something, but nonetheless it's irresponsible.

Proof is simple. If that statement were true the world would be overrun with rabbits, not humans. In fact, humans wouldn't exist at all. As mentioned, of all the species on the planet, humans are amongst the few that uses precisely the **opposite** strategy, **quality** over quantity!

Granted, in the long run the number of offspring surviving to reproductive age does 'matter' to DNA. But humans opted long ago to attain that goal by having few offspring and nurturing them lavishly and individually. If this was true in prehistory, it is doubly true today. There is a saying in South America that *"the grandfather made a fortune; the sons maintained it, and the grandsons squandered it."* Psychological explanations abound, but a simple underlying mathematical fact accounts for much of the cycle. The prosperous grandfather had ten or more kids. To simplify, let's say eight, so his 'fortune' was divided into ten parts (eight kids, the lawyers, and taxes). Each descendant, being at least middle or upper middle class, could afford four to eight kids (say an average of five, for argument's sake). So, what's left is now divided into at least 42 parts (40 grandchildren + lawyers + taxes). These sorts of numbers were common in the Americas in the early and mid- twentieth century.

The problem is simple. Grandchildren just cannot keep the standard of living they grew up with on the 42nd part of grandfather's original fortune. You might argue that money brings more money but, on average, that just compensates for expenses, taxes and inflation, which is why sons are able to 'maintain' it. Add the odd divorce, bad investments and business decisions and other contingencies, including plain squandering, to the progressive subdivision and the outcome of the cycle is virtually inevitable.

Land based fortunes fared worst. Efficiency drops dramatically as you subdivide land. Why do you think European nobility instituted the practice of primogeniture? - (the first born inherits titles and the estate). They were **not** stupid, nor cruel. They were simply aware that equanimous division amongst heirs would demolish their privileged position. Better ensure one optimal heir than squander the lot. Juniors must search for a niche in the armed forces, business, politics, or the clergy. If they made it, great! If they didn't, tough luck![23] Women didn't even count and had to be married off as well as possible.

Simply put, lack of birth controls leads to impoverished families.

Wait! Wait! But what about 'structural' poverty? Granted, in some situations poverty is the result of the *initial condition*. If you were born poor, you are likely to grow up to be poor. If you start off rich you are more likely to remain rich, right?

Well, yes and no. There's a catch! Even if you are poor, you do have some earning power. You wouldn't be alive if you didn't. If you have only one child and put all your resources into raising and giving him/her a head's start, there is a fair chance he will do as well or better than you did. Well, just one child is overdoing it. Perhaps two? - maybe three? The problem is simple, the more you have the poorer they will be! In fact, some will simply not make it at all: infant mortality is much higher in poverty-stricken communities.

Till the middle-ages people had lots of kids because most of them didn't make it. Harshly, but it balanced out. But that was before modern medical advances. Today, someone who chooses to have ten kids has a fair chance that they will all survive, and will have to be fed, clothed, sent to school and so on. No matter what you earn, that sum divided into ten parts is much less than divided in two.

It's insane to keep increasing survivorship without birth control.

---

[23] During the colonization of the Americas seeking your fortunes in the 'new' world became popular. A novel form was to buy land for the younger sons of aristocrats, sometimes called 'remittance land.'

Do you want to combat poverty?
Promote family planning and subsidize contraception.
The results are mathematically guaranteed!
===================== II =====================

Chapter II.42 –

Worldviews

At this point we need to return to the issue of worldviews that have dominated throughout history. Though they come in many guises and variations, from our point of view most of history shows us two basic forms: the descending and the ascending, or *top-down* and *bottom-up.*

The first group gathers the religious and spiritual conceptions that propose the existence of a Creator Principle. The creating agent may be called by an infinity of names: God, Allah, Krishna, the Great Spirit, the Pachamama, Cosmic Consciousness or whatever you prefer. But the basic idea is always the same. It is the Creator Principle who creates the Cosmos and who governs its subsequent evolution. The Creator Principle itself is **eternal**, it *'simply exists.'*

The second view follows the opposite path. It is the material cosmos that *simply exists*. Matter is the base. Life, the mind, and consciousness are emergent properties of certain types of organization of matter. For instance, "the real world contains only concrete (material) things: the ideas, beliefs, intentions, decisions and other things of this nature are cerebral processes" and *factual science* is based on "the ontological principle that the world is material, and its components change according to laws and exist independently of the investigator . . ." (Bunge, 1999). This materialistic view is called *ascending* or *bottom-up.*

These worldviews affect or translate to different levels of our socio-political conceptions. For instance, there are those who are convinced that *'society creates reality'* ('reality' flat), whereas for others it is this same reality that 'mandates' on society.

Yet, both conceptions inevitably remit to the mystery of existence, and **both** imply an act of faith as to what *simply exists* or to its origin. But you must also consider the possibility that both conceptions are partially correct, or that each is true for different domains of 'reality.'

We are unlikely to solve the crux of this age-old issue in the next pages, but I point it out because it's relevant to our present analyses. We need to find an operational compromise.

A change of paradigm?

In 1955 a Jesuit priest, Pierre Teilhard de Chardin, made an interesting observation in this direction. If the laws of thermodynamics that seem to push systems towards growing disorder and chaos were the only ones that govern the universe, it would not be possible for highly organized systems to evolve. Life in particular could not evolve towards growing complexity and order. There must be some 'force' that counteracts the tendency towards disorder. Pierre assigned this force to consciousness. Whatever it is 'in reality,' it seems that our perception of our own consciousness is the best approximation we have. Pierre continues pointing out that other phenomena like electricity become evident through special manifestations such as lightning but that, once the phenomenon is identified and understood, we find it is a property of everything. That is, everything has an electric charge, but it may be too weak to be perceived without special instruments or it may be in balance and not manifest externally. This uniformity repeats with every other aspect of the cosmos. This is what makes science possible.

Therefore, if consciousness and subjectivity exist in man, they must exist in some form and magnitude in everything else. This suggests a third position that at least allows us to build a conceptual and operational model that is better adjusted to the realities we observe.

> **Matter and Consciousness are two complementary components of a single reality. Neither has precedence over the other. Both '*simply exist*' (or were created) simultaneously, and they manifest in all levels of organization with the correspondences we see everywhere** (a *complimentary dualism,* expressed in simple beings as some precursor to full consciousness, such as sensing or perceiving).

Of course, here we run into a delicate, subtle distinction. On the one hand, it's clear that the division between man and nature is simply false. All the physical, chemical, and biological evidence clearly indicates that, as living physical beings, we function exactly the same as all other living beings on the planet, and have the same physical needs and limitations. In the best of cases there are small differences of degree, of quantity, but the basic 'machinery' is the same.

But when we get into the sphere of mental abstractions comparisons get trickier. The existence of a subjectal aspect as a separate domain with some degree of independence seems evident in some cultural phenomena. Mental abstractions seem to be independent of time and place, and the fact that we can create ideas and new forms make us think there is an *implicate order* hidden side by side (or beyond) matter, an order that we can become aware of at any time. Quite often the same invention or theoretical idea crops up simultaneously in two different and unconnected cultural environments, or in two cultures separated by time and space. Many mystical cosmologies speak of a manifest reality, the everyday world we are familiar with, and another sphere or domain that contains everything that could come to be. For many this is a good description of divinity. It is a fact that all inventions exist in the mind of the inventor, a Subject, long before they acquire tangible objectal (material) reality. Another aspect that suggests independence between consciousness and matter is that 'importance' in the physical domain is always associated with physical magnitude. Instead, in the subjectal domain 'volume' virtually makes no sense. Words like *mountain* and *molehill* refer to different physical magnitudes, but as concepts they are equivalent. Often the converse occurs, very powerful concepts can be expressed succinctly ($E = mc^2$).

Relativity, quantum physics, multidimensions, change of paradigms, all these wacky ideas that keep cropping up, but that most of us find difficult or impossible to fully understand. Yet, to the extent that we manage to get an inkling, we begin to see and confirm that the strictly materialistic worldview is incomplete and reductionistic in some respects. We need to change that form of thinking. A hard blow perhaps, but science is used to these changes. Change is in the very roots of the nature of existences and of knowledge itself. Paradoxically, it's the moralistic and dogmatic allegations of some religions that seem most incompatible with this expanded model of the cosmos.

To begin with, the story of creation is backwards. It was not God who created man in *His* image. It is men who have created or imagined anthropomorphic gods in **our** image! It may well be that quantum physics and relativity end up providing the most reliable proof that consciousness creates reality and that by extension Cosmic Consciousness in its most elevated form is what we perceive as Divinity.

But the grandeur and complexity of these conceptions is so far from the rather simplistic and anthropocentric visions sustained by traditional Abrahamic religions that the best they could do is to put those books in a museum and let us, humanity, start to construct new worldviews that honor the wider perspectives we have access to today. We will explore these issues further in Book III.

===================== II =====================

Book II – Ideas
Experience – Education – Preaching

As we saw earlier, almost by definition any action is inter- something, so we need to make a distinction: what does the action modify? For instance, surgery is performed by a surgeon on a Subject (the patient), but its sole purpose is to modify the physical body, the objectal. A marriage, instead, modifies the social bond **between** Subjects.

No doubt the development of the interior world of all sentient beings (animals included) follows some sort of development as the individual grows and matures, but the process is invisible to our senses. We can get some idea of the process via the development of language. The construction of knowledge follows a very specific sequence. First comes a concrete representation of the thing, usually a pictorial or material figure, and an onomatopoeic sound, which in time turn into a pictogram and a word. One can imagine that the next thing would be to identify actions (run, hunt, etc.). It takes both to construct sequences ("go hunt + hunt deer > go hunt deer"). A third component involves the characteristics of things (size, color, etc..) and the relationships between things (location, distance, etc.). You need a lot of these things before you can begin to articulate phrases, and many phrases for even more complex concepts, like *we go hunt big stag.* An abstract conceptual construct is a holarchy just like everything else, and it necessarily follows an immutable sequence of construction. In a more general sense, it follows that denomination of things and actions precedes relationships, which precede logical structures and comprehension, which precede judgments. But note that at the individual level much of this can be achieved without the use of words.

Babies begin to construct a 'theory' of how the world around them works long before they can articulate words and concepts. Most people have had the experience of vivid dreams that play out complex plots without the need of language. Thus, we can have a very rich interior, subjectal, experience without the interaction with others.

===================== II =====================

Chapter II.43 –

A 'scientific' ploy

Most modern westerners still consider science deals only with the material world. Anything related to the *subjective*, or with spirit, morals, etc. is in the domain of religion. And yet, science is becoming aware that its perceptions and the neurological tools it uses in fact affect and overlap with what was always considered to be 'spiritual.' For instance, the discovery of drugs that alter our emotions. However, since the discipline is still stuck with the notion that only the material is 'real' and that the sphere of the *'subjective'* is but an epiphenomenon of matter, they had to find a way of studying 'spiritual' issues without saying so. The solution came by way of using the term *'cognitive'* as a substitute.

The term *cognitive* effectively eludes the objective-subjective problem via the ploy of pretending that cognition is not *subjective*. But, since the last step in the sequence always requires a 'perceiver,' a person, *a Subject*, this seems to be an illusion. Even so, the sciences have managed to make considerable advances as to understanding how we construct images, feelings, and ideas from information provided by our senses; the functioning of cerebral chemistry and the influence of substances that alter the mind, love, hate, addiction and so many other topics. Another important aspect is that different mental abilities are intimately tied to certain areas of our cerebral anatomy. If these areas are damaged or if they deteriorate, we lose those abilities. It seems that many of the manifestations of 'spirit' are a lot more 'substantial' than was once thought.

But perhaps the discovery most relevant to our quest is that the mind, especially the emotional mind, at times cannot distinguish a real situation from a virtual one. For instance, a person might react with equal emotional intensity to the image of a snake as he does to the real live item. The creation of virtual *realities* has become a super sophisticated art. We create novels, movies, videogames, and all manner of virtual fantasies that entertain, move, scare and excite us, almost as if they were real life, with the unquestionable advantage that we can enjoy all these emotions and experiences without the risks they would entail if we tried to play them out in the physical world.

In a pre-cultural world this tendency to confuse our interior 'dreamworld' with exterior reality presumably was not a very serious problem because, for the most part, everything 'out there' was a flesh-and-bone reality. But once you develop culture and the symbolic representation of things (words, stories, myths, artistic images, tricked photographs, even plastic surgery) the issue gets complicated and the possibilities and opportunities to abuse our senses increase exponentially. The use of symbolic trickery to fool the minds of the naïve has a very long history indeed, most probably from the very first book ever written. The most modern version is the ever present 'fake news,' a constant avalanche of false information. Why are we so sure that they are false? When two versions on the same item or event are in total contradiction, opposed and mutually-excluding, *at least one of them must be false*. It could well be that both are false. This often happens in politics, as in the crossfire of accusations that are often all 'half-truths, half-lies.' We might not know which is which, but there are so many 'pages' and 'counter-pages' on the web that we no longer know what to believe and what not. This seems to be the latest version of the *Tower of Babel* idea.

Yet, somehow, we need to find ways to navigate through this labyrinth. And part of that process is understanding what is what, and how we construct our image of reality, both the objectal and the subjectal aspects.

===================== II =====================

Chapter II.44 –
Another turn of the spiral – the tricks of perception

As we move from hunter-gatherer societies to the pastoral (herding) stage and then to agricultural ones, what changes? How are these changes perceived in the individuals, in their physical and mental abilities? Without any doubt these changes go hand in hand with advances in the production technologies, as well as the military arts, and these in turn demand changes in our ways of thinking, of communicating, etc. For instance, when pastoral communities move on to agriculture, timekeeping becomes important, calendars evolve, as do ways to record events and quantities (fundamentally writing). Keeping track of the seasons and calendars are essential to know when to sow, and writing is needed to record crops and tithes. But going into an extensive account of these changes will not be helpful here. Better look at some features of the subjectal that have come to light in recent years. For instance, we have an innate tendency to see human faces in almost anything, including the moon. It's the basis for emoticons and the likes.

We all learn by experience, but normally we don't stop to think about how this process works. Studies of the nervous system have shown us some of these principles that are relevant here. The essential fact is that we don't perceive the outside world directly, we construct it in our minds from the codified information sent to our brains by our sensory organs. This quickly tied in with our advances in photography and computer technology, and was initially thought to 'explain' consciousness and the thought processes, but there is a catch: we don't seem to have anything that might function as an internal 'screen' on which to project the data. So far, the best model comes from an analogy to holography, the laser-based method that can record images on a holographic plate, and then project these images. The projection becomes visible to us due to light-wave interference patterns which we see as three-dimensional images floating some distance from the projector (see Chapters III.77 and .84).

A large part of our early development has to do with learning how to interpret what our senses are telling us. Even something as basic as the perception of distance and relative size, perspective, must be learned. A story of a pygmy in the Congo illustrates this well. His anthropologist friend invites him to come out of the jungle and climb a small hill that has been cleared of jungle and converted into a farm. The pygmy sees some small black dots below and automatically assumes they are ants, but in fact they are cows at a distance. Inside the jungle it's impossible to see beyond a few meters. The anthropologist explains, but after a few minutes in so much space, the poor pygmy freaks out and runs back to the familiar safety of his jungle.

One of the most important innate mechanisms that the human mind has is a remarkable ability to detect regularities, to see patterns and symmetries in the external world. Surely these abilities had great survival value for our ancestors. Both in nature as in social environments most of the significant events are relatively rare. Perhaps this is why it only takes seeing something repeat three or four times for us to assume there's a pattern. Paraphrasing Ian, *"Once is a fact, twice a coincidence, three times is enemy action"*.[24] A social psychologist colleague used this principle to interpret social dynamics in small groups. Attitudes that repeat have significance. The problem with this rule in wider contexts is that sometimes the third (even the fourth...) can also be just coincidence. Our minds are very poorly equipped to make these distinctions with large numbers and very often we see 'significant' links where there are none. This is what the scientific method was developed for, precisely to evaluate if apparent associations are simple coincidences or if they have some correlation or significance. It is very important to keep these mechanisms in mind when you look at television, hear news, listen to political speeches or to religious sermons. Repetition tricks your mind, till it ends up believing something is 'true' only because it was repeated many times. Three *testimonials,* be they marketing, political or religious, and they gotcha! With modern technology it has become increasingly easy to cheat, fake these things, trick us.

There is a counter side to this process. For you it is obvious that the plan instituted by those in office is not working, that it failed, but politicians insist that all is well, that they must persevere for the plan to work. This is called **the denial of perception.** If your perception tells you something is wrong, it's likely that it is truly wrong. Official denials will not solve the problem.

Another aspect that has been studied and validated is called **confirmation bias**. In this case we already have an idea, a prejudice or belief. Our minds tend to give more credit to events and news that **confirm** those preconceptions and to skip or **deny** those that contradict them (hence *'denialists'*). A typical case is the person who believes he has 'bad luck.' On the one hand, the slightest setback is due to his 'bad luck,' whereas the normal positive events in life he gives no value to. *Confirmation bias* plays an important role in the construction and maintenance of ethnic, political and religious prejudices. I can't give examples about humans (it would be politically incorrect), but think what

---

[24] The notion was popularized by Ian Fleming's *007, James Bond*.

pet lovers versus pet haters believe about different dog breeds, it's more or less the same.

The issue is linked to another characteristic of the mental filter. Well, maybe we should deal with the mental filter first. Our senses function and detect information all the time, at least during our waking hours. But only a small fraction of all that information reaches our consciousness. If this were not so we would be constantly distracted and overwhelmed by useless information. To avoid this problem the mind has a set of 'filters' that let some elements through and block most others. Focus and background. To a degree we manage this consciously, changing our focus of attention. But even that requires our attention, so the mind develops filters that operate below the level of consciousness. One of the mechanisms associated with this concept is what we call **search images**. Normally we don't pay attention to pregnant women. In fact, it seems rare to see them on the streets, but when we have a pregnancy in the family, we suddenly seem to see pregnancies all over the place! We changed our search image, so our mind shows us all of them because the mind somehow 'knows' they are now important to us. A year or two later pregnancies are no longer so important for us, they recede back into the background; our subconscious mind filters them out and lets them slip by unnoticed.

This is the idea behind the apps that block out unwanted messages, and the advertising algorithms that only show you things that you showed interest in previously. With this combination of an **artificial** *search image* that reinforces your *confirmation bias* in an equally **artificial** way, they can convince you of almost anything. Of the existence of extraterrestrials or of imminent Armageddon! *Deadly!*

But direct experience is only one of the ways we have to acquire information and knowledge. Another, which is very frequent in higher animals and in us, of course, is imitation, particularly when it entails **learning to do** different tasks. Kids are experts, especially for mischief. Perhaps it's our predisposition to imitate that makes us receptive (and vulnerable) to education and to preaching.

===================== II =====================

Chapter II.45 –

Teaching versus Preaching

Teaching and preaching look alike but, at least in theory, they are very different! Both aim to modify their Subjects, you, so this is really important for your well-being.

Both teaching and preaching involve the transfer of ideas, concepts, knowledge from them to you, so are they really so different? **YES, categorically!** Ask yourself: what do these actions modify?

The fundamental difference is that the purpose of teaching is to modify the knowledge and abilities of the **individual** Subject, even when it occurs in a communal setting such as a classroom. Preaching, instead, aims to modify the **affiliation** of the Subject to the institution or to the ideology in question. Besides,

- teachers show you *how* to do it –
- preachers tell you *what* to do (or not do)! It's a **'must' do** issue...

That is, what you *'must'* do instead of what might be good for you or what you might choose to do.

The ideal education for the initial levels should be free of ideologies, be they political or religious, and be free of second intentions and hidden agendas.

How to deal with your local social conventions is not a hidden agenda.

If you want to be friendly do this, if you need to be nasty do that.

Somewhat metaphorically, an art teacher should not tell what to paint, not even in what style to paint. Only **how** to paint. If you visit an art school and you see all the students are painting the same themes in the same style, you should mistrust the intentions and the honesty of the 'teacher.'

In theory, the purpose of education is to help you develop the abilities you will need to live. For instance, language is a necessary tool, an operator. So, a language teacher in school is teaching you an indispensable skill that will be useful to you in everyday life. The same goes for mathematics, urbanism, music, sports, social skills and many other abilities.

Another important category consists of the conventions of the particular place and culture you live in. A **convention** is something a society agrees upon simply because it makes life easier, such as choosing a national language or deciding which side of the road to drive on. If you drive on the right side of the road, just imagine what a mess it would be if half the folks in your town suddenly decided to drive on the wrong side of the road! Chaos! These conventions are defined by the laws of the land.

Education shows you *how* to think, preaching tells you *what* you must think. We tend to associate preaching with religions, but people can '*preach*' from many different perspectives.

All religions are based on language, especially those that go '*by The Book,*' but the language itself is clearly **not** a belief system. It's just an open-ended tool that can be used and misused for all sorts of purposes. Language is open ended, full of possibilities; ideologies are closed, limiting, binding.

So, what are preachings? - or political propaganda? Unfortunately, that's not always easy to spot. Generally, things that fall into a category called *ideology*, ideas that are relative to different points of view, a matter of opinion. Ideas that define different political and religious groups are the most typical forms of ideologies. As a rule, they include subjective valuations of things: '*I believe that ...; so-and-so says that ...*' But don't expect people to agree on *what is what* in specific cases. If they want to discredit something, they will accuse it of being an ideology ('*it's just a theory*'); if they want to give it value, they will claim it is a 'law,' nature's or god's according to which side they think is best. If you want to decide for yourself, you have to be a sharp observer and do some critical thinking. Ask who is saying this, where do the ideas come from, are they verifiable?

Pay attention, preachers can also teach, and some 'teachers' abuse you and preach.

Keep the teachings – Beware of the preachings.

At some point education must approach the analysis of these ideologies, belief systems, and the role of politics and religions in modern societies. It's the 'glue' that makes cooperation between thousands or millions of people who don't even know each other possible. It would be all but impossible to develop a school curriculum in the upper levels without touching on these issues. Besides, they must be dealt with. But the question is, when and how? The when is easy. As late as possible, when the young students have reached some degree of mental maturity, enough to understand that these things are different from the basic sciences and conventions, that these things are matters of opinion, not 'law.' As to how, it's also possible to give a couple of general guidelines. The first is to be explicit: "*Now we will consider different political ideologies,*" or "*this issue is subjective,"* or *"this is what Buddhists think."* Second, allow for a comparative analysis between the different currents and opinions, new possibilities and even some utopian variants. Preaching in favor of a specific religion is totally different from teaching **comparative** religions. I think I was never as annoyed as the day I realized there were other philosophies, aside from the Christian faiths. I was almost forty! Granted, I may be a bit slow, but how is it possible that a whole education system has systematically *'forgotten'* to mention that there are many ways of thinking and of worshiping?

Thus, a very important issue we will look into again in Book III, is that the teaching aspect of 'religion,' the guru aspect, should provide you with the tools and techniques to know the sacred domains of the cosmos directly, experientially. The preaching aspect, instead, wants you to become a believer in a specific conception of divinity and to become psychologically and materially committed and affiliated with that particular creed and institution. This is a **political** ploy which should not be confused with spirituality and reunion. In fact, it has the opposite effect: division and separation.

How can you tell education from preaching?

Education should be non-denominational (non-politico-religious).

Its purpose is to help you master the tools you need for living.

It should be free of hidden agendas.

How to cope with social skills and local rules is not an agenda.

If you want to be friendly do this, if you want to be nasty do that.

Not **what** to paint, not even what style to use. Just **how** to paint.

Education shows you **how** to think.

Preaching tells you **what** to think.

Education is (or should be) evolutionary. It is analytical.

It guides you *through* the books.

It is open to many points of view.

It carries you everywhere.

Continued development.

Preaching (political or religious) is 'revolutionary.' It is imperative.

It revolves around a single book (constant repetition of psalms, etc.)

It is closed to other visions – (this and **only** this is *'the Word of God'*).

It keeps you bound to a single spot. – Arrested development.

Abrahamic religions require the interpretation of prior experiences of ancient prophets as narrated in **The Books**, and therefore confer an **indirect** approach to the Divine, leading to a followship of believers. –

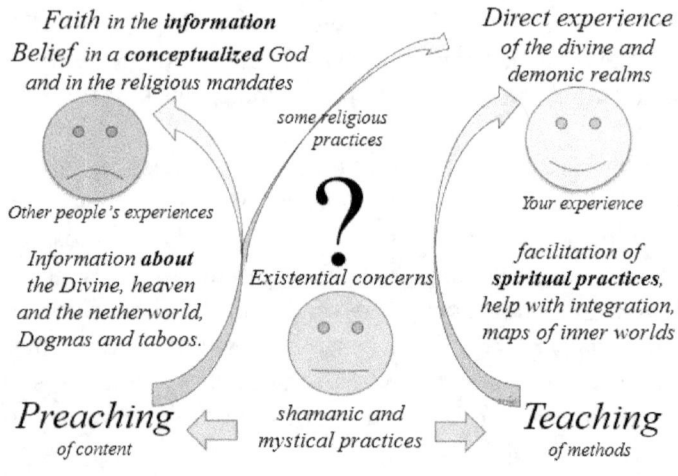

Preaching *versus* Teaching

Faith in the **information**
Belief in a **conceptualized** *God*
and in the religious mandates

some religious practices

Other people's experiences

Information **about** *the Divine, heaven and the netherworld, Dogmas and taboos.*

?
Existential concerns

Direct experience of the divine and demonic realms

Your experience

facilitation of **spiritual practices**, *help with integration, maps of inner worlds*

Preaching
of content

shamanic and mystical practices

Teaching
of methods

Figure 26. **Preaching versus Teaching.** – A sketch of some differences between the path of the believer and that of the mystic or spiritual seeker.

Mystics seeks direct contact with the numinous through personal practices and spiritual techniques, tending to a fellowship of seekers. (For an expanded notion of our inner worlds and the 'maps' of those domains, see Book III).

Preaching makes people obedient. Education makes people capable.

==================== II ====================

Chapter II.46 –

Attachment and detachment

When our affairs are running smoothly, we tend to get attached to those ideas that are associated with that progress. When circumstances change, we can find it very difficult to accept that these same ideas are holding us back, hampering us. Letting go is often painful, equally hard when it involves a person we loved, as with ideas and beliefs that we considered to be true and that we cherished. Yet, to get on with our lives we must often let them go and embrace the new, move on. Santa Claus was great, I loved Santa. But then, as I grew up, I had to accept that his time had passed.

So then, what would progress entail? There seem to be two ways to see this. Suppose you are in a forested area with a local park that has a network of outdoor paths with equipment for workouts and an old forest fire watchtower. You decide you need exercise and begin to use the circuit. You visit the park regularly and as you improve you try out different paths and props. After some time, you know the park pretty well and you have become expert in using the available equipment. But you have never seen what lies beyond the trees, have you?

One day you realize the tower has been opened to the public. Great, you can use the stairs as an extra prop. You start cautiously and add sections as you gain stamina. But it's still all forest around you. But then one day you get to the upper platform and ... **Wow!** ... the view stuns you, ... *aaaahhh!*

Welcome to a wider world!

Here you have the two ways to understand and work towards progress. The first way, the more obvious, is what we could call 'horizontal development.' You get better at doing what you already know, or adding new elements but always within the same perspective, the 'world' you are familiar with, your comfort zone.

The other alternative requires that you change your perspective and widen your vision of the world that surrounds you. Traditional education does this all the time. We start the year at some grade and spend it learning the abilities that correspond to that level. Once we have mastered them, we move up one 'rung' to the next grade, and spend that year learning new abilities. Each year incorporates new experiences and challenges. We don't lose the old ones, we incorporate and transcend them, move beyond. What's more, we really need some of the abilities of the previous levels to be able to master the new ones. But there is a difference between needing them and confusing them with the final destination, getting stuck on them or becoming **attached** to them.

Spiritual development is the same, at least in theory, but it's different in one respect. Once you get out of your comfort zone, the changes seem to be much more threatening and challenging. Passing grades is one thing, changing your beliefs is something else. And yet, to grow you must be prepared to revise your beliefs and leave some behind if you find they are out of sync with your current needs for growth. Most of us resist this sort of change, it terrifies us. This happens because we have 'identified' with our beliefs, we become attached to them. We think and believe we **'are'** our beliefs. *'If you threaten my beliefs, you threaten me, all of my being, my identity!'*

Of course, this feeling is false, but it can be very difficult to realize and accept this. Your current beliefs are very different from those you cherished when you were five years old, or even a teenager of fifteen. Without a doubt, they have changed, yet you are still 'you,' don't you think? And you can change again and again and still be who you are. It becomes easier once you realize you are not discarding your current self, just transcending it, going beyond. Suppose you have been feeling pain for some time. It slowly invades your whole body until you begin to feel you are 'pain' itself. You might say or feel like "I am pain." Surely, in that case you'd be more than happy to discard that personality. The first step is to realize you are not the pain; you just **have** a pain. Then you can begin to do something about it.

Something similar happens with ideas and beliefs. When you say "**I am** ... (such and such)" you're stuck. Any change threatens all of 'you,' your very 'being.' Saying "*I am Christian*" is not the same as saying "I believe in Christianity." There is **you** and then there is the belief. "*I believed in Christianity but then ... (I became disenchanted, or I like some of their ideas but I have problems with others...).*" You have changed your perspective, your point of view, but you are still 'you.' If you manage to **detach** from your beliefs, you cease to be their slave, a blind, passive follower. A good part of becoming an adult has to do with assuming responsibility for your beliefs and actions.

Life's circumstances change frequently. Having the flexibility to adapt to those changes is an important part of being healthy and staying healthy.

This is the fundamental problem with being dogmatic. Any form of dogma is rigid, static. It prevents you from changing to adjust to life's circumstances. It doesn't widen your world, it narrows it.

==================== II ====================

Chapter II.47 –

Not what they found, rather *how* they found it

Abrahamic books tell us what our religious heroes of the past discovered about God and the meaning of life. Religious leaders tell us that we must believe them and abide by these findings. What they neglect to show us is how these heroes of old got that knowledge in the first place. I don't want to know what they found - I want to know **how** they found it!

Yes, yes, I know: '*by the grace of God*' - 'revelations' and all that.

Just fancy ways of hiding the truth. Let's see:
Moses went to the desert alone. He returned with a fantastic story.
Buddha spent years searching for the answer, meditating in solitude.
Jesus disappeared for twenty years! He also went into the desert...
Mohammed spent years meditating in a cave, did he not?

In fact, pretty much every leader and originator of a faith seems to have followed a similar path. Much of this wisdom and the techniques to attain it come from earlier practices developed all over the world by shamans, visionaries, mystiques, and the like.[25] The particular way each culture 'colored' these practices and findings vary quite a lot, granted. But the underlying notion that **wisdom comes from within** is virtually universal. *In*-sight! All too often, shamans and high priests have kept that knowledge to themselves, no doubt.

Many of the elements of modern ritual were developed and incorporated with the express intention of producing special states of consciousness: repetitive prayers and chanting (mantras); the use of rosaries (japamalas); sacred music (especially organ music); Gregorian chants (controlled breathing); fasting (Lent, Ramadan); long services recited in Latin; the use of incense; cathedral architecture; stained glass windows; etc. Echoes of what once were spiritual practices that all too often have been reduced to mere ritual repeated mechanically. Presumably, the direct participation and the meditations that these rituals induce also produce feelings of wellbeing, a familiar place of belonging and community. But unfortunately, sermons get thrown into the bundle, including mandates that are often not to the benefit of the parishioners.

To continue moving forward in our pursuit of understanding we have to challenge ourselves. A measure of detachment allows us to view the world from a wider perspective and to better understand it. It would seem that true teachers would inspire us to look inward, to challenge beliefs, to understand our place in the wider world. The question then is, why aren't

---

[25] *e.g.*, Peter Kingsley, 2010. *A Story Waiting to Pierce You*, and references therein.

they doing this? Perhaps their motivation isn't as enlightened as they claim.

Knowledge gives us power. So does manipulating other peoples' belief systems.

Some preachers of these *Books* would like to convince you that reading and reciting other peoples' truths is the way to enlightenment, but this makes you constantly look *outwards*, stick to exteriors, which more or less guarantees you **won't** get to know the Divine, or reach enlightenment.

Oh, yes, sorry, they don't promise enlightenment, only 'salvation.'

Or the kingdom of heaven. Or a thousand virgins.

A Ponzi scheme of sorts.

===================== II =====================

Chapter II.48 –

When being subjective plays against you

Let's return to the issue of development and personal progress. We talked about the four domains of reality, remember? – mind – body – links – bonds. For each one we have different yogas or journeys, as Reverend Richardson suggested. In your personal practice you can view them as the space of Thoughts, the journey of Deeds, the yoga of Relationships, and the path of Possessions.

Each one I could approach in different ways. I might concentrate on developing one aspect (Zen archery) and cross my fingers that the rest will follow. Or I could do several practices at the same time (yoga, meditation, devotion). I could abstain or I could indulge, conquer my instincts by repressing them or by disciplining them, becoming expert in expressing them in a controlled manner. For instance, I could learn to handle food by fasting or by feasting. And, who knows, some other variant that has not occurred to us yet.

Most of the traditional approaches put the emphasis in one aspect and consider the rest as secondary, or they don't consider the rest at all. This is not good. I am not my parts, nor am I apart. When I move all my 'parts' come with me, and I move in all 'spaces' at the same time. To become whole, I need to remain whole, in contact with all the aspects of my being. Be coherent, feel, think and do in harmony, according to Pichon. But again, nothing about 'owning.'

And with both faces of me, my persona and my shadow. Cultivating the lamb that dwells in me while ignoring or repressing the lion in me is not healthy. It's very convenient for the 'shepherd' or politician, of course, because now they have a docile obedient herd of sheep they can manipulate to their bidding. Some people find that this unconditional 'surrender' is easier than facing their own responsibilities but, in my experience, they end up paying a horrendous price in exchange for this convenience. If your decision is to be a 'follower,' fine, but I hope you will not find much support here. I can only hope for a group of peers where each is autonomous, balanced, and responsible for their own choices and actions.

Where I grew up any form of aggression was criticized and repressed. *"It's not nice."* Life, however, presents us with many situations where you have to defend your space. If you have completely repressed your aggression, you are powerless, paralyzed. Granted, unrestrained aggression is not the way to go, but nobody told me there was another acceptable way to handle these situations, with assertiveness, firmness. I ended up paying a huge price as a result of this confusion. It was, and sometimes still is, a serious handicap, debilitating. The saddest part of the issue is that when you're faced with an abusive situation, you can repress the anger, but you can't avoid feeling it. It accumulates in you, it gnaws at you, it saps your energies. Sooner or later, you explode, often in the worst place and time! You were unable to put a limit to your abusive boss, so now, in response to some trivial 'offense' you discharge all your anger on your spouse or child. Not good. Your reaction was so out of proportion that you feel (or you are made to feel) ashamed, which reinforces the notion that aggression is always bad, creating a vicious cycle.

I chose aggression as an example because it is almost a social cliché. But if you are the village bully, the same might happen to you if you are polite to someone. You know, politeness is for the weak and the sissies. *Macho types like me are not polite!* If your persona is to be the aggressive macho type, then surely politeness is buried somewhere in your shadow. But it's in there somewhere. Even bullies have the capacity to be polite if they choose to, if they can overcome their fears.

Experience has shown that once you become conscious of your shadow, you accept it, then several things become easier. To begin with, you stop spending valuable energy in repressing those uncomfortable emotions. Becoming aware of your shadow, of those aspects you deny about yourself, doesn't mean you have to act them out, put them into practice. But if you manage to get in touch with, say, feelings of envy, you recognize they are there and acknowledge how it feels, then it becomes easier to recognize envy in others. Bear in mind that evaluating the attitudes and intentions of others is an essential aspect of life. Note that I said **evaluate**, which is not the same as being judgmental. To be correctly informed and alert you have to become a good evaluator, know who is reliable and who might have ulterior motives against you. 'Charm' is a very bad parameter with which to evaluate honesty. Slippery sales persons, scammers, conmen, sneakers and false preachers often present themselves as endearing, 'charming,' it's part of their show. Here again enter your shadow and your prejudices. If you are not conscious of your 'blind' side it is much more likely that you will make mistakes, misjudge people. These are not situations in which you can afford to be *subjective*, to project your biases and prejudices on others. You definitely need to be as *objective* as you possibly can, so as to see the person for what he really is. Why is he saying or doing that? What good is it to him? What does he really want? If I accept this, who pays the bill and who gets to keep the benefit?

Putting the emphasis on the issue of the shadow is a work in progress. We cannot develop a healthy spiritual relationship if we have too many buried issues. If spirituality is the search for unity, anything that tends to create and maintain a 'double personality' is the work of the devil. Unfortunately, many religious traditions and sects are designed to achieve this, or do it unconsciously. You cannot expect the leaders of these sects to tell you this. It's your responsibility to become conscious of these traps – and your ability to respond correctly, to know what to say and do about it. – For the most part, just say '*no thank you*' and go look somewhere else.

Some fortunate souls seem to be intuitive experts on these issues. Most of us need to learn as we go along. It seems to be part of the Cosmic Game. You might think you are a saint, but even saints can be easy prey to scammers. In fact, the gullible are the very best candidates for a scam. In any event, few are smart enough to evade trouble always, but a little more awareness can help shift the balance in your favor. Check out some movies like *Focus* with Will Smith and Margo Robbie, learn to read the signs of danger. There are many pages on the web, even some official government ones, that provide general recommendations and news about new scams.

For example, Wikipedia has this to say about **destructive cults**[26] (my emphasis):

Psychologist Michael Langone defines a **destructive cult** as "*a highly manipulative group which exploits and sometimes physically and/or psychologically damages members and recruits.*"

John Gordon Clark cited **totalitarian systems of governance and an emphasis on money making** as characteristics of a destructive cult. In '*Cults and the Family*' the authors cite Shapiro, who defines a "destructive cultism" as a sociopathic syndrome, whose distinctive qualities include: "*behavioral and personality changes, loss of personal identity, cessation of scholastic activities, estrangement from family, disinterest in society and pronounced mental control and enslavement by cult leaders.*" According to Barrett, the most common accusation made against destructive cults is sexual abuse.

A 1997 study by Festinger, Riecken, and Schachter found that people turned to a cataclysmic world view after they had repeatedly failed to find meaning in mainstream movements.

In 1990 Lucy Patrick commented: "*Although we live in a democracy, cult behavior manifests itself in our unwillingness to question the judgment of our leaders, our tendency to devalue outsiders and to avoid dissent.* **We can overcome cult behavior**, *he says, by recognizing that we have dependency needs that are inappropriate for mature people, by increasing anti-authoritarian education, and by encouraging personal autonomy and the free exchange of ideas.*"

- (referring to a specific example, he says that) - "it fits all the official definitions of a cult: *it indoctrinates its members; it forms a closed, totalitarian society; it has a self-appointed, messianic and charismatic leader; and **it believes that the ends justify the means**.*"

Bruce J. Casino presents the issue (of cults) as crucial: "*Limiting the definition of religion may interfere with freedom of religion, while too broad a definition may give some dangerous or abusive groups "a*

---

[26] (https://en.wikipedia.org/wiki/Cult)

limitless excuse for avoiding all unwanted legal obligations."

And quite a lot more, but let's leave all that for you to research.

The challenge, then, is to be a seeker without becoming a sucker, a victim. Learn to recognize which ideas might be dangerous or risky for you and your friends, those where it's easy to fake and use you in ways that will hurt you. Even if you think some of my arguments are flawed and you decide they are not valid for you, the time spent analyzing and discussing them should help you improve your critical thinking. Good luck!

===================== II =====================

Chapter II.49 –

The chicken or the egg? – Exploring ideas

It would seem the question of whether a god or gods exist or do not exist is the primary, central issue, but I think it's secondary. Often, 'the gods' were conceived in response to three different types of concern: where we come from; how to explain the functioning of our universe and how to influence the outcomes; and what is our destiny. Clearly, these aspects interact, but let's look from another perspective. At least in part, the gods we come to imagine depend on the questions we ask and the futures we can envision (and vice versa).

The issue of our transcendence has been important in the formulation of most religions and cosmologies. The problem is that each one has developed a different variant or version, which sheds considerable doubt about the veracity and precision of all of them. Consider the following:

1. Materialists believe there is no form of existence after our physical death. We only transcend by our merits and creations, and through our biological descendants.

2. Materialists can also find consolation with the illusion of the fountain of youth and eternal life in this world, a recurrent theme in many mythologies. A more recent variation is the one about benevolent extraterrestrials with hyper-advanced technologies that will save us from ourselves. Not all of us, mind you, only the 'chosen.' The fact that any super-advanced extraterrestrial with a mentality even remotely like ours would be much more inclined to use us as slaves or eat us for dinner doesn't seem to fit in this fantasy. I guess an illusion is better than nothing.

3. The Wachowskis came up with another 'materialistic' option. In an infinite universe there's always the possibility that at some time and place an EXACT genetic copy of you will repeat (what they call a *'recurrence'*), which is why you can specify in your will that if such an event does occur you are the heir to yourself, just in case (see the movie *Jupiter Ascending*).

4. Catholics and Muslims say that the soul survives after death, but that there is no reincarnation. What you did in this life marks your destiny for all eternity. According to the Cristian Creed: *"I believe… that Jesus … will come again in glory to judge the living and the dead, … the resurrection of the flesh and in eternal life. Amen"*. That is, your **persona** comes back to life, but according to how Jesus (or Allah) judges you, from there on you either **rejoice or suffer** for the rest of eternity! **No wonder Catholics are terrified of death**. In my opinion this is one of the most manipulative alternatives.

5. The majority of non-Abrahamic religions believe in reincarnation or transmigration of the soul. For instance, Hindus and Buddhists believe in the transition of the soul in another reality, the bardo, between incarnations, and its continuity in time by experiencing reincarnation after reincarnation. Your attachments, your merits and your sins determine the nature and the level of your next reincarnation. You can *'pay your debts'* in the next lives, and you can also free yourself from this karmic wheel by means of a spiritual practice.

6. Some people believe we have a spirit or soul, but that after death we return and dissolve into the Source, like a drop in the ocean. This is similar to what many *animistic* conceptions believe, that all beings have spirit, but that the lower beings have a shared, collective spirit: there is only one *spirit* for each species. Many lower spirits can fuse to form a higher order one. Individual spirit only occurs in higher beings like us, obviously, but we still have a collective supra-spirit for all humanity that gathers the cumulative experience of all individuals of the species, and drives the evolution of the species as a whole.

7. Another interesting alternative comes from the popular folklore of Mexico, recently portrayed in the film *Coco*. There is a beyond where individual souls live on, as long as someone living on earth

remembers them. When no one living can remember them, they dispel (or they return to the Source?) If the role of these entities is to receive the souls of those who have just left their earthly bodies, this would make sense because being met by members of your family only helps if you remember them. Perhaps when you are no longer remembered you are freed of your duties and you can return to the Source.

We could carry on, but I think this is enough to show that people, regions and religions of the world differ enormously in their beliefs and their dogmas, so much so that we can safely assume these are only cultural adaptations or inventions, crutches to make life more bearable (and in some cases, to better manipulate people). Perhaps the fundamental question that we would wish to know is whether there is or isn't life after our physical death, and what degree of continuity does our individual consciousness have. If our consciousness dissolves in the cosmic source we should be very happy. But this also depends on your degree of attachment to your current ego. More than one of us would choose to continue in emotional misery rather than let go of our beloved egos.

But in short, they are **only speculations**. What experience or experiment might we design to determine if the soul or spirit can exist without a physical body? What would be credible, convincing evidence for you? Without a doubt these issues belong to the subjectal domain, but they need not continue to be *subjective*. There must be ways to make them more objective. More on this in Book III.

If all these ideas are approximations or illusions, why not choose the one that feels best?

===================== II =====================

Book II – Bonds
Systems – Politics – Legislation®

Chapter II.50 –
The Path of Possessions

Just to remind you of the multiple manners in which we can have the experience of possessing, here goes an informal list of ways to 'win' assets and ways to 'lose' them: goods, real estate, jewelry, shares, responsibilities, whatever. A sort of 'incoming' and 'outgoing' of life.

RECEIVE – GAIN	DISCOUNT – LOSE
Natural:	
Hunt – gather	consume
Find – collect in nature	misplace – lose
Make from natural elements	use – break – wear out
Receive gift – inherit	give gift – donate
Prostitute	pay prostitute
Solicit – beg	give – donate
Social:	
Earn for work	employ – contract
Cultivate – crop	loss from hail, fire, etc.
Earn for services	pay for services
Receive compensations	pay insurance premiums
Save – hoard	overspend – squander
Receive assistance	give to charities
Rent – lease	pay rent
Cultural (business):	
Produce – make – sell	pay taxes (sales, etc.)
Trade with a profit	trade with a loss
Invent – patent	buy patented goods
Gain in the stock market	lose in the stock market
Give franchises	pay for franchises
Loan with interest	pay interests

And surely many more, but all this considering only within the sphere of what is 'legal'...

Marginal or illegal options (scams, frauds, etc.): pillage and looting; cheating; pickpocketing; snitch – steal – rob – holdup; play with marked cards, loaded dice, fixed races and casinos, etc.; usury; overcharging; dealing in drugs and other illegal products such as stolen goods; pay and receive ransom for kidnappings and the like; con with false promises and Ponzi schemes; sell with hidden flaws; undervalue or overvalue property, goods, or services; solicit for false charities...

We could go on and on, but it should be clear that the number of possible 'transactions' that in some way modify 'ownership' is huge. This multiplicity of options is intrinsic to the increasing complexity of the social and cultural levels of organization. And we keep adding new forms...!

As we saw before in Chapter I.24, another way of highlighting the importance of the interobjectal domain at the cultural level is to see the number of professions, trades and institutions that are involved in generating, registering, controlling and patrolling the **bonds** that define property, ownership and belongingness: a large part of the legislative apparatus; attorneys, escrow officers; land deed registries; mining claims; intellectual property, authors rights, patents, etc.; trade and commerce; banking; contracts, franchises; loans; accounting; tax systems; policing; patrolling of frontiers; etc., etc.

It's worth stressing that a large part of this process is mediated through numerical estimates of value. The 'real' material value that is the normal currency in the biological level is slowly replaced by virtual value systems based on a somewhat fictitious construction in the minds of a society. Direct exchange and barter with real goods (like salt, for instance, hence 'salary') is replace by payment in 'real' money (gold or silver coin), symbolic money (paper money, tokens), and then by totally virtual 'money' (a virtual transfer to your bank account, bitcoins, etc.). At the cultural level of organization **numbers** govern the world, and the subjectal is objectivized by giving it value through a fiction agreed upon and shared by all society. Of all the modern belief systems, money is surely the most widespread 'faith' of all (Yuval Harari, Ted Talk, 2021).

At a more personal level, there are several 'games' for small groups intended to increase your awareness of your personal relationship to wealth, your strengths and weaknesses.

> One 'game' goes like this. Gather a group of people who want to explore these issues in an empty, carpeted room. Each must bring a few small bills or trivia as tokens they must make available for transactions (ante, to use a poker term) and are prepared to risk and lose. Then divide into four subgroups. Each subgroup plays one of four 'roles': *solicit, offer, give, take* for five minutes, and then they rotate roles till all subgroups have acted out all the roles and everyone has experienced how they feel in each. Thus, everyone gets to experience both 'sides' of each situation (*e.g.*, steal and have things stolen).

We are often surprised to discover which role is the most difficult. Each person lives it differently, but what seems universal is that we get into the 'game' with great passion, even a game as trivial as the one I've just described. With much more passion than the trivial sums involved would seem to merit.

The issue of economics is vital. Therefore, for us...

The interobjectal domain is not in the least bit *'impersonal'*

————————— o —————————

The dance of the *goods* and their bads

When we speak of the interobjectal domain we mean issues of ownership and belongingness.

Even though it has some variants and levels, belongingness is relatively straightforward. At one level belongingness a given. We belong to the human race. It's a fact; it's not an option. Then there are a range of optative or conditional choices: club, sports team, chorus, political party, religion... Last are some situations where belonging is imposed to some degree. The most obvious and extreme is explicit slavery, but there are also a range of partial or disguised forms of slavery. Also, in any political or religious dictatorial regime, obedience to the 'regime' is imposed. You have no choice.

But this section refers more to the issue of bonds or unions with our material assets, rights and obligations, what belongs to us, what defines if we own things or not. In an underpopulated world the question of ownership is quite simple. He who finds or hunts something owns it, mostly. Romans called it *res nullius*, which means *'something that has no owner can be appropriated by anyone'* (especially for *game,* the hunter owns his catch). Most times there was no reason to quarrel because we were surrounded by nature, it provided for all. Even amongst animals there are webs of cooperation to obtain food, build refuges or harvest and store resources. Also rules for sharing and strategies for hiding resources from your neighbors. One of the most striking recent discoveries is that our cousins the monkeys have a sense of fairness and justice. Frans de Waal and his team have shown that if you train Capuchin monkeys to collaborate in some task by rewarding them with fruits and veggies, and then you give one of them yummy fruit in sight of another, and give the other *blah* cucumber, the jaded individual rebels and throws the 'prize' back at you, literally! Similar experiments have confirmed this in a variety of animals. In some way, the sense of fairness and justice is incorporated into our biology (e.g. video clip at: https://youtu.be/meiU6TxysCg).

Unfortunately, the growth and mobility of our societies has resulted in ever more unbalanced situations so that it seems resources are insufficient for all, which in turn has led to constant bickering and fighting between individuals and societies to harvest, trade and keep those resources we consider necessary or valuable. Or we can conquer them. It has been the driving force behind a large part of history, but here we can only take a quick look. The more interesting and complex problems occur in the gray area between harvest and conquest.

===================== II =====================

Chapter II.51 –

God by Decree! – Legitimizing Political Power

From a very early age kids over much of the world are told stories about gods of some sort or another. What they are seldom told is how the idea of a single ruling god came about. Virtually all early faiths recognized and worshiped many gods. The first documented worship of One God is usually credited to have appeared in Egypt ca. 3350 yb[2] or earlier. Atenism was the worship of the deified sun-disk Aten in Ancient Egypt. The Pharaoh Amenhotep IV, who reigning around 3352 to 3335 yb[2], promoted it as an arguably monotheistic state religion for Egypt. The *'Great Hymn to the Aten,'* ca. 3350 yb[2], reads so:

- *O sole god, like whom there is no other! Thou didst create the world according to thy desire, whilst thou wert alone: All men, cattle, and wild beasts (...) The lord of all of them, wearying (himself) with them, the lord of every land, rising for them, . . .*

Worship of Aten predates Amenhotep IV, but under his rule Atenism morphed from a more traditional henotheism into something that could be recognized as monotheism. He first elevated Aten as the supreme god, and later declared Aten to be the only god. All very interesting, but why? Why stop worshiping all the gods you grew up with? You need to take history one step further to see why.

By the time Amenhotep IV came to power in Thebes, the capital, the priests of the worship of Amun (another powerful Egyptian god) were on almost equal standing with the royal house in wealth and influence. "*With the exception of Ra and Osiris, the worship of Amun was more widespread* than that of any other god in the Nile Valley; the growth of Amun's cult was certainly disseminated by political rather than religious propaganda."[27] (This assumes politics and religion are different; hardly).

Amenhotep IV outlawed the old religion, proclaimed himself "**the living incarnation of a single all-powerful deity**" known as Aten and named himself 'Akhen–aten.' Atenism, however, was a very exclusive religion confined to the royal family, with the Pharaoh as **the only mediator between man and god**. Very convenient. Calling himself the '*incarnation*' of the god was clearly a rather brilliant political move, one that has been emulated under different guises by rulers ever since! What seems indisputable is that he was the first sufficiently ego-centric ruler to glorify himself as a god! The first perhaps, but not the last! The connection seems to work both ways. Even the most 'democratic' Christians seem to have difficulty shedding the allure of calling their Christ a 'king' who lives in the 'kingdom' of heaven. This is in flagrant contradiction with the image of the *poor-man's-faith* that Jesus supposedly promoted. It was the initial hallmark of Christianity.

It's impossible to understand many of the quirks of religion out of its historical context, but if you put it in proper perspective, it becomes perfectly clear that many of its 'supernatural' claims are plain and simple mundane ethno-geo-political maneuvers. Nothing holy about them at all.

Before the exodus, Moses lived in Egypt around the same period as Akhenaten (Amenhotep IV), so his version of a monotheistic religion is clearly linked to the Egyptians, and his use of the 'one god' as a unifying ethno-political glue is obvious. Judaism before that was still in polytheistic bronze-aged diapers. For the record, Christianity and Islam hadn't even been conceived. The fundamental problem posed by this little historical tour is to decide whether the biblical conception of an '*only god*' is also no more than a political confabulation, a myth (meme) that in time acquired a life of its own. Perhaps the problem lies more in the 'personification' of the concept.

Can we restrict religion into its 'spiritual' teachings and rid it of its political undertones, or would it be better to simply scrap it altogether?

---

[27] See: https://history.stackexchange.com/questions/14865/which-religion-was-the-first-monotheistic-one/14870 ; https://www.ancient.eu/Moses/ ; https://www.ancient.eu/Akhenaten/

The term has such a long and confused history that attempting to restrict the concept is unlikely to catch on.

As a guide for social socioeconomic problems, it is impossible to distinguish it from plain politics and has little to provide in favor of the believer (it is often manipulative and greedy). It could have a role in political representation, but its history and its hierarchical structure sheds doubts about its true alliances and partisanship, especially when it is very loaded with dogma. Many people prefer that religion not meddle with political issues, but it must be said that in many historical situations it has been the only force capable of facing authoritarian and despotic governments.

As a guide to structure social fabric and world views, ethics and morals, etc., it has proved to be a source of union, comfort, consolation and a great instrument of government. And for the very same reasons it has been used as a form of political domination, a dividing factor, instigator of wars, subjective, dogmatic, obsolete, castrating, manipulative, despotic and a number of other woes. In spite of the criticisms and the structural risks it has, there can be no doubt that religion has been an important force in the structuring of societies and of history, but always to the extent that it has overlapped with politics, sometimes as an actor/partner and others as a counterpoint.

As a guide for individual spiritual practice, it may be appropriate if you retain the liberty to choose and you agree with the particular style their denomination proposes. If the manner of the practice is obligatory, compulsory, then it becomes an obstacle.

This does **not** mean that the possibility of a single unifying principle ('god') is wrong. It may very well be correct for reasons that are not at all 'political.' What **it does mean is** that rulers have always taken advantage of existing belief systems to glorify their own name and buttress their political aspirations. In fact, till very recently (historically) nobody even made the distinction. If religion is no more than politics in disguise, leaving it aside would be a relief. Resting the whole theological edifice on these strongly politicized stories and the ruthless use of dogma as an excuse for subjugation and conquest is a mistake and should be abandoned (*i.e.*, *scrap the crap*).

Of course, I am deliberately leaving out an important issue, the knowledge gained from spiritual practices, which I will look into in Book III.

But there's no doubt that a large part of the rejection and mistrust towards religions comes from that mixing and overlapping of roles of religion with very mundane politics. If the existence of god or gods can't be justified on more intrinsic grounds, then the whole idea of 'divinity' is doomed.

===================== II =====================

Chapter II.52 –

The perfect Ponzi Scheme

Perhaps you know about Mr. Ponzi, perhaps not. So here is a sketch, just in case. It's simple enough. Somebody advertises an investment as excellent and risk free.

"If you invest with us, you will get twice the benefit and never lose." Tempting, so a few take the bait (or pretend to). Soon they start getting their rewards, as promised. News about these apparent 'successes' prompt others to invest and investments snowball. After some time, the scam begins to crumble, and suddenly the money evaporates, Mr. Ponzi and company elope with your money (or try to), and a great many honest suckers are left penniless.

Why does it work? Because the scammers make sure the first 'testimonials' are positive, supportive. They pay off the initial investors with the next wave of money coming in, and so on, till the pot is big enough and the promised payoffs accumulate and become unpayable. But that's its flaw.

*Ponzi schemes promise rewards in **this** life!*

With thousands of years of accrued experience, preachers and priests know better. You see, they've come up with the perfect Ponzi scheme.

Pay here and now in hard currency, and reap the benefits in the afterlife!

(No nasty promises of rewards in **this** life)

Why on earth would anybody fall for such a ruse? The rule of thumb is that the promised benefit must increase in proportion to the waiting. So, if you must wait 'forever' then the reward has to be both significant (*Paradise, gardens of pleasures*) and long lasting (forever after, *Eternal Bliss*). For good measure this option is pitted against the alternative of *Eternal Damnation in Hell*, of fire and torment no less. And of course, Judgment Day is just around the corner, could happen any day. I defy you to come up with more extreme odds than that, and a promise that is more impossible to verify!

So, according to the preacher, the solution is simple: pay now in hard cash and save yourself the horrors that *(might)* await you in the future. Too late? You're already a consummate sinner? Never too late. In fact, easy, pay an extra fee for 'absolution' and God's representative on earth will take care of the problem. This is such a nifty arrangement that you might even be advised to *Sin now, repent later*[28].

What if … it's a con? Well, if you bit with this religious bait, you must be a 'believer' (atheists don't 'bite' on this one). Putting aside the possibility that God might not exist or that there may be no afterlife—in which case you'd be a perfect sucker, though blissfully unaware—the real problem lies in trusting that the dogmas they preach about what God values and despises are actually correct. Quite frankly, I'm not in the least convinced. You see, if biology and history are any indicators, God loves winners and has little patience with losers. For many traditions Divinity is somewhat of a trickster and a joker (like the Norse god Loki, or the many personified astute animal deities like Coyote, the jackal, etc.) If you think about it, it's just as probable that Deity rejoices with nifty cons and has a good laugh with the fooled, just as we do.

Condemned to Eternal Damnation for being such a dumb sucker!

Discover ***that*** on '*Judgment Day*' and you are truly screwed!

Fair game indeed.

=================== II ===================

Chapter II.53 –

Revolutionize?

Metaphysical traditions believe the 'universe' has a nasty habit of taking your pleas quite literally.

'Beware of what you wish for' is the basic tenet. The Ancient Greek story of King Midas paints it clearly. When a god asked what he wished for, Midas wished that everything he touched should turn to gold. His wish was granted …, and he soon starved to death! Just think, ***everything*** would turn to gold, including his food.

Which brings us to **Revolutions**. Long ago the word meant: *cause to*

---

[28] From the film by Ridley Scott, *The Kingdom of Heaven (2005)*.

travel in an orbit around a central point, as is more evident in the related word *revolving*. *'Volvo' or 'volutus'* in Latin means to return or turn back, so *re-volutus* implies turning again and again. The modern political use of 'revolution' to imply *'the overthrow of an established political system'* was first recorded around 1600.

In metaphysical terms this is a most unfortunately poor choice of a word. All too often 'revolutions' end up right where they started. Well, perhaps not exactly. The names, the faces and the colors might change, but the underlying structure remains much the same, or worse! South Americans, after living through a long history of predictably failed revolutions, have a rather crude expression for the resulting regimes, "*The same shit with a different smell.*"

These results are predictable. But first we need to make a distinction. Today the term is applied indistinctly to two very different situations. Most of the first wave that started in the late 1700s and the early 1800s involved colonial uprisings against their abusive imperial overlords. Locals against invaders, quite clearcut. Those that managed to win and throw out the invaders took great pride in their feats, and their heroes were praised and honored by all those remaining in the land. In most cases some internal bickering occurred in the aftermath (the American Civil War is a case in point), but by and large the results were fairly consistent. The local populations managed to work it out, found common ground and a new prosperous nation was born.

The situations that swept much of Latin America during the 20th century are very different. Cashing into the mythos of past glories, they are often called 'revolutions,' but they are actually much closer to civil wars. Or even worse, hot arenas in a cold war between foreign superpowers. The critical issue is that these wars actually had the opposite effect. They tragically divided those countries internally, crippled their economies and stunted their growth.

But there is also another inevitable effect of internal 'revolutions,' or civil wars, in many cases. The naïve tend to think the future will be fine if the 'good guys' win, or that this or that revolution failed because the 'bad guys' won. Bullshit. It makes absolutely no difference which political color wins, because a civil war is almost inevitably a sure way of selecting the most ruthless son-of-a-bitch and his henchmen as your next ruler. You just don't win civil wars by being 'nice guys.' The whole notion of armed 'revolutions' as a way to change current affairs inside a country is a pretty iffy way to go, if not outright suicidal.

Evolution, on the other hand, means *'the gradual development of something, especially from a simple to a more complex form,'* as in *'the forms of written languages undergo constant evolution.'* We can see this at a personal level, because this is what happens to us all as we go through school, starting as simple-minded toddlers through progressively more complex stages or grades to become ever more complex thinking and sophisticated adults. Well, at least that's what most education systems aspire to. Society assigns a fair amount of value to this process, not only by investing in your education. It shows it in the amount of salary it's willing to pay you according to the level of education you've achieved!

Like everything else in the world, social systems and their means of governance also evolve. So, if you are stuck in a social system or a context you don't like, you surely want it to change in a permanent direction, for the better presumably. If what you are wishing for is a lasting change for the better, you would be well advised to reformulate your plea. Don't revolutionize -

Evolutionize!
==================== II ====================

Chapter II.54 –

Spread the Word (and keep the Numbers)

Making a living out of intangibles must have always been difficult so, from the very beginnings, cults and temples became adept at **spreading the word, and keeping the numbers**. The practice has deep roots in religious traditions. Even Christ complained about the merchants and hoarders in The Temple. Rich temples in poor communities seem to go back as far as history can trace civilizations.

Christianity started as a poor man's religion, but their priests grew out of temple traditions, it seems, because they too soon learnt to **Spread the Word (and keep the numbers)**, especially after it was adopted as the official religion of the Roman empire. This gave rise to the Roman Catholic Church, the oldest and possibly the richest institution on the planet!

How about Islam? Frankly, I don't know enough to say, but I see no evidence that wealth is distributed more equitably in Muslim countries. In fact, the rich there are stinking rich, it seems.

Or the modern versions of Christianity, televangelists and company? Granted, televangelism, (television in general), is **a great way to *Spread the Word** (and an even better way to keep The Numbers*). In fact, **spread any** 'Word' *(and keep **lots** of Numbers)*. Many built huge temples, their leaders go around in private jets, and have huge bank accounts. Not bad for 'non-profit' organizations! The total amount of wealth held by 'churches' of all denominations is simply staggering.

The trend is by no means privy to religions. Politics is all about the distribution of resources, both costs and benefits. The *(secret)* moto of any self-serving kleptocracy reads something like this:

*Spread the word **(and the costs)** and keep the numbers **(privileges and benefits)**.*

For the record, Science can hardly claim to be above it all. **Spread the Word** (publish), **and keep the Numbers *(patent any commercially useful idea you can come up with)***. Even better, the perfect score is to finance the research with public grants and subsidies (***spread the cost***), and then patent the resulting discoveries privately (***keep the benefits***)!

So hardly anyone can claim to be completely 'innocent.' However, there are some significant **ethical differences between Science, Politics and Religion**. Each in their own way claims to be a public service, a necessity, for the good of the people, and so on. And yet, . . . which violates their own ethical standards is up to you to decide.

So, are you a religious or political leader? In that case, . . .

Want to be different, radical, really e*volutionize* the world? Then
Keep your Word and spread the Numbers!
===================== II =====================

Chapter II.55 –
Kings and kingdoms have been notoriously ephemeral

Perhaps less so than other rulers, but still, a blink in the eye of history.

Which makes me wonder if speaking of the '*Kingdom*' of God is at all reasonable. For centuries before Darwin, it was thought that creation was perfect and that things were immutable, including the species of plants and animals. Considering what we have reviewed in the preceding pages, it seems incredible that generations of intelligent humans hung on to such an idea. And then, suddenly, Darwin appeared and turned the tables. At first blush the subject of evolution is just a technicism of biology, which makes it seem strange that it should have provoked such a huge outcry and ideological turmoil. No doubt, the true battle has nothing to do with biology. Not even with God. It was political, and it can only be understood if we look at the implications in the context of the politics of that era.

Centuries of imperialism (the kingdoms that survived turned into empires) generated a *status quo,* a very convenient situation for the ruling oligarchies, both the political ones and the ecclesiastical elites. For those in power, the idea of the immutability of things was a godsend. The ideal was that everything should remain the same, that the rich continue being rich, the poor poorer, and the slaves, created by 'God' as an inferior race according to the slavers, continue to be slaves. Naturally, what else? They had the whole bundle in the palm of their hands. Any change would mean an attack on their privileges, including those of 'the church.' It's hardly a surprise that the communist rooted for the destruction of the religious apparatus together with the monarchies. And yet, the communist movement saw the outer shell, but failed to modify the underlying premises, including the biological roots of social hierarchies (lust for power, greed, etc.). Actually, it unwittingly played into them.

But no one was willing to admit that these were the true reasons. Better use moral and theological arguments. The irony, perhaps, is that many of the recent discoveries in evolutionary biology may in fact undermine the underlying biological roots of imperialism, but are not as much at odds with the divine as was once thought (or peddled). Anyway, the fact is that the heyday of kingdoms has passed, and that of territorial empires is also waning. Now the true 'empires' are of another nature.

If you want to be in sync with the times, you should be speaking of the **Corporation of God**, by far the most powerful socioeconomic 'force' of the moment. The Catholic church has functioned as a transnational corporation for centuries. The modality is being emulated and is in fashion with several other 'churches' that operate with a system of franchises, a system that has also given rise to several monopolies or oligopolies (like the international pharmaceutical guild, etc.). If ground legislation is not changed, it won't be long before these corporations own the whole planet. They will even come to own the naïve humans who naively think **they** are the owners.

One of the troubling symptoms of our age is the abysmal lack of 'presence' of democracies in the popular imagery. There are many personal stories and even epics that are set in some form of government or other, but for the most part those are not *about* governments. In theory we live in a democracy, but if you look at Hollywood, novels, TV shows, the sci-fi worlds, etc., both the retrospective and the futuristic genres are largely dominated by either kingdoms or empires. On the retrospective side (either historically based or fictional), some examples include: *The First King, Vikings, Game of Thrones, The Kingdom of Heaven, Dragon-heart, The Emperor's Sword, Prince of Persia, The Tenth Kingdom*, even *The Lion King*, ... Since we seem to have run out of kings to murder and kingdoms to conquer on earth, the action has had to move out to the universe at large. On the futuristic side: *Star Wars, Dune, The Hunger Games*, even the *Matrix* series and *Jupiter Ascending* rely on the tried and tested formula of pitting the innocent against the arrogant mighty, ... And of course, always the 'empire' is the bad guy and the freedom loving rebellious underdogs are the good guys. Empires are always militarized, Hitlerian and ruthless. Even in the metaverse version of *Ready Player One*, it's the corporation's CEO who plays the role of ruthless 'emperor' – different setting – same story. Somewhere in the background is an implied form of government that is **not** a kingdom or an empire, but the details how those alternatives work are never the focus of interest. Granted, *nice humanitarian governments that run smoothly and everybody is happy* would not be much of a story for an action movie or an epic saga. But for you and me, and most likely, 99% of the world's population, a **real-world** '*nice humanitarian government that runs smoothly*' might not be such a bad idea! And the process as to how to get from here and now to there might be quite fascinating, if improbable. In any event, stop worshipping "freedom fighters." Wiser folks are *freedom seekers, freedom lovers*.

Perhaps I missed them, but if there are attempts to imagine or create alternative scenarios, few come to mind. Disney's *Tomorrowland* (2015) doesn't offer solutions, but it recognizes the problems and has the right attitude as to where and how to get the ball rolling. Veronica Roth's *Divergent* series' proposal of a society divided into functional groups based on personalities might qualify as something that is at least innovative. But our real world is very complex and has tried a variety of forms of government. For instance, Switzerland is one of the most prosperous and stable countries of the modern world. It is also pretty much unique in that it is governed by a triumvirate, three Presidents that alternate in office for periods of one year each. Other efforts (out of the artistic sphere) are projects like the DAO, Decentralized Autonomous Organizations. Technological innovations such as cryptocurrencies and e-trade in general might be changing the game to such a degree that something different will come of it without us even realizing it, but that offers little guarantee that it will be for the better. It is still hard to tell what might actually work, but we desperately need to move out of the dominating **pyramidal hierarchy** model. It was never truly healthy, and with increasing concentrations of power it is so vulnerable to derailment that it is becoming a real global liability.

===================== II =====================

Chapter II.56 –

The organizational pyramid and representation

In a primary social group, like a family, it's usually not necessary to designate *representatives*. Each is his own, save perhaps if you are ill or away. But this simple reality becomes more complicated as the number of people grows.

All populous societies have some form of social stratification and an administrative hierarchy. In the modern world it's the norm. Let's consider a relatively simple case, a factory. The owner rules through his manager or board of directors. These, in turn, delegate through section bosses, foremen, etc.

As the factory grows in the number of employees and scale, there is an ever-greater distance between the owners and the workforce. This obviously puts the individual worker in a very weak negotiating position. The solution is to name one person to represent the rest.

Something similar occurs in government structures. Everybody knows the town mayor and it would be relatively easy to get an appointment with him or her. With the mayor of a large city, we know his name and who he is, but it is unlikely we'd know him in person. Not to mention the governor of the state or the president of your country. You have to channel your voice and your vote through your representatives.

Nothing new, of course, but we need to make it explicit to see the effects of these systems.

Centuries of history in a few paragraphs. One way to sketch the situation is to see the structure as a pyramid. A simple case might be a factory with say a thousand workers. Then we have a foreman for every 20 to 30 workers. Perhaps eight or ten section chiefs, department heads, directors, and the owner at the top.

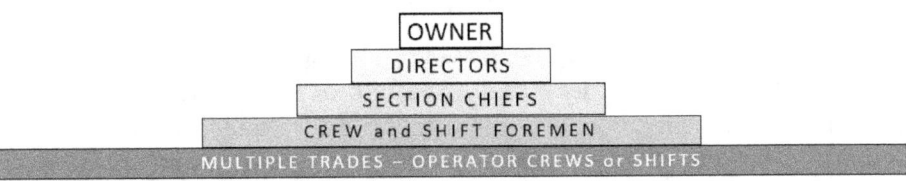

The pyramid might be flatter or steeper (with less levels, or more), but the pyramid of command, of salaries, of power and of privileges is always present.

The problem for the workers is that they don't have a way of accessing the upper levels directly. They are a bunch and for any negotiation it is almost inevitable to name speakers or representatives. Usually, you would try speaking with the foreman first. If he can't give you a solution (or washes his hands) you'd have to speak to the section chief. You'd have to ask for an interview and it's almost certain they will ask you to name a spokesperson, so you get together with your group and decide to send Joe. Joe seems to have some success and the chief takes his request (and then shelves it). The problem is important for the workers. They will have to speak with the directors. But how on earth do you achieve that? Well, getting the spokespersons from several sections together and naming a representative with enough 'votes' to get you one step higher up the organizational hierarchy. Great, some progress was achieved, and conditions improved for a time. Next time a problem arises, solving it will be easier.

Soon they discover that other factories are having similar problems and so a regional meeting is convened, so your group sends a 'delegate' (comrade, compañero, or whatever you prefer).

The workers' movement has just been born. You are saved, you now have a mechanism that will permit you all to negotiate at the same level. The movements' capacity to negotiate rests on the combined action of the many (hands-down protest, rallies, local and regional strikes, etc.). The more, the better. Syndicates and 'unions' appear.

UNITED WORKERS – GROUPS from MULTIPLE FACTORIES – AFFILIATES
SPOKESMEN and LOCAL REPRESENTATIVES
REGIONAL DELEGATES
UNION DELEGATES

Those at the very top see trouble looming, so then, what to do? Though it seems a contradiction, they permit, or even foster, the creation of a national office for the Union in question, which generates a new level in that organization and a new post, the national bigwig of the 'movement.' We'll call him 'the Boss.'

BOSS

Genius! Why? Because the guys at the capital know that the more levels an organizational pyramid has and the farther away from their constituencies the delegates are, the easier it will be to negotiate with them, intimidate them, bribe them, turn them into one of their own. Or at the very least, create an ambivalence between their personal aspirations and the needs of their constituents. **Nobody is immune to the adrenaline and the collateral benefits of power in and of itself.** All these organizations suffer an evolution that is virtually independent of their initial intention, be they good or bad. Organizations are born, grow, mature, and age, just like everything else. Sometimes they also die, but unfortunately their lifespan may exceed their usefulness by decades or even centuries. They no longer fill the role they were intended for, but they continue to suck up energies. This is just as valid for an organization as it is for some 'department' in a government structure.

It is one of the mechanisms by which kingdoms, empires, religious hierarchies, non-government organizations, enterprises and corporations, all age. It makes little difference. The case of corporations is interesting because it is a relatively new concept in terms of organizational evolution. But the indelible symptoms of that evolution are evident everywhere.

Bottom-up or top-down? The transformation of delegates

As we have seen, structural holarchies are constructed bottom-up, from the simple to the complex. Social hierarchies operate top-down. The reason is simple, the organization has more power than the individuals that make it up. He who controls the organization has much more power than any of its individual members. Obvious, right?

The problem is as follows. In those organizations that were created for the benefit of 'those on top,' such as private enterprises, the power hierarchy, and the direction of the delegation of that power are concordant with the interests and the structure of the 'pyramid' (Figure 27).

But in the case of the labor unions and syndicates, **the interests that are represented and the delegation of power are at odds with the chain of command of the resulting hierarchy** (Figure 28). In a few years or decades, these unions transform into enclaves with entrenched power structures similar to corporations and political parties.

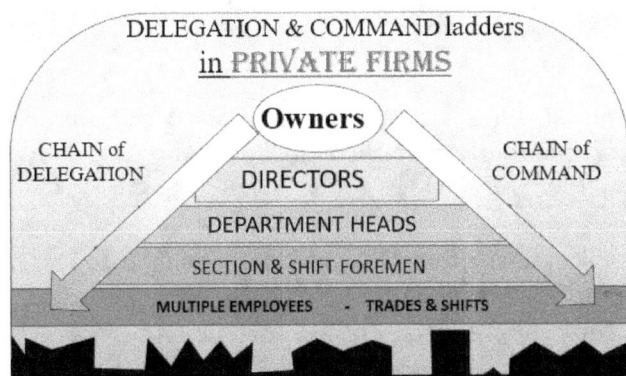

Figure 27. **Structural hierarchy in a private firm.** – In private firms (e.g., a smallish factory) the chain of delegation and the chain of command are concordant. The **Owner** has direct contact with the organization and retains its operational control.

The intermediate 'delegate' ends up being a sandwich between the interests of his constituents and the demands of the syndical bosses, so that the syndical structures end up being as coercive and oppressive as the corporations, or worse! A particularly blatant case occurred during the COVID pandemic when they asked a recently elected politician how the political strata were going to collaborate with the economic cutbacks and other restrictions. His response was clear cut:

"We give the orders, you obey"

Let's just say he showed his metal. To hell with his role as the representative of the people. From populist to fascist in the blink of an eye! I believe it was Marx himself that used to say that *"a proletarian turned aristocrat is worse than an aristocrat born an aristocrat."* In most cases this process is much more insidious, but the risk that power will *'go to his head'* is always present. The very exercise of any kind of power seems to be intoxicating, even if it is power delegated by someone else.

*Figure 28. **Structural hierarchy in a labor union**. – In labor organizations the chain of command is at odds with the chain of delegation. Delegated power soon turns into **acquired power**. The interests of the boss drift father and father from the interests of their constituencies.*

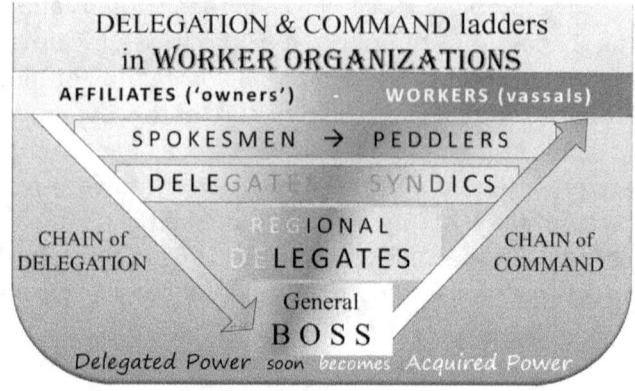

DELEGATION & COMMAND ladders
in WORKER ORGANIZATIONS

AFFILIATES ('owners')   -   WORKERS (vassals)

SPOKESMEN → PEDDLERS

DELEGATES   SYNDICS

CHAIN of
DELEGATION

REGIONAL
DELEGATES

CHAIN of
COMMAND

General
BOSS

Delegated Power soon becomes Acquired Power

The problem is structural. All structures are supported bottom-up, always. If the bases or foundations fail, they collapse. But the most complex stratum is the one that commands, almost always. Therefore, you cannot neutralize a power structure by creating another power structure, because the almost inevitable result is that now you have to deal with TWO power structures. True, to some degree one can be the counterpoint of the other, at least for a time. But if the roles and the top become entrenched, it is almost certain that it will end up being another feudal enclave with hereditary transmission of power. End of the unconditional support of the constituency's interests.

This process is particularly visible in *labor organizations*. The organization is born of a group of hardy militants who came out of the ranks. As it grows and expands, more levels crop up and the leaders occupy the resulting higher roles. One of them stands out and ends up in the capital, becoming the bigwig of the union, the Boss. Supposedly his fight is with the corporate establishment, but when the first internal elections occur, in practice most of his energies are consumed in an effort to remain in power (he and his entourage). To the original bottom-up structure we now add a top-down current of interests and impositions, and before you realize your once feisty leader mutated into a grim boss.

This is the first important symptom of distortion of the original altruistic aspirations of the movement. The second has to do with the election itself. If the current number-one was successful with the negotiations, it is quite probable that he will be reelected spontaneously in these first elections. The extra time in office allows the governing gang to consolidate alliances and power structures that then become very difficult to dismantle. The organization grows, a syndicate is formalized that is authorized to collect affiliation fees and to offer *services*. Suddenly they are handling large sums of money. Their own internal bureaucracy is born with its respective guild of workers that depend on the decisions of the bigwig. This creates the ideal conditions for political manipulation and coercion. If you are not subservient to the mandates of the reigning elite you will be marginalized, and what was supposedly a democratic venture for the benefit of its constituents, soon turns into a personal enclave commandeered by the local 'strongman,' another power structure with all its vices and woes.

The third step has to do with succession. After 15 or 20 years in power the strongman is tired or ill. His eldest son is now a young adult that grew up '*in the trenches*' and knows all the union strategies and the political ins and outs of his country (together with all the political stratagems, the tricks and internal dealings of the organization). With the support of his father, he gains political standing within the organization and ends up winning the election for union Boss. We have slowly slipped from a personal 'kingdom' to a hereditary one, with all the added problems of all hereditary systems. The father was born in a poor neighborhood in a modest home, worked since he was an adolescent, shared all his youth with other workers and knows their predicaments firsthand, *in the flesh*. But his militancy took him from those humble beginnings to live in the capital and, slowly and progressively, to better his personal situation. He barely got a formal education in a marginal school of scarce resources. But he has grit and charisma.

The son, instead, grew up in a middle-class area of the capital. He went to a larger and well supplied school and managed to complete his formal education. Maybe he even managed to get a college degree. Of course, he never went hungry or cold, nor did he have to get up at five in the morning to work twelve hours in a mine shaft, or nothing of the sort. He even hangs out with some of the sons of the business world. Perhaps he grew up immersed in the union philosophy, but he is not from the union ranks. He is a professional politician. A good advisor maybe, but it is unlikely that he will turn out to be a good Boss for the Union. He lacks grit, as a rule. He belongs to another social stratum.

Believing that the son will follow in the footsteps of his father seems to be one of the universal misconceptions of humanity, particularly of the firstborns! The number of prosperous firms that have gone broke and kingdoms that have collapsed on account of incompetent sons is uncountable. In any event, if you were about to vote in favor of some hereditary candidate, better think it over ten times.

You must have noticed that I have made very little distinction between a firm, a union, a government, a religious organization, not even a non-government organization (an n. g. o.). It doesn't matter much how they are born. They are organizations after all, and all behave as such. Sometimes people try to equate organizations to organisms, but that's a mistake.

An organization is NOT an organism

Even the names imply a relationship. Perhaps analogous, but categorically different.

The term 'organism' primarily refers to '*a group of organs that make up a living being*' and by extension, all living beings. From there comes the phrase '*organismal biology,*' for example, which refers to all aspects of the **internal**[29] functioning of a living being at an individual level. When we move to the relationships **between** individuals, or of these with the environment, we speak of social behavior, ecology and so on.

The crucial point is that an individual is a <u>closed system</u>. Even though it interacts with the environment, it is an individual encapsulated by some form of covering (cellular membrane, skin, scales, bark, etc.) None of its parts has independent existence. If any of its parts suffers harm, that always has consequences on the organism as a whole. The interests of one are the interests of all, almost. Therefore, none of its cells or organs can go against the rest without bringing harm to itself. Sometimes it happens, of course, as in the case of cancer, but the result is catastrophic even for the cancer itself, that ends up dying with the host that supports it.

Instead, an organization is an <u>open system</u>. It is analogous in as much as it is made up of numerous units organized hierarchically in subgroups that make up a functional whole.

But it differs radically because the units that make it up, the individuals, are capable of independent existence free of the organization and of all the other individuals in it. Perhaps they feel very strong ties and

---

[29] That is, from the skin inwards, but only in its material aspects.

are totally committed to the organization, but their autonomy also allows them to steal, boycott, abandon or betray the organization without that resulting in a personal suicide. Besides, in some respects the interests of each of the members are independent of the rest, even opposed in the race to advance within the organization. If the personal benefit is large enough, it might even 'justify' the destruction of the organization itself.

Aside from the direct material cost-benefit, the point of equilibrium between loyalty and betrayal is influenced by many subjective factors, such as kinship bonds, personal philosophy, the loves and deceptions of personal histories, and so many more. But the cold mathematics always underlies. As the organization grows, all these links and bonds dilute, and the potential personal benefits grow exponentially. As the cost-benefit imbalance becomes ever greater, the organizations are forced to increase the 'costs' in a variety of ways: reprimands, ostracism, suspensions, layoffs, fines, whippings, extradition and even the personal death of the offender with his whole in-group. It has never been a good idea to betray an organized mafia, but even some current governments impose a death penalty for 'treason.' *Apostasy*, the abandonment or renunciation of the faith, is still punished with death in many Islamic countries like Afghanistan, Iran, Saudi Arabia, Yemen, Somalia, Sudan, Nigeria and a few more (at least, according to Wikipedia). If the religion has been imposed, the punishment seems quite hypocritical.

Here is where the very centralized systems of governance get into serious difficulties that, historically, have contributed to the collapse of almost all the *empires*. One way or another, the empire was built based on '*honor, duty, loyalty, service,*' or similar ideologies. When they were only a few, and bound by kinships or friendships, it worked quite well. With the conquests and growth of the empire other subcultures are absorbed, other ethnicities, all Subjects with other loyalties. Sometimes they truly assimilate, but in other cases they can resist for centuries or millennia. Perhaps the most resilient and stubborn in the west are the Jews, but the same has happened in differing measures in other areas and epochs. If they have been robbed, why should they be loyal to the empire?

So then, what's the deal, loyalty or rebelliousness?

Unfortunately, the issue is truly complex. No organization functions without some degree of loyalty to its aims, and of cooperation between its members. But they also don't prosper and are unstable if their functioning is based on oppression and injustice. Loyalty and cooperation vanish.

Throughout history we have tried out many alternatives. They always oscillate between the supremacy of the individual or of the communal, between dictatorships or democracy, centralism or federalism. Everybody has their own string of 'moral,' 'ideological,' or 'political' reasons to justify one or the other. But in the end, it's a question of numbers. For the few that are at the top, the ideal is a globalized centralism. For everybody else, better some equilibrium closer to a decentralized federalism. There are some experiences with hybrid systems, like some farming federations. Perhaps they are worth looking into.

In a modern society some structure is inevitable, but to the majority of individuals, us, any form of monopoly is not good, be they religious, corporate, by a political party, or syndicate. Monopolies are breeding grounds for economic abuses, dictatorships, and totalitarian regimes.

By now it must be obvious that I don't believe in static formulas, rigid political ideologies, dogmas, and the like. Our world has become too complex and is changing too fast for a dogma to work for any length of time and the risk that it will become counterproductive is huge. But I do believe we can draw up some guidelines that should enable you to evaluate different proposals and see where they might lead. What matters here is to see what impact it has on the average citizen, let's say the middle class. Those of the privileged classes (businessmen, politicians, union leaders, the religious elites) have their advisors that surely made their calculations and can give a slew of 'reasons' to justify that the proposed measures are 'beneficial.' But it's unlikely that they will be specific as to who will be the beneficiaries and who will *pay the bill.* That should be the role of the press, but most times corporate media shun the job and play dumb. The bottom line is, it's your job.

In some cases, like a massive energy price hike, the answer might seem obvious, but in others the effects are much more subtle and the costs and the benefits more difficult to determine. The typical case involves those decisions that, according to those in power, are taken *for political reasons*. Every time you hear this 'reason' you can be sure there's shady business somewhere. You need to question who will be the real beneficiaries and who will end up paying those bills.

Common elements that lead to abuse and corruption

In any system of free trade there is an inverse relationship between unit price and volume. Unit price is always higher than bulk. It is the very basis of commerce and the retail business. The logic is simple and virtually universal. If you handle large volumes, the costs go down and even a small difference in unit price results in a large profit. If you sell only a pound at time, that same difference is likely insignificant.

The only place where this general rule gets inverted is in some political structures. In all political hierarchies the town mayor is the equivalent of a small scale 'retailer,' while the federal government is the bulk dealer *par excellence*. But in a sucker's world the town gets 2 or 3%, the state gets 8-10% and the federals get the lions' share of the overall internal product of the country. The details vary, but the tendency is widespread. It's crazy, in some countries to such a degree that you can't help wondering how what was supposed to be a 'federation' allowed it to get to that point. And it keeps getting worse. If you add the erosion of currency, inflation, and the increasing national debt-load to the taxes, some of these populist governments are eating up twice as much! 50%? - 80%? Who can know for certain. The church tithes and the aristocracies of the past seem like nothing by comparison. (Accountability? Don't even mention it!).

Now, it's perfectly clear that for the ruling political ingroup at the national level this is perfect. Huge sums of money and lots of power. What is less obvious is why the representatives of the intermediate levels approved these abuses. That is, in a federal state as is presumed to rule in most modern democracies (in theory, most of the West), the tax loads must be approved by the representatives of the convening states (municipalities, counties, states, whatever). Why do delegates (senators and representatives) approve laws that clearly deprive their own states of precious resources in favor of an abusive national overlord? Why do the constituencies, including the intermediate levels in power, tolerate decisions endorsed by their delegates that clearly damage their own interests? In some sucker-lands there is even the absurdity of a deal called 'co-participation' in which national taxes are 'redistributed' to the states. In other words, the central government sucks up most of the resources and then throws discretional crumbs to those governors who belong to 'the party' and behave well. In its more perverse form, the national government doles out 'aid' to firms and individuals, which in the long run makes them prisoners of the whims of the ruling ideology. I am not against aid per se, mind you, just fear that the excuse only exacerbates a pyramidal system that is already out of balance. In the end, supposedly 'free' citizens have to sell their souls to some ideological servitude just so they can get a meal. Bad omen.

The trend probably prospers because there are always poor neighbors who think that they may be able to get some extra money out of their rich 'brothers.' It happens a lot in countries where the distribution of resources is very uneven. But also, where there are strong cultural differences. The lazy and undisciplined are always trying to get a cut out of their hardworking and disciplined neighbors. It's far easier than having to set their own affairs straight and do the work!

But putting aside these special cases, there seems to be a more general underlying phenomenon. One issue is that we are unable to gauge the long-term effects of small changes that seem trivial, justified, something we can tolerate. But after a decade or a century a shady few are multi-billionaires and we are ruined, decimated. Elites have financial advisors who can create mathematical models to predict the long-term effects of the smallest changes, run simulations by computer and a host of technicians to measure the effects of each political nuance. By comparison, most political delegates (representatives) are inept rookies. They spend millions on their campaigns, but then refuse to spend a cent to evaluate the impacts of their decision. After all, they have already gained power.

Why waste time and money on such trivia? I already know how this works!

Hmm, maybe. Perhaps the responsibility to evaluate these proposed changes rests on the voters, those who delegated their power, rather than on their envoys. They should be the ones who control the actions of their delegates. But in all too many cases 'the people' do not know how to do this or are so oppressed that they have neither the resources nor the energy. Besides, in many modern political monopolies, the people's organizations have much stronger ties to the party bigwigs than to their constituents.

The internal hierarchy is one of the problems with unions. The other is also structural, but it has different effects. As we have seen, all the universe is organized in holarchies and thus all social structures follow these patterns. Simplifying a bit, we can visualize it as a number of small functional pyramids that amalgamate to form more encompassing pyramids. The operational and functional links are 'vertical.' The novelty of labor unions was to create horizontal links by levels or strata. No question that this is valid because it reorganizes into groups that have shared problems and needs. But it also generates other problems. When you attempt to impose general solutions to very diverse systems, that inflexibility frequently ends up destroying the resource that feeds them. The supposed beneficiaries of these measures end up being the victims of the collapse of the firm they worked for.

Too abstract perhaps? Suppose a union manages to secure a 3% raise (or 30%, no matter), which is valid for leading firms in the business, and this raise is imposed by law all over the land. It is quite likely that this degree of raise will force some of the smaller more peripheral firms to close or go bankrupt. From bad to worse. Aside from destroying local and regional workplaces, the indirect effect is that these spaces are rapidly occupied by the great corporations that, as a rule, are much more ruthless and indifferent than the 'feudal landlords' ever were. The 'solution' plays into globalization and steepens the social pyramid.

One of the greatest tragedies of the populist movements of the past century has been to foment class hatred. It always existed, granted, but now it seems to have become 'institutionalized.' It is understandable that at a given time in history this seemed the only way to put an end to brutal abuses and inequities. But when a society returns to a normal state of law and order, class hatred is a tragedy that only serves to deepen the rift and justify violations and abuses, both ways mind you.

This can best be seen in one of those sucker countries, Sucker-land for short. The *Juan Perez*, Latino for *'John Does,'* are doing quite well so they move to a bigger house in a posher neighborhood. And get some domestic help, naturally. After a time, 'the *servant*' gets fed up and disappears. Did she steal?

My God, how terrible, she abandoned us! That ......! You can't trust these _xxx_ anymore. Of course, you idiot, what did you expect? The contrast of privileges is abysmal. Emulating Abraham, you treated her like a slave, she was expected to work almost 24/7, (maybe got a Sunday afternoon off if she was lucky), you systematically underpaid her, in *'black'* (that is, off the record, without a contract, social security, health benefits or retirement plan). Your kids are hooligans that constantly mistreat her; not to mention those cases where some *macho* of the house uses and abuses her whenever he can (for free, of course), and so on. As they never bothered to make a contract, they don't even know her full name, nor can they file a police report... *But the culprit is 'the maid'!*

For sure, the flip side also occurs. As the saying goes, *"you give them a hand and they rip off your arm."* The workers do as little as possible, the indispensable; out of spite they mar, break, and abandon everything; they steal systematically; they call in 'ill' as often as they can get away with, and tag on to any strike and rally they can find an excuse for; and so on. *And then, when their firm goes bankrupt, they bitch and rant because they lost their jobs!* What did they expect? After all, they did everything in their power to destroy the firm! **Tough luck**!

When I think of modern capitalism and the corporate frenzy, the image that comes to mind is of a herd of wild buffalo stampeding down a hillside... and God looking down thinking:

Gee, look at those dumb buffalo, they're going to run straight over that cliff.

We can argue for days on the moral components of these situations, but there is a more fundamental underlying aspect that is common to these and many other situations. Both sides seem blind to the structural dependencies and functional limitations of organizations. Every social organization implies teamwork. All its members are interdependent to some degree. Without an acceptable contract for all involved the team works poorly or doesn't work at all, it breaks up or collapses. It is hard to see in something as large as a factory, but think of so many successful music groups that broke up because they could not come to a viable agreement.

How is this so?

The issue of domestic help is one of the most incongruent. They contract someone to look after them and their precious children, they bring that person into the very heart of their personal life, they spend a large part of the day with them, much more time than they spend with their own friends, for sure. They expect to be respected, cared for and pampered, **and then they treat them like shit!** Hard to understand.

As we saw, in simple societies functional structures overlap so much with personal bonds that there is a certain equilibrium. Which is not to say there are no abuses, but let's just say 'it all stays in the family.' But modern society is not a family. And it is becoming less so as time passes.

Let's start with corporations, which are easier to understand. The usual idea is that a corporation is a form of private enterprise commandeered by the owners. Many are so recent that we know the creators of the original family firm, most of whom are like gurus in the business world. But as the firm grows and these individuals retire, the nature of the organization itself changes. If the stock base is increased, or if takeovers or fusions occur, the once major shareholder participation is diluted. Eventually these original large shareholders pass away, and their fortunes are subdivided and distributed. Inevitably the firm ceases to be the typical 'private firm' and turns into a 'corporation.' So, what is the difference? Better we see it graphically (Figure 29).

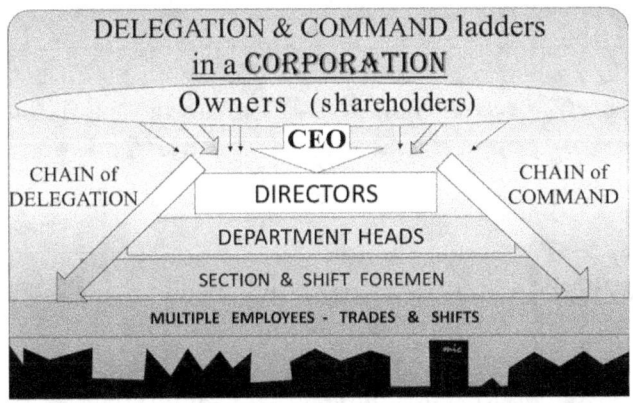

*Figure 29. **Structural hierarchy in a corporation**. – The chain of delegation and the chain of command are concordant, **but they are no longer direct**. The increase in the number of shareholders means they must delegate almost all the operational control to the board of Directors. Therefore, it is **the CEO and the Directors who have the effective power and operational control over the organization**.*

The problem here is that the interests of the directors are <u>**not**</u> the same as the interests of the owners. Slowly the board of directors will gain more and more power, better salaries and privileges, and the benefits to the shareholders will become ever slimmer. Logical perhaps, since the owners no longer have to spend time tending the business, but nonetheless the nature of the organization is no longer the same.

These asymmetries give rise to a phenomenon that was rarer in the past, that one day members of 'the board' slip off with all the money and disappear (a form of 'gutting' the firm), leaving both the shareholders and the employees stranded and penniless. But it is hardly novel either.

Delegating too much power in a satrap, a vizir, commandant or general has always been a formula for catastrophe. At some point the subordinate acquires more power than the king or emperor and dethrones him, literally.

Even though they run by slightly different rules, the syndicates and the corporations begin to look alike. The interests of the 'directors' increasingly drift away from the interests of the 'owners.'

A question of numbers...

Though it might be less obvious, these trends or processes are repeated in regional and national government structures. But with the added problem of the numbers impact we saw in the previous chapters, which turns something that was just a possibility into a virtual certainty. As the population increases the ties between the bigwigs and their people weaken, and the sums they are dealing with increase dramatically. If the risk of punishment, the 'cost,' is low or nonexistent, **corruption escalates to such outrageous degrees that even the richest and most powerful countries cannot withstand it**.

In antiquity the punishments tended to be quite drastic. If he was lucky enough not to get crucified directly, the thief ran the risk of having his hands cut off or punishments of the sort. Today these penalties seem a bit exaggerated. Besides, they don't seem to have been all that effective. So, how can we generate institutional mechanisms that lessen these problems or compensate for crimes like political corruption and similar infringements of the law? Let's return to the idea of homeostasis (or autopoiesis?). They involve regulating mechanisms used by all living organisms that usually include negative feedback loops (if it gets hot, turn off the heater). For instance, fund ex politicians' benefits using the foreign debt coupons they issued, redeeming them at their nominal value. Of course, no politician in his right mind would agree to such an act of justice. You would have to push it through with a widespread direct and binding public motion (plebiscite). Not likely to happen in the foreseeable future. Perhaps we should develop a way to pool bribes in favor of popular interests. It might not stop the corruption, but at least it would raise the stakes.

But aside from the touch of irony, it should not be necessary to go to such extremes. If you choose your politicians wisely you would not have those problems. Countries differ widely in their attitudes towards their politicians and their transgressions. In places you might hear comments like

Ha, ha, what a rogue, he had a lover and he fooled us all·

Well, it's normal· -

Normal? In Suckerland it might be normal. Some years ago, I was in a northern country in the middle of one of these scandals that rocked the political career of a candidate, and I pointed out that in South American it was common, that nobody would be bothered by an infidelity in the guy's private life. The response was categorical - *"If he lies to his spouse, he will lie to us also. **We don't want a liar as our political representative.**"* – Goodbye to his political career!

All of which takes us to a critical issue, justice. If the justice system is heavily influenced or handpicked by the ruling 'party,' it is very unlikely that justice will be impartial, objective. Political in-groups, abetting of friends, bribery, political dependence, and compliance, all these issues are enemies of impartial justice. It is one of the more nefarious aspects of all 'partisanships' (most of the ...isms, including communism). Aside from the circumstantial abuses and injustices, complex systems are stable to the extent that the internal regulatory mechanisms work adequately. If they fail or weaken, the result is analogous to the development of a cancer. Corruption ends up killing the host.

In any event, faced with all these novel situations we need to be a lot more creative. Most of the 'popular' protest methods like demonstrations and protest rallies, rapidly generate political immunity (and impunity). In third world countries we have seen these methods used for decades and little has changed. People are conveniently spurned to put the blame on the 'aristocracy' ('*oligarchy*' is often the catch word), but then they assign this role to the wrong stratum. Modern day 'oligarchs' are often politicians and their henchmen, as in all ages, really. Instead, by now many old-time traditional aristocrats are in the dumps. Few undertakings are more easily accomplished than squandering a fortune. And it is one of the few endeavors you can be sure to receive an unlimited amount of help with...

==================== II ====================

Chapter II.57 –

Politics and subjectivity

Often folks are not conscious or ambivalent about the influence of religion in matters of governance. They likely believe that having their points of view represented is a good policy, which seems perfectly OK in a democracy.

The problems become evident when those same 'points of view' constitute the dogmatic base of a theocracy. You might think that I mean some theocracy in particular, but politics is no different. They tend to follow the same evolution as empires, dictatorships, or any of those regimes with strong ideological convictions.

So then, what's the problem? Any political or religious form of governance based on dogma, on ideology, is top down by definition, either strongly or totalitarian. In this, politics and religion overlap and fuse. The same happens with dictatorships, kingdoms, empires. The most important issue is the survival of the '*head.*' As a result, decisions are inevitably **subjective.** That is, they are born of the personal interests and the prejudices of a Subject. Individualisms are born of the ego of the 'enthroned' (I did..., I say..., I..., I..., I...), rather than from ideals or the needs of the system. People aren't eternal (*thank God!*), but at times their influence can linger.

The narrower the ideology, the more restrictive are the options. Paradigmatic examples are the military governments that gripped Latin America during the 20th century. When a military junta needs to select an official, they tend to give priority to other members of the armed forces who, as a rule, haven't got the slightest idea of the specific issues they are supposed to govern. The results are all too often catastrophic, beyond the good or bad intentions of the agents. The modern world is very complex, and it is very unlikely that someone with no specific training will be able to handle these very specific roles just because of some *political decision.* This also affects many elected politicians that got to their functions more as the result of party sympathies than of their technical or administrative competence. **Political subjectivity has a price**.

So, what is wrong with this? If you are methodologically *subjective*, it is much more probable that you will make mistakes, errors of judgment. Sometimes these mistakes can be compensated by the use of force, but not all the errors are evident from the start. With time, the accumulation of these errors leads to the stagnation or collapse of the 'regime' with a huge cost to society, quite aside from its moral standing.

As this is not obvious, let's take a closer look. Suppose you need to name a bigwig to run the Agricultural office. The usual procedure would be to select a list of candidates based on their resumes (competence, work or administrative experience, academic degrees, etc.) and from there narrow it down to a 'short list.' A corporation would go ahead with this information and choose the most qualified candidate, either technically or businesswise. A political oligarchy would give precedence to an added component of political affiliation that has no bearing on the candidates' competence in that role. As this is often considered <u>very</u> important, it is not unusual that the nominee be manifestly <u>in</u>competent for the job. This is analogous to the CEO/directors problem in corporations we saw earlier. The interests of the governing elite are not the same as the interests of 'the people.' Sinking the whole economy of a country is of no concern if it is perceived as necessary to stay in power and continue to stash fortunes (after all, *the ends justify the means*, don't they?).

Something similar happens to technical decisions when they are heavily influenced by the prejudices and preconceptions of some presumed political ideal. Politics is designed to assign responsibilities and allot costs and benefits. These aspects necessarily have a subjective component, which in no way means all acts of governance should be abetted by these subjective excuses (*"… for political reasons"*). Above all, in issues that are not related to the allotment of wealth, only to its generation, and to other operational issues like traffic laws. When societies do not flow operationally, **there is ever less to distribute**.

The problems affecting dogmas are more evident with regards to religions, but they are by no means restricted to them. Politics, education, and economics are also influenced by dogmatic stances.

Even amongst scientists it is a problem. Any 'consensual truth' tends to become part of the dogma, the ruling paradigm. When someone shows that reality no longer 'fits' as it was supposed to, it is common to criticize the methods employed or even the quality of the researchers, *rather than questioning the validity of the established dogma!* In one sense, that is good. Demanding irrefutable proof is a reasonable precaution. But these rigid dogmatic structures are poorly adapted to a rapidly changing world.

Still, it is in religions where the tyranny of anachronic dogmas has its worst impact. The notion of something being a *'dogma of faith'* provides the preacher with total impunity, more than in other spheres (politics, science, etc.). To say that *"it is the Word of God"* gives unappealable authority to any crazy whim or technical lunacy on the part of 'priesthood,' no less than a question of 'God,' the most extreme form of top-downness available. Right off the bat, this is the most manipulative package of memes and therefore very dangerous. A first step is to get out of that blind 'believer' mentality.

The equivalent appeal to political dogma is to say that somebody or something is against national interests or sovereignty (*'he is a traitor'* or a spy, and accusations of the sort). But at least in these cases we are all on the same level, all within the sphere of human affairs. You only need to ask yourself: Is this true? What is he trying to sell or to impede when he makes those accusations? Who does it benefit?

What was a groundbreaking idea at the end of the 19th and beginning of the 20th century ended up creating a sort of dogmatic phobia against *'landholding aristocracies'* that today is mostly outdated. There are some, of course, but most of modern wealth is in banks, corporations, franchises, 'churches,' and the like, but not directly in the land. At least in most of the Americas, the famous *'agrarian reform'* was embedded in the equitable inheritance laws (all offspring get equal shares). After several generations of large 'Christian' family units, family-owned land holdings have been put through the mincer. The most pressing problem nowadays is the breakup of productive lands, their inefficiency, which plays into corporate greed that can now 'swallow' them up cheaply and with total impunity. A few years ago, a single forestry company owned over 165,000 acres of prime farmland made up of hundreds of small farms that had previously been 'family owned.' Between the love-hate peasant-landlord relationship of the feudal past and the corporate indifference of the present, it's hard to tell which is worse! *Once again, from the frying pan into the fire*!

Again, it has to do with complexity. In simple societies and structures the dominating tension axis are few and as a rule quite evident. In that scenario, the bipartisan system works reasonably well, efficiently. But as systems and societies get more complex, the axes of conflict multiply and it is not enough with two opinions to solve issues that involve multiple interest groups and visions. Bipartisan systems, especially when they are very politized, end up being dominated by minorities that alternate in power, producing strong fluctuations in public policies. These extremes reinforce and intensify the polarization, so that in both phases of the cycle the opinions and the interests of the *'half plus one'* of the population get ignored. We need to change our strategies.

Anyway, the problems generated by subjective visions and approaches are not just a scientific issue. They affect our everyday political and personal lives at many levels. Having a better understanding of the traps hidden in this domain is an important step to improve your personal choices, to better navigate the social sphere and your economic decisions and transactions.

===================== II =====================

Chapter II.58 –

Averroes' koan

Can God create an indestructible rock?
If he created it, can he destroy it?[30]

Can God create a land of suckers? Surely, we have examples that are pretty good approximations. Once he has created them, will God be able to save them from themselves? *Impossible!* Even the gods have their limits.

Once a country has fallen into a descending dialectic spiral, a negative vicious circle, it seems almost impossible to rescue it. At least, that's what history seems to show us. There are few or no empires that have recovered from a collapse. Many, perhaps most, of the kingdoms and empires that dominated at some point in history today are the poor kids in their block. Check a few examples from the 'old world': **Pakistan** (the first 'city states' of the Indus valley, 3300 to 1300 b. C.); **Egypt** (the Pharaonic kingdoms); **Iran** (the Persian empire, 334 b. C.); **Greece** (Alexander the Great, 336 – 323 b. C.); **India** (the Maurya Empire, 323 - 180 b. C.); **Italy** (the Roman Empire, 30 b. C.– 476 a. D.); the **Holy Roman Empire** (800 to 1800 a. D., with several reigning dynasties and changing frontiers); **Mongolia** (Genghis Khan, 1206-1368); **Turkey** (the Ottoman Empire, 1450 to 1922); **France** (the Napoleonic Empire, 1815); and many more. Even Spain and England could not hold on to the hegemonic rule they once had. Some have managed to retain a place in the 'first world'... barely. In any championship there is only one first place, but that place rotates, every now and then you can win again, and the distances between the first and the rest need not be

---

[30] Averroes (Ibn Rushd, d. 1198), Andalusian philosopher and jurist who analyzed this paradox.

abysmal.

What is striking is not so much that they have not managed to 'win' again. In many cases centuries have gone by and they don't seem to get back on their feet. You could argue that their capital cities survived as the heads of countries, whereas others were wiped off the map. But their societies seem to have remained weakened or destroyed internally. These cycles are so consistent that they demand an explanation. Here we can only speculate.

The most obvious excuse is that the fault lies in those who conquered them. There is some truth in this, no doubt. Sick of the abuses, at the first opportunity the neighbors rampaged everything they could, imposed fierce restrictions and demanded astronomic taxes. What was still standing was decimated.

But there is a flaw to this explanation. The empire was showing signs of senile weakness long before it was conquered. In fact, that is why the neighbors dared invade in the first place. So then, perhaps the more interesting question is: *Why do empires age and deteriorate?*

I don't know if anyone has a good answer to this question, but here goes my hypothesis.

The empire is born of a homogeneous tribe or ethnic group, bound by cooperative social ethics and strong cultural ties. It is not long since they came out of the hunter-gatherer stage, perhaps followed by a herding stage. But they still retain a tradition of combative tenacity. With the advent of agriculture and the increase of their resource base, their population and their power grow, but they still retain the pre-agrarian genetics and ethics, forged in the times when the very survival of the clans depended on the strength of their bonds, their courage and honesty to the group. Loyalty, valor, honor, and service... When the surrounding adversities are very severe, there is no room nor tolerance for the weak, the cowards, the cheats.

But with success the conditions change. What was once the survival of the fittest has lapsed into the survival of the less fit. The more able are enlisted to go off and die in the seemingly endless wars. Those that remain in the towns and cities are the lame, the inept, the cheats, cowards, disloyal, whatever. When this is repeated over decades or even centuries, it is very probable that even the very genetic composition of the population changes. But in any event, it does not matter much if the change includes a genetic component or if it is merely cultural. Inevitably, as the empire prospers and expands its population, all the social and cultural base that gave it birth gets diluted and weakened, including their ethnic identity. Invariably, the empire absorbs elements from the folks it conquered.

Above all, the internal structure gets more and more complex (military, government and administration, bureaucracy, etc.), and the ruling oligarchies progressively **distance** themselves from their old roots. The result is that the initial discipline is slowly replaced by institutionalized corruption and inhouse bickering. It is the beginning of the end of the hegemony. The historical details of the final collapse are anecdotal.

In a nutshell, virtually all kingdoms and empires were born of valiant warriors supported by a handful of loyal followers who were personally committed to them, leading their people into battle from the very front line. After decades or centuries, those empires died with obese rulers and their opulent retinue bunkered in their golden palaces as their kingdoms crumbled.

An important point that rests on this hypothesis is that when an empire breaks down, as a rule it gets subdivided into smaller units that frequently match those that were conquered initially, **but with a huge difference**. Those nations are reborn with all the administrative and social vices inherited from the empire according to the stage it was at when it collapsed, including a good deal of the genetic and cultural muddle. **Entrenched corruption becomes endemic**. Only the more peripheral regions that had not yet been overrun and integrated have a chance of escaping this fate. If the proportion of invaders is still low, the region has some chance of recovering its previous identity and of resurfacing as an independent power center.

Yet, to the residents all seems well. After all, that's how rulers are, it's the norm, isn't it? It did not even occur to them that there might be a better way, nor did they have any way of comparing. This probably explains why technical and social evolution has been so slow in the past. But the situation has changed dramatically over the last decades. Today the results of the different **social experiments** can be compared across countries and regions of the world. For instance, you can compare the economic evolution of different countries as a function of the degree of education they enjoy, or the degree of corruption they suffer.

But going from a better understanding to a wide enough social agreement so as to change the course of a countries' future is not at all easy. There are always 'sectorial interests' that want conditions to stay as they are. Historically, the way change has been approached is through civil wars, or as a consequence of some major upheaval such as a regional war or similar catastrophe. Clean slate and new account. But these routes are very, very costly in many ways, and there is no guarantee of success. *Troubled waters spell gains for profiteers.*

Any form of centralization of power sets the stage for increasing greed and corruption. As time in office passes and the feeling of impunity increases, the governing cliques become bolder and accumulate more and more economic crimes mostly designed to hoard personal fortunes. Silencing the accusations takes more and more energy and very easily falls into violent repression, which adds another layer of crimes to the mix. In time, ever more corrupt leaders and their henchmen accumulate such a huge criminal record that the only way to survive impeachment and jail is to hang on to power at whatever cost. The outcome is almost inevitable, a ruthless dictatorship of one sort or another.

Unfortunately, 'unlimited possibilities' includes the bad ones. If you have the misfortune of living in one of those suckered countries that seems to have fallen into a negative spiral of corruption and violence, you'd better start thinking of novel solutions, because little of what history has to teach us will be of much help to you. Most of our current political conceptions and systems were developed in the wake of the agrarian feudal system, as societies moved into the industrial age. Though agrarian–industrial may look different, they share a common feature: structurally they are both relatively simple, linear. Therefore, the old notion of command and control organized in a pyramidal structure still worked fairly well in local industrial contexts. The problem we have today is that the world, our world, is no longer 'linear.' It has become increasingly complex. In such a world, stiff pyramidal dictatorships stifle competitiveness and stunt economic growth. These politicians may win their games, but the societies they rule over end up losing the championship.

----------------- o -------------------

Money, money, money... Talking of big numbers ...

Recently there was a news item about a government scam involving sums in the order of 44 billion dollars. Mean anything to you? Or consider the gross national product of Spain, 1.244 trillion Dollars in 2019. If you are the president of this country and you must negotiate and administer deals of this magnitude you might expect to get 3% as commission, as happens in the real estate business and many others. Which means the President of Spain should be getting about 41 790 000 000 (41 billion) a year. Currently (2023 data) the richest man on earth is probably Elon Musk, who's personal fortune is valued at U$D 288 600 000 000. So, at the end of his term, the President should be about equally rich, or at least in the top ten club. Clearly this would be delirious, but I mention it to make a point. This is where many of the problems of modern governments lie. The discrepancy between the normal needs of any person and the astronomical sums a high-ranking official must deal with stretches the balance between duty and temptation to degrees that were unthinkable only a few generations ago. Our systems are simply not prepared to deal with this discrepancy. As a result, corruption easily becomes endemic.

This ties in with the notion of the upcoming 'singularity,' the moment when artificial intelligence surpasses human intelligence[31]. Data storage and retrieval has become amazingly efficient. Take a well-known citizen-science based web page that has logged over 150,000,000 bird lists representing over 2 billion sightings from all over the world, including well over half a billion photographs and recordings (to May 2025). Users can retrieve their own lists and associated media within milliseconds, or do world-wide searches for any species in minutes at most. These records also allow scientists to map and track bird migrations across the globe, including real-time seasonal movements, for instance.

If a 'simple' science program can do this, just imagine what a very well-funded national agency like the KGB or the CIA can do. The chances of anybody 'living under the radar' are dwindling rapidly. Which begs the question. If government agencies are so good at tracking us, why aren't they equally good at tracking the 'migration' of money by corrupt politicians and their scams?

Localize, parcel the cake before it gets too big.

===================== II =====================

---

[31] If you think I'm being tedious with the numbers, try reading Ray Kurzweil's *The Singularity is Near* (2005).

Chapter II.59
Politics and complexity

As we saw in Chapter II.34 about the collectival, we can order and classify the huge variety of groups and systems in several ways based on three primary variables. The **number of items**, which take us from **simple to complicated**. There are many collectives and processes that fit this category. Their structure and the organizing criterion are simple. In the case of processes, we say they are **linear.**

Complexity escalates when we move to interaction networks, the different ways in which these items can be linked. More complex webs appear when individuals are autonomous, have their own power, and this takes us to living beings. Us. A further Increase in interactions over a certain limit tends to disorganize the system, leading up to chaos. Recall Figure 23 (see below).

The industrial revolution was a profound change that promoted the creation of military style management structures, based on the notion of *'command and control,'* which led to all kinds of abuses. This in turn gave rise to a new religion, communism, and its instruments of defense (mass movements and the organization of unions). We already saw some of the structural risks of labor organizations. Unfortunately for both sides, these approaches work for linear (complicated) systems but are much too rigid for complex systems and situations.

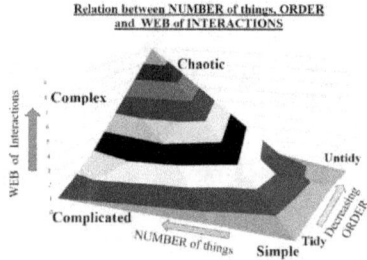

Repeat of Figure 23. relating **complexity, complicatedness,** and **order.** – Simple can have several individuals and interactions, but no crossed links. Complex systems have many individuals and interaction networks. If interactions intensify, they become chaotic. – Simple collectives are abundant (gray base). Complex ones less so. True chaos is rare in macroscopic systems.

The appropriate or necessary strategies to work in multidisciplinary teams, to adapt to changing situations, to compete in diverse markets and above all to develop innovative solutions on an almost daily basis are virtually opposite to the top-down mentality of *command and control*. **The result is that organizations and countries full of creative youths end up smothered by old cronies who don't understand the notion of complexity,** but who don't want to give way to those who do, nor let go of an ounce of the power they control (for fear they will get trampled, no doubt). Steve Jobs, the creator of Apple, pointed out that: *"It doesn't make sense to hire smart people and then tell them what to do; we hire smart people so they can **tell us** what to do."* Logical, yes, but the opposite happens all the time: "We command, and you obey."

But then, how do you handle chaotic situations?

In the beginning there was chaos and God created order. **Nonsense!** In the very, very beginning there was perfect order (very low entropy) and God decided to go ***Bang!*** (a **very BIG** bang) and generated total chaos (to have a bit of fun and see what happens, I suppose). Amongst other appeals, religion has always served as an antidote to the unpredictable, the swings of nature and the whims of the gods. It tells us how things supposedly work and that calms our fears. In this sense, whether the dogmas are true or false seems to be irrelevant. It must be something like the placebo effect. Unfortunately, this often leads us to put our expectations in the wrong place. Science has helped, because it greatly reduces the unknown and unpredictable factors in many of the areas we feared in the past: diseases, weather, volcanos, eclipses, etc.

Our modern social world has become complex, ever more complex, but we are still stuck in these old management and political conceptions, from the seventies or earlier in the case of many South American countries. Today mass productions are handled with robots and robots don't join unions. The very idea of a union or guild, in the sense of a group of people who live off a specific trade or specialized craft, is becoming ever rarer. Very narrow specialists have ever narrower opportunities. Many trades and jobs that seemed very important at one time have disappeared completely (how many weavers or rope makers do you know?). New opportunities require totally different abilities: social interaction, teamwork, adaptability, changing work chores, constant updating, etc.

Here is where modern democracies, in particular those of developing countries, are suffering grave problems. Politicians that go on ranting about old paradigms seem to have more followers than anyone who proposes innovations, which is perhaps quite foreseeable since innovators speak a language few people understand. *"This guy is delirious. He's certainly trying to pull a fast one on us. Better stay with the old and tested."* But in a competitive and changing world, hanging on to the old models is a formula for failure. An example may help. For those of us who were here before the turn of the century KODAK was a worldwide leading name in photography. According to entrepreneurial mythology, when digital photography first appeared Kodak management expressly decided to stick with their line of 'paper' products instead of switching to digital. Terrible mistake. In little more than a decade it lost its leadership and may never recover it (in 2012 it was declared bankrupt). Organizational Darwinism, those who do not adapt, perish.

---------------------- O ----------------------

But these considerations are rather macro. What about the individual, what can you do? I think one of the most difficult notions to accept is that today our everyday life is **much** more dependent on the system, the social structures, than it has ever been in the history of humanity. And this has little to do with your economic standing. In fact, the rich are often quite incompetent when it comes to fending for themselves. If they don't have energy and running water, a supermarket at hand, gas stations, home delivery of precooked foods, etc., they are completely helpless and useless! Plus, a banking system that offers credit cards to make good their worth, status, and riches, and a legal system that looks after their privileges: all is well only if we have the system to look after us.

Though it may seem a contradiction, the poor often have more personal survival skills than the rich. Unfortunately, though, this incapacity is spreading to all the population. The migration of rural people to big cities and the increasing lure of state aid sustains, and even creates, large communities that are ever more dependent on the state, and therefore on the politicians in office. If you are having a rough time, going hungry, it is understandable that you would be in favor of these measures, but it would be much better if they gave you the tools and means to fend for yourself and regain your self-sufficiency.

This is the change you have to fight for. And part of that change is to strengthen the local economies, 'localize,' the counterpoint of 'globalize.' Just in case, I am not referring to ideas like agrarian reform and the likes. Few people are willing to go back to a rural life and the sacrifices of small-time farming. I mean to recover local representation in the political system, to give back to the local and intermediate segments of governance the power and importance they once had, and to revert the tax pyramid so as to strengthen local economies. Work local, without losing sight of the global. Now, if you live in parts of Europe or North America this might sound out of place, but trust me, in other parts of the world the governments are totally top-heavy and the social asymmetries close to breaking point. I very much doubt widespread social upheaval is to the interest of the first world, especially when many of those societies are deluded into thinking they will be 'saved' by associating with your competition.

It seems societies are managed top-down, but they are built bottom-up. If the basements fail the societies crumble. **A delicate equilibrium** between the local and the global, but crucial.

And then, again... (another tedious issue, but it's important)

No matter how complex and sophisticated the systems may be, they never completely escape the basic Laws of *ah!* One of these laws is mathematical and has to do with combinations. We can see it with a pair of dice. If we throw the dice and add the points, which is the most likely outcome? And which is the least likely? Even without any calculations, I can assure you the most probable outcome is the middle or average one, and the least are the extremes, the largest and the smallest. Why?

The smallest number you can get with the throw of two dice is TWO (a 1 in each), and the highest is TWELVE (a 6 in each). The midpoint between 2 and 12 is 7. So then, SEVEN is the most frequent result and TWO and TWELVE are the rarest (or most improbable). With two dice you can add to SEVEN in six different ways: 1+6, 2+5, 3+4 and the converse, 6+1, 5+2, 4+3.

Result	2	3	4	5	6	7	8	9	10	11	12
Frequency	1	2	3	4	5	**6**	5	4	3	2	1

Table 6. Frequency distribution of the sum of two dice thrown at random.

If we use more dice, the chain of results will be longer and there will be more possible combinations, but the shape of the distribution is always similar (Figure 30). There are variants and combinations, but for additive systems the general idea is largely universal. When the number of elements is high, the distribution takes the shape of a bell, the Gaussian curve. Cassinos are experts at estimating these probabilities. That's how they make money. An important variation occurs when one end is truncated due to some limitation, which gives a similar but asymmetric curve.

This is so, it's one of *ah!*'s Laws. Take a slightly more complicated case. You have ten books by different authors on your bookshelf. You could order them by author, by title, by publication date, by subject, etc. If you chose '*strictly alphabetical by author*' there is only **one** 'correct' way out of over 3.6 million possible alternative sequences! (Mathematically, '*ten factorial,*' or 10 x 9 x 8 x 7 x 6 x 5 x 4 x 3 x 2 x 1 = 3,628,800 ways). That's why tidying up takes effort, but things seem to get untidy spontaneously. What does this have to do with politics? Simple. Social structures that approach the extremes are more improbable, more rigid, and therefore require much more energy to sustain them. Those that hover around the median disorder are more probable, more flexible, and therefore require less energy to sustain them.

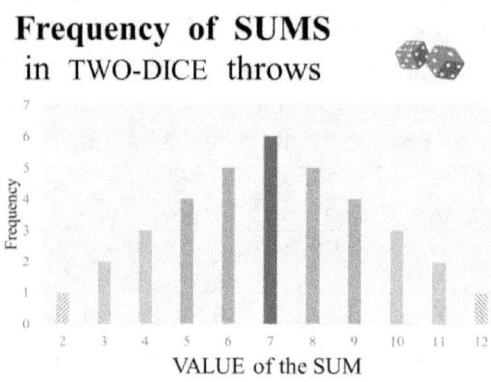

Frequency of SUMS in TWO-DICE throws

VALUE of the SUM

Figure 30. Frequency distributions.

The predicted distribution of the frequency of the **sum** of two dice cast randomly. The extreme values (2 and 12) are the rarest. Intermediate values (**5 to 9**) are the most frequent. This form of distribution dominates all systems with additive components.

In other words, structurally speaking, extreme capitalism and extreme communism are almost identical, and both tend to fall into strongly authoritarian or dictatorial regimes to sustain themselves. This includes those hybrid variants that might be called religious imperialisms. Instead, those that hover around some average, like socialisms, federalisms, and decentralized liberalisms should be easier to sustain **without** the imposition of dictatorial regimes.

All very logical, but in practice it doesn't seem to be so easy. Why? I think a central point is the combination of greed inherent to human biology, the polarization of political power structures and the difficulty we have in anticipating the cumulative effects of small changes.

As we saw above, many biological attributes result from the additive effect of many genes and circumstances. This produces traits with continuous distributions. Since the probability distribution explained above underlies all additive random process, such as coins flips, the **frequency** of individual values within this range follows a Normal (Gaussian) distribution. Average individuals are the most common. Extremes are rare, but they are, none the less, expected to occur in low frequencies.

Most of us are average, common if you will, but a few of us are off to some extreme: very tall or short, muscular or skinny, agile or clumsy, and so on. Those individuals that fall on the extremes of greed, authoritarianism, social skills, dishonesty or the likes, tend to favor equally extreme solutions or social policies. If the rest of the population doesn't develop defense mechanisms, the result is a strong polarization of society and the breakdown of the social contract.

Somewhat simplistically, political and religious extremism is often based on individuals with strong personalities that incite and drag 'the masses' (that's us), but that tend to derail once they grab power. You can boil it down to four types that affect social and political response: charisma, megalomania, narcissism, and greed (Figure 31). **Every now and then we get an extreme case**. Unfortunately, we tend to get bored with the 'average' person, but we feel a fatal attraction to these charismatic egocentric megalomaniacs. Another very captivating alternative is a populist demagogue who promises some form of 'salvation.' Most of these traits are good predictors of a future dictator. Amongst other tactics, most dictators tend to polarize power (and then destroy the opposition and assassinate the competition). We need to develop antibodies against these forms of manipulation of our instincts and sharpen the social tools to identify those features that should serve as warning or alarm signs (see box below).

Don't just listen to the content of the speech. It's equally important to observe the body language (watch the speech muted), read between the lines, see where the speech is leading to, who are and what are the candidate's buddies doing. Your future depends on the sharpness of your appraisal of the politico-religious personalities that intend or claim to govern your society.

One attempt to understand dictators is the miniseries '*How to Become a Tyrant*' –, a Netflix 6-episode event released in 2021. – But DANGER. The series is interesting, but the material is presented as a 'playbook' (*i.e.*, a *manual*), apparently intended as a satire, which is unfortunate. Prospective tyrants must have a psychopathic streak that won't get the irony, so the material is just as likely to entice them to take a shot at it as it is to deter them, or to warn us. One of the last comments in the series is that *"anybody can be a tyrant."* Perhaps, but this contradicts the fact, stressed in the series itself, that all modern tyrants have been **males**, many are pathological narcissists, and surely show other telltale symptoms, as do the circumstances under which these tyrannies emerged (*e.g.*, 'revolutions,' see Chapter II.53). Rather than a 'playbook,' we, the future victims, need an effective *diagnostic manual* to recognize incipient individuals and situations that might lead to dictatorships *before* they get out of hand.

Why does Politics tend to polarize? The mediator's predicament

Mediating between clashing postures or personalities is a noble but risky job. It's very easy to end up becoming the target of the fight. Let me illustrate the problem. There seems to be no way Black and White will ever come to agree. Someone proposes a mediator, who then starts talking to the relevant parties. Quite logically, the mediator tries to maintain a neutral stance, neither black nor white. The fatal error occurs when he becomes Mr. **Gray**. From the perspective of the Whites, a *'gray'* looks like the Blacks, for sure. But then, mixed amongst the Blacks, he looks very much like the Whites! In the end what often happens is that *everybody* shuns the 'Gray' position, and the issue polarizes again. Politically speaking, this is a real disaster because it seems the only way to achieve a measure of political stability is to reach some degree of compromise between the 'poles' (metaphorically, some shade of 'gray').

The error is to stay stuck in the same axis that generated the problem, the same polarity. To stick with the color metaphor, the mediator needs to dress with any color that is not in the range of white-gray-black. Let's say green, pink or light blue. In other words, he must **move out** of the polar opposition line that has been dominating the issue till then. Putting the emphasis out of the battlegrounds helps them find some common ground.

Polarization is the strength, and at the same time the Achilles heel of bipartisan politics. For almost a century Latin America has oscillated between capitalism and communism, between Washington and Moscow. Perhaps with some justification, dreamers want to escape the yoke of Yankee imperialism. But what is totally absurd is that the solution they propose is to submit to Russian imperialism. It's hard to understand what makes them think the Russians are going to be less 'imperialistic' than the

Gringos. An empire is an empire, and the Russians have been an empire for far longer, since the days of Ivan the Terrible, 150 years before Columbus!

Figure 31. **The Four Bulls of Discord**. Extreme expressions of features that are present in all of us. Greed, charisma, narcissism, and megalomania are additive traits that affect our social and political behavior. 'Average' guys bore us, but we feel a fatal attraction to charismatic narcissistic megalo-maniacs. Another alluring variant is a populist demagogue who promises 'salvation.' These traits portend future dictators, who tend to polarize power (divide and rule).

People are still hooked by the communist ideal, the utopia, but what is actually put into practice is not the idealized version. The Manifesto was put forth by two altruistic minded, law-abiding Europeans, Germans in fact, who clearly believed their ideals would be applied *'for the good of the people.'* Ideals, however, need to be put into practice by rulers, humans, who unfortunately are seldom simple 'altruistic, law abiding' citizens. The last hundred years of history have shown that those ideals, once taken up and into societies whose culture makes people more prone to break the rules than abide by them, more individualistic, self-centered and even corrupt, will rapidly degenerate into something else, something more in the fashion of a populist dictatorship. Once a centralized all-powerful party-docracy takes over, the interests of the 'party' and its leadership override any vestige of 'altruism.' This is what has taken over several countries, in South America at least, closer to what we might call Kremlinism. The formula peddled through the Cuban regime must be as far from the idealized utopia as you can get. The rhetoric may be populist, the practice is not.

In capitalism the danger is similar, that as an ever-richer minority ends up gaining full control of government, it turns into a plutocracy. The paths are different, the result is about the same. In theory capitalism and communism may look different, but in their more extreme forms they are structurally very similar, or at least, lead to similar outcomes. Both lie at one end on the 'order' spectrum, and hence need ever stronger controls to be enforced ('everybody owns the same amount' is just as extreme as 'we few own everything'). Both foster centralization and steepen the hierarchical pyramid. Once these regimes gain full control, they can eat their 'serfs' alive, and often do so.

The tragedy of this obsolete polarization is that it obscures any possibility of finding other solutions that don't depend on any of these imperial options (Figure 32). The economist Eric Hobsbawm tells us that every economic system has a beginning, a period of success and an end. The next system is born during the heyday of the previous one, and the previous one dies during the heyday of the next. So then, what system is being born right now? What can we aspire to, or what should we fear?

The modern world has changed, it's different. Granted, unrestrained capitalism does not bode well, but the communist 'revolution' no longer evolves, it failed, it is an empty promise. You need to allow for change. Change from shades of grey to a pallet of colors, imagine new solutions, different from any we are aware of today. Will you need allies? For many of the countries in Latin America the natural allies are the Europeans. Yes, I know, *"They were the empires that colonized us. It took blood, sweat and tears to free ourselves from them!"*

But that was centuries ago. Today Europe is not the same. They suffered the perils and hardships of several personalistic autocratic dictatorships and paid for those mistakes with devastating wars. One hopes they have learnt and have tried out several more equanimous forms of governance. Even though it's a step towards globalization, the members of the European Union have managed to retain their localisms, their identities. The few monarchies that have survived are largely parodies of their former glories, mere tourist attractions. The European Union is a federation, it flows, the members seem to respect each other, it's something else! Neither white nor black. *Golden, perhaps?*

I am not saying this is a panacea of some sort, but it's an option for Latin American countries that should allow them to get out of the Communist-Capitalist ideological tug-of-war and give them time to reconstruct in some new direction and soon, because several countries in the region are already in a very precarious situation.

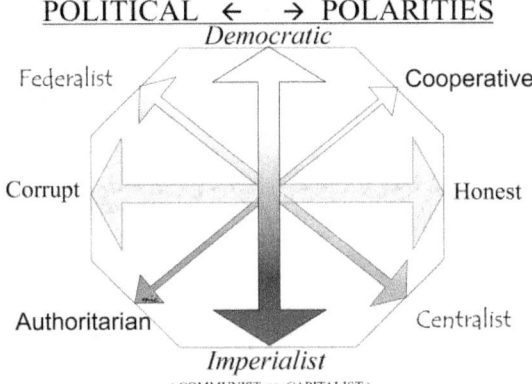

POLITICAL ← → POLARITIES

Figure 32. **A vane of Political Polarities**. – The (Latin American) obsession with the **capitalist <–> communist** polarity obscures many other oppositions and alternatives that have as much or more impact on the destiny of a country and the wellbeing of its people.

The down side of arrogance

Throughout history, rulers and even whole societies who have become dominant in some way tend to develop some form of ethnic, religious or political arrogance: *'we are the best,'* *'ours is the true god,'* *'our way of life is the best,'* and so on. Arrogance is a powerful driver, so both individuals and societies seem to thrive on it. Many would argue that it's not arrogance, just pride, but from the perspective of outsiders *that* distinction can be hard to see.

But aside from these subtleties, what are the side effects of arrogance? Arrogance is a bit like prejudice (Chapters II.57 and III.72), it blinds us to the weaknesses inherent in any system or situation.

Take the age-old practice of slavery. It was always 'justified' on the assumption that the slaves were in some way inferior (after all, they lost the war) and that the conquerors were far superior. As a result, some of those losers, primarily able males and females, were taken into the midst of the conquering society as slaves. Aside from the abuse and injustice, this amounts to the import of 'lesser' genetic variants and future problems. The inevitable genetic mixing tends to erase the original racial identities of both sides, losers and winners.

The impact of colonial abuses is not limited to slavery. Many modern European countries that once enjoyed the privilege of being colonial overlords are now beginning to face the consequences.

Even less smart was the widespread notion in the Americas of *'breeding'* their slaves. Wars and disease soon decimated the local indigenous populations. Bringing slaves across from Africa was not only brutal, but quite expensive. Better breed them locally. Biologically speaking, the net effect for those ethnicities was a 'free' ticket to the new world and the establishment of very robust populations in these lands. In Jamaica over 90 % of the local population is of African origin, close to 2.5 million; about 120 million in Brazil, near 56 %; about 40 million in the USA; and so on. Not only do they thrive: in time they might well rule the land.

This seems to be one of the general problems with complex systems. Decisions and actions at one level frequently loop back to the source, modifying or destroying the original intended effect, or creating other unforeseen problems. One current example is Satoshi Nakamoto's bitcoins, '*a peer-to-peer electronic cash system*' that was meant to avoid the need for banking institutions as intermediaries for economic transactions. Granted, it has been quite successful in achieving this, but this very 'advantage' has given every drug dealer, terrorist and corrupt politician a safe haven in which to conduct their fraudulent activities. Hard to tell what the overall net effect on society will be, but it's a good reminder that few interventions of complex systems come 'free of charge.'

==================== II ====================

Book II – Links©
Tradition – Science – Religion

Back to the intersubjectal

As we saw earlier, much of the intersubjetal has to do with communication and meaning. The development of new ideas, concepts, formulas, etc. underlies and drives the increase in complexity in this domain. New ideas require new words and mental formulations, so the basic lexicon is enlarged by the evolution of any human activity, including science, politics and religion. We dealt with many aspects of politics in the previous section on the interobjectal perspective because politics aims to modify the material bonds that structure our societies. Now we need to focus a little on science and religion which are more directly linked to the evolution of our society's world views, and the ways we interact.

==================== II ====================

Chapter II.60 –
The eternal cultural dilemma: tradition or innovation?

Tradition seems to justify itself, so there's no need to defend it. Sticking to tradition keeps you in a known and familiar space. It has been valued throughout history and proved to be useful under stable conditions. Besides, fundamental changes to our basic ways of living are scary, make us anxious. *"Better known bads than unknown goods."*

But, if conditions are unstable, changing, then tradition can be a serious impediment to an active adaptation to those changes. How about a healthy equilibrium? Sticking to routine just because *"that's how it's done"* is a good formula for getting stuck. Better test those traditions and see if they have a better solution. Here are some suggestions in that direction.

Mo Tzu, China about 2400 yb² (also named 'Mozi' - 'Mo Di' - 'Mo Ti' and other variants) argued against blind obedience to ritual and authority and postulated a three-pronged test for every doctrine:
1. Question its basis.
2. Ask if it can be verified by the sights and senses of common people.
3. Ask how it is to be applied and if it benefits the greatest number.

Ibn AL Haytham (or Al Hazen), born c. 965 to an Arab family in Basra, Iraq; died c. 1040 was an early proponent of the concept that a hypothesis must be proved by experiments based on confirmable procedures or mathematical evidence—hence understanding the scientific method five centuries before Renaissance scientists.

His guiding principles roughly translate to this:
> *Finding truth is difficult and the road to it is rough.*
> *As seekers of the truth, you will be wise to withhold judgment*
> *and not simply put your trust in the writings of the ancients.*

ا. *You must question and critically examine those writings from every side.*
ب. *Submit to argument and experiment, but not to the sayings of others.*
ت. *For every human being is vulnerable to all kinds of imperfections.*
ث. *As seekers of the truth, we must also suspect and question our own ideas as we perform our investigations to avoid falling into prejudice or careless thinking.*
ج. *Take this course and truth will be revealed to you.*

Rene Descartes (1596 – 1650), came up with a similar philosophy, which led directly to the establishment of the scientific method as we know it today.

In the opening chapter of the series *Cosmos,* astronomer **Neil deGrasse Tyson** gives us a modern version of the paradigm, summarized in a handful of basic rules that we should all take to heart:

1. Question authority. No idea is true just because someone says so... including you.
2. Think for yourself.
3. Question yourself. Don't believe anything just because you want to. Believing something does not make it so.
4. Test ideas by the evidence gained from observation and experiment.
5. If a favorite idea fails a well-designed test, it's wrong. Get over it*!*
6. Follow the evidence, wherever it leads. If you have no evidence, reserve judgment.
7. And most important, remember, **you could be wrong*!***

And adds: "This method is a way to keep from fooling ourselves, and each other."

Getting back to tradition, one of its more embedded manifestations is dogma. Metaphorically, every dogma claims the following:

Trust our map, even when you see the terrain differs from our map.

This is an excellent way to get stuck in a dead end.

It's more practical to follow the Norwegian Boy Scout Handbook on map-reading. Its advice to intrepid map-readers:

"*If the terrain differs from the map, **believe the terrain!**"*

This is the objective recommendation. The terrain mandates, the map is only a symbolic representation of the terrain, mediated by a Subject, and therefore potentially incorrect.

The same advice works when you follow the writings of the ancients with their *maps* and opinions as to how you should conduct your life to the letter, according to the visions of others. Guidelines can be very useful under specific situations, but if these conditions change you need to adapt. *'If the terrain of life differs from the mandates and opinions you are being told, believe what your life shows you.'* We cannot follow *'maps of life'* blindly because maps and books are dead static objects. They can never capture the infinite creativity of living beings, nor the unpredictable demands of a changing world.

This is particularly important in relation to the growing complexity of the modern world, both in technological matters as in the social sphere. You **cannot** continue thinking and moving at a donkey's pace in a society that moves at the speed of light and electronics.

==================== II ====================

Chapter II.61 –

About the relationship between science and religion

As mentioned, we seem to have three types of existential concerns: where do we come from; how to explain the functioning of our world and influence the outcomes; and what is our destiny. The overlap or conflict between science and religion plays out primarily in the middle sphere: how does it work and how can I influence or control it? A good solution is inextricably tied to a good understanding of how it works. This is where the 'black box' ploy comes in. When you don't understand something, especially when it's a step in a sequence, one easy and almost universal solution is to represent it as a *black box* till you can work it out. Humans have been using this *black box* 📕 trick for millennia. We used to call them "gods."

We humans could not understand why the sun comes up every morning and how it manages to go '*through the underworld*' at night. If you believed the world was a never-ending stretch of flat land, how could you? So, our ancestors created a variety of '*black box*' explanations, most of them animated by a god. For some the sun was pulled across the sky by [*black-box*] in a chariot, or ferried across the underworld by [*black-box*] on a boat. In one Egyptian variant the sun entered the mouth of 📕 and traveled through her gut to be expelled at the other end the next morning. None of these 'explanations' had a shred of truth or reason behind them, but they served to appease curiosity. Their credibility rested on tradition and faith, but also because there was no other hint of an explanation in sight. They also served priests to claim they had power over these things, and could receive 'offerings' in the name of these *black boxes* (gifts to the priests, no doubt).

Once you replace the real item with a *black box* of any kind, it becomes almost childishly easy to cheat and tell yourself, or tell others, any fantastic story you might fancy to come up with just to fill that void. And once *that* belief system is in place, new options for scams become available. But here comes one conflict of interest. If you really need to solve the problem, to get something to actually work, a phony explanation won't do. You need the real deal. Practical experience gave us hints, but progress was painfully slow till we developed better ways and special detective methodologies to weed out the phony explanations and sleuth out the ones that really worked. Today we call that bundle of tricks 'science.'

Science always starts by formulating a question and searching for a good answer. This is achieved by actually taking a good look at the problem with special protocols, research protocols. Research must focus on *'the objects of study'* and allow those objects to 'inform' the science in question. This requisite is why we say science is 'objective.' But in this context the term refers to the premises and the methods of study, **not** to science itself. The new understanding occurs inside the mind of a Subject. We refer to the spark of creativity of a new idea as an *in-sight*, meaning something that occurs inside a Subject, in this case the researcher. In this sense all scientific perceptions are *subjetal,* but hopefully not *subjective*.

Here I need to point out another semantic problem. In the preceding formulation the catch is that *'the object of study'* does not need to be *objectal,* that is, a material 'object.' Consider instead: *'the target of study.'* It is clear then that it can very well be a Subject, the *interior* of a person, or a totally subjectal issue, as is the target of linguistics, for example. This is the problem I pointed out towards the end of Chapter I.4. In the last analysis the only sense in which the object – subject pair is robust and lasting is to limit their use to refer to the grammatical roles, but this would leave us without terms to designate the other meanings we give these words.

Getting back, the scientific verification process requires a second step, which is to expose the new visions to revision by other scientists, a process usually called *peer review*. Your peers essentially repeat the process of allowing reality to inform them, initially via the publication in question, but then by repeating the process (fieldwork or experimental research), and verifying if they get similar observations and results. You can do research on your own, but you cannot do *science* alone. Science is designed to give you the most reliable explanation available as to how things really work, and thus the best tools to influence the outcomes of worldly events.

Here is where dogmatic religious preaching (and politics) moves away from empirical knowledge and science. Religions assume and claim that 'truth' is what is written in their sacred books. To know the world, you have to read the book (*their* book in particular, of course). Because reality is informed by what the Subject has been induced to believe, indoctrinated, we say this form of interpreting the world is '*subjective*,' because 'truth' emanates from a Subject. There is no possibility to go back to the source, certainly not via religious dogma in itself. But note that the beliefs only exist in the minds of some Subjects, and therefore religious perception is just as *subjectal* as scientific perception.

Now, you might think the modern use of the *black box* trick is the same as the ancient, but there's a critical difference. The modern version is just a form of shorthand. If I need to use the technology or I simply wish to know, I can open the box and study the contents because somebody somewhere actually knows all the details. The ancient *black boxes,* on the other hand, were faked ways to fill in the blanks, a sign of ignorance, a sort of Pandora's box with totally unknown content. This is where and why priests flounder, because the moment you ask them to open those *black boxes* and justify their claims they simply cannot because their *black boxes* are empty. It's just a ploy, a coverup for their ignorance. Of course, a large part of the problem is that they are trying to claim authority in spheres where they don't belong.

The critical point is this, Abrahamic religions impose a <u>subjective</u> approach to 'truth.'

Truth is what I say it is, (*or what the authority I claim to represent*
supposedly says),
And you'd better believe it, or else (we *will* punish you).

This alleged '*truth*' does not develop within you, it is imposed on you, the target of the sermons, by the preacher, who plays the role of the Subject that imparts the preaching. The relationship is truly Subject-object (you being the 'object,' not just in the grammatical sense). Since the preaching is arbitrary, the bigwigs of these religions have developed a string of safeguards to make sure you can't defy their authority. (For the use of 'Subject' to denote a person, see Chapter I.13).

Science does not impose any truth, in theory at least. It makes propositions and informs you how they proceeded to understand and verify them. That is, they provide a detailed explanation of the methods used. Then you, the Subject, are free to repeat the process and come to your own conclusions. Here the relationship is a dialectic Subject-Subject exchange. If you have good reason to disagree you are encouraged to challenge the proposition and reformulate it. In time a revised and corrected version emerges that withstands all the tests and analysis. Only when it is accepted does it become the **consensual science** of the period (i.e., agreed on by most, at least for a time).

Since both positions claim to be the owners of truth, it's worth looking into how and why these opposing views have evolved.

Religions may have had their origin in a direct experience (or a series of them), but the current versions don't rely on experience. They rely on what was written *about* those original experiences, which are then enthroned as the 'last word' on the subject. This rigid worship of the content in *The Book* is what makes these religions intrinsically manipulative. To keep his authority the preacher has to convince you that truth is in the book he peddles, even if parts are incomplete, incorrect or false. You have to 'believe,' have 'faith' in *The Book* and in the messenger (actually, in the messenger of the messenger...). The messenger rarely accepts that this whole business is of his own creation. He's only the messenger; he will always claim to have it from a *'higher'* source..., a smart way to kick the ball out of the playing field. One problem with this strategy is that once the religious operator has committed to some *revealed truth,* he cannot afford to have it debunked without losing credibility, and his precious authority.

This creates a dilemma, a double bind. The preacher can avoid errors or suspicions by being faithful of scripture to the letter, but this is a guarantee that he will repeat all the mistakes, contradictions and limitations these scriptures have accumulated. Or he can 'correct' and/or 'interpret' these scriptures to adapt them to our times. Perhaps this explains the proliferation of sects, cults and denominations, about 1,500 in the U. S. alone. Rewrite your own version and call it the TRUE VERSION. *Easy!* But also, DANGEROUS! The dangers of distortion and abuse. Where there is license to correct there's also room to corrupt. Anyone can twist meanings to his own benefit. Still, if we accept the premise that the 'original' version was corrupted centuries ago, this might be a lesser evil.

Both systems evolve, but with different dynamics. Religions through arbitrary changes, usually in attendance to the convenience of the higher echelon. Instead, the sciences do so in search of a better fit and as a response to the demands of perceived reality.

In science the motto might be "Take it or leave it."

In religion it is more like "Take it, or *leave!*"

A significant difference. Seekers prefer the first option. At least they have the right to verify the statements without anyone getting offended. Followers accept the second proposition without even questioning it. Politicians use whatever suits them best, but prefer to emulate religion.

The irony: Science converges - Religions diverge

This is a historical fact. The critical difference is that science converges by its very structure. Science is *designed* to reach a consensus. Religions, on the other hand, seem to be designed to diverge. Supremacy of one creed over the others is always the result of power struggles and domination. So-called 'unity' must be imposed by force. Crass politics masquerading as religion.

Forcing somebody to 'love you' is not love at all. It's *control.*
===================== II =====================

Chapter II.62 –

A universe without gods? – God and his creation? – Unfolding within God?

According to modern astrophysics the material reality perceived by us is presumed to represent only 4.6% of our universe; the rest is 'dark matter' and 'dark energy.' Consider also the 11 dimensions postulated by M theory. If they all really exist, there must be links between them. All this seems to provide us with plenty of room for other realms that some sensitive souls might have perceived as heavens or hells! Add the possibility of parallel realities. Or take the idea of the Akashic records as a compendium of all human events, thoughts, words, emotions, and intents ever to have occurred in the past, present, or future, encoded in a non-material domain of existence referred to as the etheric level. How different is that from the idea in modern physics that no information is ever lost, even at an event horizon?

People have envisioned these possibilities in three basic ways:

A universe without gods: the materialistic option assures us there is no god, that all there is can be explained by the basic physical laws.

God and his creation: Abrahamic religions tell us that Yahve/ God/ Allah, who exists outside of our known space-time, created this universe and will eternally preside and rule over it. Implicitly, we are not of God-stuff, we are just puppets in a Divine Colosseum in which, it is construed, our sole purpose is to praise, obey, and presumably entertain *Him*.

Unfolding within God: for many mystical traditions all the cosmos is one integrated expression or manifestation of divine essence. In this sense, we too are of divine essence, active participants in a humongous Cosmic Game, in which Cosmic Intelligence is playing hide-and-seek with itself.

Does the materialistic scientific approach know how to distinguish between these possible conceptions of reality or even how to access the realms postulated by mystics? Not for the moment, and I would wager it will never succeed so long as it continues to assume that external (material) reality is the only reality. It seems the path to other dimensions or realities is better approached via the methods developed by many of the mystical schools, the martial arts, shamans, and others. Myths? Wives' tales? Fantasies? Perhaps, but there is also the possibility that though the *interpretations* of these ancient practices may have been incomplete or incorrect, the methods used and the worlds they reveal are real, true portals to access these other realities. As a scientist, can you really guarantee that this is impossible? No way! We will look further into these issues in Book III.

Being critical is a scientific policy;

denying whole realms of possibilities is something else.

===================== II =====================

Chapter II.63 –

Conversion

Years ago, I was touring the Atlantic coast of Uruguay and drove into a little town ironically called Punta del Diablo (Devil's Point) quite late. It was off-season so the town seemed dead. I bought a snack in a deli and looked for a hotel with little success, so I was glad to find a simple but clean looking inn that had its lights on. Next morning, soon after I got up, the owner came by to see how I was doing. I made some polite conversation, with my mind mostly on getting on my way, but before I had time to wake up and react, the conversation veered from small talk to the gospel and a lengthy bout of presumably well-meant but completely unsolicited preaching. When I finally managed to extricate myself, it was close to midday and I had to accept a Spanish version of '*What Can the Bible Teach Us?*' in order to appease my tormentor, implying I had been convinced by his efforts and would look into the pamphlet.

After I had put some distance between us, I could not help asking myself what had compelled me to 'sit it out.' Was I so *polite* that he didn't realize I was uncomfortable? Or was he so enthralled with his *mission* that he was unable to see he was being invasive and was impervious to my signals? Do they teach them to be outright *rude*? In any event, the experience had a significant effect on me. I converted.

Seriously, I converted from a basically tolerant biblical disbeliever to an increasingly critical and intolerant 'reactionary' that is no longer willing to be polite in the face of rude, even aggressive, insensitive, sanctimonious, dim-witted peddlers of bronze-age lies and half-truths. For the record, that has nothing to do with my belief or disbelief in the existence of the Divine.

This stance might sound rather harsh but, as you have read in the preceding chapters, it's the result of insights gleaned over decades of reading, discussion, and mulling over these issues. Perhaps it helps clear the minds of people who are already doubting and bring together like-minded people that are equally dissatisfied with the current situation, a fellow-ship of seekers if you wish, rather than the current follow-ship of believers. —————————— o ——————————

What are the advantages and limitations of religion?

As we saw, the **intersubjectal** is what goes between Subjects, what jumps from one Subject to another Subject, and the links they imply or create. Much of this has to do with communication. We think of it as an exchange, but there are situations where it can be used unidirectionally: the boss gives orders, top-downs, religions preach. **There's no room to question**. Only obedience, adoration, submission, worship, etc. In situations where the enthroned have real physical power, obedience can be understood because the poor victim has no choice. But in those cases where power is only subjective, an imposed belief, a hypothetical threat, it's difficult to understand why individuals go with and obey absurd mandates and practices that are clearly deleterious to the practitioner, like self-immolation and mass suicides. If we ask the average western citizen what the term *religion* evokes, chances are he will think of his benevolent local preacher, church, and community. But you must keep in mind that not all 'religions' are benevolent. Some variants are outright murderous.

One reason that is frequently put forth is that we have an '**existential hole**' (yearning or emptiness), a need to understand the whys and wherefores of our lives. It is usually assumed that religion fills that gap, but it's not clear to what extent the need is real, spontaneous, or if it is a social construction. Surely, there must be aspects of religious practices that give us a sense of security, of social belongingness, of well-being (we feel good), etc. Historically, religions have provided much of the basis for moral and ethical conduct indispensable for a shared life in a modern society, including the Golden Rule (*do unto others as you would have them do unto you*, Matt 7:21)[32]. Religious practices 'solemnize' the rites of passage of the cycle of life and 'sacralize' social contracts. Temples have always been social gathering points and a refuge in times of strife. Religious beliefs help us get through tyranny, war, natural catastrophes, epidemics, and hunger.

What is **not** so obvious is that these benefits require and derive from the dogmas, mandates and taboos imposed in the bargain, or rather if these benefits are a product of the social interactions in themselves. Perhaps the same psychological and social benefits can be obtained in other ways, without the fundamentalist abuses and absurdities they want to sell you within the ideological bundle peddled by these religions. Let's take a look.

=================== II ===================

Chapter II.64 –

The owners of Truth – What do we mean by 'prophet'?

The definition of who qualifies as a 'prophet' is a bit vague. The problem with the '*messenger from God*' narrative is that it is totally dependent on what you mean by 'God.' So here we simply mean '*revealers of truth.*' Granted, we could argue forever as to what 'truth' means, but at

---

[32] The Qur'an agrees and extends it: "... and reject for others what you would reject for yourself."

least the concept is more mundane, flexible. Judaism has a few, Christianity perhaps a couple and Islam added just one. Science, on the other hand, recognizes many (not to mention the wealth of Eastern traditions).

Most Old Testament *'prophets'* were simply Jewish Kings who, like the Pharos, sought to glorify their names by claiming they were the messengers of God, but let's assume they all had some religious significance. The last one, Malachi, lived to about 2432 yb^2. Only a couple might qualify as Christian additions: John the Baptist perhaps, and Christ of course.

Starting with Adam (but not Eve), Islam acknowledges 48 of these as prophets (some say only 24), but they certainly don't count the **seven** Jewish prophetesses. However, what they truly believe is that Mohammed is the only *real* prophet. One can imagine that in his day it might have been dangerous to deny Judeo-Christianity, so they pretended, paid lip-service to it. But if we consider what Islam really did historically, all their holy wars, and still continues to do today, they clearly think otherwise. They think Mohammed is the only *valid* prophet.

Anyway, this leaves us with around 60 prophets at best, starting with Adam around 7000 yb^2 when God created the world and all the creatures on it, up to Mohammed's death about 1400 years ago[33]. That comes out to a prophet every 100 years or so. Assuming God is consistent, by this account we are now **short** by around 14 prophets.

If you consider only the Christian faith, then God blessed us with one every 85 years or so till the time of Christ and then stopped. In that case, we are now overdue on about 23 prophets! Or perhaps they existed but we somehow 'lost' them?

Allah/God/Yhwh must have a very funny sense of timing. Why would *He* only speak to one prophet every hundred years or so? Is he busy in some other galaxy meantime? Take the Islamic point of view. *He* let humanity flounder in ignorance for millennia and then, suddenly, decided to tell **only one man** what *He (Allah)* really expected of **all** humans? If *He* is really all-powerful, why in heaven would he only speak to **one** man? Perhaps *Allah* only understands Arabian and must use human assistants to translate? Not likely, don't you think?

What about science? If you were to count every *'revealer of truth'*

---

[33] The Islamic prophet Mohammed was born in Mecca about the year 570, died in 632 of our Era.

including every contributor to every area of knowledge, they'd be hundreds or thousands, so let's just concentrate on those that seem more relevant to occidental worldviews and to Abrahamic religions.

Ibn Al Haytham (or Al Hazen), died 1040. He was one of the first proponents that a hypothesis had to be tested by experimentation, anticipating the scientific method several centuries before Descartes.

Nicolaus Copernicus, d. 1543. Proposed the sun-centered model (the Sun is the center, not the Earth). He studied canonical law and was likely an ordained priest.

Friar Giordano Bruno, d. 1600, was burned at the stake by the Inquisition for upholding and expanding Copernicus' ideas about the sun, arguing in favor of an infinite universe and other '*crimes*' against the 'Church.' Soon his ideas were confirmed by Galileo.

Galileo Galilei, d. 1642, was the first to observe the heavens and the stars through a telescope. He is considered the founder of modern science. Also condemned by priesthood.

Rene Descartes, d. 1650, developed the modern scientific method. He had three visions and believed that a divine spirit had revealed a new philosophy to him.

Isaac Newton, d. 1726. He removed the last doubts about the validity of the sun-centered model of the solar system and demonstrated that the motion of objects on Earth and of celestial bodies are governed by natural laws, not by 'gods' as the ancients believed.

Carl Linnaeus, d. 1778. He created the modern binomial system of classification of living beings organized by relatedness and, anticipating Darwin, included men, apes and monkeys in a single family.

Alexander von Humboldt, d. 1859. One of the first to realize the unity that underlies diversity, relating the types of habitats and their vegetation with latitude, altitude, and climate. He is the founder of modern ecology.

Charles R Darwin, d. 1882. Also educated in the Christian faith of his time, he initially believed in the immutability of species. He later proposed '*descent with modification*' and '*natural selection*' as the driving forces behind natural diversity, demonstrating a viable natural mechanism for evolution.

Karl H Marx, d. 1883. The most radical analyst of socioeconomic reality, author of *Das Kapital*, and coauthor of the *Communist Manifesto* (with Friedrich Engels, who was also the editor of *Das Kapital*). Many consider him the founder of modern economy. Marx has historical importance here because the *Manifesto* gave rise to a sort of 'religion' that competed with the traditional ones and fused with some of the third world movements such as the *'theology of liberation.'*

Abbot Gregor J Mendel, d. 1884. He was the first to describe the mechanisms of inheritance, and is considered the father of Genetics, a fundamental pillar to evolutionary theory.

Friar Pierre Teilhard de Chardin, d. 1955. Controversial Jesuit priest who attempted to fuse Christianity and Evolution.

Albert Einstein, d. 1955. Developer of the theory of relativity, again profoundly undermining the religious doctrine of an unchanging 'creation.' Actually, he initially believed in a cosmos that was in equilibrium, but later he accepted that it is expanding. Everything is relative.

Catholic Priest Georges Lemaitre, d. 1966. In 1927 he postulated what he called *'the theory of the cosmic egg'* and the expansion of the universe, today better known as the *Big Bang* theory.

James Watson, now 97 (2025), **and Francis Crick**, d. 2004. They deciphered and described the structure of DNA and clinched the mechanism for inheritance with modification, as Darwin had predicted. This discovery marked the birth of molecular biology and our current understanding of evolution.

This is just the tip of the tip of the iceberg, but it gives us a hint of the missing prophets. People, religious or otherwise, that have contributed revelations that have helped transform our conceptions of the world, nature, life, and the cosmos number in the hundreds or even thousands. Just think of the long list of Nobel laureates.

Most preachers, priests and their faithful rely on electronic/atomic watches, use modern medicine, fly in airplanes, use computers, preach through television and cable networks, communicate with cell phones, etc., etc., etc. Yet many insist on denying some aspects of modern knowledge whose validity rests on the very same principles, and even consider some of these scientists to be 'heretics.' Needed to be said, the line dividing what is and what is not 'heretic' is totally arbitrary.

The point is simple. Either God continues to illuminate our pursuit of knowledge and these eminent scientists – and countless others – also serve as Prophets guiding us on our way to deeper wisdom, or they are truly heretics, in which case the Devil/Shaitan is gaining the upper hand and proving to be far more effective than *God/Allah/Yhwh*. It's the inevitable consequence of believing that his last acknowledged prophet appeared **1,400 years ago**, if you choose to believe the Qur'an, or over 2,000 years ago, if you choose to believe the Bible.

======================= II ====================

Chapter II.65 –

People of *The Book*

You've probably heard the expression. They've been around for quite some time. Of course, the nature of *The Book* has changed from time to time, but the human tendency to go *'by the book'* seems to endure unchanged. Some were surely lost in the mists of time, but there are at least four *'books'* that guide people's lives today. The Torah, the Bible, the Qur'an and the Communist Manifesto.[34] You may be surprised that I include the Manifesto. It seems a polar opposite and was, in theory, anti-religious. But the way people put their faith in its *dogmas*, the strategies they used to impose it and the atrocities committed in its name put it in the same category.

If you go *'by the book'* you can justify anything!

'The ends justify the means . . .'

What they have in common is a particular way of viewing the world, usually called dualistic: right or wrong, good or evil, God or the Devil, what I refer to as *excluding dualism.* You are either for us or against us. No nonsense of pretending to be neutral.

Basically, **black or white**, no room for grays - let alone yellows, greens, blues...

Did you study the same book all the way through school? I very much doubt it. You don't grow by repeating the same material over and over forever. Once you have understood what is appropriate for this level you move on to the next challenge. You grow *'through the book,'* not *'by the book.'* 'By the book' is the First Grader fallacy, falling in love with your first teacher and becoming stuck at the first-grade level.

---

[34] Many Eastern philosophies also use books, but they don't seem to enshrine any one in particular. They're more like manuals, focused on the practice, interchangeable without fuss.

We all grow up immersed in the religion professed by the society we were born in. But to become mature adults, we need to explore other religions, at least for a time. This may seem preposterous to many, but the proposition is well grounded. It is the only way you can separate the grain from the chaff. People who get stuck in one religious viewpoint lose perspective and fail to distinguish which aspects of their creed are just trivial accidents of history and which are universal principles worthy of devotion. For instance, the names Moses, Jesus and Mohammed are accidents of history. Had they been called Olaf, Brutus and Dryas it would make zero difference to their stories. And the same is true of innumerable other details. Yet people have gone to war and massacred whole generations on account of these differences! To say that this is short-sighted or narrow-minded is an understatement. Becoming obsessed with one 'book' is insane, and in complete contradiction to the fundamentals of pretty much every spiritual tradition on the planet.

Infinity simply cannot be contained in one book, any book, no matter what preachers try to make you believe! It's basic common sense. If *ahl* is truly infinite, then no book can possibly capture such vastness, not even all books ever written could. If you don't believe me, try this. Get a thick notebook and several pens, find a quiet comfortable spot with a view over some landscape or cityscape, and write down a complete description of every detail you could possibly discover about it. Write it so that someone else could read your description and reconstruct EXACTLY the same functioning reality from your account. Go ahead, try it. I defy you. If it is completely impossible to capture even a fraction of everyday *reality* with words, why would you believe a book could have the pretense and the arrogance to tell us what *ahl* **is**, and even worse, what an *infinite Divinity* **thinks**?

Don't let anybody trick you into believing that any one book is *The Book*. At best it is an approximation, a progress report, something to work **through** in your path to higher wisdom. Just like so many other excellent books available today.

==================== II ====================

Chapter II.66 –
How *respectful* is religious preaching?

We tend to be apologetic about criticizing *religion.* Any religion.

This notion is the result of religion's long-standing claim that religious beliefs are sacrosanct, a question of 'faith' above analysis or criticism. We MUST respect *their* cherished belief system. This may sound *politically correct* but it isn't, quite categorically, in particular when we are talking of the more radical sectors of the Abrahamic religions. It's a dangerous idea.

The first reason is historical, a consequence of their own track-record. Surviving religions have not just survived. They have intentionally and systematically knocked the shit out of any and all competing beliefs and practices. Most of this is very mundane politics. Centuries of unholy wars, destruction of temples of other faiths, assassination of shamans and priests, burning of 'witches,' inquisitions, torture, faked 'confessions,' jihad, wholesale genocide, appropriation of religious festivities, expropriation of property and who knows what else are a pretty lousy track-record on which to demand respect. Respect is a two-way deal.

Yes, you might think or say, "*but that is history!*" Well, it's not. It is still going on today in many parts of the world, in the name of one religion or another. Take the tragic case of New Guinea hill tribes (see Jared Diamond), or the ravages of Islamic *jihad* wars in the Middle East and the mass murders of Christians in Africa. Over the last century, every time a new tribe was discovered a horde of preachers moved in like vultures, to pick the spoils and '*convert*' them, often in the name of some creed which is just as archaic as the ones they aspire to replace.

This is the result of a deep asymmetry in the political aspect of the creeds. Some of the surviving religions actively and aggressively preach. It is a basic policy, a **mandate** of their faith to *demonize* all other creeds and to strive to further the cause of their own creed. Success is measured by the number of '*converts*' they reap. That number is equal to the number of apostates they inflict on some competing faith. Double bonus, no doubt. Those poor creeds that were truly respectful were wiped out.

Here's the catch. These are *their* rules: '*It is licit to demolish other people's beliefs and it is also licit to aggressively peddle your own.*' Great, so reciprocity entitles me to demolish their primitive beliefs and it also makes it an obligation to aggressively divulge the more evolved understandings that we profess, correct?

And they are obliged **by their own claims** to *respect* this. Fundamental.

Respect for other people's opinions and beliefs has never been a characteristic of institutionalized religions, especially those that are strongly politicized. Nor of politics, for that matter, but politics makes no claim for the same sort of *respect.*

The truth is the exact opposite, systematic ***disrespect***. The basic assumption of preaching runs something like this: "*My religion is better than yours! In fact, yours is completely shitty, ours is the only TRUE religion.*"

These religions often add a little spice for good measure: *"and I am 'saving' you by converting you. However, if you don't convert, I condemn you to Eternal Damnation"* - (anathema, whatever).

Call that respectful? If you do, you are deluding yourself.

It becomes clearer if you reformulate these religious claims as a political claim:

'*My Political Party is the only TRUE Political Party. You must accept its ideas and sign up! If you don't, you will face the Firing Squad!*'

Sounds familiar? Any political leader that rambled off with this sort of propaganda would instantly be classed as a dictator!

So, if **disrespect** is the name of the game, just **cut the crap**.

Your beliefs are just as open to question and criticism as anybody else's!

If not, let's change the game. I will respect you if you **stop** preaching.

--------------------- o ---------------------

How did that come across? You see, this is a mirror image of the more radical preaching, which most people tolerate. Instead, people often feel uncomfortable, if not outright offended, when such a critical stance is turned back towards religious preaching. Yet, as a mature adult, this is more or less what I feel when some foreigner or young preacher assumes that my faith is wrong, that I have been mindless, and that he or she is the bearer of the ***true*** faith that will correct my infidel or heathen habits and save me from sin. Quite frankly, there comes a point in life when such unsolicited self-righteousness is plainly an insult in itself.

However, the crucial issue with the religious supremacy posture is much deeper. The same excuse can justify any manner of atrocities. In the relatively benevolent West where religious freedom is a reality and the attitude is respectful, the occasional visit of some street promoter of his faith can be entertaining and even enlightening. But it is a mistake to extend this same tolerance to the more radical groups and politicized creeds. You just cannot be polite or tolerant with people who seriously think killing you or anybody else who does not profess their creed, anybody they deem 'infidels,' is a service to their god. It puts our whole culture at risk. You and your family could be next.

We cannot afford to be complacent or tolerant with political intolerance masquerading as religion. Besides, you cannot resolve conflict between competing religious ideologies by trying to eliminate one side. The only way to move forward is by eliminating the barrier that creates the delusion of separation and supremacy.

==================== II ====================

Maybe the rules of intimacy are something you have to define for yourself.
Meredith, in Gray's Anatomy.

Chapter II.67 –
Guilt

"Have you sinned in thought, word, or deed?" Tell your confessor .... but

Don't read this.
Did you read it? *Gotcha, you sinner!*

Two Hail Marys and three Our Fathers!

Sounds familiar? Guilt seems to be a very powerful and deeply embedded mechanism in humans and perhaps in other animals. Quite frankly, I still don't see how guilt could have evolved as an adaptive mechanism in natural environments. Perhaps it served as a social regulatory mechanism, as when we feel guilty because we didn't return a favor or forgot our mother's birthday. The feeling of guilt subsumes the acceptance of responsibility for some fault, omission, unkind action, etc., which explains why it is generally elicited by accusations and finger pointing. Everybody seems to get in on the game (parents, spouses, teachers, politicians, ...), but it's been the church that has converted it into a professional undertaking. Sadly, this pathology has infiltrated social discourse to such a degree that even inanimate objects are deemed 'guilty' of our misfortunes.

It seems we are designed to feel guilt. No doubt it has a biological base. It must be one of the elements of the bundle that conditions us for gregarious life. The need to interact, to keep in mind that there are always 'others,' sets a limit to pure egocentrism. This gives rise to notions such as reciprocal altruism (*today for thee, tomorrow for me*). That agreement, even if implicit, only works if reciprocity is fulfilled. The notion that 'guilt' has a biological base is also suggested by the existence of individuals that lack guilt altogether, since birth apparently, which allows them to commit even heinous crimes without the slightest remorse. These individuals are usually referred to as psychopaths. From the social perspective this is clearly a dangerous pathology, the people you need to recognize and beware of. However, every extreme must have its opposite, so we need to look at those individuals that feel crippling degrees of guilt and remorse, even for faults they didn't commit. Guilt syndrome, as some call it. The problem here is that the individual tends to assume that any situation of conflict, irresponsibility or negligence is automatically his or her own fault. If something is wrong, it must be *my* fault! This excessive guilt puts the individual in a hopelessly vulnerable position, one which any unscrupulous party can readily take advantage of. But it must be stressed that whatever predisposition an individual might have, it is exacerbated by subsequent conditioning. For the guilt-prone, excessive religious and social taboos and admonitions usually have a devastating and lasting negative effect on the victim's whole life.

A related situation occurs when, either due to excessive self-centeredness or mind-blindness, as occurs in autism, the person seems to be incapable of understanding that some other person might be an unholy scoundrel who is deliberately attempting to cause harm or pull off a scam. Although this need not involve a sense of guilt, it does put the person in an equally vulnerable position, a sort of constitutional sucker. It's generally assumed that typical neuros have an innate ability, called *theory of mind*, the capacity to understand and foresee other people's feelings and intentions. This is an essential asset needed to navigate social situations. Some people seem to lack this capacity altogether, or are very poor at it, hence they are 'mind-blind.' It's worth noting, however, that the phrase 'theory of mind' is somewhat of a misnomer. Perhaps we construct 'theories' about how other people think and act, (*e.g.,* see Alison Gopnik's

The Philosophical Baby), but for most adults these cues become internalized and operate more like an *'intuition of mind.'* For people who have this handicap, education about these facts can help them construct a truly rationalized 'theory of mind,' but it will always have the limitation of being example-specific. Chances are in any new situation they will miss the cues. Since this has negative consequence only for the sufferer, the problem is easy to overlook and seems to have received less attention.

In any event, what turns out to be an unfortunate trap for most of us is that the guilt mechanism is unspecific, so much so that any person with some authority can make you feel guilty about almost anything that crosses his fancy. Yet, for a manipulator the ideal sin is the one the person will commit almost inevitably, which puts the culprit in a vulnerable position and gives the manipulator leverage. The really 'heavy' ones, the felonies, are in a different category. The ones that are most useful are the trivial ones like petty thefts, lies and the sexually toned 'transgressions'[35], which common folks will commit for sure. Add 'confession' to the mix, which gives you a powerful espionage tool, and you have the perfect formula for manipulation.

This is particularly true with the business of sinning *'in thought.'* You're hungry and walk past this deli with posters of delicious looking apple pies. A whiff of freshly baked apple pie drifts out the door... Now **confess**, what were you thinking about just now? Apple pie of course, what else?

How can you possibly avoid thinking about the things that cross your daily life? Yet the Catholic church wants to make you believe that you must 'confess' every 'sinful' idea that ever crossed your mind. *Humm, the preacher sure is sexy!* Nonsense, you don't have to confess anything, much less your intimate thoughts. They are your private property! Anybody that tries to force you to 'confess' is trying to manipulate you. Don't, it's dangerous, anything you say can be used against you.

If you need to work over personal issues, make difficult decisions, do some therapy…, you may choose to *open up* to someone you trust or to a certified professional who has experience with the issues you need to deal with. But always check people out, be very careful who you trust. Just

---

[35] Consider for instance what different religions see as offensive in their temples: in some, ladies must cover their hair, but they can show shoulders or belly; in others the shoulders covered, or perhaps the belly. It's completely arbitrary.

because they belong to some 'church' doesn't make them reliable or safe. The annals of criminal justice are riddled with cases of abusive 'professionals,' including religious ones.

It was probably the Roman Catholic church that perfected the gambit of getting people to confess 'voluntarily,' by telling their followers that if they confessed and repented, they could *save their souls* in the afterlife. Ponzi again.

Saving your soul sounds poetic, magnanimous of priesthood, blah, blah, blah. But just think of the practical implications in **this** life. If these guys know all your secrets, they have you by the balls, or the ovaries, as the case may be. Have it from people who seem to know firsthand. The following quote refers to Ron Hubbard who invented Dianetics and founded Scientology. As the name implies, Auditing forces you to confess:

> *... Hubbard's estranged son Ronald DeWolf asserted that Auditing[36] focused on sex and the individual's sex life and could later be used as a form of control: "Auditing would address a guy's entire sex life. It was an incredible preoccupation. ... You have complete control over someone if you have every detail of his sex life and fantasy life on record. In Scientology the focus is on sex. Sex, sex, sex. The first thing we wanted to know about someone we were auditing was his sexual deviations. All you've got to do is find a person's kinks, whatever they might be. Their dreams and fantasies.* **Then you can fit a ring through their noses and take them anywhere.** *You promise to fulfill their fantasies, or you threaten to expose them ... very simple." ...*

(The quote comes from Wikipedia on *Scientology and Sex,* in turn quoted from Andrew Morton (2008): *Tom Cruise: An Unauthorized Biography*. Macmillan. pp. 128–129).

=================== II ===================

Chapter II.68 –

A recovering *catholic*

It is very difficult for a person who has grown up immersed in a culture

---

[36] To be crystal clear: in any form of 'auditing' the one who defines what you must talk about is the Auditor (the Inquisitor), not you. This is in sharp contrast to therapy where it's up to you to decide what you want to 'work' on or talk about. **'Auditing' is not a therapy.**

permeated with strong mandates, taboos and prejudices to free herself completely from their negative influences. For instance, the web of sexual taboos distorts sexual behaviors and fosters pathologies that have negative social effects. Re-education as an adult is really hard work. *"I know, I am a recovering catholic,"* as a friend dramatized the issue.

Besides, the cultural damage persists. These biases end up infiltrating popular culture, national policies, laws, etc. Some are memes that 'naturalize' postures that are not in the least natural. Many argue in favor of 'religious freedom' (for themselves, but they preach otherwise). But when the choice is the result of persistent indoctrination since childhood, the choice is not 'free' at all. It's induced.

A few misguided or failed individual decisions don't have much social impact, but when that same response is induced in thousands or millions of people, the impact can be enormous. This is just as valid for a political doctrine as it is for the political impact of religious mandates. Just see the effects on many third world countries.

In the specific case of sexuality and reproductive behavior, preachings as to what is 'correct' and what is 'taboo' directly affects personal liberties and the economic future of whole families. But it also has a huge impact on the future of all of society. Those societies that have had explosive demographic growth inevitably become impoverished and ailed by an endless string of nutritional, sanitary, educational, housing, labor, and many other problems that soon turn into structural poverty situations that are very hard to reverse. Condemning whole societies to these sacrifices just because some unscrupulous theocracy wants to peddle their own egocentric worldviews is outright criminal.

As the world stands today, the manipulation of human reproductive strategies is not an issue that can be left to the whims of any sectarian 'preacher,' because their impact affects society as a whole. I am not saying that we should impose conditions on reproduction, though in fact many governments are doing so in subtle ways, for instance with subsidies for each child. What is outmoded and nefarious is that 'commandment' that mandates that the only destiny for women is to marry and have many kids. This ties in with that other political meme that runs something like this: 'poverty → many kids,' when in fact the cause and effect is the other way around: 'many kids → poverty.'

I believe it is important that we see what is valid for each of us. It's perfectly licit to have few kids, or none if you prefer. Don't worry, no god will punish you! You have the right to choose the family that you wish for; to have a fulfilling sexual life without it resulting in a big family; to use contraception to limit the number of pregnancies to what is reasonable to your particular situation and desire.

===================== II ====================

Chapter II.69 –

Testimonials, a lure for suckers?

Faking 'testimonials' must be one of the easiest scams to pull off. Just ask Hollywood. Remember Meg Ryan faking an orgasm in *When Sally met Harry*? If faking an orgasm is easy, what makes you think faking a religious experience would be difficult? - let alone 'impossible.'

Of course, faking an orgasm is easier if your target is a naïve teenager. The problem is, a large proportion of would-be 'suckers' targeted by scammers are not teenagers. It follows that they are either truly taken in by the ruse or they prefer to lend a blind eye. This last option seems by far the more reasonable, and is the one preferred by the phonier 'preachers' to justify their operations. In one case I encountered, he justified his operation roughly thus: "*Believing in a God is less painful than thinking life has no meaning. That's what they come looking for, so that's what our 'church' gives them. So why not take their money for our 'services'? Fair game!*"

The man has a point. Our yearning for meaning makes us very vulnerable to scams.

However, the basic problem is that, as practiced today, the very structure of institutionalized 'religion' is flawed at its roots. In their idealistic youth, most spiritual practices strived for the enlightment of their congregations. Unfortunately, as time passed, gurus became priests, and the schools and temples shifted from teaching to organized religious institutions. As these grew older, idealism was slowly replaced by pragmatism. Of course, both approaches coexist to some degree, but when *the powers that were* realized they could turn seekers into believers, the emphasis and the focus shifted from enlightenment to political manipulation and 'governance' of the masses, us.

Question is, why not put your trust in a God that does not require you to believe in all the associated stories and myths, is not chauvinistic, ethnocentric, politicized and does not demand phony commandments, life-threatening commitments, and constant bribes to ensure your 'salvation.'

Do some seeking and you'll find new options closer than you thought.

But if you don't, you are free to assemble your own belief system!

Simple, *Believe in ah!*   Scrap the rest.

> The optimist prays to God
> The pessimist blames the Devil
> The realist goes to the doctor
> (Adapted from @Brainy Quotes).

===================== II =====================

Chapter II.70 –

Provincialism

Part of the problem with the archaic views of *Creation*, including the biblical version, is that 'creation' is flat, static, virtually lacking in texture and complexity, aside from the sequential nature of the process and the hierarchical grouping of living beings, with man on top, obviously. Scriptures barely begin to make a list of things created.

That 'flatness' is also visible in other spiritual and political visions, but that may be less obvious. Better try with a metaphor from the physical world.

At the start of the 18th century, the most widespread view of the living world was that '*it emanated from God*' or, if not, that Nature was mechanical. Both approaches handled long lists of things and beings piled on top of each other, each occupying its corresponding place in nature, with the implicit or explicit idea that the perfection of creation, of nature, was such that the whole mechanism could and in fact would go on working exactly the same forever, eternally. Nothing would change, and nothing needed changing. With one notable exception, **other people**, hence the compulsion to preach.

With our more extended historical perspective it seems incredible that a long list of illustrious men both from the church and the sciences, generations of intelligent beings, could have remained stuck on such an absurd idea. If there is one feature that permeates everything in the world and in the cosmos, it is constant CHANGE! Everything changes…, almost all the time. Okay, a few things don't. So long as nothing *hits* them, cobblestones and diamonds seem to be "forever." But even diamonds were in the rough when they were found and were then cut and polished! In fact, we humans are one of the most industrious agents of change. The very nature of 'civilization' is based on change, from *'primitive'* ways of living, thinking, and worshipping to the modern and *'correct'* ways of doing so (*'our'* way, of course).

So then, how can a large group of people who are constantly preaching and working to change others, fool themselves (or at least, insist on fooling others) with the idea that nothing changes, and that any mention of evolution is heresy? Maybe just hypocrisy? The naïve response is that the visible changes are taken for granted as part of the normal cycles of life and nature, but that evolution at larger scales in space and time does not exist. It may be 'invisible' to most people, especially those who never ventured far from their hometown and who lived just a few decades, but that does not 'prove' that change doesn't happen.

The other perspective is that for those in power (religious, political, economic...) things were just fine as they were and that change, almost any form of change, was seen as a threat to their privileges. Either way, the results are almost the same, a very narrow and necessarily double-standard worldview.

When did this worldview start to change? Often poor Darwin takes the brunt of the blame, but that is rather simplistic and unfair. The winds of change had been blowing for quite some time. For example, almost a century earlier Linnaeus, the creator of modern taxonomy, proposed a family of animals that he called the *'Anthropomorpha,'* which means *'those that have the form of humans,'* and grouped humans, apes, and monkeys under that umbrella. He was sufficiently smart to avoid saying that one descended from the other, only that they looked alike. But *the basic premise* of his classification is that species in one family were closer relatives to each other than to members of other families, as the name implies.

But the man who in my opinion changed the story appeared a little later, between Linnaeus and Darwin. Alexander von Humboldt, whom we met in Chapter I.10, broke the mold when he realized that in nature everything was related to everything else and that as you moved through space and time everything changed, often in predictable ways. In other words, that unity underlies diversity. It's interesting to note that his contemporaries considered he would never get far because he nibbled at too many subjects. But that's precisely the point. If you insist on reading the same book, any you care to choose, your points of view will necessarily be painfully narrow, and anything out of that narrow window will seem like a threat. Which may be perfectly okay for you. Problems arise when you start trying to impose your rules and dogmas on others. You simply have no right to impose the tyranny of your narrowmindedness on others, especially when it refers to your religious dogmatism. Clearly, *ah!* loves diversity. Who are you to deprive the *ah!mighty* of the multiple forms of worship created around the whole wide world?

So, at a personal level, what is the important issue in all this? What did Humboldt do that allowed him to develop these novel forms of understanding the world? He spoke several languages, and by the time he was thirty-five he had traveled, and often lived in different places for a time, over a good part of Europe, the Caribbean, parts of northern South America, Mexico, and eastern North America. Two hundred years ago this was quite a feat in itself! But this alone does not define him. His attitude is more important: first and foremost, he kept an open mind, traveled extensively, and always paid close attention to what nature and the world were showing him. He listened to many voices and read everything he could get his hands on. But then he chose his own path. Humboldt is to Ecology what Darwin is to Evolution. They overcame the disconnected and static views of their time and were able to develop interconnected and dynamic conceptions instead. Around Humboldt's time, Charles Lyell did the same for Geology.

Amongst those who changed our perception of the world and the cosmos we can mention Marco Polo, Galileo Galilei, Christopher Columbus, Humboldt and Darwin of course, Joseph Campbell and so many others. What did they do? Well, give and take a little, they kept an open mind, explored extensively, listened to many voices, read all they could and paid close attention to what Nature and the world was showing them. And then they did what they thought best. Each broke away from some ruling dogma of their time.

I started this journey analyzing the ideas proposed by Ken Wilber. What did he do? Well, again, he read everything he could get hold of, kept an open mind, traveled extensively, explored several spiritual practices, and paid close attention to what Nature and the world was showing him. But then he chose his own path.

A Hindu guru used to say that it's good to grow up in one religion, but to mature, to develop fully, you must get to know other forms of spirituality. It's the only way to understand which elements are merely cultural ornaments peculiar to each religion, and which are the fundamental principles shared by all spiritual practices.

If worship is free, I agree – if you impose, I oppose.
===================== II =====================

Chapter II.71 –

ah! loves evolution!

Years ago, I met someone who boasted that he *'was, is, and will always be the same.'* Long did I mull over this idea, trying to find an analogy that would fit these conditions. In the end all I could come up with was *a cobblestone.*[37] Everything else changes continually.

In fact, the one process that has become crystal clear over the last 150 years or so is that:

EVERYTHING EVOLVES

Can you see children, or a tree, grow from day to day? Of course not. Would you then affirm: "*trees don't grow*"? That would be a fallacy, wouldn't it? Every system or theme that has ever been studied in any detail shows some form of historic change, given enough time.

You might say it goes around in a circle, that it is 'revolutionary.' But at larger scales, while some parts of the systems seem to **revolve** quietly with little or no change, most don't. Though most often change is in the direction of decay, *sometimes* it is in the direction of greater complexity. Revolution without the R of rotation **becomes Evolution**. The elements evolved from simple ones like hydrogen and helium to much more complex ones. Molecules get ever more complex. Stars and galaxies change and evolve. Needed to be said, life evolves. Anybody who is honest enough to take a serious look at the natural world will see the footprint of change and

---

[37] Though *'elemental particle'* would be equally fitting. Protons are thought to have lifespans in the order of 100,000, 000,000, 000,000, 000,000, 000,000 years. Not bad.

evolution everywhere.

Languages are prime examples. Try reading ancient Aramaic, or old English sagas such as Beowulf or Latin in their original form. Take Latin, the language of the Roman Empire that dominated most of southern Europe for hundreds of years. Over time it hybridized with local languages that it conquered and then, when the empire collapsed, these local dialects quickly 'speciated' into what we know today as Portuguese, Spanish, French, modern Italian, etc. This is why Americans from 'south of the border' are called 'Latins,' by the way.

You may think you don't believe in evolution! But are you still riding a horse-drawn buggy? Look around you, is the car you drive the same as the one your father drove, or your grandfathers? Of course not, cars evolved! So did your computers and your cell phones, including the operating systems and 'languages' they run on. Do you know of any passage in the Bible, the Qur'an or any other ancient religious text that talks about cell phones, computers, jets, or X-rated movies? Of course not, none of these inventions existed back then.

Now here is the catch. I am a believer. In fact, I am two believers, I believe in Evolution, and I believe in *ah!* If Evolution is Revealed in every aspect of *ah!*'s creation that I have taken the trouble to look at, I can only interpret that *ah!* LOVES EVOLUTION. The alternative is to assume that *ah!* does not like evolution, as we are persistently told, in which case we can only surmise that *ah!* must be an incompetent idiot (and the Devil a sneaky genius!). SORRY, but I just can't buy that!

If every aspect of Creation (or 'the Cosmos' if you prefer) reveals clear signs of Evolving, then I am compelled to accept that *ah!* intends it to be so. And, by default, the 'incompetent idiots,' if there be any, must be those attempting to deny Evolution. Perhaps *they* are the Devil's advocates!

Curiously, the story of creation in Genesis is surprisingly in tune with the modern Revelations on the Evolution of the Universe. Expressed in much simpler terms and terminology, but right on target. And, as far as I can tell, there is nothing in the holy books that even implicitly **denies** Evolution. Put simply, an atheist who embraces evolution is closer to understanding *ah!* than a preacher who denies it.

===================== II =====================

Chapter II.72 –
Sexocracies, sins, and scandals

Democracies, bureaucracies, kleptocracies, theocracies, and several more, all staking claims on the theme of administration and governance. Ones that are rarely mentioned are the sexocracies, those that are strongly bent on the manipulation of other peoples' sex lives through the promotion of taboos and other impositions. Judaism, Christianity, Islam, Scientology and a few more are classic examples. What's more, dictating and moralizing on sexual life of their 'flock' is so common amongst religious sects that people don't even question it. DANGER. People who spend much of their lives preoccupied with what others do *under the sheets* are obsessed with sex. In some cases, it could just be strategic hypocrisy, but then there is even more reason for alarm. The critical question is, in what way does it benefit *them*?

Attempts to control the sexuality of other members of the group are by no means limited to humans. The phenomenon has been well studied in other species of social animals: wolf packs, hyenas, meerkats, some monkeys and even among birds, to mention some of the better known. It always involves the *alpha* (dominant) male that is super aggressive towards subordinate males that show any hint of sexual activity or interest. But it is not limited to males. In wolf packs, for instance, the *alpha* females can be equally despotic with subordinate females that come into heat (become sexually active) and can evict them from the pack if they get pregnant. As a rule, they are successful in suppressing the sexuality of their subordinates. This reproductive exclusivity gives them and their offspring many advantages. Meanwhile, subordinates simply have no option. They seem to have some innate mechanism that decouples reproduction so long as they are subordinate. Presumably the risk of suffering physical lesions or of being evicted from the clan are worse than postponing reproduction. Psychological castration.

No doubt there is a biological predisposition for these behaviors, and there are good reasons to consider that we humans are no exception. Consider for instance, those situations where parents, and especially stepparents, become increasingly aggressive to their adolescent sons or stepsons. The same goes for mothers with their daughters. Even though there is a good deal of stigmatizing and stereotyping, the cruelties of stepmothers to their stepdaughters are proverbial and are the stuff of countless fables, myths, and histories.

So, what do males, men, strive for? Status and power. And what does power bring? Power itself, status, wealth, privileges, impunity...

From the modern perspective these would be the visible objectives of those who seek power. But the Id exists, - biology is always functioning, present, underlying. All this is only the decoration of the cake, the means to an end. We cannot understand social dynamics without taking into consideration our basic biology. At this level, the underlying motivation in all power struggles is for dominance and to gain sexual opportunities, which dominance provides. *Alpha* males get all the action, or the best part of the action. At least, that is what we see again and again in the animal kingdom. Even so, more detailed studies have revealed much more complex webs of interactions. First, strict monogamy is extremely rare. Everybody cheats, and females search for opportunities just as actively as males. Rather than the puritan *death and taxes*, todays' youth say that from *"death and infidelities"* nobody is spared. In a *free-for-all* it somehow evens out. If it weren't for the *Alphas*.

So, if you don't manage to become an *Alpha*, don't give up. You can always cheat. What's more, if you happen to be one of those runts that will never make it to the top, then why not specialize in cheating from the start? Become a **sneaker**. Sneakers are a special class of males that have adopted a very peculiar reproductive strategy. They are sexually active males, but they retain their immature looks, like a female. They look and they behave like females. This allows them to move about 'under the radar' of dominant territorial *Alpha* males and fertilize eggs, in fish for instance, or steal copulations with receptive females in birds and mammals. They always represent a low percentage of the male population, often around 1%. The undisputed aces at this belong to a species of squid. Many octopus and squid species can control and change their skin colors and patterns with amazing precision, like the famous chameleon, but much faster. These smaller males hang around in the vicinity till they see a dominant male courting a receptive female. Then they slip in between the male and the female, with one side simulating a female and the other 'dressed' like a dominant *Alpha* male! This way the true *Alpha* sees a female, whereas the female sees an elegant but perfectly false *'alpha'* male! Genius.

As human beings we have more options. We can accept our destinies and resign ourselves, or we can become priests, give our life over to God, and forget about sex altogether, right? If you really think some spoiled brat who grew up with privileges in a wealthy, aristocratic family, as the third or fourth son, is going to accept the fate imposed by his father without a fight, you are truly delirious. Pure fiction.

The plots are always more complicated with us humans. As we saw above, the most frequent accusation against religious 'sects' is about sexual abuse. The more conspicuous ones these days involve the seemingly never-ending cases a child abuse, pedophilia, mostly by homosexual 'celibate' catholic priests, no doubt one of the darker sides of priesthood[38]. Other forms of deviations are well known, even amongst the popes (see Eric Frattini, 2010). Though these cases can be shocking, they may just represent the tip of the iceberg.

Still, few scandals involving women become public for several reasons. In very chauvinistic societies women are abused all the time, but attempts to denounce these abuses are either dismissed or even repressed by the authorities (all men, of curse). Besides, any adult woman who consents to have sex with a 'holy man' is going to be the last person to tell, especially if she's married. The *pact of silence* is guaranteed.

But every now and then we get inklings. A priest falls in love and elopes with his beloved (*Camila*, the story of Camila O'Gorman). Or a bishop gets caught red-handed (Hubert Wolf's research into *The Nuns of Sant'Ambrogio: The True Story of a Convent in Scandal*). Just clues, hints. We need to approach the issue from another perspective. Perhaps speculation, fiction.

Again, is this '*subjective*' or is it '*objective*'? *To err or not to err* …

Can this issue affect you personally? Yes, definitely. In academia saying "*that is subjective*" is a death sentence. The idea of being *objective* is somewhat misconceived as only relevant to science. It is just as relevant to everyday life. Our incapacity to discriminate between our *subjective* preconceptions and the objective world around us can cause disappointments, and be dangerous or even catastrophic in some situations. One frequent mistake is to think that '*to be prejudiced*' is to think negatively of some person or group who don't deserve it, such as a

---

[38] There have been many other forms of religious abuse, such as forcefully separating children from their parents (e.g., the story of *Philomena* and her 'lost' child), but one example will have to do.

race or class. For example, *'some used-car salesmen are dishonest, so all used-car salesmen must be dishonest.'*

This blinds us to a less obvious but much more dangerous mistake. Trusting or thinking highly of an equally <u>undeserving</u> person or group. *'Since most priests are good, all priests are good!'* Only to discover that one of them abused your child, slept with your spouse, or vanished with a bundle of money that belonged to the congregation.

Both ideas are *subjective,* but they entail a different kind of mistake. In the first case the mistake is probably of low risk for us because it will make us wary and cautious in any transaction involving car dealers, which might prove unwarranted, but at least it will protect us. The opposite mistake can be DEADLY. Believing someone to be 'nice' or even trustworthy lowers your guard, the prime condition for a scammer, conman, or sneaker! Lowering your guard makes you much more vulnerable, so being prejudiced (*subjective*) is not without its consequences to your own survival.

Prejudice hurts both ways.

Needed to say, we all make mistakes, but experience shows that someone who is *objectively* tuned in to the world around him is much less likely to make these mistakes and is therefore less vulnerable.

You can view the *subjective* approach as 'top-down' because the mind tells the body how to act, based on what the mind <u>presumes</u> to be happening. On the other hand, *objective* is 'bottom-up,' meaning that information coming in through the senses, the body, informs the mind. This way of looking at it can be useful when we discuss other issues such as politics and religion.

===================== II =====================

Chapter II.73 –

The perfect *lekking* system... a 'just so' story

In antiquity it was customary for the father to dictate the fates of his sons, even in such intimate issues as deciding who got married to whom, and which sons should become merchants, go to the military academy, or join the clergy. Those who were told to become priests had to accept their destinies without question, had to make chastity vows, and completely forget about sex.

A looong, long time ago, two of these unfortunate and handsome aristocratic young novices met, by a twist of fate, in a desolate corner of the wilds. One showed signs of a brutal beating, the other, half naked, with bloodied feet, exhausted and panting from so much running for his life. They soon discovered that they shared similar histories. Their wealthy fathers had decided that they should join the clergy and had sent them off as novices to receive their religious training. But their hormones had betrayed them, and both were caught red-handed. Dismayed by their predicament, but without the least intention of becoming celibate, they invented new names for themselves, *Ink* and *Boli*, and decided to move away from their past, pondering how they might continue enjoying the pleasures of life and women, but without the risk of being killed or forcefully married.

The normal options did not seem to offer much promise, but they soon realized that becoming priests had several advantages. To begin with, they would not have to work regularly as the farmers did. And officiating in a temple provided many opportunities to interact with the ladies. If only they could conjure the ideal facade! Rechristened '*Ink*' seemed enthusiastic.

—But we can't just go around flirting with any lady in plain sight, – mused the reborn *Boli*— We need to know who's who in town.

—The priest in the temple I was in kept records of all the people in his parish. He knew everything: when and where folks were born, who was married to whom, if they had kids, their next of kin, and much more! I never quite understood why, but perhaps...

—Yes, yes, that could work. Then we'd know who is available and who is taboo.

—You mean we would only sleep with unmarried girls? ...

—No, no, you idiot. That's a capital sin. What would happen if they got pregnant, who would they blame? You, of course.

—Yes, you are right. I barely managed to escape. Only married women, then. They have experience and they won't tell. But what about their husbands? They can be sooo jealous, even lethal!

—You're telling me. We have to find times when they are very busy. Humm, we could use that story about God working for six days and then taking a rest. That way we can offer the sacred rites and services on their day of rest, when they are free, and then we would be free when they are working.

Having recovered their breath, and with their hopes rising just thinking of these possibilities, they decided to head away from their homeland and put more ground between themselves and their pursuers. As they went along, they picked up sandals and clothes and other items, giving shape to the vivid image of a devoted novice that they had so hated not long ago. When they came across a caravan, they said they were making a pilgrimage to a famous temple *Boli* had heard about, and they were permitted to tag on. The temple turned out to be great indeed, but they immediately realized that the hierarchy was too complex. They would never know who to trust, so they sneaked out before they got recruited (those temples were always avid for new recruits). But they also realized they needed to gain more knowledge and experience in the art and trade of being a priest, so they continued in an undisclosed direction, searching for a more modest temple that might provide what they needed.

Soon they found themselves telling the story they had agreed upon in a temple that seemed ideal. The priest listened and chuckled between his teeth. But he had no intention of being careless. They could be spies. Yet, the town was growing, and he could use some help. He offered room and board and went along with the charade to see what would happen. *Ink* soon proved to be useful as a scribe, and *Boli* was good with people, and could cover for him when he was away on some errand. The help afforded him more free time. If they were to stay, he needed to confirm his hunch. A small fib gave him grounds.

—I consulted with a merchant friend, and he has confirmed that the story you told me is false. Now, tell me the truth or I will send letters to all the neighboring temples requesting information.

Fearing that this would give away their location, they had no option but to tell the priest the truth, providing as little detail as they possibly could. To their surprise, the older priest only listened, murmured some stern words, but did little else.

—*I must consider what is best.* — and left it at that. < *Perfect* >. — he thought to himself. This gave him some leverage, and even if they caught onto his escapades, he was now sure they would not tell.

Slowly they fell into the temple routine, learnt their chores, listened to the priest as he performed the rites, and got to know the congregation. But they dared not do any mischief. Just when they were beginning to despair, *Ink* was caught flirting with a young woman.

—*¡Don't even think of it! She's married to the butcher, and he has a foul temper.*

Shaken, and with chills running down his back, *Ink* told *Boli*. And *Boli* started to smile.

—What are you smiling at? I almost got nailed.

—No, no, don't you see. He didn't say "Don't do it," just "don't do it with **that** woman." He's protecting you, and giving you license. Just, don't screw up.

A sneaky smile came over *Ink's* face. Yes, perhaps *Boli* was right. Soon they were paying attention to the smallest details: what was the priest doing, how was he doing it, who was who. When were the men occupied with the crops, out hunting, or on trips to the markets of neighboring towns, everything! God rewards those who work hard. *Boli* started to notice sneaky looks from a young woman who seemed to have a strained relationship with her husband. Bingo. Soon they were meeting in the barn behind the temple. Some months later, when it became evident that she was pregnant, *Boli* was overcome by a wave of terror. But his fears were soon calmed. She had made sure to take her husband to bed often enough so he would not suspect. In time a lovely boy was born, and when they met alone, she would slip in some comment, "*Father, this or that...*" Soon the novices noticed that several women also called the priest '*Father*' when they thought they were alone. Heartwarming, but also dangerous, so they too started addressing him as '*Father*' quite naturally, as if it was totally normal.

After a few years, when the priest of the neighboring town fell ill, *Boli* was sent to replace him. Straight off, he was introduced as *"Father Boli."* This was clearly an opportunity, but also a crisis. He knew virtually nothing about the community and the old priest had been very careless about keeping records. *Boli* needed a way to get that privileged information as soon as possible, and a way of communication that would be above suspicions. Inspiration came to him when a mendicant mystic came by the town preaching the virtues of confession and the atonement of sins. Would it be possible to add confession to his preaching and practice? He started by *'lending an ear'* to the problems and worries of the people, and soon discovered that this made them feel esteemed, so they were quite open about it. But it was frustrating because they kept lamenting that they had not made offerings to the gods, or that they had quarreled with a neighbor, but hardly ever did they talk about the only issue that interested *Boli*, sex.

He needed to create a deeper concern about the subject of sex. The scriptures provided useful munition. Slowly his sermons became more and more 'loaded' with admonitions about sexual issues. It soon paid off. Especially women confided more and more about their love life. The *secret of confession* offered protection that assured no one would question him, and at the same time gave him a private setting for exchanges that could easily be turned into complicity. The question was: Which signs would reveal a willing and safe candidate for a sneaky encounter? He need not have worried; they made it perfectly clear.

—My child, tell me, how have you sinned today?

—Oh, Father, you are so manly. I get naughty thoughts when I see you giving your sermons. What can I do?

—Yes, dear, I understand, pray ten Our Fathers and come see me in my office tomorrow.

Ink encrypted some notes that were later passed on, giving birth to a long tradition of parallel histories.

But plans always tend to get muddled, so the beneficiaries of these practices were forced to refine their methods. After centuries of accumulated experience, of triumphs and scandals, the system evolved into a sophisticated lek style arena, and a fine-tuned system of double identity and sexual morality ideal for sneaking. A true marvel of male sneaker ingenuity.

———————————— o ————————————

Of course, as in any secret society none of this was exposed, but perhaps we can infer it. Imagine that you are hired to study the options in different societies and in nature. What would you recommend? What would such a system look like?

You could start by suggesting that they develop public notoriety. Priesthood provides this off the bat. At least once a week you have the opportunity of being the '*Alpha male*' for roughly an hour, all dolled up in fancy garbs, peacocking on a stage several steps above your public so that everyone can see you perfectly. And a whole battery of fancy props designed to impress, all paid for by the temple, naturally. Now, to be true *alphas* you need to show dominance above all those other males. Your assistants must be kids or young adolescents. Your sermons must emphasize the law. The Law of 'God,' mind you, the highest law in the land. By demanding respect, you will get all those subordinate males to kneel when you order them to. Local authorities, high ranking officials, and even kings will kneel before you! Yes, I know, in theory they are kneeling '*before God*,' but that is a rational construct. Remember, our emotional mind cannot make that distinction. For the emotional radar of any sexually active females at hand, the officiating Priest is the *Alpha male*. A seduction that for some ladies will be irresistible.

Good, so now you have the arena, the exotic dress, the perfect excuse to set up the charade, the undivided attention of your intended audience, the music, songs, etc. Surely priesthood is already well aware that there are patterns in married life. With time passions wane, husbands find themselves increasingly 'distracted' by external affairs and many wives end up trapped in very unsatisfactory marriages. All you need to do is deepen this natural tendency. We recommend the repression of normal sexuality, in particular adultery to eliminate possible escape valves and, besides, to reduce the competition. You must foment sexual dissatisfaction, generate an obsession about sexual sins, and control the possibility of damnations or absolutions dispensed by the priesthood, as needed. Good bookkeeping of all significant social events, plus the confession in *thought, word, deed and omission* will provide you with all the **privileged information** you'll need for this endeavor. If you prohibit divorce, the process will be assured.

However, even a hint of flirting in public is clearly taboo. Other strategies are needed. One option is to become the *confessor* of some aristocratic lady. But the more generalized solution we recommend is celibacy. If you manage to convince husbands that priests have no interest in sex, half your battle is won. You must develop and emphasize that other *'persona'* that comes so easily to many mystics, the devout practitioner who has sworn celibacy and poverty to *'better serve God.'* A simple drab attire, no ostentation, a humble appearance, the polar opposite of an *'alpha'* male. No masculine trousers, only gown-type 'habits,' an almost feminine look, nonthreatening, the perfect incarnation of a *sneaker*. Free of obligations when husbands are working, you can slide around the shadows without calling attention, in and out of any bed that is open to you. If you have followed our instructions diligently, for sure you will have created many more opportunities than will ever be visible to the naïve.

But at the same time, for the proceedings to be watertight and secure, we recommend that you take the following additional precautions:

That all encounters remain secret at all costs (female choice and consent, pact of silence, secret of confession, threats of (divine) punishment, damnation, the inquisition, etc.)

That your efforts result in pregnancies as often as possible (prohibit contraception).

That all pregnancies come to term (you must prohibit abortion).

That no priest ever be blamed for a pregnancy (only married women, the myths of virgin birth, the angel that descended from heaven, *the will of God*, etc.)

That you never get caught by a fatherless pregnancy, God forbid! (Only married women, prohibit divorce).

That your little bastards be well cared for (all offspring born in matrimony belong to, and must be cared for by the husband, unless it can be proved otherwise – which, of course, is always difficult – and has been next to impossible in the past).

No internal interference: men only, none of this nonsense about priestesses.

Expand the sphere of influence and possibilities: build new temples, conquer new lands.

Consolidate ways to discredit accusations and protect priests that get caught red-handed, not so much to protect the accused, but to protect the *mythos* of a celibate priesthood at all costs. Besides, today for thee, tomorrow for me, a brotherhood of sinners.

Allow name changes and the transfer to new parishes for those with problematic precedents.

And, if possible, cultivate your access to the richest and most powerful families in the area. If you are in the business of making little bastards, they might as well be born rich and well cared for!

To improve this last possibility, reserve the front pews for all the bigwigs in the area, so that their privileged wives enjoy all the authority and splendor of the Peacock strutting in his sacred garb from the very front rows. To stress your role as *Alpha,* make sure to force their arrogant husbands to '*kneel before God,*' and you will have created the perfect *lek,* if ever there was one.

If you apply all these provisions the system will provide you with ample opportunities to beget descendants with the least possible risk and without having to pay a dime, of course. Will all priests take advantage? No way! Just beware of those that don't. But have no doubts, for those who are interested, these institutional structures will facilitate the task to perfection.

Only myths, fiction, of course. Any similarity with real institutions or persons is pure coincidence. In any event though, you know, prudence is the better part of valor. Next time your congregation needs to replace its priest or preacher, better you choose amongst the options without testicles.

===================== II =====================

Chapter II.74 –

Back to the drawing board

If you had to reconstruct your life and your society from zero, but with the knowledge and experience accumulated by humanity up until now, what would the basis for your new life and our new society be? What would you like to see for the next hundred or a thousand years, besides tearing each other to pieces? How do you envision humanity surviving for the next ten thousand or one hundred thousand years? Would you use the same mandates that were put forth 3000 years ago? Not likely, don't you think?

Let's do a mental experiment. The Old Testament was lost on the way or never existed, nor the Torah. The New Testament never came to be. The Qur'an, and the teachings of the prophets and all those events never happened or got erased from the minds of all humans. Lacking these supernatural validations, the theocracies and the aristocracies never existed. Nor did the Communist Manifesto. Of course, it's very difficult to imagine because if you eliminate all these items, then 99% of the histories we were told would also not exist! So then, what are we left with?

We are left with a story of human survival and of slow technological evolution or progress, punctuated now and then by catastrophes and temporary setbacks. The result is that we are now **the masters and the landlords of Planet Earth**. In spite of the apparent regional differences, most societies have also converged to a host of basic strategies for modern living. We all dress, live in artificial caves (housing), use agriculture to feed ourselves, use money to trade goods and services, use a host of technologies and gadgets to solve everyday chores, and a whole package of conventions and standards that organize our societies. But we are also rapidly approaching the point at which artificial intelligence exceeds human intelligence, a singularity that will have a profound but hard-to-predict impact on the worldwide rules of the game.

What the future will bring will be the result of the decisions we make today, both with regards to the way we relate between ourselves as with the way we manage the relationship of humans with the rest of the living world and with the land and planet itself. Some errors we might be able to correct. Others, unfortunately, may affect our future for generations or even millennia, or be completely irreversible. Assuming we don't self-destruct, of course.

Changes are happening, so then, in what direction do we steer them?

Unfortunately, fear of change tends to worsen the outcomes. Most people who fear the 'future' tend to favor regressive solutions *(back to the old ways..., etc.)*. **History never runs backwards**. Efforts to return to the past do not work because the context is no longer the same. Try winning todays Indy-500 with a Model T Ford. When I was growing up, the country had 20 million humans. Now it has 50 million. Not the same. And it is not just the numbers. The changes affect **all** the environmental, technological, social, and political structures.

The taboo about changing your beliefs is something imposed by theocracies around the world. Once they nab a 'believer' they will do anything to keep him captive. It suits them, not us. The truth is that as we develop, we change our beliefs, we mature. The same occurs with our political views. I am not saying we should live in constant anarchy, but never relinquish your capacity and your right to scrutinize and question the ideas they are trying to sell you.

The great cycles

We all feel our personal life is unique, special, which is true to a certain degree. But if you observe at global scales, the world of humans has gone through different stages.

While our livelihood depended on nature we learned to gather, to hunt and to live in small groups. Then came the domestication of animals and for millennia thousands, perhaps even millions of humans discovered and had to learn how to tame, breed and select a variety of animals, including some truly amazing ones. Then came agriculture and millions learned to work the land, to select and cultivate useful plants, and to process the harvests. With this better resource base, the social groups grew steadily, written mythologies appeared, and languages became more sophisticated.

The accumulation of resources led to huge differences in wealth, which promoted more and more devastating wars. Hundreds of millions had to learn to fight and lived through the horrors of wars, epidemics, and famines.

Then came the industrial age and again millions had to learn to work in factories, to organize, to fight for their rights, and so on. Commerce, money, salaries, percentages, taxes, social security, retirement plans, and so many other details of modern living had to be learned by billions.

With the surge of technologies, billions worldwide are having to learn to drive vehicles, use phones, machinery, domestic appliances, radios, computers, smartphones, ... And they seem to need constant updating. Underlying our personal lives, there seems to be a *species level* global evolution.

In short, these great social cycles overlap with, or provide the backdrop for, all those billions of personal, 'unique' lives. I don't mean to dishearten you, but let's face it, your opportunities and liberties are strongly conditioned by your ability to learn to handle the world you have been born into.

The **fundamental change** that marks the 21ˢᵗ century is the passage from a world dominated by the material and objectal to a world dominated by the virtual and subjectal. Therefore, if you don't sharpen your perception and handling of the subjectal you'll be greatly handicapped.

We still cannot 'see' the human of the future, we don't know how we will be, or where we are going. But there are some trends that seem universal. Two are the consequence of globalization. Note that the term encompasses and confuses **two different processes that need to be separated**.

On the one hand, it has been a long process of **unification**, of dissolving frontiers, of growing tolerance, the search for common ground for all, the notion that somehow the whole planet is a 'communal space' for all of humanity. This is an absolutely crucial requisite for any conception of a civilized world. Codes of coexistence are indispensable for all forms of cooperation, and have given us unprecedented freedom to exchange goods, travel, and interact almost worldwide. Besides, with increasing firepower the cost of intolerance is rapidly becoming prohibitive, catastrophic.

- ℂΘ£ΧΙ$Τ-

On the other hand, an **increasing stratification** and growth of the world organizational pyramids. As the pyramids globalize, the hierarchies of the former independent pyramids get decapitated (or demoted), both in communism as in capitalism (Figure 33). As we saw in Chapter I.20, the two paths to power are still valid today. In the modern world communism embodies the subjective approach and capitalism the objective approach. Even so, as power structures they tend to converge.

In communism because the mythos itself is based on the premise that there is no private property (everything is communal property, you only have license to use 'your' house as long as you live in it). Thus, all the citizens relinquish their owner rights on their current and future wealth to the "commune," which then becomes the 'equanimous administrator' on behalf of 'the people.' This is utopian because 'the commune' is a virtual concept with no real entity in the material world. In practice, therefore, it requires the designation of communal administrators, theoretically elected by the citizens of the commune. This inevitably becomes a typical political conundrum, which the model was in theory designed to avoid. In all the historical cases I am aware of, the inevitable outcome is that the politicians in office are the effective owners of everything, with virtually unlimited powers, and are therefore free to do as they please. Turning over all property and power to a selected few represents an act of absolute faith in the prevalence of human altruism, to such an extent that it is pathetically naïve. Political leaders are not altruistic robots. They are living beings, and as such they abide by all the underlying laws and flaws of their biology. Selfish interests inevitably prevail. Considering what we have seen in the preceding chapters (I.19, I.23, II.56, etc.), powerful leaders that have been placed at the top of the pyramid by popular vote, or got there by other means, and consider themselves '*the chosen*' and thus '*above the law*' are ticking time bombs. The likelihood that they will turn into ruthless dictators is huge.

In capitalism the process is less obvious and perhaps takes longer, but the result is virtually the same, because the concentration of wealth and the successive take-overs and fusion of companies means the few surviving corporations will soon own everything. Hence, their CEOs and the board of directors end up in virtually the same position as the communist leadership. As we saw above, their interests are **not** the same as the interests of the shareholders, a situation that is completely analogous to the process in unions and the relationship between an entrenched political *partydocracy* and their serfs. As corporations become transnational, they can arm twist and elude local government controls ever more easily.

The almost inevitable result is that a handful of trillionaires will manage almost everything, and 7.99 billion *Subjects* will have to work ever harder just to survive. Granted, with some areas of the world maybe enjoying a fair degree of liberties and acceptable or even good standards of living; but also, vast regions barely scraping out a living, mired in poverty. For the one per million that wallow in the privileges, the ideal is to consolidate the model. That's no surprise. What is surprising is that the rest tolerates this. A permanent tug-of-war between cooperation and egoism. The rich and powerful demand cooperation, but they only adore the god of egoism. The poor ask for altruism, aid, subsidies, social support, and at the same time become ever more dependent and disabled. But when and if they gain power, they are often more corrupt and greedier than the 'aristocrats' they claim to replace.

Nothing new, perhaps, but it's worth projecting these trends to the future. The benefits for the ruling cliques are ever bigger, obviously, but at the same time the number of people who benefit is **ever smaller**. Taken to the extreme, we will end up being a huge 'anthill' dominated by a queen and her entourage, and 7,999,990,000 suckers who have to eke-out a living to survive. For me at least, this prospect is not at all attractive.

Quite frankly, I'm not so sure it will be all that pleasant for whoever manages to become the 'queen of the hill.' It may sound glamorous, but also pitifully lonely. The more you have to control, the greater your responsibilities, the demands on your time, and the threats. Besides, it would be murderously dangerous, especially for those who did a fair amount of murdering on their own way to the top. It's no surprise that a high proportion of dictators end up becoming totally paranoid about their own safety.

During the process you get the impression that the intermediate levels also benefit, but in the not so long run they are totally dispensable. Penny wise, pound foolish. This is happening even in the federalist democracies because, if those in the lower levels don't understand what they are doing and don't insist on adequate controls, the '*delegated*' power soon becomes **acquired power**, as we saw in union organizations and corporations. The stratified structure itself tends to generate a self-perpetuating oligarchy.

One of the tragic and at the same time comic situations is to watch how the opposition of one political system rants about not being subservient to the reigning empire in the name of 'freedom,' and then go on to propose that the solution is to become 'allied' to some other empire just as abusive and exploiting as the first one. If you are, or feel like, the last runt in the litter, changing from one hierarchical pyramid to another will not solve anything. We need to reconsider the underlying system. The usual answer is to condemn 'capitalism,' explicitly or implicitly in favor of some form of 'socialism' or even communism. In my opinion this is the wrong axis of controversy. What we need to reconsider and replace is the underlying notion of the rigid **pyramidal** *command and control* system applied globally.

Future of WORLD ORDER

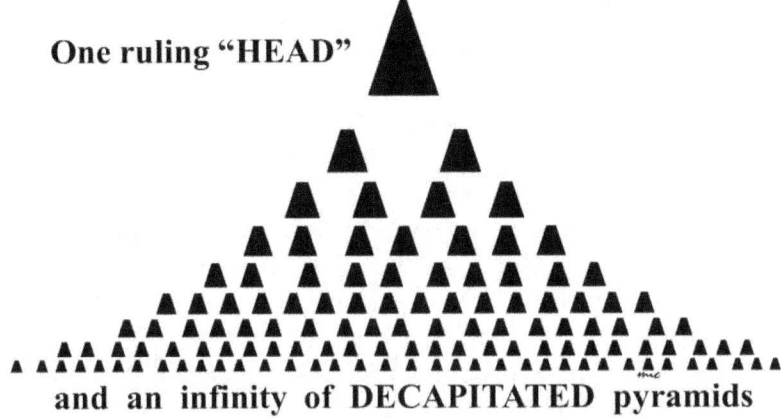

One ruling "HEAD"

and an infinity of DECAPITATED pyramids

*Figure 33. **Increasing stratification of global hierarchies**. – The progressive phagocytosis of independent hierarchies resulting from globalization leads to a rather somber future, both in the communist as in the capitalist model, or in any of the other politico-religious imperialist or dictatorial variants.*

An important aspect of this process is the distortion of the systems of representation. In the origins of federalist democracies, it was assumed that the senators and representatives that conformed the chambers acted in representation of the interests of the land and the people that empowered them. But after decades or centuries of autocratic governments (on both sides, it's much the same), the regional political coalitions have been taken over by national political parties that are more concerned with the interests of their national offices than with their supposed constituencies. The extreme is that model known as the 'unified list' hand-picked by the central offices. The traditional bipartisan 'representative' systems have passed their heyday. After the demographic explosion they no longer represent local interests. It seems no one has found a good solution to this dilemma, but the first step is to change your perspective and your expectations, and soon, because it will become ever harder to reverse the process.

How about we start 'localizing' again?

=================== II ===================

Chapter II.75 –
The laws of men

Edward O Wilson, whom we met before, posed an interesting question. Should highly evolved extraterrestrials ever reach our planet, what would they be interested in? No, not our knowledge of the basic sciences, because those are universal laws that can be deduced anywhere in our universe, so they would most likely be more advanced than us. Planets that harbor life that has reached a cultural level of evolution must be extremely rare so, for sure, they would be much more interested in how we emerged culturally, and in our humanities, because these areas are open to countless possibilities. Any species that achieved a cultural level of evolution is likely to be unique, as is our planet's history. As these things are impossible to replicate experimentally, there is much they could learn from our triumphs and from our mistakes. The thing is, can **we** learn from them? Or are we condemned to repeat the same mistakes indefinitely?

As we saw in Chapter I.31, the contradiction in the hierarchical order between the *Commandments* and the cosmic *Laws of ah!* derives from the basic structure of the cosmos: politics and religion appear and can only exist in the upper layers of the complexity scale, and are therefore the least restricted and potentially most diverse structures we are aware of. This could be interpreted as a total liberation from any sort of ethical restriction or moral constraint. Although the world is showing symptoms of such a trend, anarchy is not a viable option for a modern society. We are simply too dependent on each other and on *the system* to be able to dispense with *law and order* of some sort.

So far, we have been concentrating primarily on those Laws that are 'fixed,' imposed by the very structure of the universe, *the Laws of ah!* At the same time, I have shown that as we add levels of complexity, so do we gain in the number of available options, in 'freedom' perhaps. Now, freedom is a tricky question. As we saw, having more space, more options, doesn't mean we are freed from any of the underlying restrictions, they still apply. But at the same time, it is true that more complex organisms are capable of much more flexible responses, and therefore appear to have much more freedom. This has profound effects and gives us many advantages, but at the same time a series of complications and drawbacks. We tend to think that because we are 'free to choose' we will do fine. Well, maybe, maybe not. Mechanical robots have no freedom, but they are very good at their specific tasks and make few mistakes, if any. Instead, *free will* has a price, drawbacks, like the risks of confusion, of error, of trickery, of deceit, of making the wrong choices, at times even total bewilderment, paralysis.

Now, here is where tradition comes in handy. Of the many available options, tradition identifies the best, or at least a reasonably good one, one that has been tried and tested. No question this saves us the bother of making the same mistakes over, and over again. But, as we saw earlier, it too has drawbacks, especially if the conditions are changing significantly or if the context has become too complex for those old ways.

We tend to underestimate complexity: just how much *freedom* our biology and our culture afford us. In Chapter I.31 (Book I, in a nutshell …) we saw that *reality* is built in stages or levels of complexity, each at least one order of magnitude (ten times) more complex than the preceding. Organisms are at least a million times more complex than physics, and culture is several orders of magnitude more complex than biology. By the time you get to the level of politics, religion, and creativity, the options are virtually infinite. Even relatively restrictive notions like the messages in religious texts (bible or otherwise) could each be expressed in hundreds of different ways without losing the core message (recall the multiple wordings of the '2 + 2 = 4, …' example in Chapter I.2).

So how do societies deal with all this bewildering muddle? In many situations we are free to use any number of options, but some might be specifically banned, while others may be used more frequently as dictated by **custom** or by fads. Another important way is by defining **conventions**, of coming to an agreement and committing to one specific option. Red means danger or stop; green means safe or go ahead; yellow is transitional (things are undecided or about to change). These contrasting colors are easy to recognize (for most of us). Conventions usually define options without any 'existential' (religious or political) undertones or implications. They simply reduce the confusion and make life easier. But not all problems and options can be solved by customs and conventions.

The more general solution has been the enactment of laws, ***the laws of men***. One of the oldest and best preserved is the Code of Hammurabi, a Babylonian king who formulated and wrote it in ancient Babylonia around 3750 yb[2], long before the Bible was written. The long period of captivity in

Mesopotamia means the 'Founding Fathers' of the Jewish tradition were well acquainted with both the Babylonian laws and their mythology, from which they undoubtedly 'borrowed' freely. Add this to Moses' experience with the Egyptian dynasties and it is clear that much of the Old Testament is a mix of the earlier expertise in governance accumulated by some of the most powerful rulers the world had ever known, politics at its best for those times. And for the same reasons most of the religious rules and commandments belong to the sphere of men, not gods.

Now, here is the catch. These teachings slowly percolated down to the courts of the rulers over most of the Middle East and Europe, if not the world over. Eventually secular rulers realized they could use these commands without submitting to the whims of any 'church,' so they took up many of the practical and moral concepts and incorporated them into their own codes of behavior, which has led to yet another source of conflict of interest between church and state, basically, who rules? The end result is that most of the *'black boxes'* and many of the original social functions of religion have been taken over either by science or by politics. Science gives us tools to understand the natural world and solve practical problems, politics gives us mechanisms for negotiation and governance, each without the need to submit or appeal to any god.

Does that mean gods don't exist? Or that there is nothing left for religion? Not at all. Many people will continue to find comfort in faith and their belief in divinity. But it does mean that the old gambit of claiming superior authority by appealing to the gods has lost much of its credibility and power. You can choose to believe, but don't be fooled. In most modern countries, the rules of the game are in the legislation, and all the laws of men are subject to revision. New laws are **social experiments**: some work as expected or desired, others don't. Even well-established ones can become obsolete.

Modern societies simply cannot work without clear rules and regulations. It is the only way to balance out the need for social order and cooperation amongst strangers against our natural tendency to strive for our personal gain, self-interest or outright egoism. Thus, **the laws of men** are essential in a modern society. A few basic ideas are widespread, upheld by a majority of nations, others are only valid in specific places and times. Each society has created its own special blend of rules and regulations. This is why law degrees from one country are neither valid nor even useful in another country.

But all this has other implications. Because your life will be governed by this legal structure, you need to ensure that you and your peers (*'we, the people'*) have a reasonable degree of say in the enactment and control of legislation. Legislation in the right hands can be a blessing; in the wrong hands it can be a curse.

Perhaps the most widespread modern problem is that as countries become more populated, our current representative partisan modality becomes ever more vulnerable to political greed and corruption. Increasing power at the national level has similar effects as we saw in corporate evolution and in the power shifts that befall unions. The interests of the ruling elites tend to override the interests of the constituent states, and their citizens. This has always been the case, but as globalization advances it becomes much more acute. The new and extremely powerful instruments provided by artificial intelligence makes it increasingly likely that a very reduced number of people will have the capacity to control and manipulate millions of citizens and whole economies. Even if they are 'well meaning,' such concentrations of power are ticking timebombs. Put in a couple of psychos who want to trump democracy and the whole system can go to hell in a flash. This includes the oft prophesied risk that artificial intelligence might flip roles and take direct control, with unforeseeable consequences.

My personal hunch is that the top-down pyramidal model of command and control that has dominated politics for the last three millennia has run its course. High concentrations of power are simply too idiosyncratic and unstable, and the development of modern weapons has made them far too dangerous. Briefly: think of **pyramidal hierarchies** as the typical institutional or military hierarchy that concentrates all the power in one individual. The top-down chain of command is linear, with few or no horizontal interactions. They are efficient in some situations, but they tend to be rigid, unstable, and volatile.

We need to replace that model with a more participative and diffused distribution of power. This entails more *localizing* (counter to globalizing) and the promotion of offset power structures. I conceive **offset or diffuse hierarchies** as a web or network of hierarchies sustained by different groups or social sectors, some with a geographic base (local or regional), and others with functional links that are independent of geography and of the other aspects. The sphere of influence of a hierarchy might overlap to some extent with others, but never completely. The chains of command are diffuse, and the horizontal interactions are the norm. This web or network of 'intercrossing infrastructures' tends to mitigate the impact of hegemonic superstructures. In case you think I am a bit delirious, an octopus nervous system is organized in such a fashion, with each of its eight arms having a partially independent 'brain.' Since they have survived for over 300 million years and are considered intelligent creatures (they were declared *sentient beings* by some European countries in 2021), the strategy is not only possible but highly successful.

But these are very complex issues, best left for another day. This essay is more about us, our individual development, and our personal understanding of the world we share.

=================== II ===================

Chapter II.76 –

Beyond materialism

By the time of the reformation and the beginning of the enlightenment, the *mysterium tremendum* had been turned into an *imperium tremendum*. Dethroning the magisterium was no small feat, and seems to have required extreme antidotes. There can be little doubt that the application of the scientific method and the consequent success in understanding and controlling nature and natural processes promoted both the growing prestige of the materialistic approach and the temporary decline in the credibility of religious claims. It pulled us out of the dark ages and was at the core of the emergence of the modern world. But, like many success stories, it seems to have gone overboard.

As we saw in Book I, much of the problem originated in an unfortunate initial wording of the scientific paradigm and the polarization of the objective – subjective distinction. It resulted in an almost phobic attitude to anything 'subjective,' which fostered the genesis of passionate atheists. In an effort to get rid of *The Church* they pathologized any spontaneous manifestation of the subjectal domain and thus virtually ruled out all forms of spirituality. Any form of shamanism, mysticism, visionary experiences, etc. were deemed to be pathological manifestations of the brain. As a result, for centuries all these expressions were either marginalized or outright destroyed. In this they found a ready collaborator in *The Church*, which never had any interest or intention to allow any form of competition in the spiritual domain.

We need to change the approach. That is, we need to take a deeper look at the whole scope of our subjectal realities, the deeper roots of the many expressions of our subjectivity, before we can give science, religion, politics, legislation, government, and so on, independent definitions based on more comprehensive, less biased criteria. Once we expand our cartography of the subjectal domain, I believe it should be possible to improve our understanding and definitions. The concept of the four domains as redefined in this essay represents a good starting point for such an endeavor.

Genesis revisited

Arguing with hardcore materialists is futile. Perhaps posing a challenge helps. Consider the story of *Genesis* as an 'event' of human perception. The connection between this perception and the Big Bang theory is nothing new (*e.g.*, Smoot and Davidson, 1993), but I want to review one of the implications.

Abrahamic tradition accepts Genesis as the explanation for the origin of the universe. Without pushing the issue too strictly, this 'myth of creation' can be subdivided into a string of steps or stages. In the order postulated by scripture we have: the Unknowable before creation; God (day 0?); heavens and 'earth'; chaos and confusion, light, day and night (day 1); separate earth from sky, firmament (day 2); accumulate the waters, raise the land, plants (day 3); stars, sun, moon (day 4); sea creatures, animals, birds (day 5); land animals, man ('day' 6). Translations vary, but scholars seem to agree that the 'heavens and earth' mentioned in day 1 are not the same as 'earth and sky' of day 2. The day 1 'heavens' more likely refers to the divine realms and the 'earth' part as the manifested universe.

The modern interpretation of natural evolution, again in order, might read like this: the unknowable; infinite density (initial singularity); big bang, undifferentiated matter, light, formation of elements, clustering of matter, stars, galaxies, formation of planets, condensation of water after cooling, buildup of earth's crust, life originated in primeval seas, plants, lower animals, higher animals, humans. The idea behind the scientific 'unknowable' is that no information survives the collapse of the pre-existing universe, if any, into the initial singularity.

Several parallels are evident. The most striking is that both explanations are sequential and holarchical. And there are obvious similarities in both the holarchy and the sequence. In fact, there is only one major discrepancy, the order proposed by Genesis in day 3 – day 4: earth-land-plants appear before sun-moon-stars. Considering when this interpretation was proposed, the implicit earth-centered vision seems reasonably excusable (besides, it could also be the result of rewriting to fit theocratic dogma). The other detail is the rather sketchy taxonomy of living forms, such as whales with fish rather than mammals, but this is so trivial it can be overlooked. With these minor adjustments we have the sequence listed in Table 7 (below).

Scientists like to consider probabilities. The correlation between the two sets is very high by any scientific standard (see box).

> Considering 13 different steps there are 13! (thirteen factorial) possible orderings: about 6.2 billion, even without including the huge number of alternative myths. Kendall's Rank correlation coefficient yields a value of 0.9230 goodness of fit between Genesis and the scientific version (0 is random and 1 is perfect correlation). Sokal & Rohlf's intersection method (1969) puts the likelihood of randomness at $t \sim 0.000012$.

Now, you have to grant, neither Genesis nor the theory of the Big Bang and the expanding universe is the sort of speculation that you expect to come out of teatime gossip. So, if the similarity cannot be explained as a random coincidence, what are the options?

Conspiracy theories are always attractive, however unlikely! Perhaps orthodox Christianity infiltrated science and got it to propose this outlandish explanation so as to revalidate the bible! Or the bigshots of science came up with this trick to steal the power from the gurus of religion? It's much more interesting to consider they were generated independently, proof that they refer to the same underlying reality.

Natural Evolution	Order	Genesis 'Creation'	'Day'	Order
the unknowable	0	The Unknowable	0	0
Initial Singularity	1	God	0	1
Implicate Order – energy?	2	Heaven and 'Earth'	1	2
Big Bang	3	chaos and confusion	1	3
light and 'cloud' of matter	4	light, day and night	1	4
clustering of matter	5	separate 'earth' from 'sky'	2	5
galaxies, stars, planets	**6**	**Stars, sun, moon**	**4**	**9**
cooling, condensation	7	accumulate the waters	3	6
Earth's crust forms	8	raise the land	3	7
plankton (plants)	9	plants	3	8
lower animals	10	sea creatures, birds, animals	5	10
higher animals	11	land animals	6	11
humans	12	Man	6	12
societies		(implied)		
cultures		(Implied)		

Table 7. The order of natural Evolution and the sequence in Genesis.

The modern version is the improved explanation, no question. If so, what I would like to know is this: **can materialistic science explain how some obscure, uneducated, superstitious individual (a few at best) who barely knew how to count, sitting in a cave thousands of years ago with no instrument other than their intuitive perception, came up with an explanation (*Genesis*) even vaguely analogous to a theory as farfetched as the theory of the Big Bang and the expanding, evolving universe?**

Let me put this into perspective. The issue is not so much that the modern explanation has consumed trillions of dollars in sophisticated equipment and the entire lives of countless scores of very, very educated researchers. Consider the conceptual tools available to someone living three or four thousand years ago. Probably over 80 % of the words needed to describe the theory in its present form did not even exist, let alone the conceptual abstractions that back them up. The theory relies heavily on very elaborate mathematics. Even basic concepts such as negative numbers and zero are modern: negative numbers appeared in China about 1700 yb[2], and the concept of zero was proposed by the Indian mathematician

Brahmagupta 1305 yb^2.

Other ancient ideas are quite surprising in a modern light. Democritus (460-370 B.C.) imagined reality as composed of tiny indivisible particles, 'atoms,' that constantly move around in a vacuum, and come in different sizes and shapes that combine to make up the different physical objects. One feature, that these *atoms* are fundamental, impenetrable, turned out not quite right! (assuming he wasn't thinking of quarks). But folks, he was saying these things over two thousand years ago! How did he gain these ideas of things he could not possibly have observed directly?

Many notable modern thinkers and scientists have hinted or explicitly claimed that 'inspiration' came from within as a sort of flash, dream, or revelation. Some were noted in Chapter II.64 (*The owners of Truth*). Stan Grof mentions several more in *The Way of the Psychonaut* (Vol. II).

So, Revelation? Intuition? Insight? How could you tell one from the other? What farfetched ideas are being revealed, intuited or in-sighted today that will become the truths of tomorrow?

==================== II ====================

Book III

Boundless Mindscapes

Book III
Boundless Mindscapes

The discussions in Books I and II have stayed mostly grounded within the confines of our manifest everyday world and a materialistic cosmology. Even so, as we climb the complexity ladder, the number of possible arrangements grows exponentially, and the web of interactions cuts across all domains and levels. This is reflected in the fascinating diversity of human languages, dress, cuisine, artistic expressions, forms of governance, beliefs, religious and political creeds, and cultural diversity in general. Since politics and religion are aspects of culture, they are open to unlimited creativity and diversification. Thus, any attempt to enthrone and straightjacket religious or political ideologies is false. Even if we acknowledge Divine oneness, the claim that there is only one "true" *path* or religion is a political stratagem that has little to do with genuine spirituality.

To better understand these issues, we need to flip sides. Spirituality remits us to a profusion of phenomena and of parallel existences that cannot be experienced nor explained within the confines of the manifest material universe we are familiar with, and the materialistic cosmology. Let me be clear on this: consensual science and technology, plus politics and administration are adequate tools, the best we have developed so far, to deal with the material aspects of our universe and the phenomenology of the manifest world we live in.

However, all these insights break down when you try to apply the same criteria to the subjectal domains, just as badly as when you try to apply subjectal criteria to the material world. From the perspective of a material scientist, rejecting subjective influences and biases is justified. From the perspective of a spiritual seeker, rejecting materialist-based conceptual limitations and dogmas when applied to spirituality is equally justified.

For similar reasons, using religion as a justification for political actions is not a valid gambit. This is especially important when religious claims are used to justify and abet brutal subjugation, mutilation, rape and plain murder in the name of some presumed god or other. Physical actions in the manifest world are by definition political, **not** religious. Supporting this dictum requires a more detailed and explicit cartography of our minds and the farther reaches of our subjectal experiences, a broader understanding of 'reality' that acknowledges the existence of subtle dimensions beyond matter. often refer to as 'spiritual,' and perhaps even the existence of a reality completely out of spacetime.

In the following chapters I will sketch the growing wave of information about our rich interior worlds, our spiritual life, the methods of exploration, the ancient and modern use of psychedelics, and suggest a few lead-ins to this revitalized yet timeless approach to our interior worlds and the interpretation of the subtle spheres they reveal. With a better understanding of these aspects and how we know anything about them, we can then reconsider the role of religion and attempt a synthesis. Yet, though much of the phenomenology I describe has considerable support, most of the interpretations are still very speculative, incipient intuitions or emerging ideas that need further research and validation.

==================== III ====================

We are not human beings having a spiritual experience,
we are spiritual beings having a human experience.
Pierre Teilhard de Chardin.

Chapter III.77 –
What are we?

Risking an answer to this question is tricky. As I mentioned in previous chapters, there are many hypotheses on this issue. From the materialistic point of view, we are complex physical beings that evolved in progressive stages of increasing complexity over eons, following a long uninterrupted chain of living beings. Our physical complexity is what gives us consciousness and our perception of being, including the notion of spirituality. The physical support system is a given, it *simply existed* before life and conscious beings appeared. All this seems to be self-supporting, until you get to the issue of perception and consciousness.

As we saw in Chapter II.44 – *Another turn of the spiral, the tricks of perception*, the whole problem of perception has been the subject of much research and philosophical speculation. The prescientific intuitive notion that we 'see' directly with our eyes was replaced by the concept of light-sensitive neurons that record simple stimuli (data) and transmit it through the optic nerve to the brain. The information is processed in special areas of the brain and, somehow, the brain integrates it and creates a virtual interpretation that we perceive as the world around us, our 'reality.' However, this apparently elegant explanation had a problem: nobody could figure out what acted as a 'screen' on which this image could be projected, until the development of the holographic model. As mentioned before, a hologram is a pattern of light-wave interference that produces areas of varying brightness that we can perceive as three-dimensional images. Presumably the brain generates some equivalent form of patterns in the brain matrix or in our head. This solves some problems but creates others: can you 'see' inside your brain? Who is the perceiver, and where is this 'seer' located? One of the distinctive features of the subjectal domain is that it is non-local. In other words, you can't give precise spatial coordinates for subjectal events, as we normally do for a physical object. Even colloquially, we *'feel heavy of heart,'* have *'butterflies in our stomach,'* or got such a fright that we *'jumped out of our skin,'* and so on. Thus, the feeling of 'I' is not tied to the brain or even the whole body in any simple way.[39]

The obvious solution is to postulate our dual nature, matter and spirit, body and soul. Our body gives us the 'machine' to operate in the material domain, but consciousness is a faculty of our spiritual nature. Great, problem solved. Well, is it? Not really. How does *spirit* see? Passing the buck to 'spirit' just kicks the ball out of **this** playing field. We are again faced with the *infinite regress* problem. So now let's move to the spiritual playing field: what is spirit, why does spirit have consciousness, how does spirit 'see'? What laws govern spiritual dynamics? Well, most people, including mystics, will say things like "spirit is all-knowing," "spirit is eternal," etc. In other words, now spirit 'simply is,' the often quoted *"I am what I am."* So am I, by the way, and you. In other words, they don't really know any better than you or I do.

We need to approach the issue from a different angle. We might not grasp the ultimate *meaning* of spirit and existence, but we can certainly

---

[39] See Ed Yong on *Master of Illusion*, Nature: 480, Dec 2011, p.168-170.

take a closer look at the phenomenology that surrounds it. If we study subjectal expressions objectively, we can build a clearer picture of what is going on, even if we don't yet understand the whys and wherefores. Knowing always starts with direct experience; next we identify the components and the diversity of expressions, look for regularities and anomalies before attempting to decipher processes and mechanisms. Only then can we postulate theories and gain some understanding.

To follow up on the visual perception mentioned above, there is a growing body of evidence that under certain conditions, or with special training, we can 'see' without functioning eyes or even without a physical body. In the oriental martial arts, learning to fight with bound eyes is considered a serious possibility and it is said some gifted practitioners excelled and achieved lasting fame (something like the fictional Taoist sword master *Hundred Eyes* in the Marco Polo narratives). A more recent and tangible example is the rather special case of the French Second World War resistance hero, Jacques Lusseyran, who was blinded in an accident as a child. This, however, did not affect him as he (and most of us) expected: "*Being blind was not at all as I imagined it. Nor was it as people around me seemed to think it.*" He became aware of an inner radiance or light: "*I began to look ... from an inner place to one **further within**, ... radiance was there, or to put it more precisely, light.*" ... "*I bathed in it as an element which blindness had suddenly brought much closer.*" (Quoted in Smith, 2001). I have yet to get hold of Jacques' autobiography, '*And there was light,*' but his story sounds fascinating.

Mainstream Cartesian-Newtonian science has systematically dismissed these old stories and even the recent claims of near-death and out-of-body experiences, made more likely and frequent by modern resuscitation practices. Presumably they happened very infrequently in the past, but were seldom recorded or understood. At this point there are many studies and thousands of recorded instances, so denying the *phenomenon* just because we don't understand how it works seems foolish. This is equally true of the whole range of mystical and visionary experiences reported by cultures of all ages and all over the world.

Part of the contradiction arises from trying to apply the methods and criteria of material sciences to the subjectal domains. This doesn't work. It's like trying to hear sounds with a radar or see the stars with a microscope. You are using the wrong instrument, looking in the wrong direction. You cannot study and understand the '*interior*' subjectal domain with the instruments of the 'exterior' material sciences. Meaning and significance are not an intrinsic property of matter. Ken has a detailed analysis of the validity claims for different domains, but I had some difficulty with it because my understanding of the domains doesn't fit his classification.

Attempts to understand the subjectal domain, and especially the transpersonal aspects, can only be achieved by looking inwards. Admittedly, it is much more difficult to share and compare the resulting observations, but by no means impossible. Oriental mystical schools in India, Tibet, China, and Japan have been doing just that for centuries, even millennia, and have developed well defined protocols. Many of us can do wonders via graphic depictions of what we experienced. Validity should rest on the clarity and sincerity of the descriptions, and the consistency of the phenomena described across the spectrum of methods, practitioners and cultural backgrounds (always keeping an eye out for conflicts of interest that might distort a person's narrative). After decades of research and comparison of the modern results with ancient accounts, this actually seems to be the case. In a nutshell, the increasing number of spontaneous cases on record, plus those induced by the ancient spiritual practices, the modern methods of depth psychology, and the research with psychedelics have all shown that we humans can have direct experiential access to an unlimited constellation of information from the biographical level, our perinatal experience, historical and archetypal domains, and all the tiers of '*the Great Chain of Being*,' including occasional access to what people perceive as divine realms. Equally important is that the realms, beings and knowledge gained during these experiences are independent of the person's gender, race, beliefs, religion, or general cultural background. In other words, many of these experiences cannot be generated by material from our postnatal biography. Since this material is often completely unrelated to our current life's experiences, we must be accessing or coming into contact with an independent pool of knowledge or existence beyond our individual self and current life.

This cumulus of experience strongly supports the notion that there are other realms or dimensions in addition to the material universe we are familiar with. Of course, shamans and visionaries have known this for millennia, have developed methods to access and explore these domains and know them for a fact. Their descriptions and cartographies may vary somewhat because it is impossible for one person (or even a community) to cover all the aspects of these vast domains, but the gift of globalization and the possibility of doing in depth comparative studies over a wide range of cultures and epochs is producing a much clearer, consistent, and reliable picture than any single visionary or prophet could ever hope to achieve.

So, it seems, Pierre's dictum quoted at the beginning of the chapter is a likely interpretation. At the very least, it's a 50 – 50 situation. Let's look further.

==================== III ====================

> *Don't be a blind believer, nor an atheist, not even an agnostic.*
> *We need to find better ways to get in touch with the Divine.*

Chapter III.78 –

Honoring our spiritual heritage

As we saw, everything 'sacred' and all the great religions had their origins in shamanic or mystical practices, regarded as portals to an occult or parallel reality (or realities). I mostly avoided this topic in Books I and II. There was a time when any mention of the subject would have been discredited outright, by science because it was not 'objective,' and by institutionalized religions because they have never had any interest in fomenting ideas and practices that might compete with their authority.

Practices and techniques that affect our inner experiences of what we call *spiritual*, and the beliefs evoked by them, are so universal amongst uncontaminated societies and their cosmologies that we must pose them as possibilities to be taken seriously and explored. At the very least, recognize that the *fields* revealed by these experiences are theoretically possible and treat them as working hypotheses. Do they or don't they exist? What methods are effective to access these experiential fields? Do they require the existence of as yet 'occult' dimensions? If these other dimensions truly exist, how much do we know about how they work and what they mean? Is the nature of a *spiritual* experience or event determined by the method employed, or is it independent of the methods? What people encounter in those experiential fields, are they really a manifestation of 'deity' or do they have some other explanation? Is *'otherworldly'* truly of another world, or just an odd field of experience in this one?

To do this, we need to assume and accept that other dimensions or realities do or at least *may* exist, and that it is possible to perceive them through special techniques. This is what Aldous Huxley[40] called '*the Technologies of the Sacred*,' those that '*open the doors of perception*.' It's not for lack of precedents. World literature, including religious texts, contain innumerable accounts, from the very dawn of history to the present. The problem, rather, is to separate the chaff from the grain, and to reach some sort of consensus as to why these experiences are the way they are and not otherwise.

We seem to lack a set of terms for abstract, non-material, non-spatial concepts or realities, so everybody uses mundane terms by analogy. To add to the confusion, a profusion of terms has been borrowed and used by fantasy and sci-fi writers, often inconsistently. No use reviewing all this, but we do need to define a basic set of terms to proceed. We met several of them in previous chapters: reality, stage, arena, level, playing field, dimension, domain, sphere, realm, ...

Spiritual experiences frequently allude to *dimensions, domains, realms, worlds*, etc., but defining how different people are using them is tricky. Few terms in use are completely free of spatial connotations. Most use or imply '*dimensions*,' which originally stood for the axes that define space and time, as in *three-dimensional* space, or other variables of the physical world. Yet, today '*in another dimension*' (singular) is often used to mean '*in another universe*,' where the laws of nature might be partially or totally different from ours. Somewhat arbitrarily, I use a nested holarchy of terms, with some overlap. All are spatial, but note that we often use them to refer to virtual fields or contexts.

> **General terms,** used loosely, include:
> **Reality**: what we perceive and infer of our being and surroundings, including thoughts, dreams, etc.
> **Band:** a slice or sector in a spectrum.
> **Level**: a step or tier in a sequence of complexification.
> **Stage**: a step in a process, a sequence of manifestation, or of development.
> **Arena:** the setting or context in which an activity or perception takes place,

---

[40] All Aldous Huxley references are from a 1963 joint edition of *The Doors of Perception* and *Heaven and Hell*.

> excluding the players.
> **Field**: a combination or interaction of space, form, energy and perception.
> **Playing field:** any arena or context that includes us, the players, interacting as conscious Subjects.

You start your day enjoying the very real birds and flowers in your garden. Later you read a novel, so your *'field of perception'* is now virtual. If you switch to watching a movie, you'd be *'in another dimension'* (from the imaginary one evoked by the book to the equally virtual but distinct audiovisual one of the movie). Note, however, that the singular of the expression *"another dimension"* is figurative (*realm* would be more appropriate). In practice, even going upstairs changes the values of all three spatial dimensions simultaneously, a different *domain* perhaps, in the same sphere of your home. If you fell into the basement and had to grope around in the dark, your sensory field of smells and touch would now be very real again, but different from the garden, almost like *"another world."* But this time *"in other dimensions"* would be more accurate (from garden sights and sounds, to the smells and textures of the dungeon). Later you are asleep and dreaming. Your physical location is the same, but your inner subjectal experience is completely *'in a different world.'* So, where are *you* exactly? No intention of solving these muddles, but note how tricky all this can be, and keep these difficulties in mind.

The first item we must consider is that much of what was once taken for 'spiritual' is just stuff from the subconscious. Some types of dreams, for instance. For a culture that is not aware of the existence of our subconscious and unconscious, it is very easy to interpret dreams as messages from some other reality. There was a time in which people who suffered from mental disorders or claimed to have had unusual experiences were either considered especially virtuous or, if not, as possessed by demons. With the advent of the materialist approach, the pendulum swung from superstition to denial. Any unusual manifestation was considered 'pathological,' including any indication of contact with other realities. The person was surely mad, or suffered from a *'mystical delirium.'* Fortunately for these people, both psychiatry and social perception, in the West at least, have advanced enough as to avoid having these poor souls locked up, executed, or suffer some of the other barbarisms committed in the name of some Church, the 'Holy' Inquisition, Islam, or whatever (science included).

An experiential holarchy: – dimension – domain – sphere – realm – world – universe – cosmos.

1 Dimension: a single quantifiable or qualifiable aspect in a physical or conceptual context; an axis that can assume a range of values, such as '*temperature*' in the physical world, or '*language*' in cultures. A slice or section in the continuous spectrum of a dimension is a '**band.**'

2 Domain: an area defined by segments of two or more dimensions, as the *individual-objectal domain*.

3 Sphere: a multidimensional physical or conceptual region within a more extensive continuum.

4 Realm: a complete functioning arena or section within a world, or a level of manifestation.

5 World: a complete functioning arena in our universe, governed by the same physical laws as ours, with its own unique coordinates, evolution and history, such as a planet (*e.g., Pandora* in James Cameron's *Avatar*). At least in theory, objects can travel back and forth between worlds by conventional physical means.

  Parallel Worlds: complete functioning arenas in separate but adjacent realms (sets of dimensions), in which some of the Laws may differ from ours, but are still accessible to us; *e.g.*, those envisioned by Philip Pullman, as recreated in the HBO miniseries '*His Dark Materials*' saga. Akin to *alternate world*. Travel between them would require some sort of sci-fi style, magical, or spiritual **portal**.

6 Universe: a continuous complete functioning reality, in which the same basic Laws hold throughout.

  Parallel Universe: a complete functioning universe in a separate, disjunct set of dimensions, in which many or all the basic Laws differ from ours. We can conceive of their existence, but they would be completely inaccessible to us or our instruments.

7 Cosmos: all of the above: everything, everywhere, at all possible times.

Also relevant here is what Aldous pointed out in his essay *Heaven and Hell* with respect to the prevalence of 'mystical' and 'visionary' experiences in the past. Basically, that most people lived under much more stressful conditions than we do today, both physically and mentally. Several of these conditions are known to produce both altered (pathological) and expanded states of consciousness.[41] Our current personal, physical, and chemical

---

[41] Some texts use '*altered*' in place of '*expanded*' states of consciousness. I avoid this term because it has a negative slant: an *alteration* is equivalent to saying it is a

condition and environment is dramatically different from those experienced by everyone in the past. Most people were almost chronically undernourished, hurt, infected, ill and stressed out. Most suffered from seasonally imposed food shortages and even near starvation, vitamin deficiencies, unchecked pain, gave birth without pain killers, and suffered diseases with no known cure. Even simple wounds, fractures or dental infections often led to internal poisoning by festering in the wounds. Many of these conditions that were widespread in our recent past, are known to produce hallucinations of various sorts, including those other states that can be deemed visionary and mystical. Even a visit to the dentist, a fracture or an amputation without anesthetics must have produced excruciating pain and would have been equivalent to a flagellation, or much worse. Sensory deprivation, like spending the long winter nights in total darkness, also added to the anxiety and stress. Contact with both the beauty and the harshness of nature was much more direct, often threatening. It is difficult to imagine the cultural backdrop and mindset, but for lack of better alternatives, fantastic explanations and superstition must have run wild. In this context, perhaps it was reasonable to consider all 'mystical' claims as mere hallucinations. The pitfalls are real, they do exist.

Yet, the ancients must have been aware that these experiences sometimes produced a different kind of vision, and so incorporated many of these elements into their spiritual practices: long fasts, sensory deprivation (meditating in caves), self-inflicted pain (self-flagellation), controlled breathing, chanting and drumming, mantras, prayer, etc. For some, any amount of suffering was worth it if it afforded a glimpse of Divinity. But all too often, the mindset and the physical settings of past ages were more likely to elicit 'hellish' nightmares than blissful visions, which helps explain their obsessions with Satan, the sufferings of hell, the demonic, the possessed, and so on.

The use of these methods and conditions that provoke or at least facilitate these expanded states of consciousness, including the use of psychoactive plants (most of which contain psychedelics), was widespread

---

pathology. *Expanded* only indicates that consciousness is able to access phenomena that are not available to ordinary consciousness, without judging their nature. To a shaman they are normal. The term 'non-ordinary' covers both types, altered and expanded.

in the pre-materialistic world, but was strongly downplayed or banned for a couple of centuries, in the modern West at least. However, the rediscovery of many of our ancient shamanic practices and the discovery of synthetic drugs, most notably lysergic acid diethylamide (LSD), rekindled the interest in visionary experiences, without the sweat that many of the old methods required. Whether this is good or bad is debatable, but the widespread interest and use of these resources, virtually world-wide, should leave little doubt that we have an inner need, a yearning, for **personal** contact with the other-worldly. Interestingly, even alcohol addiction has been postulated as a misdirected attempt in search of the Divine.

However, it is easy for a staunch materialist to dismiss the claims of people who actively seek out these experiences as self-fulfilling illusions or mystical delusions, so I will spend a few lines on a glaring exception. Nobody gets up in the morning thinking it would be great if they had a heart attack or a dreadful accident on the off chance of surviving it *and* having a near-death experience (NDE), yet NDEs have been reported by thousands of individuals of all ages, from all walks of life, and virtually all cultures and countries. Most of these people were not even aware that NDE occurred or were even possible. Of course, no two NDEs are the same, but the striking fact revealed by a growing number of studies is that they all share many common features consistent with the notion that body and soul are two separate entities, and that consciousness exists and persists beyond our body. A crucial finding is that even preliterate children, too young to have been affected by cultural preconceptions, give accounts that are perfectly consistent with the narratives of adults. If you are interested, Pim van Lommel gives an excellent recent summary in his *Consciousness Beyond Life* (2010).

All these experiences seem to be much more common today than was admitted in the past century or two (NDEs alone tally an estimated 25 million world-wide, according to Pim). No wonder, if you consider that any mention of anything of the sort could have you accused of being a witch or as possessed by demons in the old days, or have you sent to the looney bin in the materialistic era. Undoubtedly the wisest response was to keep your mouth shut and handle the experience as best you could without anyone finding out. Many unfortunate souls who did speak out ended up condemned, imprisoned, or even executed. Even today it's not wise to speak of these experiences openly in public. Prudence is called for.

The field of spiritual experiences has a long history and is growing rapidly. I suggest starting with Stan Grof's *'The Cosmic Game'* as an excellent overview combining firsthand accounts and a psychological perspective with a worldwide overview of mystical literature, illustrated by examples of actual experiences as narrated by the participants, all gleaned from Stan's extensive clinical and research history.

For those who wish to delve deeper in the history of psychology, and the phenomenology produced by psychedelics and other interior techniques, Stan's more recent and extended treatment, *The Way of the Psychonaut*: *Encyclopedia for Inner Journeys,* (volumes I and II) and the references therein, is an invaluable source (*psycho-naut* means *'traveler within'*). The summary that follows draws largely from the previous chapters and these sources.

Should you delve into the field, keep in mind that no single individual was ever blessed with the complete cosmic picture. Most accounts show only fragmentary glimpses into some special aspect of the cosmic structure and dynamics. However, the emerging cartography gleaned from the accumulated experiences of many individuals covers virtually all the natural and mystical/spiritual spectrum from all cultures and ages. A place to start might be Chris M Bache's *Lifecycles* on reincarnation, and *Dark Night, Early Dawn* on the deep ecology of our minds (see full citations in Sources).

===================== III =====================

Chapter III.79
The Book of Stan

We just met Stan (Stanislav) Grof in the previous chapter. He is one of the pioneers who has dedicated his whole life to the study and understanding of the wide range of states of consciousness, with special emphasis on the nature of expanded states of consciousness (see Footnote 40 above and glossary), the conditions that produce them, and is a founding member and key contributor to the development of transpersonal psychology. Stan's basic training was in psychiatry.

In one of his conferences, he proposed a fairly simple parameter to differentiate someone with mental problems from someone who is going through an episode or experiencing what he and Cristina Grof aptly called a *'spiritual emergency.'* **Emergence/emergency** is used here in its dual sense of something that surfaces or emerges and at the same time produces a state of anguish or emotional dissonance that can be considered an existential 'urgency.' We can use *emergence* for the process and *emergency* for the episode. The person can feel overwhelmed or disoriented, but does not lose coherence.

In a conference Stan made the following distinction (my wording):

> *A person with a mental disorder speaks of ordinary matters in a disorganized and incoherent manner, often putting the 'blame' for their sufferings on external factors or people. We need not discuss the issue further, the insane say and do crazy things. There may be cases that are difficult to diagnose (those on the edge), but as a rule they show other symptoms of physical or neurological problems: senile dementia, high fever, seizures, delirium, intoxication, etc.*
>
> *Instead, a person who is going through a spiritual emergency speaks of non-ordinary or other-worldly perceptions, but in a totally coherent and clear fashion, without signs or symptoms of physical problems that might explain the episode. They also recognize that the whole situation is endogenous, coming from within themselves. It is clear that the anxiety, stress, tiredness and other symptoms arose as a **consequence** of the experience.*

Thus, "*cultures that recognize shamans and show them great respect have no difficulty in differentiating them from individuals who are crazy or sick*" (Grof, 2019, I).

Still, the medical disorder aspect is not the issue here, rather the spiritual phenomenology and its existential implications. According to Stan, the characteristics of spiritual emergencies are very similar or identical to what has been described as the shamanic crisis, to some forms of *mystical experiences* and to the discourse of many historical mystics. The presumed '*mystical delirium*' is a delirium only if we stick to the strictly materialistic view. Very similar states can be reached or induced by a list of psychoactive drugs (psychedelics) and also by relatively simple techniques such as accelerated breathing. There is no question that these experiences are real states, expressions of the *subjectal* domain. The problem lies in their interpretation, that is, how do you explain these experiences and what is their significance. As Fritz put it, "*It's a technology of consciousness we don't understand yet.*" [42]

---

[42] Quoted by Michael Pollan in *How to change your mind* (2018), page 239.

Recall that even 'myths,' 'fantasies,' 'figments of the imagination,' and similar ideas that are often disqualified as 'illusory' are nonetheless REAL states of the **subjectal** domain. They may be false, but falsehood itself is still a condition, a real thing that can have a huge social impact.

Just a background sketch. Stan found that a variety of intense or sudden emotional situations can generate spontaneous internal crises that he calls *spiritual emergencies*: accidents, giving birth, severe illnesses, physical stress, surgery, the death of a loved one, fasting, even lack of sleep. All these situations tend to lower the normal defenses of our ego, which allows stuff from our subconscious or unconscious to surface.

Aldous referred to these defenses as the *"mental reducing valve,"* which helps us keep our mind focused on our immediate biological survival. When these defenses are lowered, material from our subconscious and *"the-mind-at-large"* can reach consciousness: intense dreams, visions, physical manifestations, feelings of cosmic unity, mythological beings, dissolution of our individual boundaries... The list of possible manifestations is long. All of this can lead to a *spiritual emergency*, especially difficult when these experiences are in conflict with the person's prior beliefs, or those of the local culture.

Even apparently mundane situations, such as contact with the beauty of nature, exquisite art or architecture, music, and so on can trigger similar experiences. Expert practitioners of intense physical activities, such as martial arts, athletics, or extreme rock climbing, at their peak also report the experience of loss of ego, of fusion with their art and environment, and of oneness with what they are doing.

Stan and other researchers speak of several types of processes that can be grouped as *spiritual emergencies*: existential crises; mystical experiences; shamanic crises; kundalini awakening; unitive consciousness; psychological renewal by return to the center; psychic opening; past lives; experiences of death and rebirth; near-death or out-of-body experiences; several types of *encounters*: with spirit guides, with mythological or archetypal entities, and close encounters with UFOs and abduction; experiences of possession; alcoholism and addiction; and many variations on these themes. 'Modern' psychiatry considered most of these states or events as forms of pathology. For Stan and others, they are signs of internal processes that often lead to important healing events or spiritual growth if they are supported and allowed to play out.

The essential point is that people have these experiences, and have had them since the dawn of culture! **What has changed over time is their interpretation**. You might think they are only deliriums, mental quirks, but the people who live through a *spiritual emergency* experience it as something very real and important that produces important changes in them, their behavior and their emotional state, most often in positive ways if handled correctly. For this reason, Stan speaks of these experiences as being **holotropic**, *i.e.*, as tending towards wholeness. The other half, the cycle of cosmic unfolding or manifestation he refers to as **hylotropic**, as tending towards matter, in the direction of fragmentation, division and separation.

Many of these experiences challenge the materialistic conception of the universe. Brushing them away as symptoms of mental illness is a very deficient way of dealing with the issue. They also conflict with some religious conceptions, especially those that deny or don't recognize reincarnation. Other times they are taken as proof of one or another religious belief. But before we jump to conclusions, let's explore the phenomenology a bit further.

---------------------- O ----------------------

First, we need to make a clear distinction between the fields of infinite possibilities that become accessible under expanded (*holotropic*) states of consciousness, and the very finite interpretations, the dogmas, that form the bases of most institutionalized and politicized religions. Rather than confirm some faith or other, the growing body of experiential accounts challenge and undermine sectarian claims of the privileged nature of their specific 'revelations,' especially the claim about the **superior and exclusive nature** of their particular prophet and faith. If many ordinary folks can have a multitude of variations of these experiences, why on earth should we be forced to believe and worship only the version proposed by someone else's preferred prophet?

Let's review David Bohm's quote on the issue of 'ether' (Chapter I.3).
"I must consider the idea of something unobservable if I am ever going to find it. First, I must think about it. I must think how I am going to find it if it is there."

Given that these experiences reflect something real that does not have 'ordinary' explanations, what are the alternatives? There are several hypotheses in circulation:

a) They are abnormal manifestations of our brains, symptoms of a mental disorder.

b) It is stuff from the subconscious or unconscious that is normally 'blocked.'

c) They are spontaneous manifestations created by the particular disposition of our nervous system and brains, the product of increasing complexity. True, being conscious of what our brains are or are not capable of doing is one of the great challenges. Their study and the development of artificial intelligence have slowly eroded what was previously considered 'spiritual.'

d) They are 'memories' of past lives of our ancestors, coded in our genetic material (our DNA). This idea requires or implies at least two suppositions: first, that there is some way of transcribing records of everyday events to the DNA, and then, that we have the faculty to 'read' this coded material, that consciousness is able to access this information.

e) They are telepathic manipulations of superior extraterrestrial beings.

f) They indicate that all existence, the universe, is conscious, and that aspects of that consciousness are linked to different forms of existence (animals, plants, even material things, mings, that westerners normally consider 'inanimate'). In states of expanded awareness, we can access and experience these energies 'from within.'

g) They arise from the '*collective unconscious*' (Carl Jung). As seen from the materialistic perspective, Jung's idea also requires and implies at least two suppositions: first, that there is some corporeal or extracorporeal form of registry or memory of that collective unconscious, and then, that under certain conditions we have the faculty to access these records, something similar to point d). However, Jung and his school consider this is incorrect. Rather, they consider these archetypal realms to have independent existence (see point i. below), and that we can experience them under certain conditions.

h) That there is a parallel domain containing all the information, an energy state out of time (along the lines of akashic records, holographic files containing the memories of the soul).

i) That there are other dimensions of *real* existence, but different from the ones we normally perceive, populated by a diversity of beings. This notion has been extensively studied by Jungian psychology and, of course, it is the assumption and basis of most of our mythologies.

j) These states are produced by *'the Grace of God'* or of some other divine being (which also implies something like i).

k) Some other alternative that is still to be discovered? Linking physics and consciousness research, some suggest the whole universe is a continuous interconnected field of information and energy, perhaps structured by fractals via holographic blueprints.

l) Some combination of these alternatives …

Each religion harbors some explicit or implicit notion of this sort, including science. Since none of them have irrefutable evidence that their version is the true one and much less that their conception is sufficient to explain all the known phenomena, the healthy approach is to consider them as working hypotheses and keep an open mind. Which means that, for the moment, all religious claims and 'truths' should also be considered hypothetical. To use their own expression, *"It's just a theory."* Still, a more benevolent and practical approach is to consider the different mystical and religious claims as *'progress reports'* on our understanding of cosmology.

Points a) through d) are progressively more complex or hare-brained, but they could be considered as alternatives or 'emergent properties' within our known material reality. To be sure, when faced with any case of visions or of people who claim to hear voices, etc., we must always consider the possibility of an odd manifestation or malfunction of our neurology. For instance, it has been suggested that Jung's *'collective unconscious'* can be explained as the result of the way our nervous system develops. That is, as human beings with the same genetic background, we tend to have the same cerebral structures and therefore similar types of 'hallucinations.' Another approach is to consider perinatal experiences as the source of many of these unexpected memories. The fact that they are preverbal puts them out of reach of any talk therapy. To our conscious ego they may even appear to be alien.

An interesting category is the issue of *'extraterrestrial abductions.'* Stan considers them another type of spiritual emergency (as did C. G. Jung, John E. Mack and others). In a conference Stan was asked if he believed in U.F.O.s and extraterrestrials, to which he responded that he did not have an opinion and that as a psychiatrist the question was irrelevant. What he saw was that the **inner** experience had a great impact on the persons involved, and often a transforming influence in their lives. In other words, the experience can feel *totally 'real' in the subjectal domain*, even if it has no correlation with material realities in everyday life. This is equally valid for a whole range of dreams and imaginary experiences, like the parallel worlds created by writers and film-makers. Nobody thinks that these universes have real existence in the material sense, but we still find them very entertaining and exciting. Nor is it a question of branding Tolkien as a madman just because he had an enviable and lucrative imagination.

These types of arguments sooth the materialists, but they are not convincing. For instance, the idea that we carry the history of our ancestors written in our DNA is not realistic. There is no evidence that everyday events can modify the coded sequence of DNA. In fact, if that were the case it would be a total catastrophe to our biology! Many diseases, including cancer, have been linked to mutations in our DNA. One of the more striking qualities of DNA as a genetic coding medium is its remarkable chemical stability. What we call *epigenetic effects* triggered by environmental influences can affect the expression of a gene, but not the gene itself (the DNA). Metabolic transmission or carryover through the female ovum seems to be well established (such as the 'inheritance' of predispositions due to metabolic stresses suffered by the mother prior to or during pregnancy), but again, it does not involve the DNA. Still, some believe our large store of very variable and apparently functionless DNA ("junk" DNA) may function as a repository of information at the level of individuals (also, see box in Chapter III.85).

Problems can arise when someone starts thinking that his *subjectal* imagery, the fantasy if you wish, is a 'reality' that can be transferred or extrapolated to our everyday life. Even without considering other realms or worlds, it's clear that the dynamics of our *subjectal interior* realities operate with totally different parameters than the exterior material reality. For example, in dreams we can fly or transport instantaneously over time and space without difficulty. Also, in these domains emotional affinity seems to be a better cue than rational logic or chronology.

More serious and interesting problems arise when we are faced with events and phenomena that are clearly **not** explainable by these mechanisms. Many aspects of Jung's *'collective unconscious'* and his postulate of an archetypal realm with independent existence are beyond standard materialism. When there is the opportunity for external validation, past life experiences challenge Catholic and Islamic dogma that denies reincarnation as much as it challenges the whole materialistic cosmology. For the majority of cultures, reincarnation (or soul migration) is a given, not even a question of 'faith.' It's a fact.

Today most of these phenomena have been included in what is called *'transpersonal psychology.'* The idea is simple: all of Freudian psychology, ordinary consciousness and our unconscious material related to this life, our current ego, Jung's *'persona,'* constitutes our *personal* psychology. Stan extends these notions to the very first memories we might have from this life, memories of our earliest events including our perinatal experience. But there also seem to be a number of experiences that go beyond this life or that involve aspects that transcend the limits of our physical 'persona' (and our egos). This is why they are called *trans – personal*.

It's worth recalling that the notion first held by the Greek Stoics that we come to this world as a *tabula rasa*, a clean slate (*i.e.*, that we are born with completely blank minds), was resurrected quite recently. The idea reached Europe by way of the Persian doctor and philosopher Avicenna (*Ibn Sina*) who influenced Thomas Aquinas, who in turn incorporated it into Catholic theology. It was later picked up by the Englishman John Locke, who used it as a basis for his empiricism. This is important because it's one of the foundational concepts of the materialistic worldview and of the notion of *dialectic materialism* that underlies Marxism, for instance. According to this view everything that we are is a social construct developed in **this** life.

Even Sigmund Freud picked up on the *tabula rasa* idea, postulating not only that we come to this world with a blank mind, but that we have no recollections of our early childhood (many of his contemporaries did not agree). This seems to be an unfortunate artifact produced by his research protocol. Talk therapy is inoperant when it comes to preverbal stages of the individual's childhood development. You can only access the memories of preverbal stages by means of bodywork or experiential techniques such as holotropic breathwork and other similar approaches. The memory is perceived as a direct corporeal experience, without the mediation of concepts or words.

In a sense, recent research has provided support for one aspect of this *tabula rasa* idea. The neuronal pathways of babies are extremely rich, complex, flexible and open to novel ways of 'rewiring' to match the challenges and the environmental conditions into which they are born:

today's kids seem to come with keyboard layouts imprinted in their brains. But experiential memory and cognitive abilities go way back to the earliest infancy, if not earlier.[43]

Today we also know of a list of experiences that seem to transcend the limits of our current physical bodies. Past lives would be one kind. Extracorporeal perception would be another. The experience of dissolution of personal boundaries, of fusion with other forms of life, with physical phenomena such as the ocean, or with the universe itself; the certainty of knowing events of the past or the future; of understanding or even speaking unfamiliar foreign or ancient languages, ..., it's a long list!

==================== III ====================

Chapter III.80 –

Huston, we have a problem...

So far, we have considered the subjective-objective issue as related to the interpretation of the material world. In this context the difference is clear. However, if you accept that some of our inner experiences emanate from other realities – and more significantly, that these may actually influence and help shape our reality – then the issue of the subject-object dilemma gets transposed because, if valid, it seems we have access to a form of 'objective' reality that is distinct from our 'self,' but that we access via our interior *subjectal* field of perception. Carl Jung battled with this problem with an entity he encountered in his own spiritual emergence. This entity called itself *Philemon*, and Carl felt it could answer questions Carl himself had not consciously understood. Clearly, Carl was very cautious about his *fantasies* (in his own wording) and came to the conclusion that *"there are things in the psyche which I do not produce, but which produce themselves and have their own life."*

He is by no means the only modern medium who has allegedly channeled whole books. Some appear to be genuine; others, well, hardly! Once people accept and start believing in the 'truths' given us through channeling, control-freaks will find the temptation to fake it irresistible. Still, if you add this phenomenon to the rest of the list, the need to take other fields or dimensions seriously is undeniable.

This is where the use of *subjective-objective* becomes really tricky. We

---

[43] *e.g.*, Alison Gopnik (2009), *The Philosophical Baby*.

now have a situation that unfolds within the mind of a Subject and is therefore clearly *subjectal*, but is it necessarily subjective? I don't think so.

It seems we have the capacity to perceive other *'virtual' realities* … but this is a tricky concept, our first stumbling block! Millennials have grown up watching and living in 'virtual realities' of sorts, through television, movies and especially immersed in video games, the metaverse. But we know perfectly well how these *virtual* worlds work and how they were created because we created them ourselves. What we perceive in these inner mindscapes, instead, does not seem to be generated by us, so what exactly are we perceiving? *Virtual* originally referred to a representation of something else that has independent reality elsewhere, so that's not it. These mindscapes presumably have entity in themselves, that is, they have 'real' independent existence. Yet, at least some of these fields don't seem to have or need any tangible material support system. They have been likened to our holograms, resonating energy bundles, so perhaps *ethereal realities*? (Still, even holograms need a substrate of some kind). Western terminology is not very useful here.

Thus, the first problem we need to address is the inadequacy of our terminology to deal with and differentiate similar or analogous things and events from this reality and those of other possible fields. Many essential words in the science-religion-spirituality spectrum are particularly versatile. Webster's Unabridged Dictionary (1999) gives 24 meanings and shades of meaning to *matter*; 15 to *material*; 13 to *object*; 11 to *objective*; eight to *subjective*; around 27 to *subject* and over 30 to **spirit**! Repeat that for several realms, and you can see the potential for confusion. Different authors are already using the same words with different meanings or different words for the same idea.

The next problem is to simplify references: the manifest reality we are familiar with I will call The Practicum. For the moment, all those other domains/realms (transpersonal, astral, etheric, divine or whatever else you come up with) we can refer to as the *Mysticum*. These terms are already in use with roughly the same connotations (Figure 34).

So then, western scientists explored the Practicum, whereas modern psychonauts are at last exploring the *Mysticum*. Also, recall the growing number of first-hand experiences of the *Mysticum* that have been reported in the last few decades, gained through spontaneous spiritual emergencies like near-death experiences, past-life therapies, hypnosis, psychedelics, and all the other variants we saw above. This tsunami of direct contact with the *Mysticum* cannot be easily dismissed, and creates problems from all three perspectives: the materialist's dilemma, the believer's dilemma, and the prophet's dilemma.

The materialist's dilemma: no doubt many are still having difficulty coming to grips with all this new evidence that challenges mainstream materialism, but I've already discussed this in Chapter II.76 (*Beyond materialism*) and many other sections, so I won't dwell on it.

The believer's dilemma runs something like this: Who should I believe, the ancient prophets and the injunctions and dogmas passed down in their *Books,* or the fresh information given to us through these new seers? And, should I stick to the old practices, or should I explore new ones?

Most religious believers are convinced that it was God or Allah who instructed the prophets directly (*by the grace of ...*). It follows that every person who has been graced with glimpses of the *Mysticum* has had these experiences because *ah!* wanted it to happen. So here is the problem: if *ah!* suddenly decided to grace several thousand 'seers,' perhaps even millions, *ah!* must definitely be trying to tell us something, so we'd be wise to listen. My feeling is that the time of second-hand religions based on '*the prophets*' needs to be transcended. The new millennium will herald the age of direct personal contact with the numinous and the divine. Consider direct spirituality the new frontier.

The prophet's dilemma is treated later in this chapter, but first we need to clarify a few issues.

As we have seen, the distinction between '*subjective*' and '*objective*' is fairly straight forward in the Practicum. However, since the only access we have to the *Mysticum* is through the psyche of a Subject, everything coming from those domains appears to be '*subjective*' by definition (or by default). Hence, these terms are almost useless in a discussion of the *Mysticum.* To make useful distinctions we need a separate terminology.

To avoid the use of '*subjective*' in these contexts, we could use 'primary' in reference to the ongoing experience during an actual expanded state or event. We might not be able to visualize or feel it directly, but I assure you, when you witness someone having a kundalini type spiritual emergence or immersed in their inner world during a workshop, you haven't a shadow of doubt that something powerful is happening. For instance, watch a man in his thirties crying and sobbing convulsively, nonstop, for hours in a row. You feel exhausted just from watching, yet the man keeps on going. Eventually the energies subside and the person 'comes back.' Given time, they often give a hint or an account of what was going on in their psyche. For example, they might say they lost their young son in a car accident, but had not allowed themselves to mourn the loss. Because the experience has been translated into a narrative, it is no longer primary, but surely as close to veridical as we can hope for. The same applies to a mandala or a drawing done during or right after the experience. Thus, we could refer to these instances as a secondary stage. In this context, consider using '***unfiltered***' to replace *objective*, and '***filtered***' to replace *subjective* as a first level of discrimination. The idea is to refer to the primary expressions as unfiltered, as distinct from the narratives that issue from a mental elaboration of this primary experience. These elaborations will be affected by our mental filters to a greater or lesser degree, but it would be extremely difficult to measure or evaluate just how far or to what extent in each case. Anything involving a psychological, mythological, cultural or religious interpretation, association or suggestion is definitely tertiary, but still within the *filtered* category.

Rather than quaternary, any moralistic admonition or judgment (*God must be punishing you...*) from a bystander or third party falls into a separate class, the marred or '*tarnished*' category and should be severely curtailed and disregarded. There is absolutely no way a third party can know or understand what or why something happened to another person. For the experience to be healing and constructive, the person must find meaning and significance internally, on their own.

Occasionally someone might attempt to fake an experience, fantasize, or to embellish it (*In a previous life I was Cleopatra ...*). Hmm, maybe, but the chances of that being factually true are pretty slim. Another difficult situation occurs when the person does not understand or accept that this is an internal process of their own psyche, and '*acts out*' blaming others or denying the experience. But in most cases the person understands that everything that they experienced is internal, and are willing to own the experience and take responsibility for what transpires within their psyche.

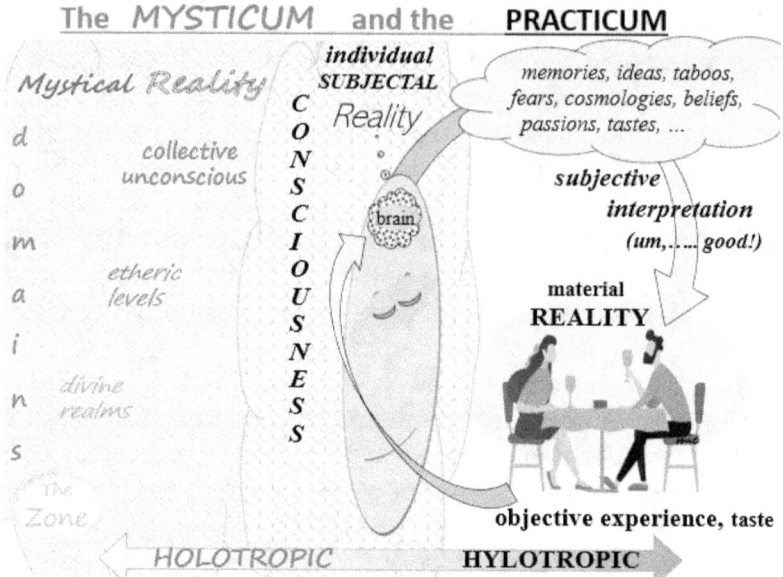

Figure 34. **The Mysticum and the Practicum.** – *Expanding 'reality' to the transpersonal domains. – Keeping to the subjectal-left – objectal-right convention, here is a sketch of the relationship between the esoteric realms and material reality, which I am calling the MYSTICUM and the PRACTICUM. The relationship between them is mediated by consciousness. – Though tricky at times, the distinction between* **subjective** *and* **objective** *is fairly straightforward in the* Practicum. *– However, these terms are useless in the* Mysticum *because everything is 'subjective' by default. Assuming these realms have entity, to make useful distinctions we need a separate terminology.*

The car accident example I used above is fairly mundane, but the categories are equally applicable to more esoteric experiences. So, let's accept that these experiences are genuine and that the realms they expose do have independent entity. Does that mean everything that was ever claimed by shamans, mystics and their religious followers is true and accurate? No, definitely not. There are several practical problems that makes this virtually impossible.

The first problem is a limitation of the experience itself. It seems consciousness always needs a focus of some sort, so even in expanded states of consciousness people's experience always seems to be limited to some aspect of the cosmic cornucopia. This limitation would apply to any mystic or prophet of times past, so their views are inevitably partial, though many don't seem to have been aware of the problem.

The second problem involves the limitations of our terminology mentioned above. When asked to describe their experience, the first thing virtually every modern psychonaut says is something like: *"Umm…, hard to put it into words…!"* Mystical literature of all ages alludes to the *ineffability* of the experience, the difficulty of describing a multidimensional experience with our very limited linear verbal language. Even the feeling of communicating with 'spirits' is usually described as nonverbal, involving some sort of mind-to-mind telepathy. The written word is worse because it lacks all the nuances of an oral narrative. People have often found analogy, metaphor, or poetry useful. The risk here is to interpret the metaphor as if it was meant literally.

The third problem is intermediation. Even when you had a direct experience, any attempt to describe it in words necessarily involves your own linguistic limitations and culturally conditioned brain. So, even when actually talking to the mystic or psychonaut in person, their *narrative* will also be colored by their mental biases. When the information is being transmitted to you via a third party or parties (scribes, preachers, mullahs, etc.) this problem escalates. It is **impossible** to do this without a subjective (in the classical sense) interpretation of the initial experience and the resulting scriptures. Again, the very act of putting the experience into words and then acquiring the knowledge through scripture involves several very mundane Subjects, and is therefore inevitably colored or distorted by the developmental perspective, understanding, mindset, personal interests, traumas, political agendas, etc. influencing those Subjects.

Needed to be said, when the prophet was the messenger, but did not actually write the scriptures himself, as was the case for all middle-eastern prophets, the limitations of language and the specter of their renderings being subjectively distorted by their scribes and compilers turns from a possibility to an unavoidable fact. All scriptures are limited and distorted by the limitations of the ancient languages in themselves, and by the inescapable intervention of scribes who clearly were **not** prophets and had no personal experience with the *Mysticum.* (If you doubt me, try this: get a friend to see a passage of a movie and then give you a detailed description. Write the description in your own words. Now see the passage for yourself and compare it with your interpretation: how much was wrong or missing?)

An added and significant problem is that most of these scriptures were written in ancient languages and then translated, often repeatedly, into their modern form. *'Translator, traitor'* as the romans used to say. And then, of course, there is always the possibility of deliberate malicious distortions for personal or political reasons. Maybe the gist is there, but taking all these writings verbatim (to the letter...) is misguided, and has led to endless abuses and the needless sufferings of millions.

Modern technology has provided us with an additional, much more compelling (and hence more dangerous) medium to transmit these ideas. There is a new and growing body of movies that fall into the mystical category. How do you differentiate reasonably factual accounts of recent experiences as narrated by the living Subject form the attempts to recreate the narratives of ancient scriptures, or from the plainly *my-fi* group? (gotcha: short for *'mystical-fiction'*). Well, you need information about the authors, producers, the origins of the scripts, etc. In other words, well-made simulations in themselves do not allow those distinctions. If this is true of our technology today, why should a naïve prophet of times past, exposed to the unfamiliar terrain of the *Mysticum,* be able to distinguish the telepathic propositions of a benevolent deity from those of a devious impostor, shaitan's advocate? This is not to say that all mystical experiences and all prophets are phony, just a word of caution to stress the need for some sort of independent verification. Yet, many historical mystics and modern psychonauts have felt and were totally convinced that their experiences were genuine encounters with spiritual beings and even with the gods 'in person.'

Here we have another terminology problem: is it legitimate to *'personify'* gods? In some contexts, 'entity' can be used instead. So then, how do we avoid the he/she/it for a nondual entity, one that exists **prior** to the emergence of gender and sex? (Some authors use 'It').

This is not a trivial issue. Personification is the basis of all religious supremacy cults, including male chauvinism and even misogyny.

Going into an in-depth analysis of the intricacies of these experiences here is out of the question, but a relatively trivial example may illustrate some of the problems. Several mythologies (and their modern *my-fi* versions) refer to the passage into the otherworld after death. Typically, this involves being ferried across a stretch of water by a boatman who must be paid in coin to afford safe passage. Well, as far as I can tell, there is absolutely zero support for this idea in modern accounts of near-death experiences. One moment you are here, and the next you are in another reality, heaven perhaps. Many (but not all) describe this as a passage through a tunnel, which you might interpret as an analogy, but none speak of a boatman. So then, where did the myth of the boatman come from? One possibility is the Egyptian *Book of the Dead*. In those days perhaps your body had to be ferried across the Nile to the Valley of the Dead. So where does the coin come in? Well, if the priests were the undertakers, the myth would be an ingenious way to ensure they got paid! (A little conflict of interests, you might say).

There is hope, however. In his discussion of *Supernatural Explanations* for near-death experiences, Raymond Moody makes the following comment: "*It seems to me that the best way to distinguish between God directed and Satan directed experiences would be to see what the person involved does and says after his experience. God, I suppose, would try to get those to whom he appears to be loving and forgiving. Satan would presumably tell his servants to follow a course of hate and destruction. Manifestly, my subjects have come back with a renewed commitment to follow the former course and to disavow the latter.*"[44]

In a similar vein, Stan says of well-integrated spiritual emergencies: ... "*successful completion and integration of such episodes brings a substantial reduction in aggression, an increase of racial, political and religious tolerance, ecological awareness, and deep changes in the hierarchy of values and existential priorities*" (Grof, 2019, I).

Note, however, that these appreciations involve *subjective* notions of value, of good and evil. Is it possible to formulate value-free criteria for these things? One option is to consider the general direction, rather than any specific detail or value. Stan's idea of Holotropic and Hylotropic may be useful, if we can agree on what we mean by wholeness and its opposite. Following Stan, I will use the sequence of manifestation as hylotropic

---

[44] Raymond Moody, 1975. *Life After Death*. Bantam Books

(tending towards matter and separateness) and the return to the Source as holotropic (moving away from mundane dualities and delusions, towards clear Spirit).

The prophet's dilemma

As embodied souls we have great difficulty seeing beyond the veil of material realities, the 'scars' of past traumas, and the limitations of our cultural constructs. This holds even for those who accept the existence of other realms and the whole Chain of Being. Remember the *taboo against knowing who we are*. This difficulty is even worse if our perceptions are very distorted by fears or subconscious traumas that we are not aware of (the *shadow* we saw in Chapter II.26). So, how can seers or prophets know if the notions they are perceiving are the influence of a benevolent deity or the machinations of a wrathful one? And how can they be sure they are not distorting those notions influenced by their own personal hangups and cultural preconceptions?

Though mystics have developed a variety of techniques that facilitate access to those hidden realms, none of them address the problem of our blind spots and the unconscious. In this I hardly have any personal knowledge, so I prefer to quote Ken directly: "*... one thing is certain: the great wisdom traditions, for all their wisdom, have absolutely nothing like this* [the concept of a shadow]. *I know, I've spent thirty years checking with students and teachers and the conclusion is unanimous: an understanding of psychodynamic repression, as well as ways to cure it, is something contributed exclusively by modern Western psychology. ... Consequently, even advanced meditators and spiritual teachers are often haunted by psychopathology, ...*" (Wilber, 2007, 119). If this is still true today, it must have been triply so in the past.

So, what might be the solutions to the prophet's dilemmas? There are several possible avenues.

The first, simplest and most obvious is to compare notes with other seers and mystics. Virtually all oriental schools have a long tradition doing precisely that, but for some historical quirk starting with the Old Testament and carried through to all later offshoots, the mid-eastern and mediterranean religions chose to enshrine individual prophets and pit them against their neighbors, who were thus seen as their enemies rather than as collaborators in a common quest.

The second aspect is to be aware of your own traumas, quirks, and prejudices, and to be mindful to overcome them. Here is where understanding the shadow can help. We often disown or 'bury' traumatic events that involve much violence, particularly when we feel victimized. As Stan has shown, this often happens during our own birth. As helpless babies we can feel brutalized during the birth process. In fact, we *were* brutalized, of course, because the natural birth process is definitely quite brutal. People re-experiencing their birth often feel trapped and powerless, and at the same time enraged and desperate to fight back (though as adults we could hardly blame our mothers for it). Still, later, as grownups, subconscious emotions from this unresolved episode in our past can resurface as an undefinable sense of rage of 'unknown' origin, making it easy to project the responsibility for the sense of suffering on others. After all, we *were* the victims, so *they* must be the bad guys. This vague sense of attribution can easily be capitalized by ignorant or unscrupulous religious or political operators and redirected to any convenient 'enemy' they chose to designate.

Experience shows that re-living these episodes and emotions in the context of holotropic experiential work allows the person to realize these feelings have their origin in a personal internal memory of the birth process. Integrating the experience as an adult can, and often will, resolve the feelings of pent-up rage. Stan believes the intensity and the reality of the life-threatening experience of birth is what produces these highly charged emotions, which can help explain some of the unrestrained violence that humans can sometimes unleash on others. We feel something or someone has to die, which in a sense is correct, but it is misdirected. What needs to 'die' is our unconscious egoic attachment to a traumatic event or belief, but since this is threatening, it is easier to project it outwards onto others. If faced and handled correctly, this process of internal 'death-and-rebirth' of some aspect of our (false) ego is an essential step in our spiritual unfolding (and it can happen many times over), but it is often very challenging. Yet, if we can work through the process and let these pent-up energies dissipate, it is often very liberating and can have profound healing effects.

All this is relevant because, in a culture that is not aware of these processes (until very recently, all of them), it is very easy to misinterpret these emotions and the imagery they evoke as coming from a demonic source, and to *project* them on some external 'enemy' (real or imagined). Of course, if you in any way communicate or demonstrate this attitude to the other party, there is a pretty good chance they will now consider *you* to be *their* enemy. A self-fulfilling prophesy! Unfortunately, all too often our notions of good versus evil are Subject dependent: *if I do it to you it's justice, if you do it to me it's evil*. For instance, priests accusing shamans of being evil and then murdering them is hardly a solution because, quite obviously, from the shaman's point of view they are the victims and the priests are the epitome of evil. We need a criterion that is relatively free of this problem. A pragmatist view might be: 'if it hurts, it's evil.' But even kids make a distinction: the hurt in a slap from a bully is in a totally different category to the pain from a tumble on a bike. To be evil it has to have intention, somehow. Intention, however, is also hard to qualify, and need not even be conscious.

Thus, **the third aspect** is to have some neutral parameter to evaluate these experiences.

As mentioned earlier, let's say holotropic is good, hylotropic is bad. Even this, though, needs some sort of parameter or measure. Hard to put a number on it, but we can give it a direction, a sequence. If reunion is the converse of manifestation, then we can invert the sequence of manifestation and see what happens. There is plenty of material on that, often referred to as *the Great Chain of Being*. However, each spiritual system has its own variants and terminology, so we can call Huston to our rescue. Huston C. Smith was another of those interesting eclectics who was born in China in a Christian minister's family, and grew till late adolescence in the Taoist milieu of that country. He became one of the leading scholars of comparative religions in the 20th Century. In his book *Why Religion Matters*, Huston gives us a sketch of the Great Chain as viewed by current religions, and the corresponding states of selfhood (also quoted in Appendix I and Figure I.2 of *Integral Spirituality,* Wilber, 2007). He includes a rich terminology, but none of those terms mean anything to you or to me. According to Huston (and Ken) there are rough correspondences in the levels, but unless you are keen to get yourself into a horrible muddle, it's best to skip the details and concentrate on the similarities. All we need is an order, analogous to the holarchy of the material world (Chapter I.31).

All perennial philosophies agree that there is a *Great Chain of Being*, and that it emanates as a specific sequence of levels/realms. The root or generative level exists (it is a real entity) but cannot be described in words, so all mystical schools stress what it is not: formless, potential, unspeakable, nameless, timeless, empty, void, and so on. None of these terms are practical or easy to relate to, so I will use '*the* (*formless, timeless, nameless, __ whatever you prefer*) *Zone*' instead (in figures, etc.). The *__Zone* is better seen as existing out of space-time altogether. Yet, it has some positive characteristics: pure, all-embracing love, a superlative cosmic intelligence, and dazzling luminosity (not the usual light, more like an intrinsic enveloping radiance). Then there are a varying number of progressively denser realms till you get to the level of gross matter, our level. This timeless chain somehow intersects the material domain on another axis.

Even physicists have now come to agree with mystics that the root of it all, the nondual ground of existence, the cloud of unknowing, the creative consciousness, *the quantum vacuum*, or whatever notion you prefer, forms and sustains all the cosmic realms. We can use *the __Zone* as the source level, a cosmic 'ground zero,' and simply number the derived levels. *Ahxioms* and the likes are tricky because they are either intrinsic qualities of the creative Source itself or must have appeared at a very early stage of manifestation.

The details of the stages are not important here, but recognizing the multilayered nature of the *Mysticum* is important. We can use the following:

0 – *The __Zone*–, the nondual ground of Being –

(1) – the level of first principles (*the implicate order, math, abstract forms, fractals, ahxioms, the Laws of ah!* etc.) -

perhaps all of which are contained or implicit in *the __Zone*

2 – the divine realms – home to *the gods* –

3 – the archetypal realms – embodied mythological archetypes, angels and demons –

4 – the astral domains – human and nature's spirits; historic and phylogenetic memories –

5 – the worldly – our normal material reality - the manifested material world –

We need to add just one *catchall* bin beyond our usual worldly affairs to accommodate any attitudes, situations or entities we feel are 'pulling us under,' away from Spirit. (This is not necessarily the 'demonic'; many mythologies place demons in the previous realms).

> 6 – the pits (illusion, ignorance, trauma, delusion, despair, attachment, fear, hate, greed, violence, war, …,) all the negative and destructive aspects of our psyche and of *creation*.

The following box gathers these approaches into a sort of guide we can use to interpret and understand different types of situations, interventions, and practices.

The Mysticum	←	holotropic | hylotropic	→	The Practicum
the Zone |< *divine* |< *archetypal* |< *astral* ‖ ← consciousness → WORLDLY → the pits
reunion ←	*numinous*	← *in-sight* | *out-sight* →	concrete →	separation

Mystical traditions agree that the way to go in the right direction is to quiet your mundane mental bustle and look to your interior (in-sight). Conversely, anything that takes you to 'the pits' moves you away from the Divine. The simplest and most compelling account comes from blind Jacques we met in Chapter III.77: *"The light that shone in my head was like joy distilled,"* and *"… from the time of my discovery light and joy have never been separated in my experience"*, **but** *"fear, anger and impatience made me blind. The minute before I knew just where everything in the world was, but if I got angry, things got angrier than I. They mixed themselves up, turned turtle, muttered like crazy men and looked wild. I no longer knew where to put hand or foot, and everything hurt me"* (Lusseryan, 1963). This general notion that our emotional state affects our spiritual awareness has been corroborated by recent consciousness research, the transpersonal states induced by a variety of modern methods, and the experience of a growing number of modern psychonauts.

> *To a mind that is still, the whole universe surrenders.*
>
> I Ching

Holding rallies, jihad, holy wars, and all those other political activities associated with 'religion' that are directed outwards to the material world will only serve to excite your mundane passions and move you *away* from the numinous. Even listening to sermons, reading *The Book* and talking about it, has a limited benefit because it keeps you looking outwards.

Murdering your neighbor is politics, no matter what religion he professes. To be religious you would have to *relinquish ('kill')* the **hate** you hold for your neighbor. This is not metaphorical. I mean it literally: this is known as the process of *death-and-rebirth* that every shaman and mystic must go through to gain wisdom. It is one of the forms of *spiritual emergence* described by Stan, that can appear spontaneously or in deep experiential work. Your false ego must *die* to its current attachment(s), to be reborn as a *new* and more integrated human (the actual experience varies, often perceived as dismemberment, dissolution, cataclysmic destruction, death, etc., followed by a rebirth into the light, if allowed to play out). The more passionately you cling to your hate, the harder will it be for you to face your own ego-death. It is sad to see generations of gullible youths being led to believe that cultivating hate will lead them to paradise and divinity. It won't.

==================== III ====================

Chapter III.81 –

Stan II – transpersonal psychology: new maps of the psyche

In Chapter I.9 we outlined the map of the psyche developed by Sigmund Freud, which dominated psychology for much of the 20TH century. Over the following decades other researchers, most notably Carl Jung, slowly expanded on Freud's findings. But it will be simpler to go directly to the most current conception which subsumes many of these previous findings.

As mentioned in Chapter III.79, as a psychiatrist and therapist Stan has spent decades studying both ordinary and non-ordinary states of consciousness. Though he basically validates most of Freudian psychology, his early research with psychedelics revealed additional domains, in part anticipated by the work of Carl Jung and others. As a result, he has developed an expanded map of the human psyche with the addition of two important domains to the basic structures proposed by Sigmund.

As often happens, a change in the research approach and tools exposes hidden aspects that were not revealed by the earlier methods such as talk therapies. In particular, high dose LSD sessions allowed Stan's patients to access much deeper layers of their unconscious and retrieve long buried memories of their early childhood, birth, and even aspects of their intrauterine life. As mentioned, these experiences surface as somatic memories, often associated with intense emotions and body movements that mimic the events being recalled. Stan was able to relate four experiential modes to the stages of the birth process, which he referred to as *'basic perinatal matrices'* (BPMs I to IV, corresponding to the late intrauterine stage, the onset of labor with a closed cervix, the passage through the birth canal, and finally the birth proper). The descriptive details and associated images can be found in several of Stan's books (Grof, 2023, 2019, etc.), but the most significant aspect of these discoveries is that even 'normal' birth is a very stressful, physically traumatic, and even life-threatening event in the life of the infant, and often constitutes some of the deeper roots of many symptoms and psychological traumas of the adult. This is in sharp contrast to the Freudian notion that we have no recollection of our early childhood and infancy (see III.79). It is worth noting that unnatural interventions that interfere with the full experience of birth, such as anesthetic depression of the infant or caesarean section, might also produce significant problems in the individual's adult life (trauma by omission?).

Furthermore, as these experiences unfold, it is not unusual to recall incidents that are perceived as experiences from past lives, or events from the collective unconscious (rather than the individual's current memories). Often the person might experience images from the world's mythologies and the archetypal domains that seem to relate to the same general experiential theme. Past life recollections are particularly relevant from the therapeutic perspective because they usually relate to and are perceived as the deeper roots of the symptoms and difficulties the affected persons are experiencing in their current life. The experience *"can thus draw on any historical period, geographical area, and spiritual tradition of the world, quite independently from the subject's cultural or religious background"* (Grof, 2023, I). These general findings have been confirmed by hundreds of researchers and facilitators working with literally thousands of patients and interested psychonauts all over the world. We can now sketch an expanded cartography of the psyche that recognizes the importance of the perinatal passage and the existence of transpersonal domains (Figure 35).

Several important points need to be made here. The first is that though inner exploration shows much variation between individuals, it tends to follow some basic patterns. As you lift the superficial layers, deeper layers become available, and these in turn are often associated with even deeper ones. The materials from these different layers are by no means random or capricious: they are usually related or linked by way of the emotional quality of the experiences and often by their connection to the different BPMs. Stan refers to these bundles as "condensed experiences" or COEX systems. Thus, an adult that suffers from crippling claustrophobia might recall a childhood event when he was trapped in a dark closet; then the experience might shift to the sensation of being stuck in the birth canal. This, in turn, may elicit images of imprisonment in a past life, or seemingly hopeless situations with no apparent exit, such as a labyrinth, drawn from the world's mythologies.

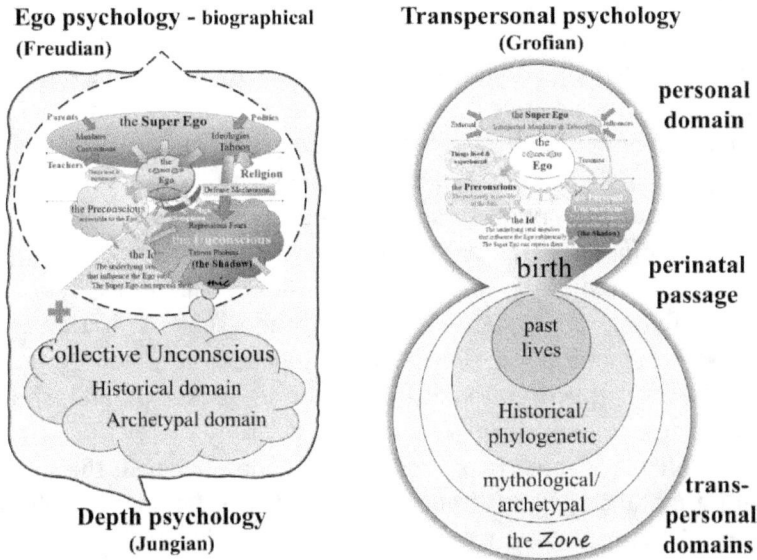

*Figure 35. **The new maps of the psyche**. – To the early Freudian map (upper left), Carl Jung added the historical and the archetypal domains of the unconscious (lower left), showing that our psyche extends beyond our ego. Stan Grof refined this model by adding the perinatal passage and the successive layers of the transpersonal domain (right half). – The constriction at the perinatal level reflects the fact that it acts both as an obstacle and as a gateway to the transpersonal, hence my renaming it as a 'passage' (see glossary).*

From the healing point of view, whether these images are 'real' or not is irrelevant. The most significant therapeutic finding is that reliving these experiences as an adult and allowing these pent-up energies to dissipate usually resolves the trauma and almost magically frees the patient of the symptoms. A similar result can occur in spontaneous *spiritual emergences* if they are allowed to play out in a protected environment.

From the existential perspective the most significant finding is that these experiences don't deal only with personal traumatic events, but can be embedded in the suffering of whole populations. We also encounter peaceful and blissful situations, feelings of oneness with others and with different aspects of our world and the entire cosmos, and even union with divine entities or energies. This often occurs *after* the negative energies of the traumatic aspects have been released and transcended. In other words, trauma seems to act as one of the veils that keep us from knowing our true nature, and reinforces the feeling of separateness and alienation.

It must be said that these experiences are by no means easy to deal with, even the more positive ones. A past life experience or a reunion with a divine being from an unexpected mythology might seriously challenge the person's prior beliefs. Part of the process of integration of these experiences, both the spontaneous ones and those induced by holotropic techniques, requires spending time immediately after the experience making sketches, paintings or mandalas of the salient aspects, writing notes and sharing the experience with other seekers. All this is not intended to elicit feedback, only a more focused, conscious integration. Feedback is only appropriate if the person requests it, and should be informative, free of any form of moralizing. From the heuristic point of view, the sketching aspect is particularly revealing because the link to the different perinatal stages is often easy to see. Other times it can allow us to connect the images, and hence the experiences, to illustrations from world mythologies or religions. These notes and drawings can also be very useful to trace and understand our own personal progress over time.

In addition to the obvious healing effects of these experiences, the more significant finding from the collected and collective transpersonal psychology field is the complete lack of connection of these spiritual experiences with the person's prior cultural and religious background. As Stan's comment quoted above reveals, anybody can connect with any aspect of human culture, history, mythology, archetypes and so on, from any period in history or region of the globe. Therefore, this category of techniques and substances can account for the *induction* of holotropic experiences, but they cannot account for the virtually limitless spectrum of their content. To the person living the experience they feel totally real.

The persistent and consistent encounter with transpersonal phenomena ties in with other developments in quantum physics and biology that clearly do not fit the classic Cartesian-Newtonian materialistic scheme of reality. Although this is a fascinating subject, it is too involved to analyze in detail here, but for our purpose we can state a few basic premises:

Reality as described by materialistic science is valid at a macroscopic and everyday level.

However, this visible domain is not the whole story. At the subjectal level we encounter several aspects that go beyond or underlie material reality:

One aspect is that the information content in matter and material processes needs to be taken into account. The entire cosmos constantly generates and is infused with nonlocal fields of information that both inform and give form to the unfolding universe.

Another issue that needs to be incorporated is the possible existence of subtle (non-material) realms of real existence populated by ethereal beings.

Underlying all this is a unified but undifferentiated 'empty' field that is at the same time the source of the creative energies and ground of all potential. Some of the more neutral ideas proposed by a variety of cosmologies include: the creative principle, the primal mind, the cosmic, formless or pregnant *void*, the quantum vacuum, the implicate order, akasha or akashic field, morphogenetic fields, the holographic universe, cosmic consciousness, the nondual Ground of existence, the Source, and several more. Collectively, ' *The__Zone.*'

Little of this is really new. The sophisticated cosmologies developed by eastern and western mystical schools have been aware of many of these realms for millennia. Much of the spiritual terminology in use today is taken directly from them. However, getting into a complicated historical analysis and comparison is not useful here.[45] Best we simply assume these ideas are possible, perhaps even valid, and see where they take us.

===================== III =====================

---

[45] For a recent overview see Ken Wilber's *Integral Spirituality* (2007).

Chapter III.82 –
The Nature of Spirit

As we have seen throughout this essay, each new level of complexity expands the possibilities and the number of variations escalates rapidly, even within the materialistic realm. But this pales as compared to the explosion we encounter when we include the possibility of subtle realms and parallel realities. The richness and diversity of experiences and possibilities just skyrockets, as is reflected in the wealth of modern experiential accounts, and in the virtual worlds envisioned and created by the ever-growing forms of 'fiction.' The down side is that it becomes increasingly difficult to choose and summarize the ancient wisdom and the wealth of recent personal reports, surveys, and overviews, so I will take a shortcut and just postulate a simple sketch that should help us move forward.

A feature often perceived in spiritual experiences and postulated by many mystical schools is that the transpersonal domain is not a simple unified field. Rather, it is made up of many embedded levels of existence or manifestation. How these levels are sustained is beyond me, but the notion of wave frequencies or vibrational levels is often used as a metaphor. This is reflected in much of the terminology: spirit is ethereal, light, luminous, weightless; matter is gross, dense, dark, heavy, and so on. Breadth is another common feature: embodied existence is narrow, confined, limited, whereas spirit is ample, open, limitless, etc. However you imagine it, the idea that the cosmos is organized in a set of embedded levels or realities is a useful model to conceptualize the observed phenomenology as reported from modern expanded (holotropic) states of consciousness and by ancient mystics alike.

So then, the primary problem is to envision how such dimensions arose, what their properties might be, and how they structure the cosmos. Let's flip the process and imagine a total blank, absolute nothingness. I know, that's impossible because there would be no 'me' to do the imagining, but just for arguments sake. So, there is absolutely nothing. Something stirs. Is it likely to have infinite mass or no mass whatsoever? If it is to develop into anything at all, is it more likely to be passive, reactive, or proactive? Passive leads nowhere. Reactive versus proactive is trickier. Let's start with proactive.

Okay, we now have a formless, weightless *speck* of proactive *something* that starts trying out possibilities. What would they be? Vibrating? Pulsating, shapeshifting, growing, dividing? Yes, cloning is good because the clones can play off each other, offering a lot more possibilities. Keep fiddling till all options are exhausted, and then multiply again, and then again... Just dividing might get boring, so try differentiating or binding together to make new combinations. This would soon lead to increasing complexity and evolution (see Chapter III.89, below).

The reactive option appears to start on a different foot, but if *specks* of reactive *something* start accumulating, you would eventually end up with a 'soup' of reacting and interacting *specks* that could also aggregate and develop into more complex structures. As any self-respecting materialist will assure you, such a system will naturally tend to evolve and eventually develop complex organisms and intelligence. But before we compare these options, we need to digress a little.

An interesting idea, which echoes some of the oriental cosmologies, was put forward by Paul J Steinhardt and Neil Turok in their book *Endless Universe: beyond the Big Bang* (2007). Much of the physics is beyond me, but the self-accelerating rebounding universe idea is tantalizing. We usually hear about one cosmic cycle, the one we are in now, but several ancient and some modern cosmologies imagine a succession of cycles, with the whole universe expanding for a time, then collapsing to a pinhead before exploding again into a new cycle. These universes might be of the same size, but some cosmologies propose that the whole system grows and accelerates with each cycle, so that the trace looks like a bouncing ball in reverse (Figure 36).

If we now envision the reactive versus proactive options in this expanded cosmology, it is conceivable that after hundreds or thousands of these ever-growing cycles of unfolding either path could develop into our current conditions. In the reactive sequence, growing intelligence would find a way to shield and perpetuate itself out of the cycles of manifestation, accumulate experience, and become what we now perceive as an infinite cosmic intelligence. In the proactive sequence, the need to generate stable arenas in which to have novel experiences would prompt the creation of a system of non-proactive or 'passive' matter-like props and, eventually, whole material universes like ours.

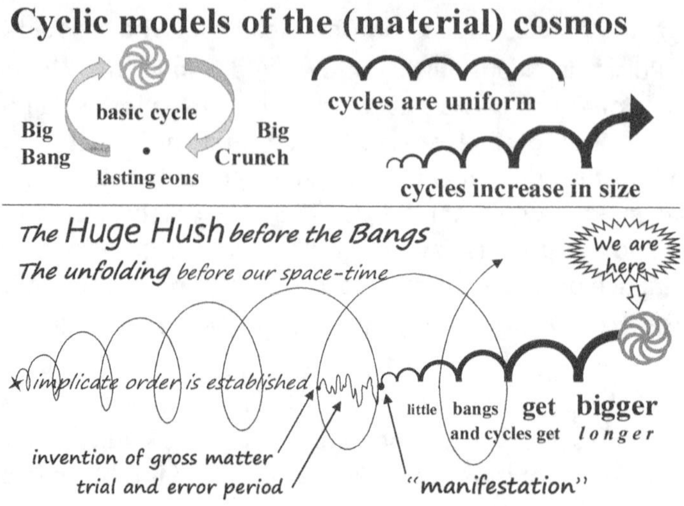

Cyclic models of the (material) cosmos

basic cycle

Big Bang • Big Crunch

lasting eons

cycles are uniform

cycles increase in size

The **Huge Hush** *before the Bangs*
The unfolding before our space-time

We are here

X *implicate order is established*

invention of gross matter
trial and error period

little bangs get **bigger**
and cycles get *longer*

"*manifestation*"

Figure 36. **A cycling cosmos.** – Several cosmologies propose that the material aspect of the cosmos is cyclic, each cycle lasting eons, but the exact form varies. – All imply the existence of a Cosmic Intelligence out of space-time, thus also implying existence before space-time, in which Spirit "*unfolded*" and generated the different levels of existence in the *Mysticum*. – *The time-spans and scale of these conceptions are mind-bending and dwarf the secular interpretations of The Books.*

Either way, we can imagine the progressive development of an entity or being conscious and intelligent enough to get bored and decide to deliberately design and explore new possibilities, new arenas. The notion that Cosmic Consciousness creates to explore all its potential and to better know itself appears in many cosmologies and in modern holotropic states. Rather than a BIG BANG, perhaps it all started with a *Huge Hush* - the exploration and elucidation of the underlying *implicate order*, and the unfolding of the subtle realms that evolved as a result.

At some point this *creative energy* decided to make a more sophisticated arena in which to have new experiences in consciousness. After some experimenting to define a workable set of *ahxioms* and mechanisms, the project was put in motion with some very, very *Big Bangs*, and the material reality we live in today came into existence (Figure 37).

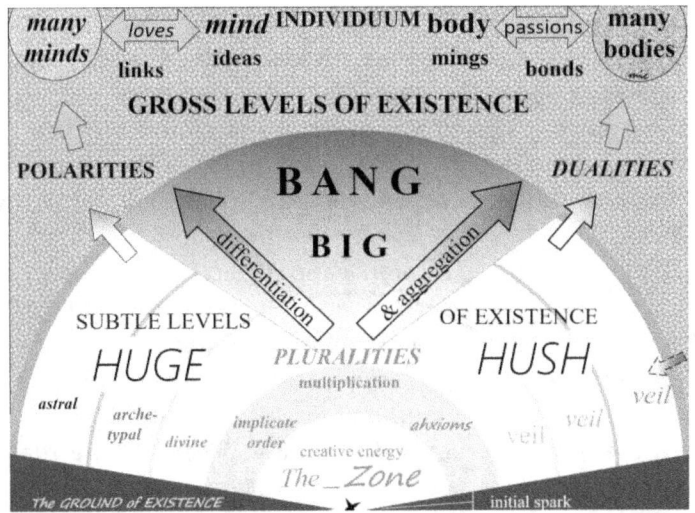

*Figure 37. **The outbound journey of existence**. A sketch of a possible unfolding of the cosmos depicting the Source and five layers of differentiation and diversification (some consider up to fifteen, others only two or three). The Big Bang and the material universe we are familiar with is just one of the cosmic realities emanated from the__Zone. Some put the 'gross levels of existence' as the middle realm and add layers beyond to represent the 'outer' realms. Transitions between levels act as veils that make it difficult to see through, especially from the gross to the subtle.*

Though very simplified, Figure 37 should help illustrate several points. I start with a hypothetical initial 'spark,' the *speck* mentioned above. But the next step, cloning or multiplication is necessary: it is impossible to have differentiation without a plurality. It may well be that it is equally impossible to have an *implicate order* that includes *ahxioms*, mathematical constants, geometry, fractal formulas, etc. without some form of differentiated medium. In the sketch all the layers look similar, but this is surely not the case. In particular, the gray band next to the center containing the *'implicate order'* would be a virtual layer contained within the__Zone, with no 'volume' at all. Even the__Zone itself could be a dimensionless dot, the 'spark' in the figure.

Also, the 'gross levels of existence' seem to envelop the subtle. In reality the opposite is more likely, with the gross level nested within the subtle levels, but it was clearer to sketch the unfolding this way. Still, it does gives us a sense of direction, from the primal creative energy to the outer reaches of the manifested worlds. As mentioned, Stan coined the terms *hylotropic* for the outbound and *holotropic* for the inbound. *Hylotropic* is moving away from the Source, away from wholeness, towards differentiation, separation, matter, and so on. Conversely, *holotropic* is moving towards reunion and wholeness. This avoids terms, such as *high* for the spiritual realms and *low* for the mundane, which are loaded with mundane connotations (*i.e.*, implications such as *highborn* or *lowborn*). Even *spirit* and *spiritual* are tricky terms. In Ken's terminology 'Spirit' is the highest level and the nondual Ground of all levels, but the term is often used with other meanings (*e.g.*, *the spirit of the party*, ... or as a synonym of soul, energy, apparition, humor, animus, effort, alcohol, etc.).

Next, everybody assumes that entities in the divine realms have no problem looking across to the *outer* realms, but the converse is not possible, or at least very difficult under normal circumstances. In the case of our normal waking state, the first obstacle is that, due to the demands of survival in this reality, we spend most of our lives focusing in the wrong direction. Whatever their nature, seeing through these 'veils' requires *insight*, connecting with our interior world with specific methods of exploration, including meditation, the use of psychedelics, and other practices.

Getting through the outer veils need not open the inner veils. This is important both for the modern psychonaut and for understanding the history of belief systems: shamans, mystics, and prophets surely had the same problems and limitations, as is reflected in their spiritual views. Even today, many supposedly monotheistic religions have difficulty letting go of worldly influences and going all the way to the pure Source. My hunch is that shamans and ancient sages had a much deeper understanding than we give them credit for. They just didn't make such a fuss about it.

A related issue is the problem of focus. Though expanded states of consciousness afford us much broader and interlinked perspectives that are not available to our normal waking mind, there is still a specific character or theme to most of these experiences, both in their emotional tone and in their content. Perhaps the ultimate Source is truly 'all knowing,' but in most other realms the individual consciousness' capacity to perceive and experience has limits. This makes it difficult for a single individual, mystic or otherwise, to get the whole picture. Perhaps this is why most advanced oriental approaches have relied on schools of practitioners, rather than any single prophet. Even Buddhism, though clearly emanated from a single source, retains the scholastic idea of leading their followers through direct experience rather than dogmatic indoctrination.

All of which brings us to the critical issue of the meaning of the cosmos and of life itself. Though we hinted at this above, it is such a fundamental issue it is worth a closer look. It's also an opportunity to see how modern experiences echo with ancient conceptions.

===================== III =====================

> *The notion that Cosmic Consciousness creates to explore all its potential and to better know itself is a motif that appears in many cosmologies and in modern holotropic states.*

Chapter III.83 –
Why did an all-powerful god create this universe?

Ever thought of that? Most creation stories state that some divine force or other created the universe and everything in it, including us humans. But few give any hint as to why, for what purpose, or reason? Studies of comparative mythologies and religions show us that there are many versions of this issue, so many that any one of them can only be considered a hypothesis at best, one of the many that us humans have come up with in our attempts to understand the ineffable.

Those that rely on 'faith' as the primary tool for manipulation tell us we were created in order to '*worship and serve god.*' Very convenient. This is one of the most blatant symptoms that these aspects of religions are not the revelations of any true god, but rather the projections of very mundane kings and high priests bent on glorifying their own name and designing ways to extract even more money and servitude from their 'flocks.' You know, as in *pastors of their flock*, in allusion to sheep no doubt, right? That lovely image of the good Shepherd looking after the lamb...! Do you know what happens to lambs, sooner or later? The 'good pastor' first castrates them, and when they are nice and fat, slaughters and barbecues them! Great metaphor, isn't it?

Anyway, do you really want to worship a completely narcissistic god? I pass. Better look elsewhere. So, why create a world, a solar system, a galaxy, a universe? Or perhaps, even a multiverse? One idea is that *ah!* (*the__Zone*) is pure potential, but being pure potential is not enough, so *ah!* desires to express that potential in order to better *know self*. Hence, *ah!* creates this simulation we call 'reality' in which consciousness can explore the possibilities, the unknowns. Now, here again is where one idea clashes with other pet ideas of creationists: Intelligent Design. Intelligent Design presupposes and requires that the designer know the best answer to the problem he is designing for. But if you already know the answer, what's the point of the simulation in the first place? If *'knowing self'* is a process, then *ah!* evolves, and must have had a stage in which that full knowledge of *self* was lacking.

Well, I certainly don't know the answers, but there is one story I like because it makes sense and gives us a hint of purpose.

As we saw, Stan has spent decades studying the different states of consciousness, both the spontaneous ones and those produced by a diversity of techniques (accelerated breathing, relaxation, meditation, etc.). These techniques produce **expanded states of consciousness** that give us access to levels of consciousness and knowledge that are not available under our normal every-day life conditions. In *The Cosmic Game* Stan quotes the vision of Gail, a modern prophetess if you wish. Briefly, in her mind's eye she is one of four ethereal beings having a very lively and erudite exchange. One proposes a game in which they could play a variety of roles in order to have different experiences in consciousness, like playing 'hide-and-seek' or feeling alone. Initially the others think this would be impossible. After all, as divine beings they have direct access to everything, so how could they possibly 'hide' or feel lonely? But after further modeling and testing they get enthusiastic about the idea.

This vision gives us an alternative explanation for the intention behind the cosmic game, the incarnation of spiritual beings, and the 'taboo against knowing who we are.' If you are unfamiliar with this last concept, it goes something like this. Spirit is all-knowing, so how can an all-knowing being play hide-and-seek with itself? Impossible, right? Unless Spirit finds a way not to be 'all-knowing,' at least for the duration of the game. Note that this apparently occurs *before* the invention of sex, violence, evil, and all the other pleasantries of our manifested cosmos. So, Spirit chooses to trick itself in order to be exposed to circumstances and adventures it cannot experience in its pure form. To enter the game, the players must forget who they really are. This is the essence of the metaphor of '*the river of forgetfulness*'- when we incarnate (during pregnancy?) our spiritual essence must bathe or drink its waters, in order to forget our true nature, and all that we experienced before, so as to start this new episode afresh. These old memories are still with us, just veiled to our present consciousness (yet, under some conditions glimpses can filter through). Later, when we regain our true spiritual nature, we can evaluate the experience and plan for the next episode. We can also learn to remember them in this life. Clearly, all this takes reincarnation as a given.

If you look around with this general idea in mind, it turns out there are many proponents and philosophies in that direction. For instance, both Sai Baba and Mother Teresa are credited with the quote: "*Life is a game. Play it.*" The Sanskrit notion of *Lila* suggests that creation is the outcome of the playful nature of Divinity. As the Divine is perfect, it could have no want fulfilled, therefore signifying *freedom*, instead of necessity, behind the creation.

Many of us spend our entire lives trying to find our 'purpose' in life. Joseph Campbell points out that many of the daring or even reckless sports and activities, those that give us an adrenaline rush, are the most meaningful to us because that's when we feel *really alive*.[46] If this is correct, trying to find the purpose of being alive is circular reasoning, redundant. We incarnate to experience being alive, whatever it takes. How you '*play the game*' is entirely your choice. In fact, some even consider we actually chose the circumstances of our next incarnation according to what we want to experience or learn. The implication is quite a sobering thought. Everything that happens to me is the result of my own choice? Perhaps, but note that Stan cautions about this being a metaphysical concept that cannot be used to excuse acts of abuse, or to belittle people's suffering. Even if the game is an '*illusion*' at a metaphysical level, to an incarnate soul the pain feels real, it truly hurts!

> *I don't think people are looking for the meaning of life,*
> *as much as they are looking for the experience of being alive.*
> Joseph Campbell

At least from our limited perspectives as humans, all these versions

---

[46] "*Fear is how I know I'm alive,*" according to illusionist Harry Houdini.

are no more than hypothetical. No version is a 'revealed truth,' much less an 'absolute truth.'

You could write a whole book on this theme. The important notion here is that we currently have many ways of looking at the issue. Don't let anybody fool you. Look around carefully and see which ideas make more sense to you. What you choose to believe will have a huge impact on the way you experience your life. If you don't choose for yourself, someone else will choose for you. There is no guarantee that others will choose to your benefit.

The purpose of your life is to enjoy and learn from your experiences.

Michael A. Singer

===================== III =====================

Chapter III.84 –

A deeper look at the cosmos: information and holography

As we saw in previous chapters, a growing body of evidence defies explanation by the materialistic cosmology, such as the whole transpersonal domain revealed by modern consciousness research and psychology. Why do some people have these experiences and not others? How do we connect? What allows us to see 'invisible' realms? What seems impossible at a macroscopic level becomes more plausible if we look at the deeper levels revealed by modern physics.

One approach is to consider all the information that can be conveyed by the versatile wave function and the multitude of vibrations, frequencies, amplitudes, modulations, and so on that it can handle. If you are vibrating at a given frequency, you cannot perceive things, beings, or events that are occurring at a higher or lower frequency, rather like our perception of sound. We can only hear a certain range of frequencies, but miss out on very high or very low ones, like the high-pitched calls of bats, or the very low rumblings of elephants. The same applies to other waves (visible light, infrared, etc.).

Brainwaves are analogous. Different mental activities occur at different brainwave frequencies. Simplifying, sleep on *delta* (0-4 Hertz), peri-sleep, intuition, creativity, lucid dreaming on *theta* (4-7Hz), concentration and creativity on *alpha* (7-13Hz), our usual waking activity runs in *beta* waves (13-30Hz), and *gamma* waves (30-100Hz) appear in deep concentration and also in kids. Any time during our normal activity, different parts of our brain can be active at different frequencies. It is now known that meditation, psychedelics, and other techniques *lower* the brainwave frequencies and synchronize them across the whole brain. This can be likened to the tuning of a radio: if you are in *alpha*, you are in a hylotropic state and can only tune into the material external world. If you want to access the dreamworlds you need to **lower** your brain's activity, say to *theta*, and so on. Exact values may vary a little, but the sequence is stable. Note that the relationship is virtually the opposite of popular lingo: if you want to be 'spiritual,' low brain frequencies are better than high.

The electromagnetic wave idea has another virtue. Compared to the usual macroscopic waves we are used to seeing in a lake or the seashore, electromagnetic waves can be extremely short. I never cease to marvel at the capacity that the space around us has to carry such a variety and number of messages all at once without mixing them up. We are most used to sound and light: sound dissipates, and though light can travel huge distances, it can also be blocked by opaque objects. But if you are in the middle of a family reunion or a bar, you can see and hear people in any direction you focus on. This means you are constantly being bombarded by light and sound from all 360 degrees around you, and all of these crisscrossing waves and rays retain enough of their individuality to be recognizable. If you are in any modern city, there are hundreds of different television and radio transmissions, and most likely thousands of cell phone and internet app conversations all occurring at the same time and streaming though you and all the space around you. With the right gadget you could selectively pick up any of these waves at any time, and take part in that specific conversation.

As the earth hurtles through space, telescopes around the globe can pick up light from groups of stars and galaxies in any location of the night sky. Thus, any outdoor spot is being simultaneously pierced by trillions of light waves from the billions of stars that are known to exist, year-round. Add the whole electromagnetic spectrum, plus sound waves and gravitational waves and the whole cosmos becomes one humungous information field. These facts become a little more believable if you recall the *Incredibly Small* section in Chapter II.35. Even without invoking other realities, there is room for many levels of worlds within worlds inside each of us, as is shown in Figure 38.

Understanding all the details of how this might actually work is another story, but matching the electromagnetic spectrum to the mass scale gives some idea of its range. The match is not totally valid as shown in Figure 38 because perceived size (length and volume) depends on a number of factors in addition to mass, but they do correlate. You cannot detect small objects with long wavelengths because they pass around the object. Very small objects require shorter wavelengths, so anything below visible light wavelengths is invisible to our unaided physical vision. Conversely, dust clouds will block short waves like light, but longer radio waves go right through, so the choice depends on what you are trying to achieve. For the same reason, long wavelengths are invisible to us, and require large antennas.

Since frequency is inversely but exactly matched to wavelength, we often refer to *frequency* instead of wavelength. Thus, to 'tune in' to a given message you need to set your receiver at the appropriate frequency. Because the electromagnetic spectrum has a huge range, a sensitive instrument can discriminate amongst thousands of different frequency bands (think of the thousands of radio stations across the planet).

Figure 38. **The Mass scale and the Electromagnetic Spectrum.**

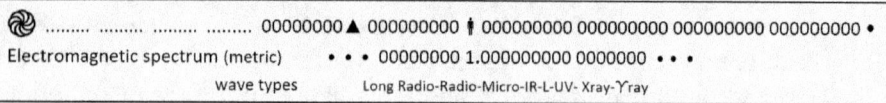

Top: our universe scaled by Mass. Zeros represent orders of magnitude (see Figure 25). - Center: the Electromagnetic wavelength spectrum roughly matched to the same base (1 human, 1 meter). Again, zeros represent metric orders of magnitude (IR = infrared — L = visible light — UV = ultra violet). Visible light is only a fraction of an order of magnitude (1 zero), and there are 9 orders of magnitude from visible light to the shortest known gamma-rays —
(• • • but there is no upper or lower theoretical limit to wavelengths • • •).

Since many of these waves are directional, we can also select only those coming from a given source (*i.e.*, any unobstructed direction in the celestial orb). Thus, the total amount of information a fistful of space can be carrying at any instant is mindboggling. Though many of these wave bundles (rays) can travel huge distance, they do disperse and eventually become too sparse to be detectable. But over short distances, extra sensitive pets or even humans could, in theory, pick up information carried by waves emitted by our bodies, assuming they can 'tune in' correctly.

The analogy has yet another virtue: even with sophisticated

instruments, you can only focus in one direction and wave type at a time. Some instruments may detect several bands simultaneously, but our own consciousness seems to have a very narrow range of attention. If we focus on one thing, we lose all the rest. Even in expanded states of consciousness, our experience always seems to be limited to some specific aspect or field. This is important to understand both our primary experience and those attributed to the prophets.

There is yet another level at which the cosmos seems to be interconnected. Physicists call it quantum entanglement: some aspects of particle pairs, such as spin correlation, mirror each other instantaneously, no matter the distance that separates them. It's truly weird, and a bit hard to grasp, but it seems to be yet another level at which there is the possibility of resonance. The bottom line is that the 'reality' that we are immersed in and the universe in general seem to be a very intricately woven, multilayered information field, rather than a disjointed jumble of 'matter.'

Footprints in the sands of time

Another crucial aspect is that many events leave lasting traces. Our world, the whole universe, is full of traces and echoes of the past. Most footprints are ephemeral, but there are many ways that records of past events persist in nature: physical traces and inclusions in ice, peat, tar, amber or rocks; petrified objects or their imprints; stratified erosion deposits; atomic decay; magnetic shifts frozen in rocks, and many others. Life does so too, in many ways, like the genetic code; ontogeny and phylogeny; metabolic and immune systems; and then consider our physical, emotional, and cognitive memories. Culture, of course, is largely the accumulation and transfer of past experience. Starting with oral traditions and then writing, we have developed a whole battery of recording systems. Increasingly compressed technologies are adding a whole new layer, the most advanced to date being our photographic and digital records.

But there is a deeper level to all this. The principle of information conservation in theoretical physics suggests that no information is truly lost, even in extreme conditions like a black hole. On another front, mystics and seers have long held that the universe somehow retains traces of past events, and claimed to have access to these information fields. The revival of transpersonal experiences is lending fresh support to at least some of their claims. Yet, how to explain these notions seemed impossible from both perspectives, until the digital age and the discovery of holography (our old notions of data recording, like writing and books, are hopelessly fragmented and inefficient).

Holography is a technology for recording and reconstructing the full three-dimensional information of an object on a two-dimensional surface using coherent light, usually from a laser. When properly illuminated, the hologram reconstructs the light field, allowing the viewer to perceive a three-dimensional image with depth and parallax, as if the object were present. The enigmatic aspects of some spiritual experiences, such as feeling both sides of an interaction simultaneously, often have a quality that can be likened to a holographic projection. Thus, this technology is a good model for understanding many of the paradoxes of the holotropic experience and the apparent contradictions in the mystical literature of all ages. But perhaps it is more than just a model. It may be an intrinsic aspect of the very fabric of the cosmos.

A striking feature of holography is that you can store many images on a single plate by changing the angle at which the laser records the image and then projects it, yet, unlike a photographic negative, none of these images can be seen directly on the recorded plate. The information is distributed evenly throughout the plate, meaning any fragment contains information on the whole image, though less well defined than projecting from the entire plate. Multiple images can be superimposed on a single plate by recording them at different angles, allowing each to be selectively viewed by adjusting the illumination angle during playback. You can also blend several images into one by recording them in sequence with the same beam on the same plate. When projected, these images will then appear to exist simultaneously in the same space-time, like the paradoxical experience mentioned above. But projecting these will not show you other images recorded on the same plate at different angles. To the extent that the analogy is valid, this is a crucial detail because it implies that no single observer (mystic or layman) will see the whole cosmic picture at once, only the part available from whatever perspective ('laser angle') they have access to. Most mystics seem to have been aware of this limitation, but their followers can easily lose track of the relativity of their guru or prophet's statements. The standard political gambit is to convince you that the revelations and teachings of their prophet represents the 'absolute truth.'

Compare this claim with the development of psychology we saw above. Sigmund used talk therapy and discovered ego psychology, the most superficial layer. Carl Jung added new approaches and discovered the collective unconscious. Stan Grof used psychedelics and holotropic breathwork to uncover the importance of the perinatal passage and even deeper layers of the transpersonal domains. No doubt some other new approach will show us realms as yet unknown to us. This notion is crucial for understanding the evolution of cosmologies. Early shamanic practices must have given us access to the first level of the occult realms (the *astral domain*, according to some), populated by the spirits of animals, plants and other natural elements. Hence, the cosmology was *animistic*. Then came the archetypal domains which presumably gave rise to the wealth of world mythologies. As the techniques and experience evolved, practitioners were able to reach deeper levels and the cosmologies changed accordingly: polytheistic, monotheistic, unitive, ... But note, in an infinite universe no mortal can possibly have 'the absolute truth.' Quite frankly, I have my doubts that even the gods can handle '*the whole truth*' simultaneously.

In a nutshell, the latest speculations posit that information and awareness are integral parts of the very fabric of the universe. In this view, matter is a special form of concentrated energy, perhaps shaped by a constellation of ahxioms, fractals, morphogenetic fields or similar notions that emanate from the basic undifferentiated 'Ground' of existence, coded in holographic templates.[47]

==================== III ====================

Chapter III.85 –

Just how intelligent is '*Intelligent Design*'?

As we saw in the previous chapter, 'reality' seems to be a very intricately woven, multilayered conscious information field, rather than a disjointed jumble of matter. This perception has led to the idea that the universe as a whole is *intelligent* in some way and has infused new life into the old religious notion that biological evolution is the result of the influence of this intelligence in the material universe, a form of '*Intelligent*

---

[47] Partly adapted from Ervin Laszlo's book: *What is Reality?* (2016).

Design' (ID), rather than a random process.

Since the process and the theory of biological evolution are both uncontroversial among biologists, you might wonder why I should insist on this controversy. Intelligent Design ties in with divine intervention and clashes with free will. Many people dislike the idea of evolution being random, but then they sign up for Divine Intervention instead. Well, the belief in Divine Intervention has been the source of many tragic events in our history, and is a questionable invasion on the notion of free will. It poses serious contradictions and difficulties, especially with regard to the existence of evil and suffering in the world. All too often it is used to justify and abet acts of unbridled violence and extermination.

All this brings us back to poor old Charles and biological evolution. In his defense, Darwin only said '*descent with modification*' (variation) and '*natural selection*' but never said anything about evolution being random. He simply recognized that individuals differ, and that natural selection acts on this variation. In fact, one of the initial stumbling blocks of his theory was that the mechanisms that produced this variation were unknown in his day, and largely misconceived (see Chapter II.37). The 'random' element was introduced later as a basic premise of the scientific method (in order to prove or disprove something you postulate a null hypothesis assuming randomness).

Why people should be so upset by the idea that biological evolution might have a random component is a mystery[48], but the idea of creation as the product of a supreme intelligence is remarkably resilient. If you postulate Divine Intervention, however, evolution should be near perfect and occur at great speed. Since it isn't, either God was very, very distracted or he had something else in mind. Ken put it more bluntly: "... *evolution... is a creative artwork, not an intelligent engineering product (because if so, that Engineer is an idiot)*" (Wilber, 2007, footnote, p.241).

Still, the issue is tricky. The more recent objection to evolution by random mutations, allegedly based on reason rather than dogma, is that

---

[48] One culprit is the Christian and Islamic denial of reincarnation. If we only live once, our attachment to our current form (body, sex, race, etc.) is absolute because our spirit appears to be inextricably tied to this specific 'being.' Once you get beyond this misconception and accept soul migration, the evolution of spirit becomes independent of our current physical body and its evolution, which then ceases to be perceived as a threat to our identity.

the biochemistry of organisms is so complex that it would take an impossibly long time for the wheel of fortune to turn over all the necessary possibilities. This has been likened to a blind man trying to solve Rubik's cube, or the likelihood of a monkey randomly typing out one of Shakespeare's plays. The Rubik's cube example was estimated by mathematician Fred Hoyle in his book *The Intelligent Universe*. At one move per second, a blind man might take over 100 billon years (10^{11}) to hit on the solution randomly. However, if he were guided by correct yes–no prompts, he might get it in less than five minutes. This discrepancy is so abysmal that natural evolution clearly **hasn't** been very intelligent. Fred Hoyle's calculations actually endorsed one aspect of Darwin's theory: the paramount importance of *natural selection*, which is nature's equivalent of a yes–no prompt. However, as a prompt, natural selection is probabilistic rather than deterministic, which would partly explain the slowness.

If we invoke God, we would have to postulate some reason or condition that explains the slowness and restricts the possibility of top-down *Divine Intervention* in natural evolution. Here is a simple example: Jews obviously think Yahweh made a mistake when *He* endowed human males with a foreskin covering the glans penis, so for the last 3000 years rabis have been cutting it off to correct *Yahweh*'s mistake (circumcision), thus mutilating every new generation. Why has *Yahweh* taken so long to correct *His* mistake? I mean, surely, *He* could just tweak Jewish DNA so that future generations of males be born with exactly the right amount of foreskin the Rabies recommend... Likewise, many Muslims clearly believe *Allah* made a mistake when *He* endowed women with a clitoris, so the wise mullahs have been correcting Allah's mistake for hundreds of years by cutting it off, generation after generation!

If our bodies have been designed by a supreme intelligence, why then do we have so many genetic malfunctions, aches and pains? There are many examples of evolution producing what seem to be suboptimal adaptations. Another feature that is hard to explain under the ID idea is that lineages often seem to get stuck in an adaptive rut, which can even lead to their extinction. These and many other cases are in complete contradiction with the idea of both *Intelligent Design* and *Divine Intervention*. Conclusion, as biologist maintain, evolution is free-wheeling and has a good quota of serendipity. Even looking at it from an existential point of view, what's the point of life and suffering if it's all digitated?

Since the slowness of evolution and its imperfection indicate that it has **not** been very intelligent, why the religious obsession with *Intelligent Design*? It's not about ID at all. Truly, who cares *how* our bodies got here? The issue underlying the battle is not biological evolution, it is about DI and ecclesiastical politics. If you do away with **Divine Intervention**, the whole edifice of religious authority and power disintegrates. The clergy, control freaks, and political manipulators **need** the top-down notion of *Divine Intervention* to justify their own claims to authority, so next time you hear "Intelligent Design" in a religious context, switch the discussion to Divine Intervention and religious authority.

I see little need for any form of ID. Rather, Ingenious Darwin figured out the design used by the Creator that, for the most part, is self-fulfilling without sustained *Divine Intervention*. Yet, considering the debate has had no clear resolution, perhaps evolution has some measure of both processes. In any event, biological evolution through spontaneous genetic variation and natural selection is a valid explanation for much of evolutionary change we see in nature, and is therefore here to stay.

What happens if we accept the existence of an intelligence developed at some higher order in our material universe as the designer? We already saw the problem with *Divine Intervention*. Postulating a self-organizing interconnected intelligence that can draw on prior experience from any region of the universe is not much different. If that were possible, evolution should be near perfect and occur at considerable speed. Since it is painfully slow and imperfect, we need another solution. (Besides, this doesn't avoid the problem of infinite regress: how did **that** intelligence evolve?)

How about the bottom-up approach? This is closer to the classic materialistic perspective, but differs in proposing that change is the product of some form of *intrinsic* intelligence present even in elemental matter, rather than mere chance. This is less farfetched than you might think. The incredible biochemical complexity and sophistication of our immune system almost requires it. It can identify and discriminate, learn and remember, and generate appropriate responses. It can also err, as in allergic reactions. It is considered a form of biological intelligence rivaled only by our brains.

Two factors could account for the more limited influence of an intrinsic intelligence in matter. First, the basic features that make up for intelligence, such as awareness, are widespread in living beings and even in complex molecules, but as complexity grows, higher intelligence levels are increasingly restricted to higher animals and humans, thus limiting its availability to these contiguous *fields*. Even if these *fields of intelligence* stretch over whole ecosystems, that would be enough to produce unique sequences of local evolution, as has been the case with biological and cultural evolution in different continents. Perhaps basic templates are widespread, but the details develop locally.

The second issue is akin to limitations of perspective. Recalling the *decoupling of scales* we saw in Chapter I.32, perhaps an atom is blind to the problems of molecules, organic molecules are blind to the possibility and the vicissitudes of cells, and cells cannot imagine or foresee the issues faced by whole organisms. In this scenario 'intelligence' at any given level will only affect horizontal evolution or progress, *i.e.*, innovations or improvements within that level of organization. The jumps to higher levels of organization are different: they need special circumstances and occur only rarely, for instance by incorporating fully functional gene clusters from other evolutionary lines, as we saw in the notion of reticular evolution (Chapter I.17). This scenario is more in tune with what has been observed in the evolution of life forms in nature. Evolution is not continuous, uniform. It occurs in spurts, followed by long periods of relative stasis, in a process known as *punctuated equilibria*. The idea that evolution is driven by its own intrinsic drives and levels of organization also helps explain why evolution seems to accelerate as complexity and self-awareness increases.

These issues merit an aside. The explosion of neurological studies that resulted from the development of new scanning techniques (PET scans, fMRI, etc.) have repeatedly confirmed very specific links of many mental and emotional processes with equally specific locations in the brain, refueling the idea that brain function itself produces consciousness and everything associated with it. At the same time, a growing body of evidence supports the notion of spirit as a real entity independent of the physical brain, one that might even be the ultimate seat of our personality, our memories, and so on. How can these apparently conflicting notions be reconciled? Well, the issue is far from clear, but one tantalizing idea is that our brain has a dual function. On the one hand, it handles the usual neurological senses, controls, and responses of our physical bodies and our relationships with the environment. At the same time, it functions as a 'transducer' between the material plane and the spiritual domain, like a two-way radio. The exquisite human diversity and the resulting specificity of our biochemical constitutions is the 'bar code' that identifies each and every one of the eight billion living humans (and, presumably, all those previous incarnations that came before us). This enables personalized exchanges between our earthly bodies and our spiritual higher Self (or soul). Because of its complexity and uniqueness, several thinkers (Laszlo, Grof, ...) assign this transducer role to our extensive repository of "junk" DNA and the very personal epigenetic combinations that each of us develops through our lives. However, in keeping with animistic traditions, this individualized contact is not possible for lower forms that only have a generalized communal spirit. Several aspects of quantum physics (entanglements, etc.) could allow for this, but the stronger active brain functions would override these more subtle energies and links. Yet, during sleep, or through meditation, hypnosis, etc., these subtle energies do filter through. All very speculative, of course, but worth investigating further.

In turn, the notion of *punctuated equilibria* in biology echoes the notion of paradigm shifts in scientific progress: occasional breakthroughs that produce a burst of progress, followed by relatively long periods of 'normal' (horizontal) science within the framework of those ideas. There seems to be a catch in material forms of existence. Spirit out of our space-time might be all knowing, but once it is trapped in a material form it loses this capacity and suffers from amnesia (or lacks the required level of energy, complexity, and fluidity).

Developmental psychologists say that as soon as babies start to interact with their parents and the environment, they begin to form *'theories of mind'* that organize and help them make sense of the reality that surrounds them. It seems we never stop adjusting these *theories*, for the most part empirically as a result of our experiences and whatever education we may receive. As we grow up, we inevitably look at reality with these conceptions as a backdrop, which helps us understand the world we are familiar with, but also distorts or shrouds other aspects. In a more formal context these conceptions or theories are called paradigms. A change in paradigm is a change in outlook that widens our view and gives those areas more clarity, while other aspects may remain shrouded (there will always be a 'beyond' that we don't yet understand). Still, a better understanding of reality will always help us better adapt to it. Humanity has come a long way, but even those at the cutting edge of progress realize that there is still an ever-broadening horizon ahead of us. As you widen your views, you realize there are new oceans to explore, new domains to understand.

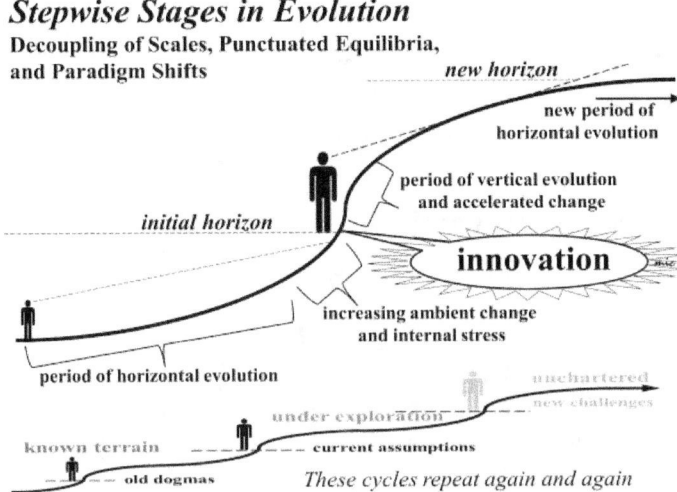

Stepwise Stages in Evolution
Decoupling of Scales, Punctuated Equilibria, and Paradigm Shifts

*Figure 39. **Evolution unfolds in steps and stages**. The global cumulus of historical data shows that evolution at the physical, the biological and the cultural level is not uniform. It occurs in 'normal' (gradual) stages, punctuated by innovations that produce bursts of rapid change and a jump in complexity (the solid line shows the increase in complexity over time). At the personal level, these major transitions are difficult and threatening, but necessary if we are to progress.*

Clare Graves – whom we will meet more fully in the next chapter – has shown that individual development follows a similar sequence. Our sense of self identifies with a given set of ideas, usually supplied by our culture, that may govern our lives for many years. As we develop and mature, these ideas begin to clash with what reality is throwing at us, or we find these ideas too constrictive or poorly adapted to our circumstances, which leads to a search for a new perspective, a change in attitude. At some point the solution hits us, we transcend the old ways and embrace these new values that embody a wider or more inclusive conception (Figure 40).

There is however, a better way to conceive the whole shebang. What we see are complementary but relatively independent lines of evolution at different levels. Consider three simple premises: the big bang vaporized everything and wiped out virtually all traces of organization and consciousness inside the bubble of matter it created. Whether this was by design or by default is debatable, but let that rest for the moment.

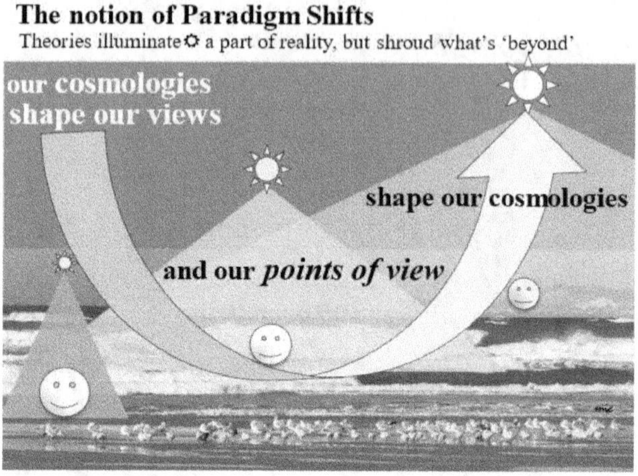

The notion of Paradigm Shifts
Theories illuminate ☼ a part of reality, but shroud what's 'beyond'

our cosmologies
shape our views

shape our cosmologies

and our *points of view*

*Figure 40. **A change of Paradigm**. – We inevitably look at reality with a conception in mind, like a street light which illuminates some areas but shrouds the rest. A change in paradigm is a change in outlook that widens our view and gives it more clarity. To achieve this, we need to 'step back' to gain a wider perspective. – But there will always be areas in shadow, a 'beyond' that we don't yet understand or even perceive.*

What followed is a slow but steady organization and complexification of 'inert' matter, driven by its own intrinsic properties, following the physical evolution laws (see Sabine's *Existential Physics* for an overview). Increasing complexity eventually leads to self-regulating biochemical systems and the birth of agency. At some point in this continuum a crucial inflection point occurs and we see a transition from inert matter to self-organizing and self-replicating organisms, life. Once life gets going it takes off on its own line of evolution that initially follows Darwinian principles. The key issue is recognizing that atomized matter by itself cannot function as an autonomous agent. It can only do so by the concourse of specific organizational plans, biochemical blueprints and anatomical templates, but even so it cannot sustain complex organization for long, so the physical body stops working, dies, and a new one has to be reassembled frequently, using these templates that must be passed on from functioning bodies to the next generation (Rupert Sheldrake's *morphic fields* perhaps, plus the drivers described below, the *software*, inklings of Spirit).

The third step assumes that increasing complexity, in this universe or in previous ones, gave rise to self-awareness and consciousness. Like memes, these consciousness bundles acquired a life of their own, and generated a third line of evolution independent of the material universe we perceive (out of space-time, extradimensional perhaps?), the evolution of consciousness itself. Its continued progress is expanded by repeated life experiences through the process of reincarnation, or soul migration. Because the physical body inevitably succumbs to decay, the trick is for consciousness to 'migrate' from the current body to a new one. Once we realize our physical bodies are just props that allow consciousness (or spirit) to have repeated experiences in the physical domain, and that spiritual progress runs on a different track than biological evolution, we can let go of our obsessive attachment to our current bodies. And once that happens, many of the ideological battles that haunt us today simply disappear.

> *Matter is the canvas that mind paints upon.*
>
> Chris M Bache

Think of matter as the raw materials on which novel forms of life can evolve, and life as the active means for Spirit to have fresh experiences in the material level of existence, thus bringing new aspects of its infinite potential into being, a process through which Spirit itself continues to evolve.

Evolution pervades everything and unfolds in predictable patterns in all domains, including paradigm shifts in knowledge and culture. *Creation without evolution is a dead end.* Thus, the patterns that underlie the evolution of complexity at all levels, including the unfolding of religious beliefs, must follow basic *Laws of ah!* – Understanding the workings of divinity is a lot more complex than we are led to believe, so be cautious of the arrogance of men who claim they know the mind of *ah!*

===================== III =====================

Chapter III.86 –

Clare Graves and Spiral Dynamics®

This belongs to the subjectal domain, but it is important here because some people think that *'going back to . . .'* is better, more religious, more spiritual. Careful, that's not always correct. If 'going back to nature' means being truly primitive, then it is not progress, it's regression. History never goes backwards. There's a Canadian film, *The Snow Walker*[49], about a cosmopolitan 'civilized' bush-pilot that takes a young Inuit girl on one of his flights. He looks down on her because he sees her as *primitive*. Then the airplane crashes in the middle of nowhere. Now he's the idiot- he hasn't a clue- she can survive just fine. After a long adventure he's dressed like an Inuit and can handle himself quite well in the wilderness. Yes, you could say he 'returned to nature,' but he keeps talking about a restaurant in Boston and can still fly an airplane! He managed to adapt, but he can't avoid belonging to a wider world.

Clare W Graves, a Psychology Professor at Union College, studied a population of university students to see how our perception of what it means '*to be an adult*' evolves over time. What he discovered is that development is not continuous. It occurs in fairly well-defined steps or shifts, similar to paradigm shifts we saw earlier, followed by periods of relative stability within that perception of self. The focus of importance alternates between an individualistic stance and communal affiliations. In one stage the person defines 'self' by personal attributes and merits, in the other by relevant affiliations. '*I am a doctor*' versus '*I belong to such-and-such community*.' Also, the process is open, so development spirals again from one phase to the other, but with different abilities and nuances, a vision that retains some of the previous abilities, but that transcends them to incorporate a wider conception of reality. This cycling in ever-widening spirals is what inspired the name *spiral dynamics*. This is somewhat analogous to Pichon's concept of a 'dialectic spiral' as referred to the evolution of groups.

Very briefly, Clare identified five or six stages that people go through as they grow up and mature. The simplest we can relate to is archaic, governed mostly by our survival instincts. The next we identify with is Kin-Spirits, with an animistic or magical tone. Later we go through an egocentric phase that identifies with Power Gods, followed by a stage in which Truth is perceived as absolute. Some stay stuck about here, but most modern adults move on to a more relativistic outlook that puts value in Human Bonds, and there are a few stages beyond. These stages roughly go hand in hand with our expanding focus of reference: symbiotic, egocentric,

---

[49] *The Snow Walker*, film by Charles Martin Smith (2003/2005), based on a book by Farley Mowat.

family-centric, ethnocentric, nationalistic, world centric, global, ..., and a constellation of associated developmental characteristics.

The essential point in all this is that people may witness the same event but give it a very different interpretation and significance according to the perspective from which they are operating. This is particularly strong or forceful when we are talking about our gods (*my God is more powerful than your god; ours is the only True God, etc.*). This may come across as very arrogant or narrow-minded (which it is, to some degree), but much of the problem lies in the person's limited perspective. In fact, from the perspective he has, the person just cannot understand the problem, his own error of judgment, and even less the possible solutions.

Unfortunately, all too often discussions both at the personal and at the political level get stuck on **what** we believe, with very little attention being given to **how** we believe, or **why** different people believe in a certain way. It requires help from someone who does understand, but all too often that help is not available in the believer's social milieu (everybody is stuck on the same problem or perspective).

An important point discovered by Clare is that people change only when their worldview is no longer adapted to their circumstances or they are forced to by changes in the context that surrounds them. These changes can produce considerable stress, so people often strongly resist them, and may even regress to an earlier stage in an effort to avoid the change. Recall the process of *death-and-rebirth* we saw in Chapter III.80 (*The prophet's dilemma*). Many of us grew up completely sold on the notion that we would marry and then *live happily ever after ...*, so the 'death' of a marriage, a divorce, is often painful, emotionally devastating. Our attachment to the illusion must 'die.' We suffer, but eventually we come to terms with our shattered illusions and move on, 'reborn' to a new, less rigid way of coping. If the conditions around us change, like it or not, we have to adapt.

Perhaps the difficulty to embrace change is why there are those who live among us and use all the commodities of modern life, but still preach Genesis, that creation occurred 6000 years ago, Adam and Eve, the flood, Noah and his ark, and all those stories and myths of the tribe of Israel. As if they really believed that nothing has changed in the last 3000 years or so since those stories began to be told and were written down. As if we were still going around on donkeys. Perhaps they are a little confused, in which case it would be prudent to keep your distance, just in case.

But it's hard to accept that a televangelist preacher that has a university level education, uses the media and television to preach, prepares his sermons on a laptop, travels around in his private jet, and manages a multimillion-dollar business on his cell phone really believes that '*nothing significant has changed*' since the bible was written. You bet he knows! Religions differ and disagree in their beliefs. Science and technology don't. If you have enough confidence to board an aircraft, you have 'faith' in the science of aerodynamics. There is no such thing as one aerodynamics for Christians and another one for Muslims. There is only one aerodynamics. That's why scientists and engineers all over the world understand each other.

Yet some preachers and mullahs want to make us believe that the same scientific principles and modern advances that are good and true for some situations, are bad and false for others. Creationists claim that *Carbon dating is not reliable*. If you use **atomic time keeping devices**, radiotherapy, you know and fear the atomic bomb, use atomic generated energy, and so on, you cannot then say that atomic dating is unreliable just because you don't like the results it produces. All these technologies are based on the same principles.

So then, ask yourself: Why insist on such obvious contradictions? If they are only pretending, why? Why such zeal, effort, and elaborations to sustain myths that are obsolete? Perhaps they are too scared to make the changes (it happens a lot to older folks). Perhaps because they have vested interests in the franchises and think they need to hold us under those spells so as not to lose their clientele. That's manipulation, by the way. Either way, keep an open mind and politely move away.

All this internal bickering within Christianity and between the Abrahamic creeds is absurd because it makes absolutely no difference. Do you believe in God because of some *book*, Genesis, or any other? Nonsense, you believe in *ah!* because you feel *ah!* is real. If these books had never existed, you'd still believe, perhaps in a slightly different *conception* of divinity, but you would be equally happy with that. From the spiritual perspective all this battle is absurd. In particular, Science is good at what it does, very good in fact, so then why not catch up with what science has to teach us about the basic Laws of *ah!* Then we can use our energies to resolve more important issues.

You can't stay stuck in a bronze age religion in the middle of the space age!

========================= III =========================

Chapter III.87 –

Old and new paths to spiritual growth (the return journey)

When we reviewed the individual psyche (Chapter III.81), we saw that experiences can be linked by emotional quality rather that logical criteria, and that continued exploration of these COEX systems often reveals a repetitive, layered system that is most easily seen at the egoic level, but that has roots at the perinatal level, and even in the transpersonal domains. This process has been compared to peeling layers off an onion. The deeper layers are hard or impossible to see until you become aware and 'peeled off' the superficial ones. Thus, the deep subconscious and transpersonal domains and phenomena appear to be protected or 'veiled' by the superficial layers. It seems we need to have those veils closed in order to operate effectively in this reality.

What has become clear in the last few decades is that both physical and existential trauma itself can act as a veil, or reinforce the effect of other veils. None of the traditional practices used by mainstream religions addresses these problems or heals them. In fact, they often compound them. This may well be one of the reasons traditional religious practices have been so inefficient as tools for enlightenment. Yes, every now and then they produce a saint or two, but for most of recent history the vast majority of religious practitioners have had little success in attaining grace, which is not to say it's easy: *"Some of the obstacles … are intrapsychic in nature. Major breakthroughs, such as psychospiritual death and rebirth, are preceded by terrifying encounters with evil forces, a consuming fear of death, and the specter of insanity"* (Grof, 2019, II).

So, what are the options? Well, you can continue reading the scriptures, going to church, hearing sermons, praying, singing hymns, and so on. These methods have been used for centuries, and surely still appeal to some folk. But you would also be wise to incorporate some of the other experiential methods either developed or revalidated in the last few decades.

There are a number of techniques and practices destined to put us in direct contact with this type of experience, some ancient and others of recent evolution. Even the use of psychoactive drugs has a very long and varied tradition. In many ancient societies the use of psychedelic plants in initiation rites and other ceremonies was the norm, and therefore *normal*, accepted. After many decades of supervised use of these substances in modern medical and scientific research, it is clear that psychedelics are not addictive, but do have powerful physical and psychological healing effects. It is therefore difficult to understand how we lapsed from the traditional situation to the current social, legal, and religious conception that these practices are perverse, demonic. Their systematic suppression during the last millennium or so must be one of the saddest human tragedies of the modern world. It only makes sense as an attempt on the part of the priesthood to retain and control this privilege for the benefit of a ruling elite, a theocracy (and the obvious racket of the drug trade). Unfortunately, in many cases the ritual context that gave these practices a safe containment was also brutally repressed and lost. Fortunately, today we can rely on a range of methods that facilitate or induce similar expanded states of consciousness without the use of substances (sensory isolation or deprivation; biofeedback; holotropic breathwork; rebirthing to some extent; hypnosis; past life therapies; fasting; meditation; yoga; etc.). The list of known natural and synthetic substances with psychedelic effects is also constantly growing.

As a result, we are seeing a resurgence of all these techniques, despite the constant disqualification and censure from some religious and social sectors[50]. Because the traditional institutional position smells ratty or hypocritical, many are moving away from those manipulative religions. For instance, in an attempt to be seen in a different light a producer claims his movie *"is spiritual, but not religious."*

'Spirituality' is gaining acceptance as an alternative to organized religion. This is by no means new. It means going back to the original roots of all religions, a personal search for direct contact with the Divine. These experiences have well defined features, recognizable in oneself and in others, like the dissolution of our ego, a sense of unity with the cosmos, the

---

[50] *e.g.*, Michael Pollan (2018), *How to change your mind*.

numinous and ineffable[51] quality of the experience, etc. Their dynamics are closer to a dream sequence than to the linear logic of our verbal thinking when awake. Often, they are linked by their emotional affinity or quality (recall the COEX idea), rather than by some logical or chronological sequence. Recall also that traumatic and violent experiences tend to be linked with 'demonic' mythological themes or energies. This echoes Jacques' perception that *"fear, anger, and impatience made me blind ... if I got angry, things got angrier than I. Everything hurt me."* Thus, anger and hate also put us in contact with negative 'demonic' energies.

The ancients put a lot of value in dream-states as portals to the otherworldly, but it is clear today that many people have these experiences in their waking state. As Aldous put it, it's like *opening the doors of perception* that allows us to see other realities or new aspects of our known reality. To operate effectively in material reality, we need to have those doors closed. But under certain circumstances those doors can open. Consciousness is always there, only expanded, more subtle or sharper. These expanded states also allow us to retrieve old issues that we had buried in our unconscious and re-live them with all their emotional charge, but as adults. For this exploration to be a positive and healing experience, you have to loosen some of the scientific, religious, and social conditionings and prejudices you might have with respect to the divine and the satanic, and on the nature of reality. It's not a question of judging, only of experiencing and understanding. This is not to deny divinity, on the contrary, it's more like opening a new experiential window to the divine, free of the personal hangups, superstitions, theories, and religious manipulations of our past.

It requires a change of attitude and expectations. Stop looking outwards, listening to sermons about what others think, focusing on what others do. An experienced meditator or psychonaut can work alone, but it helps to have some guidance while you learn the methods and practices, especially if you decide to use psychedelics. In fact, the minimum standard precaution is to work with a 'sitter,' someone who will care for your immediate needs, 'hold your space' and allow you to fully experience your

---

[51] Perhaps the most relevant notion here is *ineffable*, meaning *'difficult or impossible to put into words'* - so I will make no effort. There are many attempts elsewhere (*e.g.*, Chris Bache, *Diamonds from Heaven*).

inner world. Experienced practitioners who have some knowledge of the transpersonal domains and realms can also give you support as you progress in your own search process through the labyrinth of your interior worlds. It's the only space where you have some possibility of finding the divine, of recovering your connection with your inner *Seer* or *Higher Self*.

Going into the details is beyond the purpose of this essay, but as a general sense of direction we can use some of the common notions of the mystical schools and secular traditions. Hard to know how fundamental it is, but the general notion of karma as a cosmic law of consequence, and the tendency of the universe to keep putting the same obstacles in your path till you learn to overcome them seem to be good practical tools to measure your own experiences and attitudes.

Karma gives back to you that which you have given to others, so

Do *unto others as you would have them do unto you* (Matthew 7:21)

(... but be mindful of what *others wish to do unto you*,

and reject from others what you reject for yourself).

The good news is that over the last decades, we humans have rediscovered many of the old *technologies of the sacred*, the power of natural psychedelics, synthesized new ones, gained a better understanding of how these substances work, and developed a whole battery of new drugfree methods to produce similar effects with less effort and better results. The bad news, or at least the cautionary note, is that like any other tool, these methods can be misused or abused, and lead to very difficult or even dangerous situations (the 'bad trip' phenomenon). Experience has shown that mindset and setting are important, as is working with adequately trained facilitators that hold the space for a safe journey (safe, mind you, not necessarily easy).

It is worth recalling the list of notions or conditions we saw in Chapter III.81 (the creative principle, the Source, cosmic consciousness, the primal mind, etc.) Though the names and ideas have changed over time, there are several underlying qualities that seem to be recognized by all schools. This cosmic ground or essence is nondual, formless, eternal (or more likely, outside space-time), abstract, impersonal, immanent, hard to describe with words, usually silent but can be felt or sensed, 'empty' but full of potential (a plenum). Thus, the creative principle, the true *ah!mighty*, is prior to and devoid of any form, duality, sex, gender, race, ethnicity, skin color, politics or religion, but contains the **potential** for all these things.

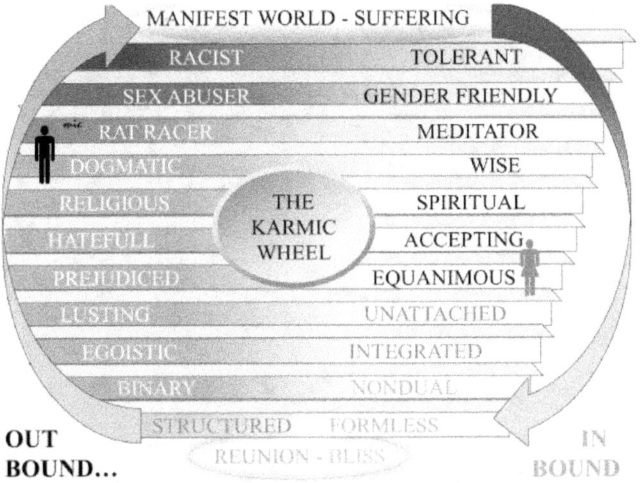

Figure 41. **The Wheel of Karma.** – *The staircase to heaven or to hell. According to the Hindu tradition, your actions in each life determine your next incarnation. – On the right, some of the Holotropic attitudes and qualities that foster steps on the return journey to the Source. – On the left side, some of the Hylotropic attitudes and actions that increase your separation and deepen your alienation from the Source, sinking you ever deeper into the Wheel of Karma.*

Which means that if your deity is masculine, racial, speaks only one language, favors some form of ism and imposes one specific form of worship, you are definitely dealing with a lesser deity. Which is fine, of course, if you prefer to worship and sacrifice your life to a second or third order deity, you are totally free to do so. Conflict ensues when you are led to believe that yours is the one and only "true" alternative, and are instructed to impose it on everyone else, by brute force if need be. If that's your persuasion, you are much more likely to be in the grip of the devil's or shaitan's advocate, than in the service of divinity.

Moving towards wholeness, re-union, entails a process of removing the sense of separateness which veils the underlying unity. Each polarity that you integrate and transcend takes you a step closer to *ah!* Instead, creating and perpetuating polarities, such as sexual and racial discrimination and hate, moves you **away** from the divine.

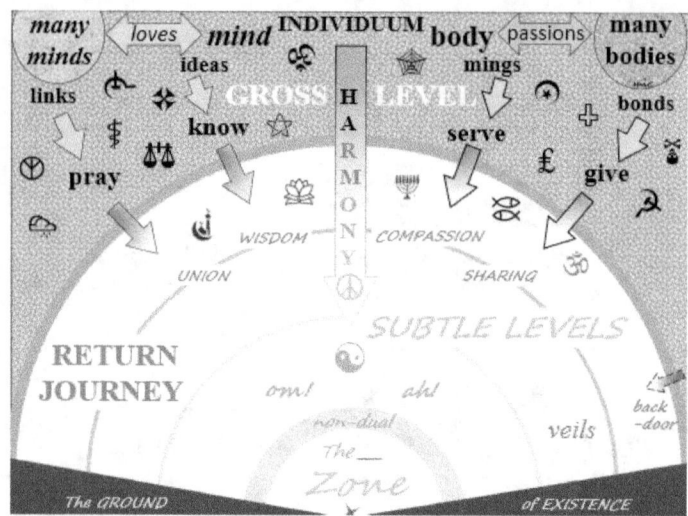

*Figure 42. **The Return Journey**. – The reverse of manifestation (Fig. 37), reflecting our craving to reunite with the Source. Spontaneous awakening, spiritual practices, and psychedelics can all help open our awareness of the numinous domains. Transitions between domains are barriers that are difficult to move through, especially from the clutter of the gross level to the subtle realms, and beyond to the __ Zone that is the Ground of existence. Contrary religion turns your attention to the mundane, the Practicum. Phony politics turns mundane conveniences into dogmas.*

This is not to deny that these differences exist. They do, of course, and make up much of the richness and color of the world we live in, but they are not fundamental. You are moving ten steps or stages up the ladder of manifestation. They do not represent the immanent Ground of existence, only some of its outer and less significant expressions.

===================== III =====================

Chapter III.88 –

Wisdom in the nature of Water

- ma'an - wasser *- i -* **eau** *-* 水 (mizu) *- ... ...* ءﺎﻣ *-* **water** *-* ☁ *-* **agua** -

We could go on with the 2000 to 5000 variants that occur worldwide, but the incredible fact is that all these words have the same meaning. They identify the same substance, and if you use the correct translation and ask for that word in the correct place, no matter how strange it may sound to you, you will obtain exactly what you were thinking. Nobody is going to ask if you meant this or that. Water is water, everywhere! What's more, we don't even need to say it. There are many memes, even simple gestures like cupping the palms of your hands and moving them to your mouth, that will get the idea across anywhere. Everybody understands water because water is the universal support of material life on this planet.

Water is truly amazing. It can be pure as crystal or harbor the filthiest gutter; make any shape imaginable or be shapeless; be a part of every living thing, from the lowliest to the mightiest; reside anywhere from the sky above the highest mountain to the deepest sea; be soft as a cloud caressing that mountain or hard as a glacier that bulldozes it. Its plasticity and creativity know no bounds, both as the container and as the actor. Almost like Spirit.

If we are to believe all the mystical schools and traditions, everything is made of Spirit. We *are* Spirit. But here is **the paradox**. Even those who can understand the fundamental unity and plasticity of water are often totally incapable of grasping the equivalent sameness of the *Spiritual* essence that underlies all of reality. *Oh, yes,* they talk about it all the time, "*Jehovah is everywhere,*" "*Allah is infinite,*" "*there is only one true essence*" (referring to their chosen name, obviously). Aaahh, yes, but then, when the time comes to accept that "*my essence is the same as your essence*" all hell breaks loose:

—*But didn't you know? My essence is the good one, yours is crappy, dummy!*

—NO, NO, NO, mine is the good one, yours stinks, infidel!
(..., idiot, heretic, ...the list of possible insults is as long as the list of creeds and religions).

These ideas contradict their own conception of deity. Anyone who thinks that his deity is different from mine (or yours, for that matter) is admitting that he or she adores a third order god, a partial god. Do you believe in a god? *Yes, of course, the creator of this world and universe.* Me too! So then, since we are in the same world, we must be speaking of the same *being*.

Now, we could argue for ever and a day if a pantheon of gods of different ethnicities, sectors or hierarchies even exists. But that does not matter in the least. The important issue here is that *they believe it. Oh, yes!* As I said, they argue that their god is THE one and only 'universal,' 'infinite,' 'supreme,' etc., which can only mean one thing, that **everything** in this universe is made of the same divine essence. Alleging that 'our god' is better than 'your god' (or *vice versa*) is to admit a belief in an excluding duality – God/ not God – God or Satan – Allah *versus* Jehovah – good or evil – etc. This lowers the discourse to a political level. Yes, there is good and evil, but don't blame Divinity for it.

Any form of excluding duality means that neither part is whole, infinite. Capitalizing names of deities has the same effect. Capitalizing is equivalent to personalizing, as if to say "*bring me Water, please, I would rather die before drinking Agua.*" It is also difficult or impossible to give a Name without an implication of sex or gender. The only deity worth speaking of is *pre-* any sort of *dualistic* notion (nondual).

All spiritual schools avoid names when they refer to ultimate causality, as do the esoteric branches of more traditional religions. Giving a Proper Name limits your mind and takes it to the preconceptions about your deity that you were raised with, which truly hampers your chances of knowing deity experientially. If you have any illusion of knowing the numinous, you'd do well to avoid names and preconceptions. Accept my gift. Every time you read, hear or think 'god' of any kind replace it with *ah! – om! – the__Zone* – any abstract equivalent you feel comfortable with.

A blank frees your mind and allow you to experience *spirit* in new ways.

In a nutshell, all these politicized creeds that stress the otherness and divisions also strengthen the pathology. If religion derives from the Latin root '*re-ligare*' meaning 're-tie' or 're-unite,' then all that separates is satanic. It's frightening to see how easily we let ourselves be swept away by these excluding polarities.

==================== III ====================

A note on imagining cosmic dynamics: I considered adding chapters on modern visionaries and their visions, but I could never do justice to such a vast topic in a compressed form. We struggle to grasp the immensity of an *infinite* cosmos. Still, gleaning from humanity's accumulated perceptions of cosmic dynamics, we can piece together plausible scenarios as food for thought, including the unfolding of divinity itself.

Chapter III.89 –

Creating the Creator

So, absolute nothingness.

Something stirs, a formless, weightless *speck* that comes 'alive' and starts tinkering.

What essential assets would enable *speck* to manifest a cosmos? Being (there has to be 'something' present); energy, the capacity to do work; definitely needs to be proactive; awareness? Many say everything is form and energy, but this idea falls short of explaining all of *reality*. Perhaps form and energy interact to give us entities and motion, but you need a third aspect, attractors or links, to produce patterns that underlie the *inter*-aspect, the forces that hold entities and collectives together. And what about consciousness? Tricky.

> So far, my model has things and links, but doesn't consider energy, purpose. Some speak of trilogies: the Tao creates two, the two create three, and these three create everything else. But of course, "the Tao" is already *something*. Being, form, breath – Ground, Logos, Spirit? Or think of *ah!* as the ground of *entity*; *om!* as the ground of energy and action; and the *yin-yang* binode - ☯ - or - S - the implied force *splicing* them together, the ground of interactions and patterns: awareness, love? … (Figure 43). – About here is where we all run out of imagination, so the black-box trick invariably comes into play: the *Tao*, *Spirit*, the *Source*, *speck*, matter, whatever you prefer, is **ETERNAL!** – End of story! –
> (You didn't seriously expect me to solve that one, or did you?)

The first thing *we* think of is moving about, but if there is no other point of reference or 'space,' that's meaningless. *Speck* shapeshifts, wiggles, vibrates, pulsates, grows, divides … and divides, … or did more *specks* arise out of *the __Zone?* Clones begin to interact, offering a lot more possibilities. More and more *specks* appear, and carry on acting and interacting till it seems all options are tried out and exhausted. And so, a variety of basic shapes, numbers, actions and interactions are discovered. *Speck* start trying ways of binding together to form combinations. As this mass of *specks* grows, a subtle type of space takes form, and new options appear: moving about, playing, synchronizing, and so on, all of which leads to inklings of complexity and evolution. If you start from scratch, simple must appear before complicated and complicated before complex; slow, low-energy vibrations (low frequencies) come before fast, high-energy frequencies, and so on.

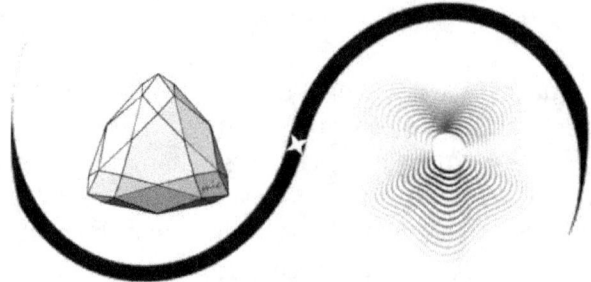

*Figure 43. **At the base of manifestation are three essentials**: form (geometry, the **amplituhedron**, ah! perhaps); energy, vibration, om! – ; and the S factor, splice, or Spirit - the invisible, intangible 'inter,' the threads that mesh it all together: awareness? - consciousness? - love? - (see box above). – And then, of course, the initial 'spark' always leaves a gap (a rabbit hole, a worm hole, a portal, ...) leading to a deeper level of reality, and another, and yet another ...*

Whether consciousness as we know it was the ground of all this, as some postulate, or was an intrinsic property from the beginning, or perhaps developed later, is anybody's guess. The point is crucial though, because it's so hard to grasp that virtually all elude the issue by kicking the ball out of our reach (*"the all-knowing is eternal"*). This is really a stretch. Religious folks can be quite derisive about the idea that complexity can evolve out of simpler things, such as our material brains (our *squishy meat*) creating thoughts and being the seat of intelligence, but they have no qualms about a total vacuum, the *Void*, thinking intelligently. When you ask for more detail or a credible alternative they mumble evasively.

One way or another, *specks* become conscious and intelligent enough to develop fairly elaborate designs, activities, and so on. Perhaps by trial-and-error, *specks* learn that wave motions dissipate and disappear, but certain interference patterns last longer and can be made more stable, a trick that allows the creation even more dazzling designs. Out of sheer enthusiasm, *specks* increase their vibrational frequency, which also increases their perceptual acuity, and permits the creation of new playing fields. And so the unfolding of the subtle realms gains momentum. *Specks* have covered the lower frequency bands with so much activity that a new arena is needed to diversify in, one that won't interfere with what's already done. This is achieved by elevating their own frequency band a few octaves higher, opening more 'room' to tinker and play in without destroying all the previous artwork. If you are alone in the cosmos with nothing much else to do, what better than to create, and then create some more.

This might please creationists, but if they took their proposal seriously and really sat down to figure out how things might have come about, they would soon realize the picture drifts ever closer to what we understand as evolution. It's impossible to imagine a one-step 'creation' of something as complex and fine-tuned as our universe out of absolute nothingness and, besides, quite unnecessary.

So, we begin to get a feel for *primal tinkerer*. We can envision *pt* fiddling with some new idea, fleshing it out and then deciding it doesn't work quite right, so scrapping it to try something else, perhaps a bit more ambitious. *Pt* would soon accumulate experience and create a system that grows and improves with each cycle, an incipient version of the bouncing ball in reverse we saw in Figure 36.

At some point *pt* decided to make a more complex arena, affording a variety of novel experiences, so used the accumulated knowledge to generate another level of vibrational resonance, with much more elaborate differentiations. The growing mass of cloned *specks* gets large enough to split into what amounts to two budding *pts* that begin to entertain a sort of telepathic exchange about the artworks and the games they can play. And so appeared the first tier of what would, with further elaborations, become what we perceive as the subtle realms (keep in mind, solid matter hasn't appeared yet, so it is a poorly differentiated plasma, or 'ether' …).

Several cycles later, and *pt* has become quite proficient at cloning (or perhaps, at materializing *specks* out of *the __Zone?*) But, as complexity grows, diversity finally comes into play and these all-knowing plasmas start morphing into more polarized entities of the next level of differentiation that don't really *need* anything, but can't seem to avoid competing with one another (the jealous gods of Buddhism, perhaps?) An intrinsic diversity of sorts can appear in several ways, such as opposite spins or polarities.

It seems *pt* can't stop generating more stuff and ever more energy, so this once dimensionless bundle of nothingness keeps growing, thus generating subtle 'fields.' We can't conceive of existence out of space, but in our current cosmic scale it would be infinitesimal, with no 'volume' at all. *Pt* continues elaborating new ways to generate better playing fields, in part by increasing the vibrational frequencies. Because these new domains are still close to the basic vibrational level of the various differentiated beings that emerge, they can drift in and out of these 'theaters' to try them out, so the novelty affords a lot of fun. But the lower vibrational levels are still non-local and a bit fuzzy, overlapping, so you can't really forget that it's just a game. Much thought is given to figuring out how to veil the player's perception so they really immerse themselves in the experience.

(A note in passing: trying to write this account of primal evolution before *space-time* and before *dualities* is a struggle. Our language is so dominated by these notions that I keep having to do some linguistic somersaults to avoid falling into personifications, dualisms, and spaciotemporal implications. Try it, it's fun).

Pt notices higher frequencies enable sharper and better differentiated artwork (in our world, higher frequencies equate with shorter wavelengths, which can detect small objects more precisely), and if you immerse at those frequencies, their intensity shrouds other modulations, so in effect you sort of forget your true identity. But in the first attempts there is still a certain fluidity between levels. After much exchange with *alter tinkerers, pt* comes up with a model that creates a bigger gap between levels, acting as a sort of veil, so that once you move out there you can no longer see back, at least not directly. This entails the generation of much higher vibrational frequencies, so that *pt* needs to develop ways to handle these higher levels, in the process evolving and transforming into them. Still, when treading new fields some uncertainty as to how the whole shebang might work is inevitable. The first attempts fizzled out with a plop. Some sort of blow up and evaporate. After some further experimenting and adjusting the parameters, the project gets in motion with a *Bang*. This first try isn't as nifty as *tinkerer* had hoped, so it gets scrapped and a bigger try is attempted. After several of these adjustment cycles, things seemed to be working smoothly, so the whole illusion is retracted once again.

This iteration notion is an important point: amongst the arguments in favor of Intelligent Design is the incredible '*fine tuning*' of the physical parameters in our universe, but *finetuning* can come about faster than you might imagine. If you have a range of possible values, just take any around the middle and try it. Too fast? OK, take a second stab around the middle of the remaining 'slow' range. Too slow? Great, in two steps you have limited the options to a much narrower range, and eliminated around 75% of those options. The preceding formulation still implies an intelligent operator, but in practice if it can cycle (iterate), any system with negative feedback loops tends to a natural equilibrium point spontaneously. The trick would be to figure out how such feedback loops might have influenced the early cosmos and universes.

Pt's project is ready for a much more ambitious effort, so *pt* puts in *infinitillions* of new *specks*, infuses them with unimaginable amounts of energy and creates a much, much **bigger Bang**, the one that gives rise to our space-time and the arena we live in today. Pure amazement, it works stupendously, outrageously, fantastically! The initial steps in the whole process might look something like Figure 44.

One intriguing point is the issue of divine intervention, or not. Consider the proposed motivations that might lead to the creation of universes: divine enthusiasm and playfulness, the need to discover and express its full potential, boredom, curiosity perhaps, ..., and the tragedy of being alone in the cosmos! My hunch is that loneliness plays an important role in some of the design details of our material universe and its evolution.

Put yourself in that place: you are acutely conscious, yet totally and absolutely alone in the cosmos. What are your options? Creating your double would be a start, but it would be like talking to your own image in the mirror. You would need to figure out a way to generate an independent conscious entity that is **not** exactly like you, not your clone, one in which imperfection and error *can* exist. Perhaps creating us "in *ah!*'s image" just won't do the trick.

A self-evolving universe in an isolated compartment, like our space-time, might just come up with some innovations you had not yet thought of. But for that to really remain independent, you would have to refrain from meddling in the process, and forbid any form of intervention by any other echelon in your crew. This non-interference idea actually crops up quite a lot in mystical literature, and is essential to afford us *free will*.

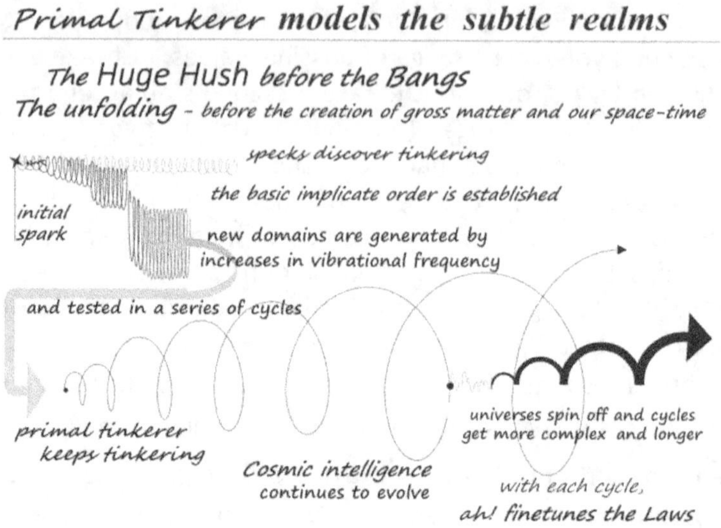

Primal Tinkerer *models the subtle realms*

The Huge Hush *before the Bangs*
The unfolding *- before the creation of gross matter and our space-time*

specks discover tinkering

the basic implicate order is established

initial spark

new domains are generated by increases in vibrational frequency

and tested in a series of cycles

primal tinkerer keeps tinkering

Cosmic intelligence continues to evolve

universes spin off and cycles get more complex and longer

with each cycle, ah! finetunes the Laws

Figure 44. **Creating the creator.** *– Everyone seems fixated on what happens after 'creation' of our universe. – How did ah! unfold from the__Zone before the creation of space-time, and how did cosmic consciousness evolve and generate the different levels in the Mysticum? – A system based on the control of tiers of modulated vibrational frequencies and stabilized interference patterns using something on the lines of fractals and hologram technology is a nifty proposition.*

Pure *my-fi*, but see how easy it is to weave a new mythology.

This is getting longer than I had intended, but take heart, we are almost there. The two-by-two model proved useful to organize and understand the Practicum, but some aspects seemed to overlap, and there is no place for the *Mysticum,* in part due to a limitation of the spatial disposition the model, or perhaps its representation as a two-dimensional surface. It's easier to grasp, but the domains are just conceptual abstractions. I've just speculated on the creation of levels in the *Mysticum* using vibrational frequency bands. This is valid for many phenomena in the Practicum, so perhaps we can extend the notion to the whole cosmic spectrum.

Think of it as an ocean. What we see on the surface (the swells, the passing waves, the crashing surf, the calm seas and swirling typhoons occurring on the surface and all their inhabitants) represents the

Practicum. Below the surface, but still in the light zone, are the ebbs and flows of the tides and long-range swells, with their own residents and visitors from the surface. Deeper in the twilight zone the slow but inexorable oceanic currents that mark the flow of time and history, conventionally separate oceans but ultimately all interconnected. Much deeper in the darkness of the abyssal zone you find total calm. Yet the place has its own luminescent denizens and vents through which bubble the primary components emanating from a seemingly inexhaustible reservoir hidden even deeper, out of our reach, upwellings that furnish the components that sustain and enrich the surface phenomena.

Imagining a similar 'ocean' with layers made up of frequency bands or zones permeating the matrix gives an expanded conception of the cosmos. We usually represent the frequency bands as separate, but as we saw in Chapter III.84, '*A deeper look at the cosmos…,*' they all coexist interlaced in the same matrix. Thus, we can conceive of *reality* as an intricately woven, modulated, layered mesh of vibrations. If we could *tune-in* to the right frequencies, we would find all the cosmos reflected inside us.

Adding *depth* to the notion of the domains allows us to visualize reality as a multi-layered volume rather than a flat surface. The objectal and interobjectal domains make up the most accessible layer, the conscious subjectal and intersubjectal aspects of our everyday mind making the next layer, the 'deeper' (usually unconscious) psyche acting as a portal to the deepest layers of the *Mysticum* beyond, which also shows several recognizable levels, but may lie on another axis (another 'dimension'). Even though we don't yet know the details, each of these layers or domains must have their own *breadth* ('horizontal' expanse), with their own individual holons, links, collectives and dynamics (*as above so below, as without so within*). Elements or aspects of these contiguous layers would be linked 'vertically,' with the deeper layers giving form to the outer ones ('in-forming' them). But we cannot perceive these 'internal' links directly from the outside, the Practicum, only through introspection and our inner Seer.

Thus, the path to introspection starts by temporarily shutting out the external material world, relaxing the body, quieting the mental bustle, and turning our attention inwards. If we succeed in letting go of our usual egoic controls, the process takes on its own dynamics and will likely takes us ever deeper into the inner world of our subconscious mind, through the perinatal, and eventually into the successive levels of the *Mysticum*, a cycle that would look something like Figure 45.

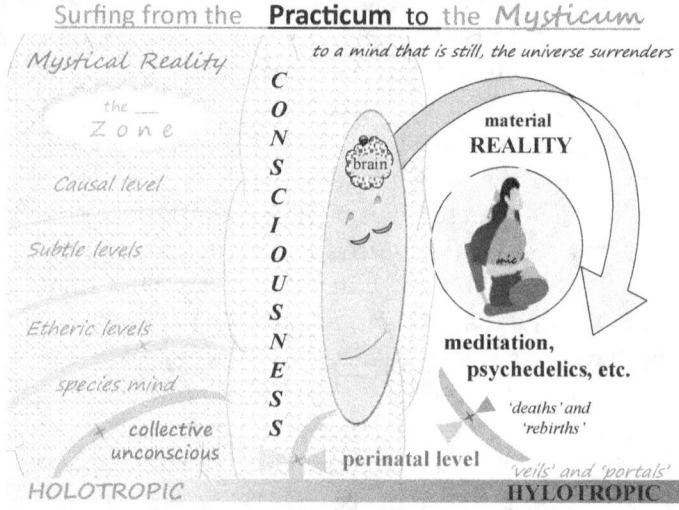

Figure 45. **Surfing from the Practicum to the *Mysticum.*** Moving from our usual hylotropic attention to deep introspection requires focus and special techniques that shut down normal brain activity, thus allowing expanded states of consciousness and a recurring cycle of 'death' of our attachment to our current realities, and 'rebirth' into successively 'deeper' and more 'spacious' experiential levels, which retain a semblance of material reality as far as the 'species mind.' To go beyond requires relinquishing any and all attachments to our sense of individuality and human form. Sustaining all is *the__Zone,* the Ground of being, home to *primal tinkerer.*

The tough part is that breaking through the successive 'veils' often involves difficult and even terrifying 'deaths' and 'rebirths,' a process that can be likened to an insect shedding its constricting exoskeleton in order to grow. As we deepen into the *Mysticum*, the energy-fields that felt 'individual' in the material plane begin to lose their borders, and slowly fuse into ever more interconected 'collectives,' all the way to a global *species-mind* and beyond. But this progresive 'fusion' into larger cohesive groupings is as seen from our perspective. If we reverse the flow and imagine the process from *primal tinkerer*'s perspective, this layered sequence supports the notion that 'creation' is not a magical burst of creativity, but the result of an intricate succesion of subdivisions of the creative principle occuring in steps and stages over vast cycles of existence.

Much of this is speculative, of course, but it is worth noting that some firsthand descriptions give the impression that at some point in these transitions we are no longer dealing with shifts within the standard material electromagnetic spectrum. Rather, what we perceive is a subtle intrinsic radiance often described as a substance or 'ether' that retains some degree of spatial structure, but seems to be of a different category that does not interact directly with our material world, and is thus not perceptible with our normal senses or instruments attuned to ordinary matter. This seems to be the only way to interpret the narratives and avoid contradictions. The deeper levels of the cosmos are built of a radiance that can attain very high levels of intensity or charge, but that is neither hot nor blinding when our consciousness is exposed to it. Of course, with over 95% of the cosmos composed of 'dark matter' and 'dark energy,' postulating this embedded medium/dimension is hardly a surprising claim.

The only problem with all this is that *pt* forgot to put in a safety feature and now doesn't know how the devil to stop the whole delusion from expanding endlessly. To some, this might seem a little far-fetched, but remember Averroes' koan (Chapter II.58). Some things may simply be impossible, even for the gods. Truly, there is no reason to suppose Divinity is infallible. Infallibility is a pretty tall order! Of all the stuff I've read on these lines, I'd like to close with a quote from a recent essay by Christopher, a very experienced and committed seeker, a modern mystic:

> *... finally, I was lifted into a particularly spacious and peaceful dimension, ... a sense of homecoming, and felt fully the tragedy of having forgotten this dimension for so long. ... I asked what had happened and It [the Consciousness I was with] explained that we had left time. Then It said, "**We never intended so many to get caught in time.**" It felt like time was simply one of the many creative experiments of the multidimensional universe I was being shown* - (my emphasis).

========================= III =====================

Wisdom was chasing them, but they proved to be a lot faster.
Nigerian proverb

Chapter III.90 –

Beyond *The Books*

From the beginning I posed the problem of defining the roles and activities that rule our lives. Most were easy, but religion seemed as elusive as they come. The problem is simple: you cannot separate the domains of psyche and spirit (and thus separate the roles of politics, religion and mysticism) on the flat surface we've used so far for the domains. Categorizing the Practicum can be handled as two-dimensional. To include psyche, spirit and the *Mysticum* we need three or more dimensions.

Now we can reconsider the issue and see if we can better separate the different aspects of religion and politics. Actually, it's quite simple, really. If it aims and claims to affect and modify worldly material affairs, it's politics. To be called spiritual or mystical it has to afford you the context and guidance to facilitate your <u>personal</u> experience with the *Mysticum*, because that is the only path that can put you in direct communion with the numinous and the Divine.

The Mysticum	←	**holotropic | hylotropic**	→	The Practicum
reunion ←	*numinous* ←	*in-sight* | out-sight	→ concrete	→ separation

Introspection and the aim of all forms of mystical practice is **subjectal**, and thus personal, never institutional (the practice may be communal, but the aha experience is personal). They allow us to dive below the surface and delve into the depth, so the perceptions they reveal needs to be incorporated by science and philosophy. They seem to be the **only** genuine source of spiritualty.

In this scenario, politics and the political aspects of religion, such as preaching and indoctrination, deal with and belong to the surface phenomena. Perhaps religion was born of philosophy, but the moment religion is institutionalized, dogmatized, and turned into an instrument of governance it transforms into politics. The interest, the agendas and the survival of the institution and its hierarchy take precedence over the alleged mission, as we saw in other political arenas, so we need to make a clear distinction. "Religion" is a Mediterranean concept. We have extended it to encompass other forms of dealing with the *Mysticum*. But that is our bias. Because of its Middle Eastern and Mediterranean roots, the notion conveyed by 'religion' is inextricably tied to *The Books*, theocracies, dogma and politics, to be used as instruments of governance. To be fair, this occurred at a time when most folks did not follow any agreed form of law or government, so the use of 'religion' as an organizing principle may have had its merits, but the costs were horrendous.

Today most of these functions have been formalized as different modes of government. In this context, the meddling of religion in these affairs is outdated. In fact, institutionalized religion as a whole may have become outdated.

In a perfect world, religious practices should still be the interface between our world and the *Mysticum*, but they are so distorted and contaminated by racial and political infiltrations that, in my opinion, the whole approach is no longer redeemable. At a local community level, it should be possible to salvage the community, reunion, and service aspects, but best call it something else, a gathering place for social and spiritual practices, on the lines of *ashram* or spiritual center, perhaps?

Inasmuch as it delves into the fundamental structure of the universe, science ranges back and forth from the surface to the depth, the very *ground of being*, as does philosophy. In fact, science and philosophy cannot be separated in any meaningful way (after all, Ph. D. stands for *Philosophy Doctor*, lover of wisdom). But again, science and philosophy are just the social manifestations of a deeper process that can only take place within the individual psyche: introspection, *in-sight*. Consider this essay as a stab at **integrative philosophy**, our never-ending quest in search of a holistic field of understanding.

To be clear, the problem is not *God*, **the problems lie in the stories we make up about our gods, and the abuses and atrocities they serve to justify**. As we have seen, the cosmos is managed bottom-up by adjusting the underlying *ahxioms* of the *implicate order*, not top-down. In other words, God doesn't go around the countryside hammering things, clobbering trees, and torturing humans to get them to do His Will. Only humans do that.

Beyond re-litics and po-ligion

I have been asked how might we move forward. People think that if one religion prevailed, the problems would go away. Unfortunately, they won't, because the problems are intrinsic to the premises and structure of organized religions in themselves.

One issue is the association of religious belief systems with ethnicity. Few things are as misguided and have been as disruptive. Hopefully, I have made it as clear as possible that ethnicity is a delusion. If you had a magic wand that could go back far enough in time and **simultaneously** erase ethnic and tribal identity from the minds of both Jews and all the neighboring Arab tribes, what would remain of the middle-eastern crisis? To heal, BOTH sides have to relinquish their ethnic and religious attachments.

Next, the differences between the three Abrahamic belief systems are so absurdly superficial that it is unforgivable to keep going to war and murdering millions over them. Amongst the tragedies of the political distortions incorporated into their *Books* is the denial of reincarnation and the threat of an imminent 'judgment day.' Both these assertions are unfortunate. The earth is scheduled to go on spinning for the next billion years at least, so the prospect of remaining in suspended animation in some limbo till some hypothetical 'judgment day' should not appeal to anyone. Besides, if you are in the bliss of heaven, would you want to be resurrected back into the same old crummy physical body? If you believe your soul gave life to your current body and will survive after your body's death, why in heaven might it not reincarnate time and again in new, improved, physical bodies?

Another aspect that has marred all these religions is their false promises, their Ponzi schemes. Humans, all of us, can be incredibly gullible. Tempting for sure, but no excuse for institutionalized scams. Spirits don't need nor use food, nor sex, nor riches, and so on, so tell me please, where is the compassion of having some gullible young kid of your own blood commit some brutal act, even sacrifice his own life, in the pursuit of a promise (eternal life) his spirit already has, or one (a thousand virgins...) his spirit does not need and will not be able to enjoy? If they die, their religious instigators are the ones who will enjoy the earthly virgins that were meant for the poor kids.

The path forward is to acknowledge that **The Books have passed their heyday as instruments of spiritual instruction, and the sectarian divisions they foster are persistent political liabilities**. This goes for all forms of institutionalized and/or denominational religions. Theocracies are political operators, not 'religious,' and should be awarded the same credit and status as any other politician. If someone were to burn all the bibles or all the qur'ans, all hell would break loose. But what if each community had the courage to burn their own books on some designated day? At the very least, rewrite them free of all the historical, ethnic, and denominational garbage. The road to *ah!* should be simple, clean.

Here is where we need to switch sides. Expecting entrenched religious orthodoxy to correct their devious ways is unrealistic. They will always defend the status quo and their own privileges. It is up to you, the potentially uncritical believer-come-sucker, to be more discerning and stop feeding perverse systems that will only damage you and your family. Believing in the existence and the compassion of *ahl* is natural, but you don't need to submit to the manipulations and mandates of any theocracy or religious sect to get there (all current religions are sects, both in their partial views and their partial followship). Spirituality is a largely personal search, which you can pursue in many different ways.

Faith, a good servant, a terrible overlord

For over 3000 years religion has been telling us what we can and cannot do. Perhaps it's time we tell "religion" what IT can and cannot do. We need to make a categorical distinction between the political and the mystical sides, the preacher and the teacher aspects.

Preaching is essentially a political approach: it's main aim is to condition other people's behavior and create a link between the audience and the institution. Talking about the Divine may catch people's attention, but it does not modify their direct experiential contact with the Divine. It can, in fact, act as a barrier to a direct spiritual experience, particularly if the preaching is loaded with moralistic admonitions, racial hatred, gender inequality or other discriminatory components. All these attitudes stress the differences, foster alienation, and go against *reunion*. It also keeps your attention focused on the external.

When preaching shifts to outright forceful indoctrination in a specific cult or doctrine associated with an ethnic or nationalistic overlord, often including compulsory affiliation, the process has moved from anything we could admit as *religious* to the very mundane imposition of a **political agenda**. Of course, finding excuses to overpower, pilfer, rape, torture, murder, and preferably exterminate your competition is perfectly legitimate and acceptable in the political arenas of all ages. However, when 'faith' turns **you** into a political weapon in the service of someone else's agenda, you have been led astray and have become a consummate sucker. You need to overcome the tragically naïve notion that these abuses are excusable 'on religious grounds.' Abuses are **not** *excusable* at all, and should not be accepted by you personally, nor in any civil forum.

Religions also claim to offer the context for practices, rites and rituals that, in theory, promote the union with the Divine. But note, it is possible to do this without indoctrination nor affiliation. In fact, at least initially, most spiritual practices are personal, and thus do not need any form of institution, religious authority, officiating priests, books, or dogmas.

Strong affiliation, whether by choice or by imposition, is a fundamental contradiction in the current religious approach to spirituality. At least since Buddah's time, attachment is known to be one, if not the principal, cause of human suffering. Even more importantly, both mystical traditions and recent experiential work point to an inexorable condition in the path to spiritual development: the need to let go of our worldly attachments, a demand that most of us find almost impossible, so hard in fact that we experience it as death itself. But it is not the 'I' that needs to 'die,' only its attachment to aspects of our embodied selves. Unfortunately, 'ego' has become synonymous with personal identity, but innumerable accounts of 'death' and subsequent 'rebirth' show that we continue to perceive our sense of 'I'ness, even though the ego-identity we once cherished was demolished in the purifying kiln of what is better called ego-death. This ties in with an inescapable condition of a freed spirit: we cannot be one with an infinite spirit if we are constrained by a multitude of attachments, each of which confines us in different ways. Like many critters that have to shed their skin as they grow, expanding from this entrapped condition without 'letting go' of our worldly beliefs and passions, loves *and* hates alike, is impossible. The stronger our attachment, the harder and more painful it is to let go. Should we struggle to hang on, it would be devastatingly painful, literally felt like our constrained 'self' is being torn apart. This suggests we look at 'religion' in a different light.

As instruments of spiritual instruction, *the Books* may have served their purpose, but once you have become aware of the existence of the divine, a believer perhaps, it is time to expand your search and your practice. Getting stuck on one *book* is a form of attachment, no different from any other attachment, even if the book is perceived as promoting religiosity. Imperceptibly but inexorably, we get more and more caught up in a confined way of doing and thinking, till in the end, rather than being attuned to the Divine, we are married to the Church, the creed, or *The Book*, all forms of constricting attachment. When being Jewish, Christian, or Muslim becomes more important than being spiritual, we have been led astray. Time to let go and find new paths to spirit.

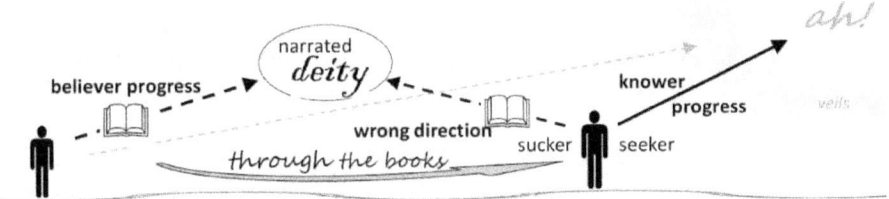

Figure 46. **Through the books.** *The Books* help the uninitiated, but they can be an obstacle later on. *At some point you'll need to readjust your direction and explore better practices.*

Considering mainstream religious practices have been employed or imposed for centuries, the number of enlightened 'graduates' seems dismally low. This may be the result of the different aims of religious practices. According to Stephen Prothero, for Buddhism, for instance, the primary aim is *awakening, enlightment*, truly a personal approach. But for Christianity it is *salvation* and for Islam, *submission,*[52] so both approaches have strong political undertones (*be a good boy, submit to authority*).

But it is also possible that the differences in results stem from the actual practices, the techniques they use. Reading and writing, in particular, are known to have very distinctive effects on the mind and even the structure of brain. As we saw with the right hand/left hand issue, certain functions of the brain are seated in only one hemisphere. The primary handling of language, writing, reading, recognition of letters and numbers, logical thinking, math, all usually lie in the left hemisphere. Shapes, faces, music, social cues, color and patterns, artistic and emotional response more often go with the right hemisphere. Although these trends are not absolute, people with very strong **laterality**, as it is called, may have difficulty switching sides or integrating both hemispheres at the same time. Since this integration is essential for achieving meditative states, the persistent reliance on language and the written word, *The Books*, may strengthen *laterality*, which would work against a numinous or Holotropic experience. If this is correct, the irony is that these *Books* may have actually *promoted* the emergence of rationality, science, and materialism. Reason is

---

[52] Stephen Prothero, 2010. *God is not One.*

discriminatory, spirituality is integrative.

The teaching aspect is better represented in the more esoteric branches of the dominant religions and is especially visible in oriental schools. If you want to come in contact with the Divine, follow this practice... Focusing on the practice, rather than on the politics, greatly increases the chance for a transformative process and of direct experiential contact with the numinous nature of the cosmos. This is the basic idea of the shaman and his apprentice, the guru and his ashram, the Zen master and his disciples. These modalities can provide a group of supportive fellow seekers and the guidance of teachers who are more advanced in the practice of inner journeys than we are. The hitch lay in the rather arduous nature of the more ancient *technologies of the sacred*. Few people could afford the time to spend months in meditation, do extended fasting, prayer, isolation, and so on. For the ordinary folks, contact with the numinous was mediated to some degree via special events, the rites of passage or initiation ceremonies, often enhanced by the use of natural entheogens. But that is changing rapidly, in part spontaneously, and in part through advances in spiritual technologies.

Spontaneous contact with the numinous must have occurred occasionally since the dawn of advanced consciousness, and certainly since the earliest stages of civilization, but it would have been difficult to connect and make sense of these chance events occurring in small isolated populations. Even if their frequency had remained constant, the sheer increment in human population and the world-wide interconnectedness has turned these once freak events into what seems like a delusional epidemic (if you stick to the materialist view). To thicken the plot, several of our medical advances have had the unexpected and unintended side effect of creating conditions that produce profound spiritual experiences, most notably the NDEs we discussed earlier. According to many polls and population studies, these experiences are now being reported by the thousands, and surely add to millions world-wide. If this is all due to '*divine grace*,' *ah!* must be sending us an important message. We need to listen.

If properly handled, there is growing evidence that even one deep experience of this sort can have a profound effect on a person's psyche and produce a significant change in attitude and their inner sense of balance and well-being. It also helps widen the person's outlook on the meaning of life, death and the possibility of an afterlife.

Additionally, the revival of some old and several new *technologies of the sacred*, plus the ever-growing expertise in the treatment of psychological trauma and related problems, is offering new hope for the spiritual seeker. I don't know of any concrete estimates, but if you add the numbers of people initiated in shamanic practices, meditation, holotropic breathwork, past life regressions, the growing therapeutic and experiential use of psychedelics, and many other alternatives, the total number of seekers experiencing these new avenues to spirituality must be huge.

Quite significantly, even if some people encounter entities they attribute to deities they are familiar with, in general these experiences are either unspecific or relatable to mythological entities from anywhere in the world. Perhaps they are the underlying source of our mythologies, but not limited to any one in particular. The majority of these experiences seem to be beyond any specific creed, *Book* or religion.

> *Converting a guide into a destination bungles it.*
> *It's like sailing your ship into the lighthouse.*

==================== III ====================

Chapter III.91 –
What's next...?

Most analysts would agree that humanity as a whole is undergoing rapid change driven by a succession of fundamental paradigm shifts, and that our world is poised on the verge of a major transformation. How all this will play out for us depends on whether we embrace these changes or resist them. Periods of major change are always risky and can cause of much strife, anguish, and pain, but even so, it is clear that the more we resist, the harder it gets, for ourselves and for those around us.

The obvious question is: Where is all this headed? We tend to get lost in the tangled immediacy of cataclysmic predictions of ecological and social collapse. I prefer to look at the broader picture, over longer time frames. However we negotiate these changes now, they *will* play out, and our species as whole *will* have to evolve to adapt to them. So, consider this: since reincarnation is supported by a growing body of evidence, we will do ourselves a service to accept it as a fact. Hence, we should take excellent care of the environment, of biological and human diversity, and the health of humanity as a whole, not so much for the sake of some abstract notion of "future generations," but because our souls will be the inhabitants of those renewed bodies, and of the world we bequeath for them, ***in our own future incarnations***! In this light, healing the planet and, above all, healing ourselves has a completely different ring to it, don't you think?

We know genes get passed on to the descendants of our physical bodies. Much of the variation needed to build the improved human bodies of the future already exists in our current global genetic diversity, but we have no way of knowing where those key variants occur today, and thus little control over this extremely complex process at a global species level. Hence, all the racial arrogance and bickering is misguided and pointless. The evolution of our physical bodies is best left to its own designs.

Instead, there is compelling evidence from reincarnation studies and other transpersonal exploration methods that our souls do 'inherit' traces of past traumas, karmic debts, and our unfinished business, so it is fitting to focus on our personal affairs because what we do today can definitely influence our spiritual future. Though this might sound individualistic, we are all so deeply interconnected that our individual actions do affect the whole. So, let's move on with this broader perspective in mind.

First and foremost, *if* the primary commitment is to help people to open up to their full spiritual potential, then the path that works best for them, or the one you choose to follow, should be of little or no concern to others. Unfortunately, this is not what many people and some dominant religions believe in or preach, so it is up to you to decide whether their approach serves your needs, or whether you might be better off someplace else. Getting beyond outdated religious mandates and practices may be necessary, but it's pointless if the outcome is a vacuum. It's not a question of becoming an atheist, not even an agnostic. You simply need to find new ways to explore the *mysticum* and commune with the Divine. Perhaps the most significant recent achievement in our path to spiritual freedom is not so much what we believe, but rather in the ever-broadening availability of *technologies of the sacred*, and the resulting freedom to choose ***how*** we pursue our spiritual practice. A new blend of ancient mystical practices and modern experiential approaches is providing us with a broad spectrum of techniques for personal and spiritual growth.

Our knowledge of the laws that govern nature, mechanized food production, weather forecasts, medicine, and so on have given predictability to a large part of the old uncertainties. Most of our basic needs are assured, so it is no longer necessary to believe and to make offerings to 'the gods' on these issues. But there are other benefits that only come through spiritual practices. The certainties they provide, belonging to a well-defined social group, the support and consolation that this group affords us, and so on. Some feel an existential emptiness, which appears more vigorously when we have our basic needs covered, and can spend time thinking on the future, on the beyond. In the past few had that privilege, but we are all attracted to *the promise* of some miracle that will save us from our evils.

So, let's assume you feel the need to gain more wisdom and that you have full liberty to choose your practice. What shape would it take?

A first step is to replace the path of a 'believer' for a more proactive approach of personal internal search. You can work on your inner life on your own, in solitude. In fact, for certain stages of meditation it may be indispensable, but there are processes that are difficult to handle without the support of others. Working with people who have experience also makes the work easier and shortens the search, but be cautious of those who demand that you conform to their whims.

As for the context, I can only speak for myself. To feel supported in my practice, I **do not** need a group that spends all its energies telling me what I must do or criticizing what I have already done. I need a group that is willing to share a spiritual path with me, accept my limitations and give me support so that I may persevere. Facing my fears, or exploring new terrain of my interior worlds can be terrifying. To progress I need to let go of my repressions and mental control, explore, allow myself to touch on issues that make me vulnerable. I can only do this if I have complete trust that the people around me will '*hold my space*' and that they **will not make any value judgments** (they won't moralize) on the experiences that might surface during my inward search. I, in turn, am willing to *hold their space* and be free of moralizing judgments for them, accepting their process in a similar fashion. Trust is crucial, and therefore gossiping is a fatal blunder.

In my experience this plays out constructively if the people involved understand that my process is exclusively mine, and that no part of what I say, write, draw, think, or ask is directed at them. It's not about them (the people who are assisting me), it is about me. When I am in a support role for them, the same applies: it's about them, not me. It's easier said than done. Society has conditioned us to find fault with everybody except ourselves. We need to re-educate ourselves, accept that useful change only occurs when we take responsibility for our actions and our lives. Curiously, this seems to be easier to learn when you work with complete strangers or, at least, with people with whom you are not involved on a daily basis. It's hard to sustain a neutral position when the accusations and the blames refer to real situations in which both of you were involved, which pretty much eliminates family and friends, at least as you begin to learn how to. You might go with a friend, but don't do the 'work' together.

An important point: to be of help, the person in a support role must keep in mind that, above all else, the seeker needs to feel empathy. Doing without doing. Empathy is not permissiveness. I can understand and accept what is happening to you, even if I don't agree or if I think you made a mistake. Committing mistakes is part of the human condition. I want to have the opportunity to learn from my mistakes, without getting crucified for them.

Of course, if I abuse that privilege and use it as an excuse to cross the line, it's up to society to step in and impose the appropriate limits. But in the context of spiritual learning, being moralistic or judgmental has a negative effect. It reinforces the pathology, the alienation, and the victim will surely close in on himself again. End of progress.

Spiritual growth ties in with the need for a therapeutic 'mirror.' Undoing old traumas and destructive habits is very difficult without help. There are many new technologies designed to diagnose problems within the workings of our nervous system, and techniques to understand personal traumas, fears, phobias and the likes that we carry within us. Unfortunately, traditional practices such as prayer and meditation rarely solve these issues, and in many cases stigmatizes them, makes them worse. We still hear of cases accused of being 'possessed,' of witchcraft, and accusations of the sort, when in reality the person was suffering from a perfectly treatable psychiatric or psychological problem.

We talked about progress. Becoming more expert in what you are already doing is progress, no doubt. Sooner or later, you are likely to hit a ceiling. You feel there's no room for progress in the place or situation you are in. Or your surroundings are hostile to any significant change. You are expected to follow dogma, to continue doing what that culture mandates.

Perhaps it's time to seek a change. You could change your job, your profession, try a new sport, read some new author you are not familiar with, travel, expand your vision of the world, change your beliefs, adopt a new religion, or abandon religion altogether, move to another place or country... The possibilities are endless!

So then, where's the trap? It varies, obviously, but a common theme is that these changes are of little help if you continue to drag your traumas, prejudices, misconceptions, and failings with you. Life seems to have an irritating way of putting the same obstacles in your path till you learn the lessons they have for you and learn to overcome them, even if it takes you a hundred lifetimes. Better learn to overcome them in this life and give yourself permission to move on to the next challenge free of these handicaps. This notion is nicely sketched in the now classic *Groundhog Day,* starring Bill Murray and co., by repeating the same 'day' over and over again till he learns the lessons it holds for him. The implication is that one lifetime is not enough to ensure our spiritual evolution, which again brings the issue of reincarnation to the forefront. Reincarnation constitutes an indivisible part of most native cultures and oriental philosophies, but has been systematically denied by our more manipulative religions. If you can correct your mistakes and pay your debts in future lives, all those threats about eternal damnation and rotting in hell become quite empty, don't you think?

When the negative patterns in your life keep repeating, you need to look inwards. Since your obstacles can be lodged in any of the domains, there's no way that I, or any other person, can be wiser than you as to what you need to do (assuming that you are mentally functional[53]). Others may help you research the options or mirror you to help you better understand yourself, but in the last analysis you must decide for yourself. Trust your process, your intuition, your inner healer, your emotional positioning system, or whatever you prefer to call it.

Though each of us must find their own path, there are some tricks that might help a range of people. Consider a popular metaphor: '*You can't see the forest for the trees.*' Einstein pointed out that you can't solve a problem from the level in which it is perceived. These are limitations of perspective. Some problems cannot be solved from your current perspective, which is

---

[53] The exceptions to this notion are people who are suffering from any form of mental collapse, are victims of severe addictions, prey to abusive or alienating cults, paranoias, or who suffer deliriums and other similar woes. First, they need professional assistance to stabilize them, allow them to recover their identity.

why you see them as a problem. Insoluble issues at one level are often easy to solve from another viewpoint. But we tend to be more stubborn than a mule. *We prefer to die rather than change our perspectives*, and betray our precious *beliefs*.

But if we are to grow, to move ahead, we must change. Our world is changing, rapidly. It's difficult to see exactly where it's heading. But it's becoming increasingly evident that, as currently stated, the old traditions clash with today's realities or simply don't work at all. Abandoning archaic religious dogmas does not mean denying *ah!* God is not a religion, and no religion **owns** God. We might be accused of being 'atheists,' but it's just a slander. We need to overcome old dogmas and the narrow vision they want to impose on us. ... *ah!* is something else. There are many ways to commune with *ah!*

A sure way of getting past many of these problems is being eclectic. Listen to other voices, to other points of view, and try out different practices. Study sciences, meditate, practice sports, yoga, join a choir, learn to handle a business. It's your choice. If your ingroup turns out to be intolerant of your new choices, that's not a good sign. Look for more open-minded people who can accept your process.

ah! is all things, everywhere. There are many paths you could take.

Find those that work for you.

> *I've seen good men do bad things and bad men do good things.*
> *It is not God's plan; it's your own.*
> The Reverend, from John Favreau's *Cowboys & Aliens*.

========================= III =========================

Chapter III.92 –

Boundless mindscapes

When I started this, I thought that I was studying and writing to solve age-old riddles, to change the world perhaps. But when all is said and done, I realize it was always about my personal journey of discovery. It was I who needed answers to these dilemmas. Perhaps you have struggled with similar issues, so I hope that at least some of the answers I found will be of value to you too.

When Columbus returned to Europe with news of the discovery of the "western Indias," all of Europe went into a frenzy of exploration. Columbus opened their eyes to the existence of other worlds. The West shifted from being a prisoner of Europe to being citizens of those worlds, but it has taken 500 years to explore them, and we still have a long way to go.

About a century later another aperture of similar magnitude occurred. In 1609 Galileo made his first observations of the heavens aided by a telescope. He was the first man to confirm what others had only imagined or dreamt of. With his telescope he transformed our vision of the known universe. Many of the beliefs we held before the telescope turned out to be very poor and often erroneous descriptions of the universe that surrounds us. We had to resign our illusion of being at the center of the universe, but this discovery opened incommensurable spaces that we still barely know and comprehend.

The conscious recognition of the subconscious, unconscious, and transpersonal internal spaces of our mind, the subjectal domains, puts us in a similar position to Columbus and Galileo. Our physical bodies may be earthbound, but the interior spaces of our psyche, our imagination, and our creativity know no bounds. This new understanding opens spaces within, mindscapes, that are at the same time boundless. We begin to see a huge panorama almost unknown to us (in the West at least), but fascinating, alluring... and at the same time terrifying! Only shamans and artists had license to explore them. For common folk they were either forbidden or mostly out of reach, somewhat like exploring the frontiers of outer space, which has been, and will likely continue to be, the privilege of a select few. Instead, new tools and technologies are bringing the exploration of the inner dimensions of the Cosmos well within the reach of *ordinary* folks like you and me. For many of us, this has become our *new frontier*.

Science gives us the best explanations available as to how material things really work. In a practical sense, science is a shortcut. It reduces a multitude of subjective 'godimistic' and rather temperamental notions into one which is 'mechanistic' and mostly neutral. But perhaps not just mechanistic. As we add complexity, these interpretations become ever more flexible, till we reach the zany level of quantum physics, relativity, chaos theory, and the study of consciousness itself. At this point the gap between philosophy, science, and 'animistic beliefs' is vanishingly small. In Chapter I.4 we looked at the apparent progression from animistic through magical, mythic to religious, scientific, unitive, and vision-logic worldviews.

Somewhat teasingly I suggested the 'ultimate' explanation might be Zen. But truly, if we are to trust Clare Graves and other developmental researchers, life and culture tend to spiral back to earlier conceptions, just a step more inclusive in the complexity of the approach. Perhaps the next step is to combine our old animistic views with our very modern quantum views, a totally zany yet much more enchanted vision of reality, into an *'animated science,'* or what I like to call a *zanimistic* cosmology.

The Escherboros

*Figure 47. **The Escherboros.** - M C Escher's version of the ouroboros or eternal return. – Worldviews spiral back to earlier conceptions, just a step more inclusive than before. Thus, an updated **zanimistic** cosmology needs to take the valid elements from earlier mystical conceptions and harmonize them with the new cosmological insights into a unified field of thought. ("Spirals", M C Escher, 1953.)*

We come from a long historic cycle during which these perceptions were cloaked in religious taboos, 'scientific' prejudices, social and political mandates that demonized any vestige of deviation from the accepted norms. These norms are like screens, the opaque glass of tiny fish-tanks immersed in the middle of a vast ocean. Yes, they structure our lives, and they protect us from the immensity, but they also limit us severely. Lift the veils and swim in the cosmic ocean.

Assume the control of your interior life, delve in it, become a seeker...

Gee, no. That leaves me prey of my free will. Horror...!

Hmm, yea, it is scary. But it's worthwhile. Just be safe. Good luck.

================= III =================

Appendix:
Summary of **the Michael Christie Integrative Model**

This section gathers the fundamental points made along the preceding chapters. I used the classic framework, as summarized by Ken Wilber, to lead into a discussion of the nature of reality (Chapter I.2). Those ideas have proved useful as organizers of the bewildering diversity of natural and cultural phenomena. However, the classic approach has left several key issues unresolved.

The framework I developed in these pages differs in several of its founding principles to such a degree that I consider it a different model. Those points are:

1) The incorporation of several new terms needed to avoid the overlaps and ambiguities of the past (see Chapter I.3 and 'Definitions and Glossary' below).

2) The replacement of 'collectives' in Ken's individual-colectival dimension by the underlying forces (links and bonds) that generate and govern the dynamics of those collectives (Chapter I.10).

3) A classification of human endeavors based on a new criterion: **What does it modify?** (Rather than the traditional: What is it about?) This seemingly simple change results in a radically different and improved attribution and organization of human activities and fields of study (Chapter I.21).

4) The radial, layered representation of the colectival domains (Chapter I.12). Perhaps this idea is not new, but the novel representation in Figure 14 makes it easier to visualize. Tied in with the complexity ladder (point 8, below), it becomes clear that culture is an organizational level, not a domain, and that religion and politics are amongst its least restrictive expressions.

5) Treating the nature of object-subject as a dynamic complimentary binode (Chapter II.42), so replacing the current materialist idea that the 'subjectal' is an epiphenomenon of matter.

6) Ken's model handles 'breadth' (the 'horizontal' dimensions), but not volume. The incorporation of *'depth'* as an independent dimension allows the overlay of the domains and the addition of new levels (Chapter III.80, III.89). This moves the model from a bidimensional surface to a multidimensional layered *'volume'* with a *'vertical'* aspect, perhaps the *axis mundi* of the ancients, where each level can have its own expanse of *breadth*. But keep in mind that these spatial references are figurative props to aid description and understanding. In *reality,* somehow, it is all meshed together and happening simultaneously here and now.

7) The reticular nature of biological evolution (Chapter I.17), and of the structure of the universe in general. This was not developed fully above, but it is worth noting briefly here: any level of complexity has a baseline of separate, identifiable holons (individua, Figure 14). Variable mixtures of these form bands of loosely aggregated collectives (*e.g.,* atoms form variable mixes such as air). But at some point, selected groups of these holons can come together to form higher order holons (atoms bind into molecules), thus constituting a new baseline of individual holons. Decoupling of scales in physical evolution, punctuations in biological evolution, and paradigm shifts in cultural evolution (Chapter I.32) seem to correspond to these transitions into increasing levels of complexity.

8) The growing complexity of holons forms a well-defined 'complexity ladder' (Figure 22, Chapter I.31). On the other hand, no such order can be found in collectives, which can be a mixture of holons from almost any level of complexity (*e.g.,* an ecosystem). But the underlying forces that generate these collectives at each level of complexity are unique and constant. This fundamental distinction motivates and justifies the change from descriptive treatment of the *colectival* dimension to one focused on the generative forces that underlie 'aggregatedness,' as introduced and discussed in Chapter I.10 and mentioned in point 2) of this list.

As a result of these changes and additions, it is possible to resolve the issues alluded to above and make clear distinctions between teaching and preaching (Chapter II.45), and between art, science, technology, politics, religion, spirituality, and mysticism (Chapter I.21, I.24, III.90), amongst other things. These distinctions should offer new perspectives on the age-old deadlocks that plague our current discussions on these crucial issues. In turn it will, hopefully, aid the search for viable solutions to some of the current global problems and affairs of states.

===================== III =====================

Definitions and glossary

The model presented in this study rests partly on the definition of new terms that resolve some ambiguities of the past, and on the reclassification of human endeavors. As a guide for comparisons, I provide a brief list of related sets of words, grouped by issues, followed by an alphabetical glossary with the definitions of new terms and the meaning given to some unusual or ambiguous words.

Aspects of reality

Reality, consensual reality ; **Entity** ; **Ming** ; **Field** ; **Level** ; **Band** ; **Arena** ; **Playing Field**.

Dimension ; **Domain** ; **Sphere** ; **Realm** ; **World**, parallel world ; **Universe**, parallel universe, **Cosmos**.

Exterior ; **Interior** ; **Internal** ; **Mind and Psyche** (see also Object – Subject below).

Duality–dualism ; **Polarizing or excluding Dualism** ; **Complementary dualism** ; **Binode, binodal**.

Cosmos ; **Infinite** ; *Mysticum*; **Practicum** ; *Ahxioms* ; *the Zone.*

Branches of human endeavors - What do they modify?

Art/arts ; **Esthetics** ; **Investigation (research)** ; **Science** ; **Technique** ; **Technology** ;

Integrative philosophy ; **Mysticism** ; **Religion** ; **Sexocracies** ; **Spirituality** ; **Politics** ; **Corporation** ; **Hierarchy** ; **Offset or diffuse hierarchies** ; **Pyramidal hierarchies**.

Cosmology ; **Lore** ; **Mythologies** ; **Zanimistic**.

Human aspects

Psychology (Individual) ; **Social Psychology** ; **Statistical Psychology** ; **Psychological contract**.

States of Consciousness: ordinary, non-ordinary, pathological, altered, expanded ;

Object ; **Objectal** ; **Objective** ; **Interobjectal** ; **Subject** ; **Subjectal** ; **Subjective** ; **Intersubjectal** ;

Holotropic ; **Hylotropic** ; **Numinous** ;

Individuality and complexity

Holon ; Holarchy ; Hierarchy – Simple ; Complicated ; Complex ; Chaos – Chaotic ; Disorder ; Order.
Collective ; Collectival/ Relational ; Collectivity ; Individuum ; Individual ; Series ;

Glossary

Ahxioms: refers to the intrinsic elements, constants, constraints, relationships and processes that underlie and generate the structure of reality, including the fundamental Laws of physics. The elements of David Bohm's *'implicate or enfolded order,'* perhaps.

Arena: the setting or context in which an activity or perception takes place, excluding the players.

Art/arts: physical actions that create or modify material things that are useful, and/or pleasant to our senses. The activity modifies objects. It is objectal (in dance or martial arts, the 'object' is our body).

Band: a slice or section in a continuous spectrum, as in *the infrared band*.

Binode – binodal: a complimentary duality, as in the yin-yang symbol ☯, or a binary star system.

Chaos, Chaotic: random disposition of things. Zero predictability. 'Perfect' chaos is very rare.

Collectival: refers to the properties and characteristics of groupings of holons of any kind. The 'collectival' aspect constitutes one of the basic domains of reality.

Collective: refers to groups or aggregates of independent entities of any kind.

Collectivity: grouping or association that results from some form of internal attractor that maintains the individuals bonded or linked in some way. It is the counterpart of a *series*.

Complementary dualism: when the two aspects are integral parts of a single interlinked reality. Complementary dualism is at the very base of existence: particle-wave, yin-yang, object-subject, ...

Complex: several or many things or individuals, with **webs or networks of interacting relationships.**

Complicated: many things or individual beings, with **linear relationships**.

Corporation: a power structure specifically based on economic management and the accumulation of wealth. Its aim or function is primarily **interobjectal**.

Cosmology: the understanding of the laws that govern the cosmos, including the possible ethereal domains and divine realms. Mysticism, science, and philosophy are different approaches to, or aspects of, cosmology that cannot be in contradiction. Attempts to separate one from the other are false. The rules put forth in Chapter II.60 should apply to all areas of understanding. If a favorite idea fails a well-designed test or contradicts persistent facts, its either wrong or needs revising. There is no reason to exempt religious claims from these constraints.

Cosmos: everything, everywhere, at all possible times (see **Infinite**).

Cosmos versus **Universe**: the dictionary says they are 'almost' synonyms, but opinions differ. For practical reasons I use cosmos and cosmic as the wider notion that subsumes universe and its derivates. Cosmic rings *infinite*. Nobody speaks of multi-cosmoses, parallel cosmoses, meta-cosmoses, etc. There is only one Cosmos. Instead, Universe has been fragmented into many types.

Dimension: a single quantifiable or qualifiable extent or aspect; an axis in a physical or conceptual context with a range of values, such as '*temperature*' in the physical world, or concepts like '*levels of complexity*,' *e.g.*, Mass and Complexity:

🌀00000000 000000000 000000000 000000000 00000000 ▲ 000000000 ✝ 000000000 000000000 000000000 000000000 •

ahxioms > physics > chemistry > organic > biology > society > culture > politics > art

Disorder: disposition of things without any discernible criterion. Low predictability**.**

Domain: an area or space defined by segments of two or more dimensions, as we saw in Chapter I.2 (*e.g.*, the *individual-objectal domain*).

Domain versus Realm: perhaps arbitrarily, I use realm as the wider term (*the realm of dreams*), and domain an aspect within a realm (*the individual domain*), with **Sphere** somewhere in between.

Duality - dualism: the notion that things, processes or situations have two well defined and absolute aspects or sides. In some contexts, this is referred to as 'binary.' There are different forms of dualism.

Entity: loosely, denotes an object, being, or abstract thing, *with distinct and independent existence.*

Esthetics: sensorial perception and the appreciation of beauty (or not) of the world that surrounds us, including human creations. This appreciation is <u>a faculty of the Subject</u>. It is subjectal.

Exterior: refers to the material, concrete dimensions of reality.

Field: a combination or interaction between space, form, energy and perception. *A* visual *field* needs the conjunction of a context with visible objects, a light source, and the perceiver. Experiential *fields can be abstract*, as in a *field* of knowledge.

Hierarchy: social structure with assigned levels of power within a given level of a holarchy, such as an organization. It is possible to add or remove intermediate strata. The structure can change and the individuals that hold power are interchangeable.

Holarchy: a natural structure composed of scaled and inclusive levels of complexity. The sequence of levels is fixed, and the more complex levels **cannot exist** without the simpler ones.

Holon: an item or composite that constitutes a whole and at the same time is a part of a larger aggregate.

Holotropic: tending towards wholeness; healing, integration, reunion with the divine.

Hylotropic: tending towards separation; disintegration, matter, attachment to the worldly.

Individual: refers to the properties and characteristics of holons of any kind. The *individual* aspect constitutes one of the basic domains of reality.

Individuum: each holon of any kind. It alludes to some form of unity.

Infinite: everything that ever was, everything that is and everything that will ever be, in all possible dimensions, both material and abstract, spiritual or whatever you might imagine. Sometimes we use the word **cosmos** with a similar connotation, but perhaps leaning more to the material side (*e.g.*, Carl Sagan in the miniseries *Cosmos*, where I picked up the basic form of the definition). Both terms encompass the more restricted variants like universe, multiverse, metaverse, parallel universes, etc.

Integrative philosophy: our never-ending quest towards a holistic field of understanding, the spirit underlying this study. Though it does not seem to have been formally recognized as a field, I like the notion of *wisdom as a process* implied by the phrase, an open ended, dynamic, continuing quest.

Interior: refers to the abstract, nonmaterial dimensions of reality.

Internal: refers to the parts and functions that are contained inside an organism or individual structure, usually referring to the material aspect.

Interobjectal: refers to the forces or bonds that affect, unite, or disperse independent material entities, resulting in dynamic aggregates. The interobjectal constitutes one of the basic domains of reality.

Intersubjectal: refers to the links that affect, bind, or disperse independent non-material entities, resulting in dynamic aggregates. The intersubjectal constitutes one of the basic domains of reality.

Investigation (research): a process of study that is **designed to change (enlighten) the Subject**, the investigator or researcher. It includes studies based on empirical observation of nature: descriptions, measurements, chemical analysis, etc. practiced on the targets of study; experiments on those entities and related methods designed to describe and understand the things, issues, and processes of our reality. What is modified is the comprehension that the Subject has. The eureka moment is a personal experience. Therefore, this aspect of what we usually include under the umbrella of 'science' **is individual-subjectal**. Investigation and research can be applied to any domain of reality, including the abstract and subjectal aspects of human nature and endeavors.

Level: loosely, a step or tier in a sequence of complexification.

Lore: the predominant, usually unwritten, way to imagine and relate to the world, including how it functions, that dominates a given society for a period (*imaginario social* in Spanish).

Mind and Psyche: used interchangeably by some, or as distinct by others. Since it is useful to consider '*mind*' as the narrower expression of the material brain, and '*psyche*' as the wider term including the transpersonal, I go by this convention, mostly. (But note that some consider '*Mind*' as the more fundamental concept, sustaining and independent of brain function).

Mings: short for 'material things,' used in figures, or in lieu of 'things' when restricted to material items.

Mysticum: that part of reality that appears to exist within our subjectal perception and beyond the material domain of our everyday world and life: the collective unconscious, astral domains, mythological realms, heavens, hells... and their inhabitants. Because they have a profound impact on our life and culture, these states definitely have entity, regardless of whether they are 'real' or imagined in the materialistic sense.

Mysticism: the processes and the conditions that foster a direct **personal** experience of the transpersonal realms; practices that provide the most appropriate ways to perceive and reunite with the numinous and divine nature of existence. The term overlaps with *Spirituality*, but refers more to the knowledge and the techniques, rather than the primary experience.

Mythologies: stories with some special ethnic, historical, practical, or moral significance for a given culture or religion. We need to change and modernize our mythologies.

Numinous: having a strong spiritual quality; indicating or suggesting the presence of divinity. Similar to: spiritual, divine, mysterious, otherworldly, awe-inspiring, transcendent, ...

Object: refers to concrete, material elements or things (mings). When referring to the anatomy or physical aspect of a person, it is useful to capitalize Object: *Ted is the Object of my study* (rather than *'the subject ...,'* see Chapter I.13). – The passive element of an interaction.

Objectal: refers to objects and their material, external attributes or aspects. The objectal constitutes one of the basic domains of reality.

Objective: denotes information proceeding from an object external to the person who is speaking, and to the characteristics of those objects. Also, to the generalizations and theories constructed with that type of information. It qualifies appreciations, methodologies, beliefs, and attitudes.

Offset or diffuse hierarchies: a web or network of hierarchies sustained by different groups or social sectors, some with a geographic base (local or regional), and others with functional links that are independent of geography and of the other aspects. An individual can belong to or be affiliated with several different hierarchies, and any hierarchy might overlap to some extent with others, but never completely. The chains of command are diffuse, and the horizontal interactions are the norm. This web or network of 'intercrossing infrastructures' mitigates the impact of hegemonic superstructures.

Order: disposition of things following some criterion. High predictability.

Parallel Universe: a complete functioning universe in a separate, disjunct set of dimensions, in which many or all the basic Laws differ from ours. We can conceive of their existence, but they would be completely inaccessible to us or our instruments.

Parallel Worlds: complete functioning arenas in separate but 'adjacent' realms (sets of dimensions), in which some of the Laws may differ from ours, but are still accessible to us; e.g., those envisioned by Philip Pullman in the HBO miniseries 'His Dark Materials' saga. Travel between them would require some sort of sci-fi style, magical, mystical, or spiritual **portal**.

Perinatal passage: perinatal refers to events occurring during and around the birth process. This experience has often been referred to as a 'domain'. However, this seems incorrect because we cannot *reside* in this state, we can only pass through it. Following Chris Bache's lead in *Dark Night, Early Dawn*, (2000), I propose calling it the 'perinatal passage,' with its dual implication of a constriction, and the process of moving through it.

Polarizing or excluding Dualism: when the two aspects seem to be or are perceived as mutually excluding, disjunct: black or white, friend or enemy... This is what bipartisan politics tries to achieve, with the exclusion of all other options. When applied to social or political issues, these polarizations are usually false.

Politics: a power structure based on the management of objectivity. The process that leads to the creation, modification, and custody of legal (documented) and material bonds that govern the rights and responsibilities of physical or legal persons, and those that determine the benefits and obligations on the material and intellectual (virtual) assets. That is, who is responsible or owns what (or, if you prefer, to whom does it belong and who pays for it). In a nutshell, **it aims to modify interobjectal bonds**. Though the final aim is to create or modify the country's laws and legal system, much of the process relies on intersubjectal tools and strategies that overlap with those of religion (and vice versa).

Practicum: that part of reality formed by the material domain that constitutes and deals with our everyday world and life, including the usual subjectal brain states and functions.

Psychology (Individual): the study of the 'interior' aspects (as defined above) of a Subject, the subjectal aspects of a person, and the corresponding methods of study and intervention.

Psychological contract: what each person **believes** that applies or governs their relationship with other people or institutions, and what they assume about the ethics of the other party. These expectations often differ from what the other party thinks, and even from what is written in the contract.

Pyramidal hierarchies: institutional or military hierarchies that concentrate all the power in one individual. The top-down chain of command is linear, with few or no horizontal interactions. They are efficient in some situations, but they tend to be rigid, unstable, and volatile.

Qualifiers: the preferred term referring or pertaining to objects is '**objectal**,' and the one referring to Subjects (people's interior) is '**subjectal**.' The terms '**objective**' and '**subjective**' must be used only to qualify notions such as statements, methodologies, beliefs, and attitudes.

Reality: loosely, all that we perceive or infer of our being and our surroundings, including thoughts, dreams, etc. Perceptions of reality can be quite personal. When aspects of these perceptions are shared by a community, we speak of a '**consensual reality**.'

Realm: a complete functioning arena or section within a world, or a level of manifestation.

Relational: forces or processes that underlie groupings of holons of any kind. *Collectival* refers to the groupings of things; *Relational* to the links and bonds that shape collectives (*i.e., individual – relational*).

Religion: historically, a power structure based on the management of subjectivity. It modifies the links through the manipulation of mythology and the psychological social contract, as a means of controlling the behavior of people. It is hard to find an exact niche that would clearly separate it from politics, save that at present, in the west at least, its role is more restricted to the inter-subjectal domain. Basically, **it aspires to modify our intersubjectal links**. In its origin religion had a different role, providing the means for a personal connection with the *Mysticum,* but for the moment at least, it seems unlikely that many entrenched theocracies will be willing to restrict their actions to this role, and forsake their current political power.

Science: a systematic body of knowledge on a holon of any kind, a process, or a theme, including the acceptable criteria and methods of study and validation of that kind of knowledge, the scientific method. **It modifies aspects of the intersubjectal domain**. It differs from politics and religion in as much as it **is not concerned** with or has any relevance on issues of ownership or belongingness.

Series: a nonspecific plural without any implication of order or relationship amongst its components, other than the feature that defines it (*e.g.*, 'a series of accidents'). Also, aggregates or groupings formed by external forces, like leaves blown by the wind. It is the counterpart of a collectivity.

Sexocracies: sects or politico-religious institutions that are strongly oriented to the manipulation of the sexual lives of others through the promotion of taboos, confessions, punishments, auditing, and other forms of control. Since they tend to be male-dominated, they have also been called *phallocracies*, but not all sexocracies are male-dominated.

Simple: one or a few things or individuals, without links or only linear ones.

Social Psychology: the study of the 'interior' aspects of the **interactions** between Subjects, the intersubjectal, that which passes from Subject to Subject, and the corresponding methods of study and intervention.

Sphere: a multidimensional physical or conceptual region within a more extensive continuum.

Spirituality: the personal inner experience and relationship we have with the transpersonal, including the perception (or not) of the numinous and the existence of subtle entities (deities, etc.). The current religious approaches to this field of experience are complex and are very contaminated by mundane political interests. There must be more direct and simpler ways to commune with the divine.

Stage: a step in a process, or in a sequence of manifestation or development.

States of Consciousness: different states or functioning modes of our consciousness. Terms in current use include: ordinary, non-ordinary, pathological, altered and expanded. **Ordinary** is our every-day type. **Non-ordinary** includes or subsumes expanded, pathological, and altered. **Pathological** denotes malfunction, illness, dementia, etc. **Altered** is sometimes used as a synonym of non-ordinary (as defined here), but is best restricted to pathological states (and **not** used for expanded states). **Expanded** refers specifically to special states (attained spontaneously, through meditation, psychedelics and other techniques), in which we can access memories or fields that are not available to ordinary consciousness, states a shaman or a mystic would consider normal.

Statistical Psychology (individual) is a sub discipline that studies the prevalence of functional and dysfunctional psychological traits across populations, but it is not 'social.'

Subject: an individual as a conscious actor, but only the interior aspects: consciousness, the ego, our 'being,' my sense of 'I' and so on. The confusion of '**subject**' as an area of study and '**Subject**' as a person is avoided by capitalizing this last use (see Chapter I.13). – The active element of an interaction.

Subjectal: refers to Subjects and their abstract, interior attributes or aspects. The subjectal constitutes one of the basic domains of reality.

Subjective: denotes a statement or judgment that is born of the interior perceptions, pre-existing concepts, prejudices, or interests of the Subject who is speaking. Also, to the generalizations and dogmas constructed with that approach. It qualifies appraisals, beliefs, attitudes, and stratagems.

Technique: loosely, methods or practices used or applied in the mental/spiritual arena. Many don't require any special support (prayer, meditation, accelerated breathing); others rely on new technologies (biofeedback is a mind-training technique that relies on a technology).

Technology: the application of knowledge to the solution of practical problems by means of tried and tested procedures to modify objects or their components. It includes the arts as defined here. **It is designed to modify objects** (though some are becoming ever more abstract).

Universe: a continuous complete functioning reality, in which the same basic Laws hold throughout.

yb²: '*years before 2000.*' (This avoids adjusting for a shifting '**present**').

Zanimistic, zanimism: a novel cosmology that combines elements of shamanic animism and perennial mysticism with the latest zany scientific advances (quantum physics, relativity, consciousness research, transpersonal psychology, etc.), an *animated science*, perhaps.

Zone: I use *Zone* or '*the ___ Zone*' to stand for '**the** ... *formless, timeless, nameless, ... Zone* that is believed to be the ground of existence, the quantum vacuum, the source, ..., etc. – As a personal beacon, I find it easier to relate to *the ___ Zone* than to other notions that stress no-thingness (emptiness).

A searchable INDEX for this edition is available in www.zanimistic.com

==================== IV ====================

The problem is not God, the problems lie in the stories
we humans make up about our gods,
and the abuses and atrocities they serve to justify.

Acknowledgements

In an endeavor that stretched over decades it is close to impossible to remember and mention every person who directly or indirectly contributed or influenced the outcome (authors, professors, peers, friends, family…). Indeed, due to the nature of some of the issues, I should include all the manipulators, scammers, scoundrels, thieves, and charlatans that I have had the dubious privilege of encountering, but that in their own way provided many of the experiences that prompted me to write this essay. Yet, I fear that should I name them explicitly, I might become liable to several lawsuits for defamation. So perhaps better extend my sincere generic thanks to all those teachers and travel companions in this fantastic cosmic game for those experiences that we shared, both the good ones and the bad ones.

To those who deserve it, *if the shoe fits, wear it!*

It would also be the norm to thank the editors and all the other links in the technological chain that makes an effort such as this possible (internet, email, Wikipedia, WhatsApp, the folks at the printers, etc.). But I must say that in the post-COVID age of '*work at home*' the issue of the facelessness of the interactions has become a serious handicap towards any attempt at personification. All too often you are not sure if you are emailing to some impersonal algorithm, or if the guy is just overworked and tired. Even the signatures are electronic! Nonetheless, at least for the moment, we can assume that behind all that facade there are real people of flesh and bone! To all those anonymous and faceless collaborators that make these modern miracles possible, again, my most sincere thanks.

Much of the material is the result of events, talks and discussions transpired within family, amongst friends and in work settings. In particular, the notable transformations of perspective and vision between the generation of our parents, ours, and those of our children. Above all our children, who are the ones that keep us young in spirit. I would like to mention them all, but they are a bunch. So, fondly, thank you all!

More specifically, several people reviewed and helped improve sections or chapters of the book: Patricia Liljesthrom R. proofed the original Spanish version and contributed significantly with the psychology aspects, especially Chapters 9 and 11; Eileen Lacey reviewed Chapter 23 on altruism; Tomas Christie contributed to chapter 34 on complexity; Mark Seelig reviewed Chapters 79 and 81 on Stan Grof and psychonautics, and made valuable suggestions. Mindy Conde and Natalie McDonald of *The Crimson Quill* proofread an earlier MS. Their questions and insights prompted me to expand Book III to include spirituality more in depth than in the Spanish version. Eric Larson of *Studio E Books* helped with the cover design and layout of the final version. I am especially grateful to John Wieczorek, who proofread the entire English version, made many valuable suggestions, and was a great help with my rather rusty physics and astronomy.

To one and all, my sincerest thanks.

But it's important to stress that having discussed or proofread the issues doesn't mean we agree on every detail and therefore, in general, that the subject matter included in the book and the final position and wording adopted was my decision and is my responsibility.

Michael I Christie

===================== IV =====================

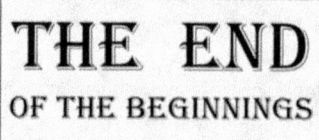

THE END
OF THE BEGINNINGS

Sources
Citations and notes: authors, books, movies, videos, and web pages
(Original titles in *italics*, translations "between quotes")

Aldous L Huxley, (1894 – 1963), English writer and early experimenter with psychoactive substances, author of *The Perennial Philosophy*; *The Doors of Perception*; and *Heaven and Hell*.

Alexander von Humboldt, (1769 – 1859), German geographer, naturalist and explorer. An avid student of nature and a prolific writer, he is considered the 'father' of ecology and environmentalism.

Alison Gopnik, 2009. *The Philosophical Baby*. Picador.

Andrea Wulf, 2015. *The Invention of Nature: Alexander Von Humboldt's New World*.

Arthur Koestler, 1967. *The Ghost in the Machine*. Random House.

Averroes (Ibn Rushd, d. 1198), Andalusian Muslim philosopher and jurist.

B. Alan Wallace, 2004. *The Taboo of Subjectivity: Toward a New Science of Consciousness*. Oxford Univ, Press.

Barry Stevens, (1902 – 1985), American writer and gestalt analyst, somewhat rebellious for her time, author of *Don't Push the River, it Flows by Itself*, amongst other works.

Carl G Jung, (1875 – 1961), Swiss psychotherapist who founded the school of analytical psychology and developed many new terms and notions (*psychological types, collective unconscious, persona, shadow, synchronicity, archetypes, etc.*); author of *The Red Book*, and many others.

Chris M Bache, 2019. *Diamonds from Heaven. LSD and The Mind of The Universe*. Park Street Press. Also from Chris are two excellent earlier books, *Lifecycles – Reincarnation and the web of Life* (1990, Paragon House), and *Dark Night, Early Dawn – Steps to a Deep Ecology of Mind* (2000, SUNY Press).

Clare W Graves, (1914 – 1986). Psychology Professor at Union College (New York State), developed an open-ended cyclic model of human ethical development, which is the foundation for Spiral Dynamics™. Author of *The Never-Ending Quest* and many other writings.

Dave Snowden, (1954 – ___), Welsh consultor, creator of Cynefin – see: *Cynefin – Weaving Sense-Making into the Fabric of Our World*, 2020.

David Bohm, 1978. *The Implicate Order: A New Order for Physics*. Process Studies, pp. 73-102, Vol. 8, Number 2, Summer, 1978.

David Christian, 2011. *Maps of Time, An Introduction to Big History*. Univ. of California Press.

Dmitri Ivanovic Mendeleev, (1834 – 1907), Russian chemist best known for organizing a disjoined jumble of knowledge on the elements into a coherent system, the Periodic Table.

Ed Yong, 2011. *Master of Illusion*. Nature: 480, Dec 2011, p.168-170, on Henrik Ehrsson's research.

Edward O Wilson, 2014. *The Meaning of Human Existence*. Liveright Pub.

Enrique Pichon-Rivière (1907 – 1977), Swiss-Argentine psychiatrist and psychoanalyst, creator of the Argentine School of Social Psychology. Some relevant titles are (all by Editorial Nueva Visión, Buenos Aires):

_____, 1985. *Del psicoanálisis a la psicología social (I): El proceso grupal*.

_____, 1987. *Del psicoanálisis a la psicología social (III): El proceso creador*.

_____, 1985. *Teoría del vínculo*.

Eric L Bernstein (1910 – 1970), Canadian born psychologist, better known as **Eric Berne**, creator of *transactional analysis* and author of *The Structures and Dynamics of Organizations and Groups* (1961) and *Games People Play: The Psychology of Human Relations*, 1964, amongst others.

Eric Frattini, 2010. *Los Papas y el Sexo*. Espasa/Planeta. ("The Popes and Sex"). According to his tally (Anex, p 303) out of 261 Popes studied: 12 were married; 6 were sons of married priests; 4 were sons of Popes; 7 were fetishists; 22 were homosexuals; 10 were incestuous; 17 were pederasts; 10 were procurers; 20 were either sadists or masochists; 9 were rapists and 1 was a zoophile.

Eric Hobsbawm (1917 – 2012), English historian and economist.

Ervin Laszlo, 2016. *What is Reality? The New Map of Cosmos and Consciousness*. Select Book, Inc. (Includes short opinions and essays contributed by 18 leading thinkers).

Frank J Sulloway, 1997. *Born to Rebel: Birth Order, Family Dynamics and Creative Lives*. Vintage Books.

Frans de Waal, (1948 – 2024), ethologist and primatologist at Emory University (Georgia, USA), born in Holland.

Fred Hoyle, (1915-2001), was the English astronomer who coined the phrase "Big Bang" (intended as a slur). Author of *The Intelligent Universe (1983)*, and many other books and papers.

Frederick W. Taylor, 1911/19. *The Principles of Scientific Management*.

Friedrich Engels, (1810 – 1895), German philosopher and political theorist, and a revolutionary socialist. He was also Karl Marx's closest friend and collaborator, with whom he coauthored the *Communist Manifesto* in 1848, amongst other writings.

Fritz Perls (1893 – 1970), Esalen psychotherapist (originally from Germany), creator of 'Gestalt' therapy.

George Orwell (1903 – 1950), pen name for Eric A Blair, English critic and novelist, author of *Animal Farm* (a satire on communism, where the paraphrased quote in Chapter I.5 comes from).

Hubert Wolf, 2013. *The Nuns of Sant'Ambrogio: The True Story of a Convent in Scandal*. Alfred A. Knopf.

Huston C. Smith, (1919 – 2016), born and raised in China of missionary Christian parents, moved to the US to pursue an academic career in comparative religious studies. Author of 17+ books, most notably *The World's Religions,* 1958, and *Why Religion Matters,* 2001.

Isaac Newton, (1642 – 1727), English mathematician, astronomer, and creator of classical mechanics and other basic laws of physics, which he gathered in his *Principia…* (*"Mathematical Principles of Natural Philosophy"*, 1687).

James Burke, 2007 (1995). *Connections*. Simon & Schuster.

Jacques Lusseyran, 1963. *And there was light* (autobiography). [2014, New World Library].

Jim Baggott, 2015. *Origins, The Scientific Story of Creation*. Oxford Univ. Press.

Joseph Campbell (1904 – 1987), American mythologist, in an interview series with Bill Moyers.

Ken E. Wilber, (1949 – ___). American philosopher and writer. See publication list below.

Leo Buscaglia (1924 – 1998). The 'Love Professor' from Los Angeles, California.

Lucy Cooke, 2022. *Bitch, on the female of the species*. Basic Books.

Luiz S A DeRose, (1944 – ___), Brazilian yoga practitioner and creator of the DeRose method.

Mario Augusto Bunge, (1919-2020). Argentine-Canadian professor and philosopher. – 1999. *Las Ciencias Sociales en Discusión,* University of Toronto Press.

Michael A. Singer, 2007. *The untethered soul: the journey beyond yourself.* New Harbinger Pub.

Michael Pollan, 2018. *How to change your mind.* Penguin Books. In 2022 Netflix also produced a documentary series under the same name, hosted by Michael Pollan.

Miguel I Christie, con la colaboración de Patricia Liljesthrom R., 2022. *Las Leyes de ¡ah! Una brújula para navegar el Siglo 21.* Ed. Círculo Rojo. –

Patricia Liljesthrom y Miguel I Christie, 2001. *La psicología social en la Educación y la educación de la Psicología Social.* Congreso 200 Pensadores en Psicología Social, 6° Encuentro, Tandil, Argentina, p. 53-61. - ("Social psychology in Education and the education of Social Psychology").

Paul J Steinhardt and Neil Turok, 2007. *Endless Universe: beyond the Big Bang.* Doubleday.

Paul Watzlawick, (1921 – 2007). Austro-American Psychologist from Palo Alto, California, specialist in the theory of communication, amongst other subjects.

Peter Reason and John Rowan, eds. 1981. *Human Inquiry: a source book of New Paradigm Research.* J Wiley & Sons, England.

Peter T. Richardson, 1996. *Four Spiritualities: Expressions of Self, Expressions of Spirit.* Nicholas Brealey Publishing.

Pierre Teilhard de Chardin, 1955. *Le phénomène humain.* Éditions du Seuil, Paris. – 1959. *The Phenomenon of Man.* Harper Collins.

Pim van Lommel, 2010. *Consciousness Beyond Life:* The Science of the Near-Death Experience. HarperOne.

Ramiro A. Calle, 2008. *Yoga para el mundo de hoy.* Editorial Sirio, Málaga, Spain. (And many other books).

Ray Kurzweil, 2005. *The Singularity is Near.* Viking, Penguin Books edition.

Richard Brodie, 1996. *Viruses of the Mind: The New Science of the Meme.* Hay House.

Richard Dawkins, 1976. *The Selfish Gene.* Oxford University Press.

Richard Dawkins, 1991/ 92. *Viruses of the Mind.* Conference and paper.

Rhonda Byrne, 2006. *The Secret.* Atria Books/ Beyond Words Publishing.

Roderick Ninian Smart, (1927 – 2001), Scottish educator and writer who defined the Seven Dimensions of Religion. See https://www2.kenyon.edu > Sevendi: The Seven Dimensions of Religion.

S. Frederick Starr, 2013. *Lost Enlightenment: Central Asia's Golden Age, from the Arab conquest to Tamerlane*. Princeton Univ. Press.

Sabine Hossenfelder, 2022. *Existential Physics. A scientist's guide to life's biggest question*s. Viking Press.

Stanislav Grof, 1990. *The Cosmic Game*. – (for Stan's bio and publication list see below).

Stanislav Grof, 2019. *The Way of the Psychonaut. Encyclopedia for Inner Journeys.* Volumes One and Two. Multidisciplinary Assoc. for Psychedelic Studies (MAPS).

Stephen Prothero, 2010. *God is not One*. Harper One.

Steve Jobs, (1955 – 2011), creator and cofounder of Apple.

Swami Sivananda, (1887 – 1963), Hindu guru well known in the West.

Tav Sparks, 2009. *Movie Yoga*. Hanford Mead Publishers.

Temple Grandin, 1995. *Thinking in Pictures*. ; _____, 2013, *The Autistic Brain*, with R Panek.

Tess Wilkinson-Ryan, 2023. *Fool Proof. How Fear of Playing the Sucker shapes our Lives and the Social Order – and what we can do about it*. Harper Collins.

Thomas Alva Edison, (1847 – 1931), American inventor and entrepreneur, best known for the invention of the electrical light bulb, amongst hundreds of electrical technology patents and others.

Yuval N Harari, 2015. *Sapiens, A Brief History of Humankind*. Harper Collins.

"¿Qué nos enseña la Biblia?", 2017. (anonymous) – (Spanish Version of: *What Can the Bible Teach Us?*), Watch Tower Bible and Tract Society of Pennsylvania, EEUU.

Movies, TV series and videos : (original titles in *italics*).

Avatar – by James Cameron, 20th Century Fox, 2009.

Camila – the story of Camila O' Gorman, by María Luisa Bemberg, 1984.

Coco – Disney-PIXAR animation, 2018.

Cosmos - A Spacetime Odyssey – by Carl Sagan, Ann Druyan, and Steven Soter, 2014, narrated by Neil deGrasse Tyson. Updated remake of Carl Sagan's original 1980 television miniseries.

Cowboys & Aliens – by Jon Favreau, Universal Studios, 2011.

Focus – with Will Smith and Margot Robbie, Warner Bros., 2014.

Groundhog Day – with Bill Murray, Columbia, 1993.

Heal – Kelly Noonan, director, 2017. Documentary on complimentary approaches to health and healing (featuring: Anita Moorjani, Anthony William, Bruce Lipton, Darren Weissman, David Hamilton, Deepak Chopra, Gregg Braden, Jeffrey Thompson, Joanne Borysenko, Joe Dispensa, Kelly Brogan, Kelly Turner, Marianne Williamson, Mark D Emerson, Michael B Beckwith, Rob Wergim).

His Dark Materials, HBO 2019 - 2023 miniseries, on Philip Pullman's trilogy.

How to Become a Tyrant – a Netflix 6-episode docu-series, 2021:
I. How to gain Power: Adolph Hitler.   4. Control the Truth: Joseph Stalin.
2. Crush your Rivals: Sadam Hussein.   5. Create a New Society: Muammar Gaddafi.   3. Reign through Terror: Idi Amin.   6. Rule Forever: Kim Il Sung.

Jupiter Ascending – by the Wachowskis, Warner Bros, 2015.

Kingdom of Heaven – by Ridley Scott, 20th Century Fox, 2005.

Mary Poppins – with Julie Andrews and Dick van Dyke, Disney, 1964.

Pay it Forward –on the story by Catherine R Hyde, Warner Bros, 2000.

Philadelphia –Denzel Washington and Tom Hanks, TriStar Pictures, 1993.

Philomena – with Judi Dench et al, Weinstein Co, 2014, based on the real-life story *The Lost Child of Philomena Lee* by Martin Sixsmith.

Soul – Disney-PIXAR animation, 2020 (2024).

The Gods Must be Crazy – by Jamie Uys, 1980.

The Shack – by Stuart Hazeldine, 2017, on the book by William P Young.

The Snow Walker – by Charles Martin Smith, 2003/2005.

Tomorrowland – with George Clooney, Britt Robertson, Raffey Cassidy, Disney, 2015.

When Sally met Harry – with Meg Ryan and Billy Crystal, Columbia, 1989.

Videos and web pages:

Video of Frans de Waal and his capuchin monkeys – https://youtu.be/meiU6TxysCg

Wikipedia on Destructive Cults – https://en.wikipedia.org/wiki/Cult seen 2018.10.04

On Egyptian monotheism –
https://history.stackexchange.com/questions/14865/which-religion-was-the-first-monotheistic-one/14870 ; https://www.ancient.eu/Akhenaten/ ;
https://www.ancient.eu/Moses/

=================== IV ===================

Ken Wilber and his publications

A recent **summary** of the world's religions, philosophies and cosmologies both East and West, is the one developed by Ken Wilber, starting in 1977. I use the arrangement of reality he proposes to kickstart the discussion for this essay (but then I modify it substantially).

The list below has most of his titles up to 2007, the year of publication and the number of pages, totaling over 6,000 pages of his personal output (not counting his contributions as Editor, and many shorter essays in editions shared with other authors, a few listed here as '---- p.'). There is repetition, but the point is that it takes this much just to summarize and produce a synthesis of the accumulated wisdom of world religions, philosophies, and spiritual practices.

Compare that with any of our current religious *Books*. I hate to break this to you, but if you are still stuck on one of these you are being horribly short-changed.

1977	388 p	*The Spectrum of Consciousness.*
1979	162 p	*No Boundary: Eastern and Western Approaches to Personal Growth.*
1980	260 p	*The Atman Project: A Transpersonal View of Human Development.*
1981	372 p	*Up from Eden: A Transpersonal View of Human Evolution.*
1982	---- p	*The Holographic Paradigm and other Paradoxes.* (KW and others).
1983	190 p	*A Sociable God: Towards a New Understanding of Religion.*
1983	338 p	*Eye to Eye: The Quest for the New Paradigm.*
1984	---- p	*Quantum Questions: Mystical Writings of the World's Great Physicists.* KW et al.
1986	---- p	*Transformations of Consciousness: Conventional and Contemplative Perspectives on Development.* (KW and others).
1987	---- p	*Spiritual Choices: The Problem of Recognizing Authentic Paths to Inner Transformation.*
1991	422 p	*Grace and Grit: Spirituality and Healing in the Life and Death of Treya K Wilber.*
1995	---- p	*---- Sex, Ecology, Spirituality: The Spirit of Evolution.* (See Revised Edition 2000).
1996	339 p	*A Brief History of Everything.*

1997	415 p	*The Eye of Spirit: An Integral Vision for a World Gone Slightly Mad.*
1998	240 p	*The Marriage of Sense and Soul: Integrating Science and Religion.*
1998	----- p	*The Essential Ken Wilber: An Introductory Reader.* (a compilation).
1999	356 p	*One Taste: The Journals of Ken Wilber.*
1999 – 2000	-----	*The Collected Works of Ken Wilber.* (prior titles in 8 volumes).
2000	851 p	*Sex, Ecology, Spirituality: The Spirit of Evolution.* Revised Edition.
2000	303 p	*Integral Psychology: Consciousness, Spirit, Psychology, Therapy.*
2001	189 p	*A Theory of Everything: An Integral Vision for Business, Politics, Science and Spirituality.*
2002	464 p	*Boomeritis: A Novel That Will Set You Free.*
2004	272 p	*The Simple Feeling of Being: Embracing Your True Nature.*
2007	313 p	*Integral Spirituality: A Startling New Role for Religion in the Modern and Postmodern World.*
2007	232 p	The Integral Vision: A Very Short Introduction to the Revolutionary Integral Approach to Life, God, the Universe and Everything.

It is worth noting that to date (late 2024), Ken has maintained his basic model of the quadrants, the terminology, the assignment of human endeavors to the quadrants, and the corresponding holarchies essentially unchanged (see figures 11.2 and 11.3 in his latest book *"Finding Radical Wholeness,"* June 2024, Shambhala, 488 pp.).

================== IV ==================

Stan Grof and his publications

In my opinion, the best approach to the spectrum of psychology and spiritual experience is the one developed by Stanislav Grof. Much of the material presented, especially in Book III, is based on the experiences, theory and practice developed by Stan.

Stan is a Czech psychiatrist born in Prague in 1931, who has lived and worked in the United Staes since the sixties. Shortly after he graduated, he became one of the first researchers ever to work with lysergic acid diethylamide, LSD, soon after it was discovered, an experience which marked the rest of his extensive career in psychotherapy and consciousness research.

Currently there is an explosion of books, techniques and theories on the connection of psychology and spirituality. Still, I think Stan's work is the most reliable overall cartography of the subjectal domains as currently understood. Besides, his work deserves a special place as a founding member and leading pioneer in the field of transpersonal psychology.

Equally important, his approach is as well grounded in our current scientific understanding as it is in the world's spiritual cosmologies.

Here is a partial list of his work, mostly those which are more readily available:

1975. *Realms of the Human Unconscious*. (Redone as *LSD: Doorway to the Numinous, 2009*).
1985. *Beyond the Brain: Birth, Death, and Transcendence in Psychotherapy*.
1985. *Ancient Wisdom and Modern Science*. - S Grof, Editor –
[a compendium of papers by over 20 scientists and spiritual leaders].
1987. *LSD Psychotherapy*.
1989. *The Stormy Search for the Self*. - Christina and S. Grof -
1989. *Spiritual Emergency*. – S. and Christina Grof – (reprinted in 2021).
1990. *The Cosmic Game*.
1993. *The Holotropic Mind. The Three Levels of Human Consciousness and how they shape our lives*. - SG with Hal Zina Bennett -
1994. *Books of the Dead*.
2000. *Psychology of the Future*.
2002. *The Call of the Jaguar*.
2006. *The Ultimate Journey*.
2006. *When the Impossible Happens*.
2009. *LSD: Doorway to the Numinous*. (Reprint of *Realms of the Human Unconscious*, 1975.)
2010. *Holotropic Breathwork*. – S. and Christina Grof -
2012. *Healing Our Deepest Wounds*.
2015. *Modern Consciousness Research and the Understanding of Art*.
2019. *The Way of the Psychonaut. Encyclopedia for Inner Journeys. Volumes I and II*.
2023. *Holotropic Breathwork*, Second Edition. S and Christina Grof – (1* edition in 2010).

==================== IV ====================

Suggested reading and viewing

I hesitate to recommend. Seekers need to find their way around, trust their intuition and the synchronicities that occur for them. Still, perhaps a few that I mention in the text and found helpful, might be appropriate as lead-ins (alphabetical by author's name).

Chris M Bache, 2019. *Diamonds from Heaven.* LSD & The Mind of The Universe.

Ervin Laszlo, 2016. *What is Reality? The New Map of Cosmos & Consciousness.*

Ken Wilber, 2007. *The Integral Vision*.

Michael A Singer, 2007. *The untethered soul* – the journey beyond yourself.

Michael Pollan, 2018. *How to change your mind*.

Peter Kingsley, 2010. *A Story Waiting to Pierce You*.

Peter Richardson, 1996. *Four Spiritualities*. Expressions of Self, ... of Spirit.

Pim van Lommel, 2010. *Consciousness Beyond Life* (... on NDEs).

Rhonda Byrne, 2006. *The Secret*.

Sabine Hossenfelder, 2022. *Existential Physics*. A guide to life's biggest questions.

Stan Grof, 1998. *The Cosmic Game*.

Tav Sparks, 2009. *Movie Yoga*.

For those who are not readers, here are few movies to get your *movie yoga* going (alphabetical by title):

Avatar, 2009, sci-fi on another world: by James Cameron, Fox.

Casper (the friendly ghost), 1995, my-fi classic; by S Reit & J Oriolo, Universal.

Children of the Sea, 2019, holotropic style; by Ayumu Watanabe, STUDIO4°C.

Cloud Atlas, 2012, my-fi/sci-fi on reincarnation: from the Wachowskis, Warner.

Coco, 2017, my-fi on afterlife's light side; by L Unkrich and L Molina, Disney-Pixar.

Cosmos, a Spacetime Odyssey, 2014, on our physical universe: miniseries, from Carl Sagan et al., hosted by Neil deGrasse Tyson, Fox.

His Dark Materials, 2019, my-fi on parallel worlds; Philip Pullman's sagas, HBO.

Mama Mia, here we go again, 2018, the joy of life in the Practicum; Universal.

Philomena, 2014, on religious abuse; The Weinstein Co. based on the book *The Lost Child of Philomena Lee* by Martin Sixsmith.

Soul, 2020, my-fi on soul migration; from PIXAR animation, Disney.

The Legend of Hei, 2019, Pure my-fi; by MTJJ Mu Mu, Beijing, HMCH Anime Co.

The Matrix, 1999, the universe as a data field; from the Wachowskis, Warner.

The Shack, 2017, my-fi on divine intervention; book by William P Young, Summit.

The Sixth Sense, 1999, my-fi on afterlife, not so light: by M N Shyamalan.

-------------------- O --------------------

About the author

Custom dictates a formal tone: **Michael I Christie** was born in New York, but grew up in a bicultural family setting in Argentina, at a time when the newer scientific and materialistic frame of thought was gaining ground in a Roman Catholic dominated social backdrop. He shunned religion when he was seven or eight and pursued a scientific education in **organismal biology** and **behavioral ecology** through university, and married with the fairytale illusion of living '*happily ever after*.' Life was objective, direct, and obvious.

This little worldview soon shattered. He lost his job, divorced, and was forced to review almost everything. Counseling ('therapy') allowed him to revisit religion and philosophy. A friend gave him Ken Wilber's *Up from Eden*. More of Ken's books followed. In the 90's he studied **transpersonal psychology** with Stan Grof and certified as a Holotropic Breathwork facilitator. He later worked with social facilitators in consensus building around conservation and environmental issues. As a complement, he studied **social psychology** and mediation. Done with the formalities.

I prefer a more personal tone. Though much of my life has been associated with academia and I have taught various courses, I am neither an educator nor an academic by profession. This might be a limitation, but it has also freed me from many of the constraints imposed by institutional settings. Thus, the insights gained and presented here are the result of decades pursuing my own path fueled by a deep interest in the fundamental issues of life. Wisdom may come from constant mindfulness, but sharing and validating these often-complex ideas has more to do with crafting precise yet accessible explanations and illustrations, and then exposing them to open scrutiny. I offer them here both as a contribution to our never-ending quest, and as an opportunity to test their validity.

------------------- O -------------------

www.ingramcontent.com/pod-product-compliance
Lightning Source LLC
Chambersburg PA
CBHW070903130626
46555CB00001B/9